ELEVENTH BRIEF EDITION

PRINCIPLES OF

SPEECH COMMUNICATION

Bruce E. Gronbeck
The University of Iowa

Kathleen German
Miami University—Oxford, Ohio

Douglas Ehninger

Alan H. Monroe

HarperCollinsPublishers

Sponsoring Editor: Melissa A. Rosati
Development Editor: Bob Nirkind
Project Coordination, Text and Cover Design: Proof Positive/Farrowlyne Associates, Inc.
Photo Researcher: Carol Parden
Production Manager: Michael Weinstein
Compositor: Graphic Typesetting Service, Inc.
Printer and Binder: R. R. Donnelley & Sons Company
Cover Printer: The Lehigh Press, Inc.

For permission to use copyrighted material, grateful acknowledgment is made to the copyright holders on p. 363, which are hereby made part of this copyright page.

Principles of Speech Communication, 11th Brief Edition

Library of Congress Cataloging-in-Publication Data

Gronbeck, Bruce E.
    Principles of speech communication/Bruce E. Gronbeck, Kathleen M. German. — 11th brief ed.
       p.   cm.
    Includes bibliographical references and index.
     ISBN 0-673-46508-X (student edition)   ISBN 0-673-46603-5 (teacher edition)
     1. Public speaking.   I. German, Kathleen M.   II. Title.
PN4121.E36   1991
808.5'1—dc20
                                             91-19247
                                           CIP

91 92 93 94 9 8 7 6 5 4 3 2 1

Contents

Preface

Origins of Text

Principles of Speech Communication, Eleventh Brief Edition, traces its parentage back to 1935, when Alan Monroe first assembled *Principles and Types of Public Speaking.* The so-called "brief" edition was born in World War II, when a shorter, more direct, practically oriented book was needed for schools training military officers. Alan Monroe thus came out of the great war with two books: one more broadly grounding public speaking in the humane and social-scientific research traditions of communication; the other focusing more narrowly on the technical decisions speakers must make when rising to say a few words.

Text Distinctions

In some ways, the two books have grown closer together over the last 45 years: they have similar structures and they share certain sample speeches. Yet *Principles of Speech Communication* is distinctive in three ways:

1. *This text works hard at getting you into speaking situations and on your feet quickly and easily.* While every college-trained speaker needs a communication vocabulary to prepare and critique speeches, students in more practically oriented classes need less conceptual background.

2. *Our textbook draws its examples not only from student government and campus organizations, but also from the worlds of work, politics, and social activism*—examples of students' present and future experiences that prove to be highly motivating.

3. *Within the safety of the college classroom, this textbook challenges you technically, intellectually, and morally.* Throughout your life you will be expected to know how to accomplish goals (technical skills), how to analyze situations and propose courses of action (intellectual skills), and how to lead your social and professional life in trustworthy ways (moral development). Stretching your skills and thought processes now will make you a more

effective communicator later. For these reasons, our textbook challenges you to try speeches on different topics and to use speaking techniques you've never tried before.

Regular Features

A textbook stays around as long as this one has because (a) it has a solid theoretical base and (b) because it rolls with the times. This textbook employs a time-tested method of teaching public speaking skills. *The "Monroe formula" for teaching public speaking was the most innovative idea that Alan Monroe had. It is now the standard organizational pattern in the field—and it still works.* This book's organization allows you to gain an overview of the process of public speaking (Part I, Public Speaking and Critical Listening), then to learn the basic principles of speech preparation (Part II, Planning and Preparing Your Speech), and finally to put those principles into practice as you prepare and deliver speeches tailored to a variety of audiences and occasions (Part III, Presenting Your Speech; Part IV, Types of Public Speaking). Other long-standing features of this textbook include

1. Monroe's *Motivated Sequence,* the greatest formula for putting together a speech this century has seen
2. a critical examination of forms of supporting materials and of the factors of attention
3. an emphasis on speeches to inform, persuade, and actuate (to move to action)
4. an exploration of types of imagery and of various kinds of introductions, organizational patterns, and conclusions

New Features

This textbook has always taught the basics, and it always will. Nevertheless, *Principles of Speech Communication,* Eleventh Brief Edition, like its predecessors, is still evolving. It strives to keep up with the latest thinking of scholars in rhetorical and communication theory and research and blazes new trails in speech communication pedagogy. What follows are descriptions of some of the newest features of this textbook:

1. An *increased awareness of ethics in speech communication* that manifests itself in a discussion of speech ethics in the first chapter and, more importantly, in a series of special features entitled Ethical Moments (these features pick up on today's concern with the ethics of communicating and help you to explore your own thinking about do's and don't's when speaking).
2. A *chapter-opening vignette* that offers a real-world application of the topic to be discussed and sets the tone for the subject to be explored.
3. A *separate chapter on finding supporting materials* (in recognition of the special information skills that you need in the electronic age).

4. A *chapter summary* that enumerates the main concepts of the chapter to facilitate your review.

5. A *Key Terms list* that highlights the important new terminology introduced in each chapter and provides a page reference to help you locate the definitions in the text.

Rewritten, Revised, and Restructured

In addition to adding new features to the Eleventh Brief Edition of *Principles of Speech Communication,* we've kept the text alive and vital by rewriting, revising, and restructuring the following five elements and features:

1. *Full color printing.* The last edition of this book was the first college-level public speaking book to be printed entirely in full color. Given the overwhelming success of that change, we've increased the use of full color in this edition, making the book easier to read, its main points more understandable, and the design more attractive.

2. *Critical thinking emphasis.* With critical thinking becoming an increasingly greater part of speech instruction, we've introduced it into many of our chapters, and featured it in two: Chapter 2 on critical thinking and listening and Chapter 14 on critical thinking and argumentation.

3. *In Pursuit of Excellence feature.* The popular In Pursuit of Excellence feature of the last edition has been expanded in the Eleventh Brief Edition to include special challenges and encounters with interesting ideas.

4. *Sample outlines and speeches.* As always, a key feature is the large number of sample outlines and speeches. In this edition, you'll find a number of new outlines and speeches that allow you to see how others wrestle and (usually) overcome the problems that all speakers face.

5. *Skillbuilding Activities.* The Skillbuilding Activities at the end of each chapter have been consolidated, rewritten, revised, and expanded from the last edition to accelerate your development as a speaker.

The Plan of the Book

Principles of Speech Communication, Eleventh Brief Edition, has been organized into four parts, reflecting the four major emphases of most contemporary courses in public speaking.

1. Part I, Public Speaking and Critical Listening, provides you with *an orientation to the communication process.* Most teachers help you to relate the particular skills involved in public speaking to a variety of real-world contexts. They want to see how those skills impact on your success at work and in society; to show you the underlying conceptual or theoretical explanations of what's going on when you speak publicly; and to adapt what you say and how you say it to the folks who make all the difference—the people in your audience. Part I of this book introduces you to important ways to think about speechmaking even as, with the help of Chapter 3, you give your first classroom speeches.

2.   If you try to think about all of the things you should be doing as you research and assemble your speeches, you'll drive yourself crazy. That's why Part II, Planning and Preparing Your Speech, offers a *step-by-step approach to speech preparation.* If you break down any complex task into its component parts, you can conquer it. Setting purposes and articulating central ideas or claims, finding and assessing supporting materials, organizing and outlining these materials, and building introductions and conclusions can be accomplished one task at a time with the aid of Part II.

3.   Building a speech is only half your battle. The other half is actually giving it—*putting your presentation into words, gestures, bodily actions, vocal patterns, and visual aids.* That's what Part III, Presenting Your Speech, is all about. You're communicating by way of four channels—language, sounds, movements, and visuals—every time you speak, so you've got to learn how to set and control the messages flowing through each channel. Even if your teacher doesn't assign each of these chapters, you're well advised to read them, especially if you sense you're having trouble with one or more of the channels.

4.   So, you think, you finally know how to build a speech. In reality, of course, there are many different kinds of speeches, each with its own demands on you and with its conventional rules for talking. In Part IV, Types of Public Speaking, we introduce you to *four broad types of speeches—* speeches to inform, speeches to persuade and actuate, argumentative speeches, and speeches for special occasions—as well as the particular formats you will often use when addressing certain kinds of groups. In Part IV, as a result, you really start to refine your speechmaking skills, learning how to adapt them to the demands of particular speaking occasions.

Resources for Instructors

The resources program for *Principles of Speech Communication,* Eleventh Brief Edition, has been expanded to include the following seven instructional supplements:

1.   *Instructor's Edition.*
2.   *SpeechMaster Test Package.* Contains over 3000 test items: true/false, multiple choice, short answer, and essay questions. The program contains editing features to create new questions or to modify existing items. Available for the IBM or Mac.
3.   *SpeechMaster Test Package.* Print version of the computerized program.
4.   *SpeechMaster Video Series.* Includes the classic speeches of our time as well as coverage of preparation tips and presentation techniques. Instructor's Video Guide available.
5.   *Great Ideas for Teaching Speech (GIFTS).* A short guide to assignments successfully used by public-speaking instructors.
6.   *Instructor's Resource Guide.* An extensive bibliography and reference for media resources.
7.   *First Choice.* A multipurpose software program available at a substantial discount to students. Because First Choice's applications (word processor,

database, spreadsheet, graphs, and electronic communications) are integrated, students learn how to use these features to create comprehensive reports or presentations.

ACKNOWLEDGMENTS

This book is not simply the product of two professors and their predecessors. *Principles of Speech Communication* is the result of the efforts of many instructors and students who have evaluated and reevaluated its many features for over half a century. Feedback is as important for writers as it is for speakers. We thank a nationwide network of users who graciously completed questionnaires for us: Diana A. Brehmer, University of Iowa; Dan B. Curtis, Central Missouri State University; Phillip W. English, University of Wisconsin—River Falls; Robert Friedenberg, Miami University of Ohio; Darla Germeroth, University of Scranton; Irvin David Glick, SUNY—Oswego; Pat Goehe, Southern Illinois University of Edwardsville; C. T. Hanson, North Dakota State University; James E. Jones, University of Northern Alabama; Bradford Kinney, Wilkes University; W. Faye Kirchen, University of Missouri—Kansas City; Leonard Leary, Eastern New Mexico University; Suzanne E. Lindsay, University of Alabama, Birmingham; Barbara Marder, Anne Arundel Community College; Robert Martin, Indiana-Purdue-Ft. Wayne; Sujanet Mason, Luzerne County Community College; Donovan Ochs, University of Iowa; Michael R. Palmer, Samford University; Mary Pelias, Southern Illinois University at Carbondale; Paula Tompkins Pribble, St. Cloud State University; Robert W. Renshaw, Jefferson State Community College; Anthony B. Schroeder, Eastern New Mexico University; Tom Smiley, Troy State University; Deborah Smith-Howell, University of Nebraska at Omaha; Jill Voran, Anne Arundel Community College; Carol Wilder, San Francisco State University; Jerry L. Winsor, Central Missouri State University.

We also want to thank the following manuscript reviewers whose detailed advice helped us to bring this edition to you in its final form: Arnold Abrahms, Thomas Nelson Community College; David Axxon, Johnson Community College; Dorothy Beimer, New Mexico Highlands University; Thomas Biggers, University of Miami; Ronald Bode, University of North Dakota; David Bradbury, Wilkes University; Nancy Buerkel-Rothfuss, Central Michigan University; Patricia Comeaux, University of North Carolina; Patrick Devlin, University of Rhode Island; Sam Edelman, California State—Chico; Robert Edmunds, Marshall University; Raymond Fisher, University of North Dakota; Mark Gring, Ohio State University; Lucia Hawthorne, Morgan State University; David Henry, California Polytechnic State University; Gerald Hundley, South Suburban College of Cook County; Carl Johnson, Metropolitan State College; Gloria Kellum, University of Mississippi; David Knapp, Northeastern University; Joseph Lamp, Anne Arundel Community College; Leonard Leary, Eastern New Mexico University; Suzanne Lindsay, University of Alabama, Birmingham; Judy Lukes, Northern Illinois University; John McKiernan, University of South Dakota; Shirley

Myrus, Onondaga Community College; Donovan Ochs, University of Iowa; Larry O'Kelly, John Brown University; Donna Pawlowski, University of North Dakota; Valerie Schneider, East Tennessee State University; Anthony Schroeder, East New Mexico State; Gwen Schultze, Portland Community College; Joy Seibert, University of Louisville; Henry Sheele, Purdue University; Ralph B. Thompson, Cornell University; Beth Waggenspack, Virginia Tech; June Wells, Indian River Community College; Tom Willett, William Jewell College; Donald E. Williams, University of Florida; Gary Woodward, Trenton State College.

A special thank you is due to the Gronbeck children. Christopher, Jakob, and Ingrid are collegians all and possess research skills useful to textbook writers. Their library research was especially important, as was their help in coming up with examples from a world younger than the one inhabited by the authors.

Finally, we owe our greatest debts to HarperCollins, a newly formed company that took this revision on as its first large-scale project in communication studies. In part, this revision was so successful because several Scott, Foresman professionals made the transition to the new company. It was especially helpful having the assistance of Director of Development Barbara Muller, who had worked on this book since the 1960s; Anne Smith, Vice-President and Editor-in-Chief of Humanities, Art, and Home Economics Education, who had been an English editor at Scott, Foresman and knew about the book; and Melissa Rosati, another former Scott, Foresman editor who became Acquisitions Editor for the speech and mass communication lines. Special thanks must go to Bob Nirkind, the HarperCollins developmental editor who not only helped coalesce the new writing team of Gronbeck and German, but who also brought a reservoir of ideas to the book; his hours of thinking about and shaping our work are evident on every page.

A publishing company with the size and reach of HarperCollins brings to its major books a tremendous array of talent, resources, and energy. The company is committed not only to its authors and books, but to its users as well; that commitment includes concern not only for achieving excellence in products, but also for inspiring excellence in the students who use those products day after day, term after term. If you come away from your class in speech with improved communication skills and a desire to make the world a better place by using those skills, all of us will have accomplished our goals. Good luck!

Bruce E. Gronbeck
Kathleen M. German

PART ONE

Public Speaking and Critical Listening

CHAPTER ONE

The Process of Public Speaking

"I can't believe they require a public speaking course at this place! It's not an academic subject, and I'll certainly never make my living giving speeches. I get nervous when I give speeches, I hate to raise my voice, and I can't stand it when people ask me questions." Kim was really fighting his school's oral communication requirement. Samantha wasn't going to let him get away with self-pity, however. "Listen to yourself! Repeat what you just said and you'll see why public speaking is a graduation requirement. No matter what you do, you'll have to give talks to people. And if you're nervous, afraid of disagreements, and thrown off by questions, you'd better get some speech training. Work those problems out now, among friends, rather than later, when you'll be surrounded by people who want your job. Speak now, Kim, or forever go to pieces."

THE ROLES OF SPEECHMAKING IN SOCIETY

For centuries, public speaking has been the glue that holds societies together. The Latin root *cum-munis* of the English word *communication* means "to work publicly with," and, indeed, communication bonds people together. Public communication enables people to organize into work and living groups, mark the passage of individuals from childhood to adulthood to retirement, debate and make decisions about perplexing issues, and change their societies in positive ways. Because oral communication flows directly between individuals in face-to-face settings, it's the preferred form of communication in times of solemnity, celebration, and crisis. Because speech unites people, speaking and listening skills are important to you.

Specifically, public speeches perform four important functions for a society:

1. *Speeches are used for self-definition.* Especially on such occasions as Memorial Day, the Fourth of July, Labor Day, dedications of monuments, and centennial celebrations, people define their communities and themselves by proclaiming "what they stand for" and what it means to be a member of the community. Just as churchgoers recite aloud their creeds, societies regularly review their defining tenets through speech.

2. *Speeches are used to spread information through a community.* Though much information is distributed by pamphlets, newspapers, and letters, spoken information is more personalized. This is one reason that the president outlines legislative proposals through public announcement, the Surgeon General holds a press conference to update AIDS research findings, and the mayor uses a radio interview to spread the word about the town's upcoming "Pioneer Days."

3. *Speeches are used to debate disputable questions of fact, value, and policy.* Human beings always have fought over their differences with each other. As civilization advanced, however, verbal argument emerged as an alternative to physical combat, and the art of public debate was born. From government to the workplace, oral communication serves an important role in settling disputes.

4. *Speeches are used to bring about individual and group change.* Persuasion has always been a part of public talk. The earliest books about public speaking dealt exclusively with persuasion as the most important kind of speech. As societies have experienced changes in their environments, values, and practices, people have used speech to persuade others to accept those changes.

Speechmaking serves many purposes, but by fulfilling these four broad social functions, speechmaking enables entire societies as well as communities of friends to exist and function.

PUBLIC SPEAKING SKILLS: PERSONAL SURVIVAL

Communication skills will enable you to contribute positively to society in numerous ways: you'll be able to spread much-needed information clearly and powerfully among your associates, to challenge others to arrive at the best solutions to their problems, to persuade listeners to change their beliefs, attitudes, values, and behaviors when you feel that they do not contribute to the good of society, and to participate in the definition and redefinition of society on celebratory or solemn occasions.

The Need for Speech Training

Altruism, however, may not be enough to persuade you to work on your communication skills. Consider, then, another powerful argument: *public speaking skills are necessary for personal survival in society.* (See Figure 1.1.) You must become an effective speaker to grow and prosper.

At some point in your life, you might be called upon to react to proposals to close schools; you could let others do the talking, but then you'd be putting your children's future in the hands of others. You might be asked to choose among candidates for city council; you could let others make the choice, but then the quality of your neighborhood, public library, and public transit system would depend upon the whims of others. You need social communication skills to convince neighbors to sign petitions to stop rezoning, and you need communication skills to argue with the door-to-door salesperson. You must learn to speak publicly; if not, instead of controlling your social environment, you will be controlled by it.

The need for communication skills is, if anything, even more important in the world of work than it is in your social environment. Essentially, work is communication—committee discussions, employment and appraisal interviews, instructions from supervisor to their subordinates, inquiries for

Figure 1.1 Public Speaking Skills Are Survival Skills
Your social world demands that you develop effective communication skills to influence neighborhood projects and community organizations. Your workplace also requires that you apply your effective communication skills as you participate on committees, supervise others, and relate information. What are your personal and career objectives? How will effective communication skills help you pursue your personal and career objectives?

information and advice, lunches and conferences with clients, and efforts to close sales and other deals all consist of some type of communication. It makes sense that employers would be interested in prospective employees' specialized college training when they are interviewing them for entry-level jobs. However, a study found that once a prospective employee had some work experience, employers were less concerned with that individual's college training than they were with his or her interpersonal relations skills, oral and written communication skills, and business know-how. Another study found that speaking with others clearly and forcefully is important in almost all occupations of college graduates and that it is crucial for administrators, managers, sales personnel, allied health workers, educators, social workers, and counselors. It is little wonder, therefore, that graduates of liberal arts programs, as well as business schools, engineering colleges, and other professional programs, list oral communication training as a determining factor in work-related success.[1] All in all, your paycheck and sense of achievement in the workplace are tied to your ability to talk.

The Goals of Speech Training

If you will accept the proposition that you need public speaking skills to survive on and off the job, you might still wonder about the necessity for a class in public speaking. Why not just learn those skills as you go, as you have all of your other communication skills? There are three good answers to that question:

1. *Bringing your communication skills to consciousness allows you to examine and then to either keep or change them.* All of your life most of your social learning has occurred "out of awareness," without you giving much thought to it. Most of your social education has consisted of formal learning or admonition—when people have told you what to do—and informal learning or imitation—when you have copied the behavior modeled by others. Now, however, you're old and mature enough to move to the next stage of learning, technical learning, when you learn from the explanations of others.[2] You can now handle a more technical analysis of your speech, and you can understand rationales for why you should try this or that speaking technique in a particular situation. A classroom makes you self-conscious—but this effect can be positive. In thinking about your speaking behavior and in listening to others discuss that behavior, you can make some decisions about techniques to keep and techniques to change.

2. *A speech classroom is a laboratory and, thus, an ideal place for experimentation.* Most of us have a comparatively limited repertoire of communication skills. You can try out new ones in the safety of a classroom, if you like, rather than in a workplace situation where your skills may cause you to gain or lose a major client. Use your classroom as a lab where you can experiment with different introductions and conclusions, special organizational

patterns, varieties of kinds of evidence, and even different delivery styles. You'll probably find numerous ways to improve your skills by trying different approaches and by evaluating their usefulness to you and your styles of speaking.

3. *Studying oral communication not only makes you a better speaker, but it also helps you to become a more perceptive consumer of oral messages.* You undoubtedly spend more of your communication life listening than talking. In your lifetime you'll be exposed—in person, and via phone and mass media—to literally thousands of oral messages. You'll meet or hear hundreds, even thousands, of people who want some of your time and effort, your money, and your commitment. To protect yourself, you'll need to become a critical listener and critical thinker. You'll have to reason your way through complex appeals, often quickly, and decide how to proceed. That means that you'll have to listen—not just hear, but listen—to others carefully so that you can apply substantive and formal tests to what they say. As you listen to speech after speech in this class, you will be making yourself into a critical listener and critical thinker. You're here to become better at both sending and receiving messages.

Overall, then, you must learn to speak effectively in public because if you don't, who will? And, you must improve your speaking and listening skills because if you don't, your ability to progress and grow as an individual will be threatened. Now is the time for you to start growing as an oral communicator.

Before you plunge into the activities that will improve your speaking and listening skills, however, visualize the whole process—think about the various elements that make up the public speaking process. The remainder of this chapter will examine those elements, the competencies they demand, and matters of fear and ethics that you face as a speaker.

BASIC ELEMENTS IN THE SPEECHMAKING PROCESS

It's time you started thinking seriously, and more technically, about the speechmaking you are about to study. Speechmaking is comprised of a number of elements: a *speaker*—the primary communicator—gives a speech—a continuous, purposive oral *message*—to the *listeners,* who provide *feedback* to the speaker. Their exchange occurs through various *channels,* in a particular communication *situation* and *cultural context.* (See Figure 1.2.) Let's examine each of these elements individually.

The Speaker

From the speaker's viewpoint, there are four key elements in every speech transaction: (a) communicative purpose; (b) knowledge of subject and communication skills; (c) attitudes toward self, listeners, and subject; and (d) degree of credibility.

Figure 1.2 Basic Elements in the Speechmaking Process

All speeches entail an interaction among seven primary elements: message, speaker, listeners, feedback, channels, situation, and cultural context. They work together in a complex process or transaction. Identify each of the elements present when you give your first classroom speech.

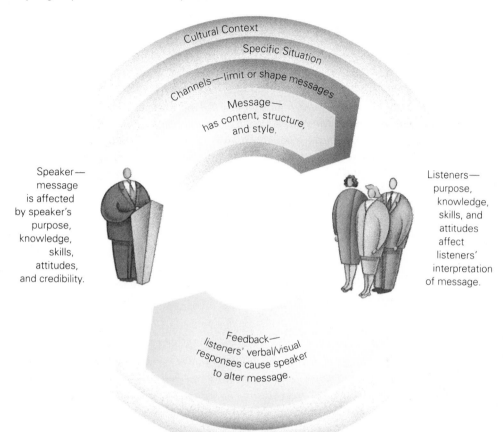

Cultural Context

Specific Situation

Channels—limit or shape messages

Message— has content, structure, and style.

Speaker— message is affected by speaker's purpose, knowledge, skills, attitudes, and credibility.

Listeners— purpose, knowledge, skills, and attitudes affect listeners' interpretation of message.

Feedback— listeners' verbal/visual responses cause speaker to alter message.

The Speaker's Purpose

Every speaker has a purpose. Generally we speak to achieve a goal. That goal can be as simple as social intercourse or as complex as an attempt to alter someone's ideas. Additionally, you may wish to entertain, call attention to a problem, refute an assertion, ward off a threat, or establish or maintain your status or power.

The Speaker's Knowledge

Your knowledge of the subject and mastery of communication skills affect the character of your message and your effectiveness. If you have only surface knowledge of a topic, listeners feel cheated; you had better say something important, new, relevant, interesting. Also, to succeed you need to acquire and refine a series of fundamental speaking skills. The communication skills addressed in this book include a wide variety of abilities—setting communicative goals, finding and assembling relevant information, organizing messages in coherent and powerful ways, illustrating them visually, and delivering them with clarity and punch.

The Speaker's Attitudes

Your attitudes toward your self, your listeners, and your subject significantly affect what you say and how you say it. All of us have mental pictures of ourselves as persons—self-concepts, or images of the kind of individuals we are and of how others perceive us.[3]

Your self-image influences the way you speak in particular situations. If you have little confidence in your abilities or are unsure of your information, you tend to speak hesitantly. Your voice becomes weak, your body stiffens, and you watch the floor rather than your audience. If you're overly confident, you tend to move in the other direction, becoming overbearing and overly familiar, disregarding listeners' needs, and riding roughshod over others' feelings. Ideally, you'll find the middle way, with enough self-confidence to believe in yourself and enough sensitivity to treat your listeners with respect.

Part of your treatment of your listeners comes from your *power relationship* with them and the way you perceive them—as parents or children, instructors or students, supervisors or employees, subordinates or equals. Giving a report in front of a teacher who's grading you involves an unequal power relationship. Giving a report in front of a student committee of which you're a member involves a relationship of equality. Your attitudes tend to differ from situation to situation, and you adjust your speaking style to take into account your status relative to members of the audience.

Other attitudes that you hold may also affect your talk:

1. *Are you comfortable in the speaking situation, or does it make you feel strange?* A speech classroom, for example, at first will make you feel awkward, and that feeling will affect your performance, but, as you grow more comfortable, your attitudes will improve—and so will your skills.

2. *Are you comfortable with your subject and your mastery of it?* Do you believe what you're saying? Is the subject interesting to you or did you pick it because an article in *Newsweek* set it up for you? Does anyone else care about it? Your answers to these questions will be reflected in the ways you use your voice and body, in the intensity of your language, and even in your selection of materials. Your attitudes affect your manner of speaking.

The Speaker's Credibility

The listeners' estimation of a speaker's credibility will affect the speaker's success in winning agreement, inspiring confidence, or promoting ideas. Speaker **credibility** is the degree to which an audience judges a communicator trustworthy, competent, sincere, attractive, and dynamic. The idea of credibility is rooted in the classical Greek concept of *ethos,* a word that

A speaker can heighten the impact of a speech by increasing the audience's estimate of trustworthiness, competency, sincerity, attractiveness, and dynamism. How are these elements of credibility probably influencing the listeners in this setting?

means *character*. Research has repeatedly demonstrated that a speaker who can raise an audience's estimation of his or her trustworthiness, competency, sincerity, attractiveness, and dynamism will heighten the impact of the speech. Research has verified the following generalizations, among others:

1. References to yourself and your own experience—provided they are not boasting or excessive—tend to increase your perceived trustworthiness and competence; references to others (authorities) tend to increase your perceived trustworthiness and dynamism.
2. Using highly credible authorities to substantiate your claims increases your perceived fairness.
3. If you can demonstrate that you and your audience share common beliefs, attitudes, and values, your overall credibility will increase.
4. Well-organized speeches are more credible than poorly organized speeches.
5. The more sincere you are, the better chance you have of changing your listeners' attitudes.[4]

As these generalizations suggest, you and your message are inseparable in people's minds; your audience's perception of you is the key—Aristotle called it the most important aspect of persuasion—to your effectiveness.

The Message

Messages are often referred to as *ideas* or *information*. In public speaking, the message the speaker communicates is made up of three variables: *content*, *structure*, and *style*.

The Content of the Message

The message of a speech does not consist merely of facts and descriptions. A speech's **content** is the substantive and valuative material that represents the speaker's view of the world. A message is always controlled by speakers who cull through mounds of material to come up with ten minutes' worth of content. This book seeks to help you to select that content wisely.

The Structure of the Message

Any message we transmit is necessarily structured or organized in some way, simply because we say some things first; others second; and still others third, fourth, and so on. Even if you seem to ramble, listeners will look for a coherent pattern in your message. It's important, then, to provide a pattern in order to guide the audience's search for coherence. That structure may be as simple as numbering points—"First, I will discuss . . . , next I will . . . , and, finally, I will. . ."—or as complex as a full outline with points and subpoints.

The Style of the Message

The third variable in every spoken message is style. Just as you must select and arrange the ideas you wish to convey to audiences, so too must you select words, arrange them in sentences, and decide how to reveal your self-image to that group of listeners. Selecting and arranging words, as well as revealing oneself to be a certain sort of person, are matters of style. Given the innumerable words from which to choose, the great varieties of sentence structures, and even the many kinds of self-images available to the speaker, many styles are possible. Styles can be personal or impersonal, literal or ironic, plain or elevated, and even philosophical or poetic; such labels refer to particular combinations of vocabulary, syntax (sentence arrangement), and images of the speaker. What we call style, therefore, really has nothing to do with elegance or stylishness; rather, it has to do with those aspects of language use that convey impressions of speakers, details of the world, and emotional overtones.

The Listener

Like speakers, listeners have goals or purposes in mind. The way they think about what is said is affected by their (a) purpose; (b) knowledge of and interest in the subject; (c) level of listening skills; and (d) attitudes toward self, speaker, and ideas presented.

The Listener's Purpose

Listeners always have one or more purposes that they want to fulfill; no less than speakers, audience members come to speeches looking for rewards. You may, for example, attend an on-campus presentation by actor-activist Robert Redford in part to be entertained, in part to learn something about the environmental causes he champions, and in part just to see what a star looks and sounds like in person. Such purposes form listeners' expectations; speakers must take such expectations into account or risk rejection.

The Listener's Knowledge and Interest

In speech situations, the listener's knowledge of, and interest in, the subject significantly affects how they respond to the message. When speaking, one of your jobs is to figure out how much the listeners know about your subject and if they have any personal stake in it. You can give only the most elementary speech on prestressed concrete and its uses to an audience that knows nothing about cement; talking about cement with your speech class is one thing, but with a structural engineering class it's quite another. You must assess the level of knowledge and interest of your audience.

The Listener's Command of Listening Skills

Listeners vary in their ability to process oral messages. Some people were raised in homes in which complex oral exchanges occurred, and others were not. Some people have acquired the ability to follow long chains of reasoning, while others struggle to get the point. Most younger children cannot yet concentrate on difficult speeches, while most college students already have been taught to do so. As a result of these differences in listeners, you must constantly scan your audience, looking for signs of comprehension.

The Listener's Attitudes

Listeners' attitudes toward themselves, the speaker, and the subject affect how they interpret and respond to speeches. Listeners with low self-esteem, for example, tend to be swayed more easily than those with a stronger self-image. Listeners whose opinions seem to be confirmed by the views of the speaker are also more easily influenced. Moreover, as a rule, people seek out speakers whose positions they already agree with, and they retain longer and more vividly those ideas of which they strongly approve.[5] *Audience analysis* is one of the keys to speaking success because you need to know much about people's attitudes before you can reach your listeners.

Feedback

You may think of public speaking as communication flowing from speaker to audience. But information, feelings, and ideas flow the other way—from audience to speaker—as well. That flow is called feedback. **Feedback** is information about the clarity and acceptability of ideas that is returned by listeners to the sources of messages. Two kinds of information are provided by feedback. Speakers can learn, by looking for frowns or other signs of puzzlement, or, in the case of educational settings, by seeing how well students do on tests, whether their ideas have been comprehended clearly. Speakers can also look for cues about the acceptability of their ideas; audiences can boo, look disgusted or antsy, or even leave the room. Being able to read feedback is an important weapon in a speaker's arsenal, especially since the speaker is often able to make some mid-course adjustments in the speech.

Suppose you're giving a speech on child abuse. You might, for example, discuss the difference between punishment and abuse by referring to spanking. If you see frowns after your first example, you might try a second and third example, each time distinguishing between legal and illegal discipline until the listeners understand. Or, if you quote one authority on the subject and some members of the audience still look skeptical, you might add another authority, as well as descriptions of some incidents of abuse. You might not be able to convince all your audience that there is a difference between punishment and abuse, but at least you might convert a few people. Speakers typically make these moves in response to feedback.

Public speaking is not a one-way street; it has intellectual and emotional traffic flowing in two directions. Both speakers and their listeners produce messages during a speech transaction.

The Channels

A communication exchange between speakers and listeners occurs simultaneously through multiple channels. The **verbal channel** carries the words, the culture's agreed-upon symbols for ideas. The **visual channel** transmits the gestures, facial expressions, bodily movements, and posture of the speaker and listeners; these tend to clarify, reinforce, or add emotional overtones to the words or to transmit important information to the speaker. At times the visual channel may be supplemented with a **pictorial channel**— visual aids such as diagrams, charts, graphs, and objects. The **aural channel**—also called the **paralinguistic channel**—carries the tone of voice, variations in pitch and loudness, and other vocal modulations produced by the speaker's stream of sounds. Similar to the visual channel, the aural channel heightens some meanings and adds others. Because these four channels are seen and heard by listeners simultaneously, the message is really a combination of several messages flowing through all of the pathways. You must learn to shape and control the messages moving through all four channels.

The Situation

If you think about it, you may realize that what you say and how you say it are affected seriously by the situations in which you are speaking. You don't talk the same way at work as you do at a dorm room party. Your speech is affected by the *physical setting* and the *social context* in which it occurs.

Physical Setting
The physical setting of the speech influences the listener's expectancies as well as their readiness to respond. People waiting in the quiet solemnity of a cathedral for the service to begin have very different expectations than do theatergoers gathered to witness the opening of a new Broadway play. Listeners at an open-air political rally anticipate a different sort of message than do those gathered in a college classroom to hear a lecture on political theory.

The furniture and decor of the physical space also make a difference. Comfortable chairs and soft-hued drapes tend to put discussion groups at ease and to promote a more productive exchange. The executive who talks to an employee from behind a large desk set in the middle of an impressively furnished office gains an advantage from the nature of the physical setting.

Social Context

Even more important than physical setting in determining how a message will be received is the social context in which it is presented. A **social context** is a particular combination of people, purposes, and places interacting communicatively. In a social context, *people* are distinguished from each other by such factors as age, occupation, power, degree of intimacy, and knowledge. These factors in part determine how one "properly" communicates with others. The degree to which people are seen as superior to, equal with, or inferior to each other in status helps determine each one's communicative style. You are expected to speak deferentially to your elders, your boss, an influential political leader, a stranger whose reactions you cannot immediately predict, and a sage. Certain *purposes,* or goals, are more or less appropriately communicated in different social contexts as well. Thus, a memorial service is not a time for attacking a political opponent—a "meet the candidates" night is. Some *places* are more conducive to certain kinds of communicative exchanges than others. Public officials are often more easily influenced in their offices than in public forums, where they tend to be more defensive; sensitive parents scold their children in private, never in front of their friends.

Societies are governed by customs, norms, and traditions—or communication rules. A **communication rule** is a guide to communication behavior; it specifies what can be said, how, to whom, and in what circumstances. "Stand up and speak loudly" is a very general rule; "Always address the president of the United States as 'Mr. President'" is a very specific rule. Some communication rules tell you what to do—"An audience will better remember what you have to say if you break it into three to five main points"; others tell you what to avoid—"Don't wander aimlessly across the stage because it will distract your audience." Such rules, of course, can be broken; some wandering speakers are nevertheless listened to, probably because they have so many other virtues. Occasionally, such rule breaking is inconsequential; sometimes, however, it determines success or failure; and it always involves a certain amount of risk.[6]

The Cultural Context

Finally, elements of communication may have different meanings depending upon the culture or society within which the communication is taking place. Each culture has its own rules for interpreting communication signals. A hearty belch after a dinner in Skokie, Illinois, is a sign of impoliteness, but in other cultures, it's a supreme compliment to the host or hostess. Negotiating the price of a T-shirt is unheard of at Sears in Atlanta, yet it's a sign of active interest in an Istanbul bazaar or at a Cleveland garage sale. Communication systems operate within the confines of cultural rules and expectations of members of a given society.

Cultural rules and expectations become important in two situations: during *intercultural contact* and *cross-cultural presentations.* When talking to members of other cultures on your home turf, you might offend them by violating some rule that they bring with them to your speech. A common violation that occurs during intercultural contact is too much familiarity or informality with a new acquaintance. To call people by their first names publicly, for example, is simply not acceptable in many countries. Your problems may be even greater, of course, if you attempt to speak publicly in another culture. During such cross-cultural presentations you risk violating not only personal standards of interaction but the rules of the situation operating at that time. Americans soon learn that they cannot joke publicly about royalty in England in the same way that they can joke about the president in the United States. If you are going to speak in various countries, you have to learn the communication rules governing the ways to introduce a person to an audience, to quote authorities, and to refer to yourself and audience members; rules for such communication situations tend to vary from country to country.

To tap into the cultural context for public speaking is to grapple with the most fundamental questions of sociality—how people in various countries interact with each other and transact public business. The cultural context for public speaking is the ultimate source of the communication rules you've been taught.

Because speeches almost always represent transactions whose appropriateness is determined by cultural rules or expectations, you will throughout this book find explicit pieces of advice—do's and don'ts. It's not really "wrong," for example, to skip a summary at the end of your speech, but most audiences expect one. If you omit it, the audience might question your **communication competence**—your ability to construct a speech in accordance with their expectations. These sorts of expectations do not have to be followed slavishly, because conditions and even speaker talents vary from situation to situation; however, you should follow the rules of communication most of the time because you want listeners to evaluate your ideas, not your communication skills.

Speakers and listeners, messages and channels, feedback, context, and culture—these are the primary elements of the public speaking process. Sooner or later you need to become expert at managing all of them in ways that make you a more effective communicator for the following reasons:

1. *A change in one element usually produces changes in the others.* During a speech on learning to use the campus computer system, for example, your attitude will affect your language and delivery, your listeners' attitudes toward you, and even the feedback that you receive from them.

2. *No single element controls the entire process.* You may think the speaker does control the entire process, but, of course, the speaker doesn't because listeners can tune in or tune out and because cultural expectations often affect the listeners' perceptions of the speaker's talents.

Overall, therefore, public speaking is a *transaction*. Inherent in the idea of transaction is the notion of exchange: you prepare a speech to give your listeners, and, in turn, your listeners give you their attention and reactions or feedback. From among all of the things you could say, you actually select only a few and tailor them to the listeners' interests, wants, and desires, so that they can absorb and accept them. And, just as you assert your right to speak, they assert their right to listen or not listen. *Public speaking is a communication transaction, a face-to-face process of mutual give-and-take.*

SKILLS AND COMPETENCIES NEEDED FOR SUCCESSFUL SPEECHMAKING

Because public speaking is an interactive process through which people transact various kinds of business, you must acquire certain skills (psychomotor abilities) and competencies (mental abilities to identify, assess, and plan responses to communication problems). Four basic qualities merit your attention: (a) integrity, (b) knowledge, (c) sensitivity to listener needs and to speaking situations, and (d) oral skills.

Integrity

Your reputation for reliability, truthfulness, and concern for others is your single most powerful means of exerting rhetorical influence over others. Integrity is important, especially in an age of electronic advertising and mass mailings—when every pressure group, cause, and special interest can make its way into the public mind, often with conflicting analyses and recommendations for action. Listeners who have no personal experience with a particular subject seek information and advice from speakers they trust. You must earn their trust if you want to succeed.

Knowledge

Expertise is also essential. No one wants to listen to an empty-headed prattler; speakers should know their subjects. So, even though you know a lot about a topic through personal experience, take time to do some extra reading, talk with local experts, and find out what aspects of the topic interest your potential listeners.

Rhetorical Sensitivity

Sometimes we talk publicly for purely *expressive* reasons—simply to be talking. Usually, however, we speak for *instrumental* reasons—to pass on ideas or to influence the way others think or act. The most successful speakers are "other directed," concerned with meeting their listeners' needs and solving their problems through public talk. These speakers are rhetorically sensitive to others.

Rhetorical sensitivity refers to speakers' attitudes toward the process of speech composition.[7] More particularly, rhetorical sensitivity is the degree to which speakers (a) recognize that all people are different and complex and, hence, must be considered individually; (b) avoid rigid communication by adapting their messages and themselves to particular audiences; (c) consciously seek and react to audience feedback; (d) understand the limitations of talk, sometimes even remaining silent rather than trying to express the unexpressible; and (e) work at finding the right set of arguments and linguistic expressions to make particular ideas clear and attractive to particular audiences.

Being rhetorically sensitive does not mean saying only what you think the audience wants to hear. Rather, it is a matter of careful self-assessment, audience analysis, and decision making. What are your purposes? To what degree will they be understandable and acceptable to others? To what degree can you adapt your purposes to audience preferences while maintaining your own integrity and self-respect? These questions demand that you be sensitive to listener needs, the demands of speaking situations, and the requirements of self-respect. Rhetorical sensitivity, then, is not so much a skill as a competency—a way of thinking and acting in the world of communication.

Oral Skills

Fluency, poise, control of voice, and coordinated movements of your body mark you as a skilled speaker. These skills don't come naturally; they are developed through practice. Such practice is not a matter of acquiring and rehearsing a bag of tricks. Rather, your practice both inside and outside your classroom should aim at making you an animated, natural, and conversational speaker. Many successful public speakers—discounting those speaking in the high ceremonial situations of politics and religion—seem to be merely *conversing* with their audiences. That should be your goal: to practice being natural, to practice conversing with others in public.

OVERCOMING SPEECH ANXIETY

As you think about speaking publicly in front of a group, you're likely to feel some anxiety because you don't want to fail. At times, though, this fear of failure or embarrassment may be even stronger than your desire to speak.

Research distinguishes between two kinds of speech anxiety: *state apprehension* and *trait apprehension*.[8] **State apprehension** refers to the anxiety you feel in particular settings or situations. For example, perhaps you can talk easily with friends but are uncomfortable when being interviewed for a job. This sort of apprehension is also known as *stage fright* because it's the fear of performing that leads to your worries about failure or embarrassment. Extreme stage fright has physiological manifestations—clammy hands, weak knees, dry mouth, and a trembling or even cracking voice. Its psychological manifestations include mental blocks—forgetting what you're going to say, vocal hesitation and nonfluency, and an internal voice that keeps telling you that you're messing up your speech. The knowledge that you're being evaluated by others brings on these anxious moments.

While some aspects of nervousness are characteristic of the situation, others are a part of your own personality. This kind of apprehension, called **trait apprehension,** refers to your level of anxiety as you face any communication situation. A high level of anxiety may lead people to withdraw from situations that require interpersonal or public communication with others. By attacking your trait fears of speaking before others, you'll be in a better position to reduce your overall level of anxiety. Although there's no foolproof program for developing self-confidence, there are some ways to achieve the confidence necessary to complete the speaking task:

1.   *Realize that tension and nervousness are normal and, in part, even beneficial to speakers.* Fear is a normal part of living; learn how to control it and make it work for you. Remember that the tension you feel can provide you with energy and alertness. As adrenaline pours into your bloodstream, you experience a physical charge that increases bodily movement and psychological acuity. A baseball pitcher who's not pumped up before a big game may find that his fastball has no zip. Similarly, a speaker who's not pumped up will undoubtedly come across as dull and lifeless.

2.   *Take comfort that tension is physiologically reduced by the act of speaking.* As you talk and discover that your audience accepts you and some of what you're saying, your nervousness will tend to dissipate. Physiologically,

Some anxiety about performing publicly is normal. Symptoms of anxiety are experienced both physically and psychologically. How can you cope with the anxiety that accompanies performance?

your body is using up the excess adrenaline it generated; psychologically, your ego is getting positive reinforcement. Shortly after you've begun, you realize that your prior preparation is working in your favor and that you have the situation under control. The very act of talking aloud reduces fear.

3. *Talk about topics that interest you.* Speech anxiety arises in part because of self-centeredness; sometimes you're more concerned with your personal appearance and performance than with your topic. One means of reducing that anxiety is to select topics that are of deep interest to you, topics that will take your mind off yourself. By doing this, you make the situation topic-centered rather than self-centered.

4. *Talk about subjects with which you are familiar.* Confidence born of knowledge increases your perceived credibility and helps control your nervousness. Have you ever wondered why you could talk at length with friends about your favorite hobby, sport, or political interests without feeling anxious, only to find yourself in a nervous state when standing in front of an audience to talk about something you just read in *Newsweek?* Knowing something about the subject may be part of the answer. Subject mastery is closely related to self-mastery.

5. *Analyze both the situation and the audience.* The more you know about the audience and about what is expected of you in a particular situation, the less there is to fear. In the speech classroom, students are usually less nervous during their second speech than during their first. They are more comfortable with the audience and are more aware of the demands of the situation. The same is true in other settings as well: careful analysis of the audience and their expectations goes a long way toward reducing a natural fear of the unknown.

6. *Speak in public as often as you can.* Sheer repetition of the public speaking experience will not eliminate your fears, but it will make them more controllable. Speaking a number of times in front of the same group can help reduce anxiety. Repeated experiences with different audiences and situations also will help increase your self-assurance and poise, which, in turn, will lessen your apprehension. Force yourself to speak up in class discussions, join in discussions with friends and others, and contribute in meetings of organizations to which you belong. Find time to talk with people of all ages. Attend public meetings on occasion and make a few comments.

There are no shortcuts to developing self-confidence about speaking in public. For most of us, gaining self-confidence is partly a matter of psyching ourselves up, and partly a matter of experience. The sick feeling in the pit of your stomach probably will always be there, at least momentarily, but it need not paralyze you. As you gain experience with each of the essential steps—from selecting a subject to practicing the speech—your self-confidence as a speaker will grow.

Shyness and Public Speaking

Do you think of yourself as shy? If so, does shyness affect your willingness and ability to speak in public? Many people think of themselves as shy, but some people suffer from heavy-duty speech fright to the point of paralysis.

A leading psychologist, Stanford's Philip G. Zimbardo, defines shyness as "an apprehensiveness about certain social situations due to excessive preoccupation with being critically evaluated, resulting in a variety of behavioral, physical, cognitive, and emotional reactions." Shyness comes in many forms. It's a matter of bashfulness at one extreme, social paralysis at the other, with the middle ground being a state in which you lack self-confidence and are easily embarrassed. About 40 percent of American college students describe themselves as shy, another 40 percent say that they used to be shy, and about 15 percent see themselves as shy in certain situations. To get at the roots of shyness, Zimbardo and his colleagues developed *The Stanford Shyness Survey*, a tool used to diagnose shyness and its sources in specific individuals.

Using such instruments as the Shyness Survey, therapists can tailor treatment programs to individual needs: (a) They can help individuals build new social skills, teaching them *how* to act in situations that are new or strange. (b) They can suggest exercises to boost self-esteem if it appears that a person consistently thinks of him- or herself in negative terms. (c) If a shy person's physiological reactions are dominant, therapists can teach the individual anxiety management—breathing exercises, relaxation techniques, muscle-flexing, and so on. (d) Occasionally, therapists organize group and individual sessions devoted to "cognitive reorganization"; here, individuals learn the bases of their shyness, come to understand that it need not destroy social relations, and attribute different sorts of significance to it than they had before. (e) Group sessions can also be used as practice arenas, just as your speech classroom is, where shy people can be guided through their interactions with others step by step.

Shyness is probably at the base of what we usually call "speech fright" or "communication apprehension." If you are shy, one of the goals you ought to set for yourself in this classroom is the control and redirection of those feelings. Talk with your instructor, and perhaps other professionals on campus, if you want help.

For more information, see Philip Zimbardo, Paul Piklonis, and Robert Norwood, "The Silent Prison of Shyness," Office of Naval Research Technical Report Z-17 (Stanford, Calif.: Stanford University, November 1974); and Philip G. Zimbardo, *Psychology and Life*, 11th ed. (Glenview, Ill.: Scott-Foresman, 1985), 447–450.

THE ETHICS OF PUBLIC SPEAKING

No introductory chapter to a public speaking textbook is complete without a reference to the ethics of public speaking. In helping people define who they are, in assembling and packaging information for others, in seeking to persuade them to think a certain way or to act on your recommendations, you run into many ethical questions. Is it ethical to make explicitly racial references when defining a people? Should you tell both sides of the story when you are giving people information on a new wonder drug? Can you ethically suppress certain kinds of information when you're trying to change people's minds? These and hundreds of other ethical questions face you as you prepare and deliver speeches. Whether you want to or not, you make decisions with moral implications many, many times—even when you are building a comparatively simple speech.

No one can presume to tell you precisely what ethical codes you ought to adhere to when giving a speech. Given a textbook's educational mission, however, we will regularly raise ethical questions to urge you to deal with them. Throughout the book, you'll encounter Ethical Moments, features that will confront you with a problem and ask you to think through it. Confronting and working through ethical dilemmas will make you a more thoughtful speaker.

CHAPTER SUMMARY

1. Speaking skills are important to society because people use speeches for collective self-definition; for information giving; to debate questions of fact, value, and policy; and for individual and social change.

2. Public speaking skills are survival skills because your growth and progress in social and workplace environments are affected by your ability to speak effectively.

3. There are seven primary elements of the public speaking process: *the speaker* (purpose, knowledge, attitudes, and credibility); *the message* (content, structure, and style); *the listeners* (purpose, knowledge of subject, command of listening skills, and attitudes); *feedback; the channels* (verbal, visual, pictorial, and aural); *the communication situation* (physical setting and social context); and *the cultural context* (during intercultural contact and cross-cultural presentations).

4. To be a successful speaker, you need a range of skills and competencies: integrity, knowledge, rhetorical sensitivity, and oral skills.

5. You can control speech anxiety—state apprehension (stage fright) and trait apprehension—through counseling, hard work, and practice.

6. Speakers face ethical decisions that they must make if they're to maximize their impact on others.

KEY TERMS

aural channel (p. 12)

communication competence (p. 14)

communication rule (p. 13)

content (p. 10)

credibility (p. 8)

feedback (p. 11)

paralinguistic channel (p. 12)

pictorial channel (p. 12)

rhetorical sensitivity (p. 16)

social context (p. 13)

state apprehension (p. 16)

trait apprehension (p. 17)

verbal channel (p. 12)

visual channel (p. 12)

SKILLBUILDING ACTIVITIES

1. Interview the leader of a local group that schedules public lectures, the director of the campus speakers' bureau, or another person in a position to discuss the speech skills that are characteristic of professional speakers. Bring a list of those skills to class and be prepared to compare your notes with those of others.

2. Meet with another classmate to prepare to introduce him or her to the rest of the class. Concentrate on obtaining, selecting, and ordering your information for public presentation.

3. Prepare an inventory of your personal speech needs and speaking abilities. (Your instructor may make this the first assignment in a personal communication journal that you will maintain throughout the term.) In your inventory, offer thoughtful responses to the following items:
   a. I am _____
   b. I am not _____
   c. I want _____
   d. I can _____
   e. I cannot _____

REFERENCES

1. Conclusions about skills in the workplace appear in N. L. Ochsner and Lewis C. Solmon, *College Education and Employment—The Recent Graduates* (Bethlehem, Penn.: College Placement Council Foundation, 1979); Carol A. Carmichael, "Most College Grads Satisfied with Jobs," *Chicago Tribune,* September 16, 1979; Ann Stouffer Bisconti and Lewis C. Solmon, *College Education on the Job—The Graduates' Viewpoint* (Bethlehem, Penn.: College Placement Council Foundation, 1976), esp. 43; Carol H. Pazandak, "Followup Survey of 1973 Graduates, College of Liberal Arts" (Minneapolis: College of Liberal Arts, University of Minnesota, 1977), multilith; Jack Landgrebe and Howard Baumgartel, "Results of the Graduation Requirement Questionnaire for College of Liberal Arts and Sciences Alumni" (Lawrence: College of Liberal Arts and Sciences, University of Kansas), typescript; "Instruction in Communication at Colorado State University" (Fort Collins: College of Engineering, Colorado State University, July 1979), multilith; Edward Foster et al., "A Market Study for the College of Business Administration, University of Minnesota, Twin Cities" (Minneapolis: College of Business Administration, University of Minnesota,

November 1978), multilith. These and other studies are reported in Samuel L. Becker and Leah R. V. Ekdom, "That Forgotten Basic Skill: Oral Communication,"*Association for Communication Administration Bulletin,* No. 33 (August 1980).

2.   Edward T. Hall, *The Silent Language* (New York: Fawcett World Library, 1966), chap. 4, "The Major Triad," 63–92.

3.   For a discussion of the interrelationships between self-concept and communication, see Gordon I. Zimmerman, James L. Owen, and David R. Siebert, *Speech Communication: A Contemporary Introduction,* 2nd ed. (St. Paul: West Publishing Co., 1977), esp. 32–43; and Gail E. Myers and Michele Tolela Myers, *The Dynamics of Human Communication: A Laboratory Approach,* 3rd ed. (New York: McGraw-Hill Book Co., 1980), chap. 3, "Self-Concept: Who Am I?" 47–72.

4.   Generalizations about source credibility are most usefully summarized in Stephen W. Littlejohn, "A Bibliography of Studies Related to Variables of Source Credibility," *Bibliographic Annual in Speech Communication: 1971,* Ned A. Shearer, ed. (New York: Speech Communication Association, 1972), 1–40; cf. Erwin P. Bettinghaus and Michael J. Cody, *Persuasive Communication,* 4th ed. (New York: Holt, Rinehart & Winston, 1987), Chapter 5, "The Influence of the Communicator," 83–104.

5.   See the personality analysis of receivers in Michael Burgoon, *Approaching Speech Communication* (New York: Holt, Rinehart & Winston, 1974), 64–69.

6.   Much of the research on physical setting and social context is summarized in Mark L. Knapp, *Essentials of Nonverbal Communication* (New York: Holt, Rinehart & Winston, 1980), chap. 4, "The Effects of Territory and Personal Space," 75–96. The determinative aspects of social expectations in human communication are discussed in John J. Gumperz and Dell Hymes, eds., *Directions in Sociolinguistics: The Ethnography of Communication* (New York: Holt, Rinehart & Winston, 1972); and Peter Collett, ed., *Social Rules and Social Behavior* (Totowa, N.J.: Rowman & Littlefield, 1977). A review of research on communication rules is found in Susan B. Shimanoff, *Communication Rules: Theory and Research,* Sage Library of Social Research (Beverly Hills: Sage Publications, 1980), 97.

7.   See Roderick P. Hart and Don M. Burks, "Rhetorical Sensitivity and Social Interaction," *Speech [Communication] Monographs,* 47 (1980), 1–22.

8.   James McCroskey, "Oral Communication Apprehension: A Summary of Current Theory and Research," *Human Communication Research,* 4 (1977), 78–96.

22   •   Part One / Public Speaking and Critical Listening

CHAPTER TWO

Public Speaking and Critical Listening

> *"I didn't hear the professor say that Chapter 12 would be on the exam. I didn't even read that stuff. That's not fair! I got a zero on that entire question. I didn't have a clue how to answer it."*

In your daily life, you spend more time listening than you do reading, writing, or speaking. Yet, you probably spend little time listening carefully. While you may assume that you're a good listener, you don't realize you weren't really listening carefully until you miss something important. You have probably never been trained to listen. Nonetheless, you're expected to be a good listener—and often, your performance depends on your listening skills.

Listening accounts for over 40 percent of your communicative time.[1] Through conversations, classroom lectures, group meetings, electronic media, and other forms of communication, you acquire an amazing amount of information. You also learn to anticipate the expectations of others and to gauge their feelings and moods through listening.

Listening is the central conduit in the communication process. As a speaker, you reach out to your audience through that conduit, and, in turn, listeners respond. In particular, listeners can provide two kinds of feedback—immediate and delayed. **Immediate feedback** consists of verbal or nonverbal responses during a communicative exchange. **Delayed feedback** consists of oral or visual signals received after the message has been transmitted.

This chapter will discuss listening behavior in general and then focus on both speaker and listener responsibilities more thoroughly. Finally, to help you refine your listening skills, the chapter concludes with some advice on effective listening.

The speaker receives verbal and nonverbal feedback both during and after the communication transaction. What other examples of immediate and delayed feedback can you think of?

Immediate Feedback

Delayed Feedback

HEARING AND LISTENING

Hearing is the first step in the listening process. To listen to a message, you must first hear it. **Hearing** is the physiological process of receiving sound waves. Sound waves traveling through the air set up vibrations on the eardrum and these vibrations, in turn, are transmitted to the brain. Hearing is affected by both the laws of physics and the neurophysiology of the body. Any number of factors can interfere with hearing—distracting noises in the environment, sounds too loud or too soft for the aural mechanism, or physiological impediments such as illness or hearing loss. Generally, the hearing process is beyond the speaker's control except for the ability to change speaking volume and to eliminate distracting sounds.

Listening, on the other hand, is the cognitive process whereby people attach meanings to aural signals.[2] After sound waves are translated to nerve impulses by the middle ear and the auditory nerve, they are sent to the brain for interpretation. The process of interpretation—registering impulses, assigning them to meaningful contexts, and evaluating them—constitutes listening.

Barriers to Listening

Listening is a joint responsibility of both speaker and listeners who must make sure that intended messages are taken in, comprehended, interpreted, and evaluated. Few people are good listeners. Although researchers vary in their assessments of the average listening comprehension rate, most agree that people do not utilize their listening potential. Some studies indicate that people may be listening at only a 25 percent comprehension rate; that is, they understand only about one-fourth of all information received aurally.

There are several reasons why people are poor listeners.[3] One reason is that the complex human mind can comprehend many more words per minute than speakers can produce. Listeners can process more than 400 spoken words per minute, yet the average speaker only produces between 125 and 175 words per minute. This time lag between slower speaking rates and faster rates of thinking is known as the **speech-thought differential.** Stated in a different way, the listener needs only 15 seconds of every minute to comprehend the spoken message. The resulting time lag creates special problems. In this excess time, listeners' thoughts may begin to stray. Can you recall a time when you began listening to a speaker, but soon found yourself thinking about lunch, or an upcoming test, or a date? This tendency for our thoughts to stray poses many problems for the speaker trying to convey an understandable message, especially if the subject matter is complex.

A second reason people are poor listeners is that attitudes, values, beliefs, and memories trigger personal interpretations and reactions to spoken messages. Sometimes, a thought or word reminds you of a past experience. At that point you may start to think about that experience and lose track of the message being presented. Or, if you don't agree with the speaker, you may be distracted by mentally debating the ideas instead of listening for their full development. At times, your feelings color your reception of messages so much that you attribute ideas to the speaker that were not actually presented. All of these thoughts, feelings, and emotions are part of your **internal perceptual field.**

A third reason for poor listening is that people tend to be passive listeners. Listening is an active process that requires energy. Recall the last time you enjoyed a movie. When you left the theater you have felt tired even though you did nothing more than watch and listen. Because you empathized with the characters, you were actively engaged in the flow of events. This type of empathic response takes energy—the same sort of energy you use when you are actively listening. Being passive is much easier than concentrating on the speaker's message. However, passive listening is ineffective listening.

A fourth reason people are poor listeners is that physical setting can interfere with listening. Seats are uncomfortable; rooms are too cold or too hot; people cough and sneeze; outside doors slam. Physical well-being and comfort often take priority with the listener.[4] Just as distracting thoughts can invade your internal perceptual field, so too can external distractions draw your attention away from the speech. Your **external perceptual field** includes stimuli from the surrounding environment. (See Figure 2.1.)

The fifth reason for poor listening is that listeners can become frustrated when the speaker uses unfamiliar language or presents complicated ideas. Dealing with words or concepts that are unfamiliar requires mental and physical energy. If the ideas are not clearly explained or the organization is vague, confusion results. Often, listeners simply give up.

The sixth and final reason for poor listening consists of the listeners' predetermined ideas about the topic, the speaker, or the occasion. **Selective perception** is the process of filtering multiple stimuli through a narrow set of expectations. Columnist William F. Buckley, Jr., is known for his intellectual sneer and well-turned phrases. His listeners wait for both, and were he not to provide them, people would wonder what was wrong with him. Many speakers aren't given a fair opportunity because their audiences accept conclusions about them or their topics before they even speak.

What, then, can you as a speaker expect from your listeners? You already know that they can think much faster than you can talk. You must contend with competing thoughts that your listeners might feel are more important than the information you want to share. Your listeners' internal and external perceptual fields may divert their attention. Their preconceived biases about you, the topic, or the words you use may block their acceptance of your message. Now that you're aware of the problems you may face, you need to know how to make some adjustments and adaptations in your speaking to assist your listeners. You'll explore speaker responsibility for adjustments and adaptations later in this chapter.

Figure 2.1 The Perceptual Fields of the Listener
Competing demands on our attention guarantee that we usually listen with only partial discrimination. That is, we hear and process only part of a spoken message. We rarely listen with full discrimination.

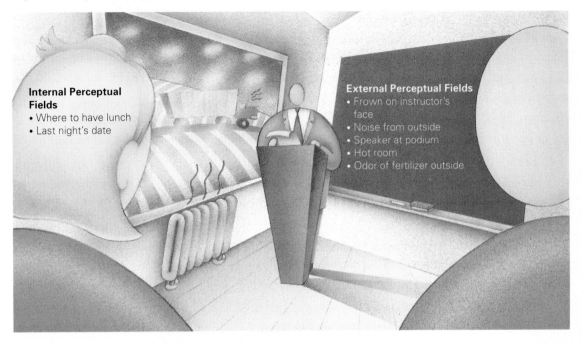

Internal Perceptual Fields
- Where to have lunch
- Last night's date

External Perceptual Fields
- Frown on instructor's face
- Noise from outside
- Speaker at podium
- Hot room
- Odor of fertilizer outside

Purposes of Listening

Speakers' motivations for speechmaking vary from situation to situation just as listeners' purposes for paying attention vary. Researchers have identified five types of listening (each serving a different purpose): (a) appreciative, (b) discriminative, (c) therapeutic, (d) comprehension, and (e) critical.[5]

Appreciative Listening

Appreciative listening focuses on something other than the primary message. People who are principally concerned with participating in the experience are appreciative listeners. Some listeners enjoy seeing a famous speaker. Other listeners enjoy the art of good public speaking, pleasing vocal modulation, clever uses of language, impressive phraseology, and the skillful use of supporting materials. Still other listeners simply like to attend special occasions such as inaugurations, dedications, and graduations.

Discriminative Listening

Discriminative listening requires listeners to draw conclusions from the way a message is presented rather than from what is said. In discriminative listening, people seek to understand what the speaker really thinks, believes, or feels. You're engaging in discriminative listening when you draw conclusions about how angry your parents are with you, based not on what they say, but on how they say it. Journalists listening to the way that a message is presented often second-guess the attitudes of national leaders on foreign policy. Performers, of course, can convey emotions such as anger or exhilaration to audiences through their delivery alone. In each of these examples, an important dimension of listening is based on relatively sophisticated inferences drawn from—rather than found in—messages.

Therapeutic Listening

Therapeutic listening is intended to provide emotional support to the speaker. It is more typical of interpersonal than public communication—the therapeutic listener acts as a sounding board for a speaker attempting to talk through a problem, work out a difficult situation, or express deep emotions. Sometimes, however, therapeutic listening occurs in public speaking situations such as when a sports star apologizes for unprofessional behavior, a religious convert describes a soul-saving experience, or a classmate reviews a personal problem and thanks friends for their help in solving it. In therapeutic listening, special social bonding occurs between speaker and listener. Consider the communication of joy that occurs when listeners react to someone who wants to tell others about a new relationship, a new baby, a promotion at work, or an award at school.

Listening for Comprehension

Listening for comprehension occurs when the listener wants to gain additional information or insights provided by the speaker. This is probably the form of listening with which you are most familiar. When you listen to radio or TV news programs, to classroom lectures on the four principal causes of World War II, or to an orientation official previewing your school's new registration process, you're listening to understand—to comprehend information, ideas, and processes.

Critical Listening

Critical listening requires listeners to both interpret and evaluate the message. The most sophisticated kind of listening is critical listening. It demands that auditors go beyond understanding the message to interpreting it, judging its strengths and weaknesses, and assigning it some value. You'll practice this sort of listening in your class. You may also use critical listening as you evaluate commercials, political campaign speeches, advice from career counselors, or arguments offered by controversial talk show guests. When you listen critically, you decide to accept or reject ideas. You may also resolve to act or delay action on the message.

The evaluation of messages through critical listening requires that you take advantage of the speech-thought differential to mentally identify the key ideas and phrases. You might rephrase or organize the key ideas and note the signposts and other clues provided by the speaker. Summarize the message periodically. Ask yourself crucial questions about the information

Listeners have many purposes for listening. Can you identify several different purposes for listening in this situation?

provided. Do I understand the ideas? What's the main thrust of the speech? Does the speaker's message coincide with other things I know to be true? Does the speaker provide supporting material or reasoning and explanations? Do these explanations lead to the conclusions reached by the speaker? As you continue with this course, you'll learn other techniques for improving your critical listening skills.

The variety of listening purposes has serious implications for both listeners and speakers. Appreciative listeners are highly selective, watching for metaphors, responding to speaking tones, and searching out memorable phrasings. At the other extreme, critical listeners work hard to catch relevant details, to judge the soundness of competing arguments, and to rationally decide whether to accept ideas. Therapeutic listeners decide when to positively reinforce speakers through applause or other signs of approval, and those listening for comprehension distinguish between important and unimportant information. Finally, discriminative listeners search for clues to unspoken ideas or feelings that are relevant to themselves. As you think about your own listening purposes, you'll find yourself adapting your listening behavior to the speaking situation more carefully.

STRATEGIES FOR EFFECTIVE LISTENING

It's the responsibility of both listener and speaker to make speech communication a rewarding experience. We'll begin by exploring ways to improve listening skills through the analysis of self, speaker, and message.

Listener Self-Analysis

To become a better listener, you must first identify your listening patterns and preferences and then decide what changes to make to enhance your listening behaviors. Think about the times when you have felt that you were a good listener, when listening was easy for you, and when you retained most of the message content. When did this occur? How did you keep your attention focused on the message and on the speaker?

Think also about those times when it has been difficult for you to listen for comprehension and critical analysis. Why was it so difficult to listen? Were you uninterested in the subject? Were you bored or tired?

In addition to reviewing your listening behavior, you can begin to correct poor listening habits by preparation. Before a speaker begins, ask yourself the following series of questions:

1. *What is my purpose in listening?* Do you expect to gain information and understanding to make a critical decision? Think about your listening behavior when a teacher announces, "This material will be on the next test." You probably pay closer attention to that material.

2. *What can I expect from the listening environment?* Become aware of the physical environment. If your classroom is always chilly, you can better prepare for this distraction by bringing a sweater to class.

3. *What do I know about the speaking situation?* You can better focus your attention if you're able to anticipate the length of and the occasion for the speech. If you know that the scheduled speaker is the focus of the meeting, you probably won't be surprised when the speech takes most of the regular meeting time.

4. *What do I expect from this speech?* Be realistic. If a classmate gives a speech on the stock market, you'll be disappointed if you expect to learn the secret to doubling your investments in 30 days. On the other hand, if you expect to increase your understanding of the way the stock market operates, your expectations may be more easily satisfied.

5. *How much do I know about the topic?* If you're relatively uninformed about the topic, you can listen for details and information. If you're an expert on the topic, be prepared to compare the speaker's information to your own knowledge. Such comparison may provide you with additional motivation for listening.

6. *Am I impartial about the topic being presented?* If you're unwilling to let the speaker fully develop ideas before you begin to draw conclusions, you may miss the message. This doesn't mean you can't disagree. It simply means that you should suspend judgment until all of the ideas have been presented and fully developed.

7. *What* trigger *words or ideas cause me to stray from the listening situation?* As you listen, take note of particular words or ideas that seem to pull you away from the speaker's message. After the speech, try to analyze why those particular words or ideas caused your attention to be redirected.

Listener Analysis of the Speaker

Speaking does not occur in a vacuum. The listener's past experiences and expectations can influence the communication event. From the listener's vantage point, the speaker's credibility is an important component of the speech transaction. The following questions may help you to decide how to view the speaker and how to determine what impact that view will have on your reactions:

1. *What do I know about this speaker?* Rightly or wrongly, the reputation of the speaker will influence how you listen to the message. If you know that a lecture will be presented by a popular and entertaining university professor, you'll expect to enjoy it. Unwittingly, you may allow prior knowledge of the speaker to color the way you receive the message.

2. *How believable is the speaker?* Does the speaker have a reputation for honesty? Does the information presented seem to coincide with what you already know? If not, you may listen more carefully for unfounded conclusions, weak supporting material, and suspicious explanations. In doing so, you may focus on details rather than on main ideas.

3. *Has the speaker adequately prepared for the occasion?* As a listener, you're more likely to accept messages that you perceive as carefully planned and researched. However, the mere fact that the speaker cites a source does not mean that the speaker has carefully researched the topic. You need to listen to the total presentation of ideas, noting the relationships between the message and supporting materials. Suppose you decide to buy a new car. You enter a showroom eager to learn about fuel efficiency and car maintenance. The salesperson, however, begins a prepared speech about the new models, citing commendations from a sales brochure. Your interest will probably wane because the salesperson skirted the topics that concerned you.

4. *What is the speaker's attitude toward this presentation?* As a listener, you take cues from the speaker to guide your own responses. A speaker who appears flippant, bored, or disinterested creates an obstacle to productive listening. You must take care that the speaker's demeanor does not mask the message.

Listener Analysis of the Message

The message should be the principal focus of the listener's energy. The receiver can more critically assess the message being communicated by adjusting listening behavior in response to the following three questions:

1. *What are the main ideas of the speech?* Determine the thesis of the speech and look for the statements that help the speaker to support that thesis. The main ideas should serve as the foundation upon which the speaker builds the speech. The next time you listen to a commercial, listen for the main ideas. What sort of information does the advertiser give to encourage you to buy a product? Transfer that same listening behavior to a speech. By focusing on the main ideas, you can better understand the message.

2. *How are the main ideas arranged?* Once you've identified the main ideas, you can determine the relationships among them. If the speaker is using a chronological pattern, it's obviously easy to identify the progression of topics. For example, you can expect that a speaker discussing the history of rock music will follow discussion of the 1950s, 1960s, and 1970s with an exploration of musical developments in the 1980s.

3. *What kinds of materials support the main ideas?* Consider the timeliness, quality, and content of the supporting materials. Ask yourself whether these materials clarify, amplify, and strengthen the main ideas of the speech. Make sure the supporting materials make sense to you.

To focus your attention on the main ideas, the pattern of development, and the use of supporting materials in the speech, you should be an *active* listener. You should constantly *review, relate,* and *anticipate.* Take a few seconds to *review* what the speaker has said. Mentally summarize key ideas each time the speaker initiates a new topic for consideration. *Relate* the message to what you already know. Consider how you would use the information in the future. *Anticipate* what the speaker might say next. Use this anticipation to focus on the content of the message. By reviewing, relating, and anticipating, you can make good use of the extra time generated by the speech-thought differential and keep your attention message-centered.

PRACTICING CRITICAL LISTENING SKILLS

You can practice the basic principles of critical listening in most of your classes. Critical listening is focused, organized listening that takes advantage of the speech-thought differential. You can begin to train yourself to become a more critical listener by focusing on note-taking.

You need to take a few steps to prepare to become a better note-taker. First, get organized. It's easiest to take useful notes if you have a system. A loose-leaf notebook works best because you can add, rearrange, or remove notes for review. If you use spiral or other permanently bound notebooks, use a separate notebook for each subject to avoid confusion and to allow for expansion. Second, set aside a few minutes each day to review the syllabus for your course, to scan the assigned readings, and to review your notes from the previous class period. If you do this just before each lecture, you'll be ready to take notes and practice critical thinking. Finally, prepare your note pages by drawing a line down the left margin approximately two inches from the edge of the paper.[6] Leave this margin blank while you take notes so that later you can use it to practice critical thinking.

During the class, apply the strategies for analysis of self, speaker, and messages. In particular, concentrate on the message. You'll need to identify the key ideas and organizational progression of the lecture as well as the supporting material used to bolster each idea. Give yourself plenty of room on each note page. Skip lines if necessary and fill in ideas later. Many experts recommend that you develop a system of abbreviations for common words. Some of these abbreviations are obvious, such as using the sign *&* for *and* or writing *btwn* and *w/o* for *between* and *without*. Come up with your own symbols to improve your speed while taking notes.

You've probably been wondering what to do with the two-inch margin in the left hand of your note page. After class, you should review your notes. However, rather than being a passive reader, react to the material. If your instructor said an idea was important, star it in the left margin. If you don't understand something, write out your question or place a question mark by it so that you can ask your instructor for clarification during the next class period. As you consider course assignments, record ideas in the note-page margins to help you integrate classroom lectures with your work. Add your own examples to clarify theoretical material. You're no longer passively rereading them, but integrating, challenging, and adapting them to your own needs. At this stage you've begun to engage the critical response process. If you practice this system, you'll soon find yourself reacting critically as you listen to classroom lectures and engaging the critical listening process in other forums, such as the television news, friendly arguments, and presentations in your public speaking class. Soon you'll be automatically applying the review, relate, and anticipate strategy.[7]

THE RESPONSIBILITIES OF THE SPEAKER

Even though it's the listener who finally judges the transmitted message, there are several steps that you as the speaker can take to help the listener. Concentrate your efforts in three areas: preparing the speech, capturing and holding attention, and presenting the speech.

Preparing the Speech

Keep in mind that it is difficult for the listener to follow the structure of your speech *and* keep track of what you are saying. Listeners can't see your notecards and probably don't have a detailed outline of your speech. Plan to share your main topics with your audience in an initial preview or **forecast.** This will help guide your listener as the speech unfolds. You might say, for example, "I want you to understand the two most common types of eating disorders—anorexia nervosa and bulimia. I will discuss the symptoms, the causes, and the cures for these two devastating diseases."

Keep your listeners in mind during the preparation stage of your speech. Try to anticipate points where your listeners will probably need special guidance. Forecasts and internal summaries will help listeners focus on your ideas. Think about concepts that may be especially difficult for listeners to understand. Try to present them several times, using different wording each time. Or, add illustrations or visual aids to clarify your ideas.

If the audience is expecting a five-minute speech, tailor your presentation to that expectation. If you know the environment is going to be uncomfortable for your audience, try to adapt your speech topic and length to accommodate the physical situation—in other words, be interesting and, above all, be brief.

Preparation also includes practice. While practicing your speech, work out awkward phrasing, get used to the sound of your own voice, and convince yourself that you're ready to take on an audience.

Capturing and Holding Attention

There are many elements competing for the attention of the members of your audience. Essentially, you need to convince your listeners to listen to you. And even when you have listeners' attention, you'll find that their attention tends to ebb and flow in response to the thoughts and sensations moving through their internal and external perceptual fields. So, you must constantly be on the lookout for lapses in attention—slumping, fidgeting, or squirming, for example. James Albert Winans, a twentieth-century pioneer in public speaking instruction, expressed this problem succinctly: "Attention determines response." Your first step in achieving your speaking purpose is to gain and hold your listener's attention.

Attention is the ability to focus on one element in a given perceptual field. When attention is maintained, competing elements in the perceptual field fade and, for all practical purposes, cease to exist.[8] For example, near the end of his rock concert, performer Billy Joel breaks into the song "Innocent Man." The fans go wild, and you join them. After all, you love that song. The audience is hushed during the middle verses, but, by the end, you can't help yourself—you're singing the chorus at the top of your lungs. The arena erupts and Billy Joel obliges the audience by repeating the last verse and chorus. Again the audience explodes. As the screaming finally ebbs, you look around only to realize that you've spilled your soft drink on your new jeans, that the person sitting to your right is sobbing uncontrollably, and that you have to use the bathroom. Now that's paying attention!

How can you capture and hold attention without putting on a rock concert? You must capture and hold listeners' attention through the types of ideas you present. Ideas can be presented in nine ways that have high attention value. These nine **factors of attention** are *activity, reality, proximity, familiarity, novelty, suspense, conflict, humor,* and *the vital.* (See Figure 2.2.)

Activity
Suppose you have two TV sets side by side. On one set, two congressional representatives discuss American domestic policy; on the other set, there's

an exciting car chase involving flying debris, near-collisions, and a very fiery conclusion. Which set will you watch? Similarly, active verbs and colorful adjectives tend to attract attention.

Your speech as a whole should "move"—it should march or press forward. Nothing is as boring as a talk that seems to stand still or that meanders around a topic. Speeches of instruction and demonstration, particularly if visual aids are used, demand orderly, systematic progress. Keep moving ahead, and your audience will be more likely to stick with you.

Reality

The earliest words you learned were names for tangible objects such as *daddy, milk,* and *cookie.* While the ability to abstract—to generalize—is one of the marks of human intelligence, don't lose your audience by becoming too abstract. When you speak, refer to specific events, persons, places, and happenings. Turn back to the paragraph comparing two television programs. The paragraph could have read, "Compare a TV show with little action to one with lots of action." Language that lacks concrete detail fails to generate much interest.

Proximity

A direct reference to a person in the audience, to a nearby object or place, to an incident that has just occurred, or to the immediate occasion usually helps you to command attention. Talking about specific people in the audience—"Take John over there. Imagine what he'd look like with his hair

Figure 2.2 The Factors of Attention
Speakers can use the factors of attention to capture and hold the interest of their listeners. Which can you use in your next speech?

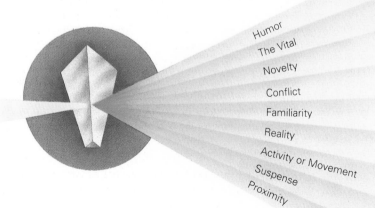

styled, and with a three-piece suit, a Brooks Brothers shirt, a silk tie, and a black leather briefcase"—involves all of your listeners in your message. If people are sharing in a speech, they're more likely to listen to it.

Consider the following introduction: "Do you realize how much fast food is consumed by our student body? Within four blocks of this classroom are nine restaurants, including a McDonald's, a Wendy's, a Godfather's Pizza, a Kentucky Fried Chicken franchise, and a Best Steak House. Two of the others are local submarine shops. Even the student union runs a fast-food counter. Should we start wondering what our lunch habits are doing to our nutrition—to our bodies and to our minds?" Such an introduction commands attention because it involves your audience personally.

Familiarity

References to the familiar are attention sustaining, especially in the face of new or strange ideas. A device that is useful in establishing familiarity is an **analogy.** Analogies compare the similarities between two things, using the familiar to explain something unfamiliar. For example, you could compare London postal or zip codes with directions on a compass, since the initial letters of the codes indicate directions and the next set of numbers represent degrees of longitude or latitude.

The familiar is also comfortable. During the holidays, you like to sing the songs you know, such as "Rudolph the Red-Nosed Reindeer," for example. You like to reminisce about the good old days. Sharing brings people closer together—hence, a comfortable anecdote holds people's attention.

Novelty

Novel happenings, dramatic advances, or unusual developments attract attention. Think of typical tabloid newspaper headlines—"Bigfoot Sighted in Shopping Mall" or "Grandmother Gives Birth to Quadruplets." Two special types of novelty are *size* and *contrast.*

While size demands attention in and of itself, large and small are even more compelling when thrown into *contrast* with each other. In an address at the University of Virginia, Henry W. Grady, a famous nineteenth-century Southern spokesperson, used novel and startling contrasts to focus attention on the gap between the rich and the poor:

> *A home that cost three million dollars and a breakfast that cost five thousand are disquieting facts to the millions who live in a hut and dine on a crust. The fact that a man . . . has an income of twenty million dollars falls strangely on the ears of those who hear it as they sit empty-handed with children crying for bread.*[9]

When using novelty, be careful not to inject elements so bizarre that they are entirely unfamiliar to listeners. Your listeners must at least know what you're talking about. Otherwise, their attention is certain to waver. A proper combination of new and old, of novel and familiar, will most likely yield the best results.

Suspense

A large part of the interest people take in mystery plots arises from an uncertainty about their outcomes. Films such as *Death Trap* and *A Fish Called Wanda* have so many twists that they leave viewers spellbound. When giving a speech, you can create uncertainty by pointing to puzzling relationships or unpredictable forces. Introduce suspense into the stories you use to illustrate your ideas, building up to a surprising climax. Hint that you will divulge valuable information later in your talk after you provide some necessary background information first. For example, you might begin a speech on retardation with the scenario of a developmentally disabled child; then, after describing the causes of retardation and care for the retarded, reveal that you had been talking about your brother.

Conflict

Controversy compels attention; consider the ratings for prime-time TV soap operas that emphasize extremely strong interpersonal conflicts in their plots. Conflict, like suspense, suggests uncertainty; conflict, like activity, is dynamic. When President George Bush wanted to get Americans involved in the fight against drug abuse, he talked about "the war on drugs" and promised an "assault on every front."[10] The word *war* gave him a dynamic conflict metaphor.

In an informative speech on metropolitan renovations, you could easily introduce conflict by describing the struggle between downtown merchants, who want parking lots and wide sidewalks, and suburban mall owners, who argue that such projects waste tax dollars. Discussing urban renewal and fiscal responsibility will not attract the attention that a description of the fight between downtown and suburban shopowners will.

Humor

Listeners usually pay attention to a speech when they're enjoying themselves. Humor provides a change of pace and a chance for listeners to participate more actively in the interaction by sharing their laughter; in this way, it provides a link between you and your audience. In addition, humor relaxes both speaker and listener. When using humor to capture and hold attention, observe two guidelines:

1. *Be relevant.* Beware of wandering from the point, and of telling a joke just for the sake of telling a joke. If your joke does not reinforce an important idea, leave it out.

2. *Use good taste.* Consider the occasion. You don't want to tell a knee-slapper during a funeral, and you should refrain from telling off-color stories in most speeches because you may offend audience members.

The Vital

Finally, people nearly always pay attention to matters that affect their health, reputation, property, or employment. When you hear, "Students who take an internship while in college find jobs after graduation three times as fast as those who don't," you're likely to pay attention. Appealing to *the vital*, therefore, is a matter of *personalizing* your speech, making it unavoidably relevant—not just to the group, but to specific individuals in your audience. In 1838, while Angelina Grimké addressed a general meeting of the abolitionist societies, a mob raged outside, preparing to destroy the meeting hall. Grimké referred to the tumult in her speech saying, "What if the mob should now burst in upon us, break up our meeting and commit violence upon our persons—would this be anything compared with what the slaves endure?"[11] At that moment, every individual in her audience most likely felt the horror of slavery.

Each of these nine attention getters should be in your arsenal of rhetorical weapons. They give your speech sparkle and spunk and they keep you and your words squarely in the listeners' external and internal perceptual fields. The nine factors of attention are designed to keep audiences curious and alert.

Presenting the Speech

As a speaker, always remember how it feels to be a listener. Consider your own positive and negative reactions to the ways other speakers have presented ideas. Make use of the best strategies from other speech presentations. Remember that good speakers are also good listeners.

Interpreting audience feedback during your presentation will help you to modify, adapt, or recast any ideas you feel are being misunderstood or doubted by your listeners. If your listeners notice that you're making a sincere effort to communicate your thoughts, they may be more receptive and try harder to be good listeners. Your use of listener feedback is one way that the audience assesses your desire to communicate effectively. If several of your listeners frown or express confusion, you can quickly think back over what you've said. Then, try to rephrase the main points of your speech in simpler language. A brief review of the points you've already covered is also a good idea. If the situation allows, you can ask your audience for questions following the speech.

DEVELOPING CRITICAL LISTENING SKILLS IN THE CLASSROOM

Critical listening skills can be developed through understanding and practice. These skills are vital because it is the listener's responsibility to understand and evaluate messages. Sometimes the skills we develop in critical listening can affect the quality of our lives. Imagine, for example, that you are listening to competing offers from home loan companies. The way that you understand and evaluate the companies' messages can end up costing you or saving you thousands of dollars over the 30-year period of the mortgage.

Figure 2.3 Speech Evaluation Form
Use this form to evaluate your own speeches.

The Speaker

☐ poised?

☐ positive self-image?

☐ apparently sincere?

☐ apparently concerned about the topic?

☐ apparently concerned about the audience?

☐ apparently well prepared?

The Message

☐ suitable topic?

☐ clear general purpose?

☐ sharply focused specific purpose?

☐ well-phrased central idea or proposition?

☐ adequately supported (enough, varied, trustworthy sources)?

☐ supporting materials tailored to the audience?

☐ introduced adequately?

☐ concluded effectively?

☐ major subdivisions clear, balanced?

☐ use of notes and lectern unobtrusive?

The Channel

☐ voice varied for emphasis?

☐ voice conversational?

☐ delivery speed controlled?

☐ body alert and nondistracting?

☐ gestures used effectively?

☐ face expressive?

☐ language clear (unambiguous, concrete)?

☐ language forcible (vivid, intense)?

The Audience

☐ all listeners addressed?

☐ their presence recognized and complimented?

☐ their attitudes toward subject and speaker taken into account?

The Speech as a Whole

Audience's expectations met?

_____

_____

_____

_____

_____

Short-range effects of the speech?

_____

_____

_____

_____

Long-range effects?

_____

_____

_____

_____

_____

Possible improvements?

_____

_____

_____

_____

_____

Use the Speech Evaluation Form in Figure 2.3 on page 39 as a checklist of listening concerns in your classroom. The speech classroom is a good place to begin practicing critical listening skills. What follows are several suggestions for ways to improve your listening skills:

1. *Practice critiquing the speeches of other students.* Take part in postspeech discussions. Ask questions of the speaker. Determine the primary strengths and weaknesses of each speech.

2. *Read the sample speeches in this book.* Look for forecasts, internal summaries, transitions, supporting materials, and other key elements of the speaking process.

3. *Listen critically to discussions, lectures, oral presentations, and student-teacher exchanges in your other classes.* Identify effective and ineffective communicative techniques used by individuals in these different contexts.

4. *Make an effort to listen to speakers outside of class.* Carefully observe their successes and failures, analyzing the reasons for each.

5. *Examine the supporting materials, arguments, and language used in newspapers and magazines.*

Undoubtedly, you will become a more effective speaker after you've studied this book and carried out your classroom speaking assignments. You can start now to become a more proficient listener. First, use the Speech Evaluation Form. Depending on the particular assignment, the nature of the audience, and the demands of the occasion, some of the checkpoints on the form will be more relevant than others. For now, use the form as a general guide; later, concentrate on those aspects that are relevant to your specific speech assignment.

Also, participate regularly in postspeech evaluations, even of early classroom speaking assignments. Don't hesitate to provide direct feedback to your classmates, pointing out what worked and what didn't, what was clear and what wasn't. Good, constructive classroom criticism can be either positive or negative—but it should always be supportive. Oral critiques accomplish two goals: They provide a beginning speaker with much-needed feedback, and they force you, the listener, to verbalize your thoughts and recognize your standards and expectations. In this way, both you and the speaker gain: the speaker acquires a sense of the audience reaction, and you gain a better sense of your own thoughts.

Listening, then, is a two-way process, a joint responsibility of speaker and listener. When both parties are sensitive to techniques for enhancing oral communication, the interaction between speaker and listener will be a successful transaction. Much of later chapters is based upon the premise that listening is a two-way process.

CHAPTER SUMMARY

1. Public speaking is a two-way transaction. Speakers reach out to their audiences through their speeches and listeners respond. This response may come through either *immediate* or *delayed feedback.*

2. *Hearing* and *listening* are two different processes. Hearing is physiological. Listening, on the other hand, is a psychological process in which people attach meanings to aural signals.

3. Listening is a joint responsibility. Both speaker and listener must make sure that intended messages are taken in, comprehended, interpreted, and evaluated. There are seven barriers to effective listening: (a) *distraction from competing stimuli in the internal and external perceptual fields;* (b) *past associations which may interfere with the present message;* (c) *passive rather than active listening;* (d) *the physical setting which may make listening difficult;* (e) *physical needs which may compete with the message;* (f) *unfamiliar language which may cause frustration;* and (g) *preset ideas about the topic, speaker, or occasion which may interfere with comprehension.*

4. Just as a speaker's motivations for speechmaking vary from situation to situation, so, too, do a listener's purposes for paying attention. There are five types and purposes of listening: (a) *appreciative listening,* (b) *discriminative listening,* (c) *therapeutic listening,* (d) *listening for comprehension,* and (e) *critical listening.*

5. It's the responsibility of both listener and speaker to make speech communication a rewarding experience. The listener can improve listening skills through an analysis of *self, speaker,* and *message.*

6. You can practice critical listening skills by focusing on notetaking in your classes. To become a better notetaker, you need to (a) get organized by developing a notetaking system, (b) set aside a few minutes each day to review your notes, and (c) record your reactions in the margins of your note paper.

7. When preparing a speech, try to anticipate where your listeners will need special guidance. To help your audience overcome these obstacles, *prepare the speech well, capture and hold attention by considering the factors of attention,* and *present the speech in ways appropriate for the audience, topic, and occasion.*

8. The key to effective public speaking involves capturing and holding the attention of your audience. Ideas can be presented in nine ways that have high attention value. These nine *factors of attention* are *activity* or *movement, reality, proximity, familiarity, novelty, suspense, conflict, humor,* and *the vital.*

KEY TERMS

forecast (p. 33)
hearing (p. 25)
immediate feedback (p. 23)
internal perceptual field (p. 26)
listening (p. 25)

listening for comprehension (p. 28)
selective perception (p. 26)
speech-thought differential (p. 25)
therapeutic listening (p. 28)

SKILLBUILDING ACTIVITIES

1. To check the listening abilities of your classmates, conduct a class discussion on a controversial topic. Before the discussion begins, establish the rule that before anyone can speak, he or she first must summarize to the satisfaction of the previous speaker what that person said. As a result of this exercise, what conclusions can you draw about people's ability to summarize accurately and satisfactorily? How do good listening and feedback reduce the amount and intensity of disagreement?

2. List some ideas that trigger preset ideas. Choose one of them as the subject for a two-to-four-minute speech. In that speech, concentrate on discussing what causes the preset ideas and how analyzing the preset ideas affects listening skills.

3. Keep a Listening Log. For two or three days, record your oral communication interactions, noting (a) who you were listening to, (b) what your listening purposes were, and (c) how effectively you listened. After completing the log, look it over, focusing on your listening patterns. What changes should you make to improve your listening habits?

REFERENCES

1. Andrew Wolvin and Carolyn Coakley, *Listening* (Dubuque, Iowa: William C Brown Co., 1982), 3–11.

2. Thomas Lewis and Ralph Nichols, *Speaking and Listening* (Dubuque, Iowa: William C Brown Co., 1965), 6.

3. Carol A. Roach and Nancy J. Wyatt, *Successful Listening* (New York: Harper & Row, 1988), chap. 1; Kittie W. Watson and Larry L. Barker, "Listening Behavior: Definition and Measurement," *Communication Yearbook 8,* Robert Bostrom, ed. (Beverly Hills: Sage, 1984), 178–197.

4. This discussion of internal and external perceptual fields is adapted from Wayne C. Minnick, *The Art of Persuasion* (Boston: Houghton Mifflin Co., 1957), 38–41.

5. The discussion of purposes for listening is drawn from Wolvin and Coakley, *Listening*, chaps. 4–8.

6. This has sometimes been called the Cornell System for taking notes. See Walter Pauk, *How To Study in College*, 3rd ed. (Boston: Houghton Mifflin Co., 1984), 127–129.

7. Tom Willett and Toni Willett, "Be Quick to Listen," *New Horizons*, 4 (1990), 1–2.

8. Psychologist Philip G. Zimbardo has compared attention to "a spotlight that illuminates certain portions of our surroundings. When we focus our attention on something and thus become conscious of it, we can begin to process it cognitively— converting sensory information into perceptions and memories or developing ideas through analysis, judgment, reasoning, and imagination. When the spotlight of attention shifts to something else, conscious processing of the earlier material ceases and processing of the new content begins." In *Psychology and Life*, 11th ed. (Glenview, Ill.: ScottForesman, 1985), 191.

9. From an address by Henry W. Grady, presented to the Literary Societies of the University of Virginia, June 25, 1889.

10. "Text of President's Speech on National Drug Control Strategy," *The New York Times* (September 6, 1989), A-10.

11. Angelina Grimké [Weld], "Address at Pennsylvania Hall, 1838," reprinted in *Man Cannot Speak for Her*, vol. 2, Karlyn Kohrs Campbell, ed. (New York: Praeger, 1989), 27.

CHAPTER THREE

Getting Started

"*Well, yeah, I knew what I wanted to say. It just didn't come out right. I made a fool of myself in that class.*" "*I don't think you really knew what you wanted to say, Jeff,*" Bo replied. "*Sure, you might have known something about the topic, what aspect of it you thought was interesting, and even your attitude toward it, but you still didn't know what you wanted to say.*" "*What do you mean?*" Jeff asked. "*What I mean is,*" Bo responded, "*knowing what you want to say is a matter of knowing the precise point you want to make, knowing your specific supporting arguments, knowing what your evidence is, even knowing how to phrase your most important ideas. You'll never get anywhere in that marketing class or anywhere else until you're really ready to talk. You can't bake a cake till you've got the ingredients!*"

Part I of this textbook has oriented you to public speaking and listening. Now it's time to get you on your feet. While you can't learn everything at once about the intricacies of speech preparation and speechmaking processes, you can learn enough about the basics to get yourself thinking and acting in more rhetorically sound ways. Having a *rhetorical frame of mind* means thinking your way strategically through decisions you have to make about: (a) selecting and narrowing your subject, (b) determining your purposes, (c) analyzing your audience and the occasion, (d) gathering your speech material, (e) making an outline, (f) practicing aloud, and (g) delivering your speech. These may seem like a lot of decisions. That's true, but systematic planning and purposive decisions are the keys to platform success. They save you time and keep you from wandering aimlessly through the library or waiting endlessly at your desk for inspiration.

There's no magical formula for getting ready to speak; the job can be irksome and frustrating. However, if you generally follow the series of seven steps—either in the order presented here or in another that works for you—you'll be ahead of the game and ready for an audience. At the end of this chapter, you'll explore another subject you ought to think about before speaking: projecting self-confidence.

SELECTING AND NARROWING YOUR SUBJECT

The most difficult task for many speakers, especially in a classroom situation, is to choose a subject. Three important considerations should guide your selection process: (a) what do you know something about?; (b) what are you interested in talking about?; and (c) what topics can you relate to the audience's situation and interests?

You might begin by listing those topics that you have knowledge of, circling the ones you're willing to talk about in front of others, and thinking about ways you can relate them to your listeners. Before committing yourself to a firm choice, though, check your possible subjects in the next two steps; be sure that your choice fits the purposes your instructor intends and that you can phrase it as a strong central idea or claim.

Once you've selected a workable topic, narrow it so that you can cover it in the time allowed. How much can you say about a particular subject in five minutes? You certainly can't tell your listeners everything there is to know about next month's charity marathon, but you might be able to discuss (a) differences in strategy among five kilometer, ten kilometer, half-marathon, and full marathon races; (b) simple conditioning techniques to help students prepare for a five kilometer race; (c) what happens to runners physiologically and psychologically during a race; or (d) how students can sign up sponsors for races in your school's town.

Next, narrow your subject to meet the specific expectations of your audience. An audience that comes to a meeting expecting to hear a talk on gun safety will probably be upset if you lecture instead on the need for stricter gun-control laws. The announced purpose of the meeting, the demands of the particular context, and the audience's traditions all affect the audience's expectations of the speech.

Suppose, for example, that you've agreed to give an informative talk on gardening to a learning extension class at a local high school. Within that general subject are countless narrower topics, including

- the growth of personal or hobby gardening over the last decade (facts and figures on clubs, seed sales, the home canning industry, and so on);
- methods for preserving homegrown vegetables (canning vs. freezing vs. drying vs. cold storage);
- soil enrichment (varieties of natural and artificial fertilizers, the strengths and weaknesses of each);

- factors to consider when selecting vegetables to plant (plot size, family eating habits, amount of time available for tending, cost of supermarket vegetables of each type);
- available strains of any given vegetable (selection of seeds based on geography, climate, soil characteristics, regional pests/bacteria, uses to which vegetables will be put, germination and heartiness);
- literature on gardening (library books, television programs, governmental pamphlets, magazines, seed catalogs, fertilizer company brochures);
- varieties of gardening tools (inexpensive hand tools, medium-cost hand tools, expensive power machinery); and
- year-round gardening (window-box gardening, "grow" lights, cold frames, hot frames, greenhouses).

Given this list of subtopics, your procedures for narrowing might run as follows:

1. *Subjects I know something about*
   a. methods for preserving homegrown food
   b. soil enrichment
   c. literature on gardening
   d. varieties of gardening tools
   e. year-round gardening
2. *Subjects interesting to me*
   all except soil enrichment
3. *Subjects interesting to a learning extension class*
   a. methods for preserving homegrown food
   b. literature on gardening
   c. year-round gardening
4. *Subjects appropriate to occasion* (demonstration speech)
   all three are appropriate
5. *Topics I can talk about in the available time* (note narrowing)
   a. *one* or *two* methods of preserving homegrown food
   b. *two* or *three* kinds of gardening literature
   c. *one* kind of year-round gardening
6. *Topics I can fit to the audience comprehension level*
   a. do not discuss home food preservation, as most of them already know a lot about this subtopic
   b. do not discuss gardening literature, as few participants want to spend more time reading about gardening; in the past they have found it easier to learn from other gardeners than from books
   c. they have shown interest earlier in the course in the topic of year-round gardening
7. *Topics that will meet their expectations for a project*
   year-round gardening, specifically, how to build an inexpensive home-made greenhouse

Selecting and narrowing a topic involves assessments of yourself, your audience, the occasion, available materials, and other speakers. A focused but not too technical topic, adapted to your knowledge and attitudes and those of your audience, can make you a success behind the lectern. A good, systematic start to the preparation process will pay off by the end.

DETERMINING YOUR PURPOSES

Once you know what you want to talk about, you need to ask yourself some more questions—questions that require you to consider the reasons behind your choice: (a) why do *you* wish to discuss this subject?; (b) why might an *audience* want to listen to you?; and (c) why is what you're discussing appropriate to the *occasion?* You should approach these why's in three ways: (a) first, think about *general purposes,* the reasons people speak in public; (b) next, consider your *specific purposes,* the concrete goals you wish to achieve in a particular speech; and, finally, (c) focus your thoughts on a *central idea* or *claim,* the statement of the guiding thought you wish to communicate. In addition, you'll probably want to put into words a working title of your speech. Selecting a provisional title early in the preparation process helps you to keep sight of your primary emphasis and lets you announce it to others ahead of time.

General Purposes

If you turn the speech functions discussed in Chapter 1 into generic purposes, you'll come up with three **general purposes** for speeches: to inform, to entertain, and to persuade or actuate.

General Purpose	Audience Response Sought
To inform	Clear understanding
To entertain	Enjoyment and comprehension
To persuade or actuate	Acceptance of ideas or recommended behaviors

This book emphasizes two types of speeches: speeches to inform and speeches to persuade or actuate. The reason is that these types of speeches dominate the speaking occasions you'll face in life. This is not to say that speeches to entertain aren't important—they are. Even the comedians of the A&E cable network regularly criticize social and political practices, point out human shortcomings, and attack human ignorance in their sets. Speeches to entertain often combine information and assaults on attitudes or inaction, and, consequently, they are very potent. That is why rhetoricians since the great Roman orator Cicero have referred in their writing to speeches that were meant "to delight" *(delectare).* Chapter 14 explores these speeches for entertainment in more detail.

To Inform

When your overall object is to help listeners understand an idea, concept, or process, or when you seek to widen their range of knowledge, the general purpose of your speech will be to inform. Such is the goal of scientists who report their research results to colleagues, of public figures who address community groups on subjects on which they are expert, and of college lecturers and work supervisors.

To create understanding, you must change the level or quality of information possessed by your listeners. By providing examples, statistics, illustrations, and other materials offering data and ideas, you seek to expand or alter their knowledge. Not only must an informative speech provide raw data, but its message and supporting materials must be structured and integrated in such a way that listeners perceive the whole. For example, an informative speech on how to assemble a stereo must include the necessary instructions in an orderly sequence of steps. Understanding in this instance depends not only on learning *what* to do, but also on knowing *when* to do it and *why*. Some of your listeners may already be familiar with the information that you're presenting but have not put the pieces together coherently. Your job as an informative speaker is to impart both knowledge and overall understanding.

To Persuade or Actuate

A speaker whose purpose is to persuade or actuate seeks to influence listeners' minds or actions. While it may be argued that all speeches are persuasive to some degree,[1] there are many situations in which the speaker's primary purpose is outright persuasion. Promoters and public relations experts try to make you believe in the superiority of certain products, persons, or institutions; lawyers seek to persuade juries; social action group leaders exhort tenants to believe in landlord collusion; politicians debate campaign issues and strive to influence voters' thinking.

As a persuasive speaker, you usually seek to influence the beliefs and attitudes of your listeners. Sometimes, however, you will want to go a step further and try to move them to action. You may want them to contribute money, sign a petition, or participate in a demonstration. The distinguishing feature of an actuative speech is that instead of stopping with an appeal to their beliefs or attitudes, you ask your listeners to alter their behavior in a specified way.

Because the speech to persuade or actuate is usually designed to influence or alter listeners' beliefs and actions, you should fill it with well-ordered arguments supported by facts, figures, and examples. But you'll have to go beyond the facts. Persuasion is a psychological as well as logical process. You'll need strong motivational appeals to tap into the needs and desires of listeners.

To inform, to entertain, and to persuade or actuate are the general purposes a speech can have. By thinking about general purposes you begin your orientation process, your assessment of the task you face. Immediately, however, you should focus your thinking on more specific purposes or goals.

Specific Purposes

Specific purposes are the actual goals you want to achieve in a speech. They can be extremely wide ranging. While you can tell others about your public purposes, some specific purposes are private, known only by you. For example, you probably hope you'll make a good impression on an audience, although you're not likely to say that aloud. Some purposes are short-term, and others long-term. If you're speaking to members of a local food cooperative on the virtues of baking their own bread, your short-term purpose might be to get people to try out your basic recipe tonight, while your long-term purpose could be to have them change their food-buying and food-consuming habits.

Theoretically, you have any number of private and public, short-term and long-term, specific purposes whenever you speak. Practically, however, you need to reduce that mass of goals to a dominant one that can guide your speech preparation. Grabbing onto *a* specific purpose, one that you can articulate for an audience, focuses you on precisely what you want that audience to understand, enjoy, feel, believe, or do.

Suppose you wanted to take on the challenge of getting more of your classmates to actually go into your campus library. Consider various ways of wording your overriding specific purpose:

- "To tell students about the variety of library services" (understanding).
- "To relate in a humorous fashion my initial troubles in using the library" (enjoyment).
- "To reduce students' levels of anxiety about going to the library" (feelings).
- "To destroy the old belief that librarians are mechanical automatons who care only about silence" (beliefs).
- "To get half of the class to agree to come on a library tour" (action).

All of these purposes involve student use of the library, yet each has a different specific focus that will demand of you different materials, appeals, and speaking styles. Locking onto a specific purpose zeros you in on your primary target.

Central Ideas or Claims

Once you've settled on a specific purpose for your speech, you're ready to translate that goal into concrete subject matter. You first need to cast into words a central idea or claim—sometimes called a **thesis statement**—that will be the controlling thought of your speech. A **central idea** is a statement that captures the essence of the information or concept you wish to communicate to an audience. A **claim** is a statement that phrases the belief, attitude, or action you want an audience to adopt. Central ideas are characteristic of informative speeches and some speeches to entertain, while claims form the core of persuasive, actuative, and some entertaining speeches.

The precise phrasing of central ideas and claims is very important because wording conveys the essence of your subject matter, setting up audience expectations. Examine Table 3.1 for examples of ways to word speech purposes. Then consider another example—assume that you've decided to give an informative speech on building an inexpensive composting bin. You might phrase your central idea in one of three ways:

1. "With only a minimum of carpentry skills, even a teenager can build a composting bin."
2. "With some careful searching around the house and neighborhood, anyone can build a homemade composting bin for less than $50."
3. "Building an inexpensive composting bin will permit you to dispose of yard waste and to create nutritious mulch and fertilizer cheaply."

Note that the first version stresses an audience member's ability to complete the technical aspects of the task. Presumably, the speech would offer a step-by-step description of the construction process. But the second version

Table 3.1 Speaking Purposes

This table provides a guide to the relationships between the general purpose, specific purpose, and thesis statement of your speech.

General Purpose	Specific Purpose	Thesis Statement
To help your listeners understand an idea, concept, or process (to inform)	To teach your listeners about the Federal Reserve Board	"The most important influence on interest rates in this country is the Federal Reserve Board."
To influence your listeners' actions (to persuade)	To get your listeners to walk to classes this week (short-term goal) To get your listeners to develop a fitness program (long-term goal)	"You should start a fitness program today to improve the quality of your life."
To influence your listeners' thoughts (to persuade)	To increase your listeners' appreciation of the role of pure scientific research	"While science doesn't always yield a better mousetrap, it is still an important human activity."
To increase your listeners' enjoyment (to entertain)	To recall the lighter moments of going to school	"Remembering your first day of school makes you realize how much you've really learned!"

Ethics and Public Speaking

Occasionally, we'll include a boxed area devoted to "ethical moments"—ethical decisions public speakers must make in preparing and delivering their talks. Some of these moments will fit you and your circumstances, and some won't. In either case, we hope that you'll take an ethical moment and think about the problems presented and their solutions in your life. Some of these problems might be discussed in class. Here are some typical ethical questions that you might face in the speeches you'll give this term:

1.   When is it fair to borrow other people's ideas and words, and when is it not? Need you acknowledge everything you learned from others? Must you cite sources for everything?

2.   You recognize that a major portion of a speaker's informative speech came from an article that you read last week. The speaker does not cite the source. During the critique session, should you blow the whistle on the speaker? Should you instead talk with the person later? Or tell your teacher? Or let it go?

3.   An article says exactly what you intended to say about the use of pesticides on garden vegetables. Then you find a more recent article claiming that new research contradicts the first article. Should you ignore the new evidence?

4.   An authority whom you wish to cite uses the words *perhaps, probably, likely,* and *often.* Should you simply strike those words from a quotation that you wish to use to make the statement sound more positive? After all, you're not tinkering with the ideas, only the strength of assertion.

5.   There are four minutes left in your class period. If you keep talking, there'll be no time left for a critique of your position. Should you extend your speech by four minutes?

6.   A student in your class disagrees strongly with your analysis of the crack problem in the United States. You know that he was in a substance abuse program a year ago. You expect that if you bring this student's past up in response to his challenge, it will deflect focus from his point of view. Should you go for the deflection?

Ethical moments such as these will face you regularly, both in your speech classroom and throughout the rest of your life. Taking a few moments to consider such situations, and even articulate your position in discussion, can save you many, many embarrassing times later. Know what your moral stands are and know why you take them *before* you face ethical dilemmas on the platform.

---

suggests quite a different speech, focused on obtaining free or inexpensive materials. In contrast, the third version discusses the actual construction of the bin only superficially, concentrating instead on use and design—how to layer various kinds of yard waste, how often to water, when to shovel cured materials out of the bottom, and so on.

Wording a central idea is key in the planning of your speech because it controls the way you end up developing the whole talk—your main points, the data and information you'll need to find, the organization you'll give them, and the ways you'll hook the points together.

Phrasing a claim or thesis statement is an even more crucial preparatory act than phrasing a central idea, because the words you select can control several aspects of your relationship with your audience. For example, each of the following claims would vary the audience's perception of the speaker's intensity:

1. "Do not eat cured pork because *it is unhealthy.*"
2. "Do not eat cured pork because *it is carcinogenic.*"
3. "Do not eat cured pork because *it will kill you.*"

As you move from version 1 to version 3, you are phrasing your feelings in progressively more intense language: each successive version expresses your attitude more harshly.

The following claims would vary the impact of a speech on each member of the audience:

1. "Make use of our school's Division of Career Planning because it can help you *plan your curriculum.*"
2. "Make use of our school's Division of Career Planning because it will help you *select your major.*"
3. "Make use of our school's Division of Career Planning because it will teach you how *to prepare résumés and to interview for jobs.*"
4. "Make use of our school's Division of Career Planning because it will put you *in touch with employers.*"

These four examples vary the rationales behind the actions you wish listeners to take. Presumably, one can take some course of action for any number of reasons: your claim should be phrased in a way that captures what you think will be the most compelling reasons for this *particular audience.*

The following claims would vary the approach of the speaker:

1. "The city's new landfill is an *eyesore*" (aesthetic judgment).
2. "The city's new landfill is a *health hazard*" (personal-safety judgment).
3. "The city's new landfill is a *political payoff to the rich companies that supported the council members' campaigns*" (political judgment).

Each of these claims condemns a civic project, but in a different way. The first version judges the landfill negatively on aesthetic grounds, the second on safety grounds, and the third on political grounds. Were you to advocate the first version, you would need to demonstrate that (a) aesthetic qualities are important criteria for judging landfills and (b) the landfill indeed will be visible to a significant number of community members. For the second version, you would need to argue successfully that health hazards are a matter of public concern and that this particular landfill allows hazardous materials to be deposited. In defending the third version you would want to document (a) the campaign contributions and (b) the fact that major users or beneficiaries of the depository are the companies that gave the most money to the successful candidates. In each case the selection of a particular evaluative criterion controls the main features of the speech.

What follows are examples of general and specific purposes and central ideas or claims:

Example 1
Subject: Cardiopulmonary resuscitation (CPR)
General purpose: To inform
Specific purposes:
- To explain the three life-saving steps of CPR
- To interest the auditors in signing up for a CPR course
- To impress on listeners their social responsibilities relevant to CPR

Central idea: "Cardiopulmonary resuscitation—CPR—is a three-step, life-saving technique for use in emergencies that anyone can and everyone should learn."

Example 2
Subject: Household technologies
General purpose: To persuade
Specific purposes:
- To make members of the audience care less about their own personal comfort
- To convince them that non-electrical appliances such as mechanical can openers, hand-operated egg beaters, and knives work as well as or better than electrical versions of the same tools
- To create a concern for the wastefulness represented by many household technologies

Claim: "You can still live the good life even if you abandon many household technologies."

Work on your general and specific purposes before you construct your speech. Being sensitive to general purposes guides your thinking about needed materials and your relationship to your audience. Exploring the full range of your specific purposes helps you to come to grips with yourself, the importance of this speech to your life, the range of effects you want to have on your audience, and the measures by which you can gauge those effects.

ANALYZING YOUR AUDIENCE AND THE OCCASION

This book has emphasized the notion that communication is a two-way street. If you accept that concept, you need to act as if it made a difference—that is, you need to take listeners consciously and systematically into account when you are preparing to speak. It's tempting to focus only on yourself—your goals, your fears, and your own interests. However, if you believe you're speaking so that others will know what you know, believe what you believe, feel what you feel, and do what you believe is in their best interests, then you've got to construct the speech from the viewpoint of members of your audience.

You must regularly ask yourself questions such as these: "How would I feel about this topic if I were in their place?" "How can I adapt this material to their interests and habits, especially at points where their experience or understandings are different than mine?" Putting yourself in your listener's shoes is what researchers call **receiver orientation.**[2] A receiver orientation will push you to construct speeches from the receiver end of the communication process, investigating what aspects of the audience's *psychological* and *sociological background* are relevant to your speech.

Chapter 4 takes up the topic of receiver orientation in detail, but, for now, you should find out what you need to know about the people who compose your listening group—their age range, gender balance, social-economic-political status, origins and backgrounds, prejudices, hopes and fears. As suggested in the first chapter, you should also find out how much they know about the subject so that you pitch it at the right level. In a public speaking class, this type of investigation is easy enough to conduct—you can ask. In other circumstances, you'll have to be more creative. Start asking those questions early; audience analysis is *the* crucial step in speech preparation because your receiver orientation will determine how successful you are at reaching your audience.

Almost equally important to the need to analyze your audience is the need to analyze the occasion on which you're speaking. The occasion is what brings people together, and, consequently, it usually determines listeners' expectations. Do they expect to hear a comic monologue on race relations or a lecture on the relationship between minority status and socio-economic achievements in this country? You had better be meeting the audience's expectations. In addition, you had better follow the communication rules that govern the specific occasion. If parliamentary procedure is being used in a meeting, for example, you'll have to follow those rules to know what you can talk about and when. Other rules aren't written: no one tells a president-elect that the inaugural address must contain a citizen greeting, a call for unity, discussions of both domestic and foreign policy, and a final appeal to the deity. Yet all presidential inaugural speeches do, for rules flow out of earlier speaking practices. Those rules are every bit as powerful and constraining as the written rules of parliamentary procedure. When analyzing occasions, ask yourself the following questions:

1. *Nature and Purpose.* Is this a voluntary or captive audience? How should I adapt to that fact?
2. *Prevailing Rules and Customs.* How must I adapt to the rules and customs of this group?
3. *Physical Conditions.* In- or out-of-doors? Hot or cold? Audience sitting or standing? Public address system or not? Good audiovisual facilities or not? Outside noise or not?

Answers to such questions affect your delivery style.

The occasions that bring people together help to determine their expectations. There are usually communication rules that govern such occasions and reflect those expectations. What questions can you ask yourself to help you understand and analyze these occasions?

GATHERING YOUR SPEECH MATERIAL

Once you've considered the subject and purpose of your speech and analyzed the audience and occasion, you'll be ready to gather the materials for your speech. Ordinarily, you'll start by assembling what you already know about the subject and deciding roughly what ideas you want to include. Nearly always, however, you'll find that what you already know is not enough. You will need to gather additional information—facts, illustrations, stories, and examples—with which you can develop your speech. You can acquire some of this information through interviews and conversations with people who know something you do not know about the subject. You can gather other materials from newspapers, magazines, books, government documents, or radio and television programs. In particular, you should consult such sources as the "News of the Week in Review" section of *The New York Times,* as well as *U.S. News and World Report, Wall Street Journal, Harper's,* and *The Observer* if you plan to deal with a current question of public interest. Many magazines of general interest are indexed in the *Readers' Guide to Periodical Literature;* numerous encyclopedias, yearbooks, government reports, almanacs, and other reference materials can be found in your college library. This important topic—supporting materials—will be covered in detail in Chapter 5.

MAKING AN OUTLINE

Early in your preparation you may want to make a rough sketch of the points you wish to include in your speech. A complete outline, however, cannot be drawn up until you've gathered all of the necessary material. When this material is at hand, set down in final order the principal points you expect to present, together with the subordinate ideas that will be necessary to explain or prove these points.

In Chapter 7, you'll find a number of specific patterns according to which the ideas in a speech may be arranged. There, too, you'll find the form that a complete outline should take. For the present, remember two simple but important rules: (a) arrange your ideas in a clear and systematic order and (b) preserve the unity of your speech by making sure that each point is directly related to your specific purpose.

PRACTICING ALOUD

With your outline completed, you're ready for the most terrifying task of preparation: practicing your speech. (See Figure 3.1.) This is not easy! You can feel like a fool talking aloud in your room; the sound of your voice seems to ring hollow; and, you find that some of the materials you wrote out come off as simplistic, clichéd, or silly. Nevertheless, you must practice aloud (a) to improve some of the decisions you've already made and (b) to work on your delivery skills.

Give practice a chance. It can save your rhetorical life. Talk through your outline aloud, in a full (not a mumbling) voice; that will help you to get used to the sound. Repeatedly read through the outline until you've made all the changes that seem useful and until you can express each idea clearly and smoothly. Then, putting the outline aside, think through the speech silently, point by point, to make sure that it's fixed in your head. Now, try to talk through the outline without looking at it, but by looking at a card with only a one-word cue for each idea. On your first trials, you may inadvertently leave out some points; that's okay. Practice until all of the ideas come out in their proper order and the words flow easily, all the time talking in full voice. Finally, if possible, get a friend to listen to your speech, give you direct feedback, and help you practice making eye contact with a real person.

DELIVERING YOUR SPEECH: COMMUNICATING SELF-CONFIDENCE

Now you're ready to present your first speech. Even if you've read over the material on speech anxiety in Chapter 1, you still might be asking, "How can I deliver this speech? Even if I'm successfully fighting speech anxiety inside myself, how can I convey a sense of self-confidence to an audience?" The following guidelines should help:

1. *Be yourself.* Act as you would if you were having an animated conversation with a friend. Avoid a rigid, oratorical, or aggressive posture. At the same time, don't become so comfortable in front of the group that you lean on the wall behind you or sprawl all over the lectern. When you speak, you want your listeners' minds to be focused on your ideas, not on the way you're presenting them.

2. *Look at your listeners.* People tend to mistrust anyone who doesn't look them in the eye. They also may get the impression that you don't care about them and that you aren't interested in their reactions to your message. Watch your listeners' faces for clues to their reactions. Without this essential information, you cannot gauge the ongoing effectiveness of your speech or make minor adjustments as you go along.

3. *Communicate with your body as well as with your voice.* Realize that as a speaker you are being seen as well as heard. Bodily movements and changes in facial expression can help clarify and reinforce your ideas. Keep your hands at your sides so that when you feel an impulse to gesture, you can do so easily. If there is no lectern, don't be afraid to let your notes show. If you're working from an outline, use a hard backing to hold the papers firm (this will make your nervousness less visible). If you have notecards, hold them up so that you can see them clearly. Don't hide them so that referring

Figure 3.1 The Essential Steps in Planning, Preparing, and Presenting a Speech
Systematic planning and preparation will save you time and frustration as you develop your speeches. These are the seven basic steps involved in effective speech preparation. Do you usually prepare your speeches in this order? Which steps are the easiest and which are most difficult for you?

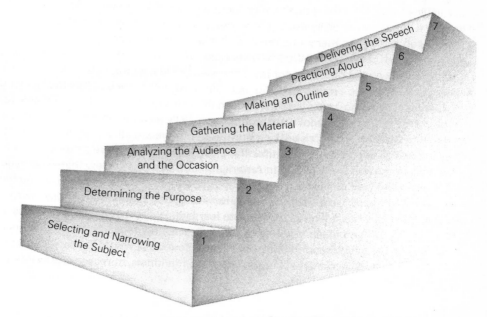

the role you allow it to play in your lives. To best accomplish this task I will first examine the influence of our society on our perception of success. Second, I will explore how these societal attitudes contribute to a fear of failure. Finally, I will describe ways to reevaluate our attitudes about success in order to greatly diminish our fear of failure. In order to achieve, then, this new perspective on failure, we must first understand America's perspective on success./2

American cultural factors influence our attitudes about success in three ways. First, whether we are aware of it or not, our society places an extraordinary emphasis on success. An article in *U.S. News and World Report,* August 24, 1987, states, "Winning, it is true, is the American way. In a society that prides itself on equality, we have a peculiar obsession with being No. 1." In America, being good is not enough—you have got to be the best to be considered a success—because No. 2 is the same as No. 10. This is glaringly evident by our treatment of the Olympics. For instance, an American news reporter approached Inga Benedick, an American cyclist, saying she must be terribly upset over her loss. Inga, however, looked pretty happy, after all she had just placed 8th in the world. The American reporter was completely baffled by her response; how could she consider herself a success? She did not win a gold medal. As a matter of fact, you probably do not know who Inga is because she didn't win a gold medal. Do you know who won the silver medals? The bronze? Do you know who the No. 2 ranked tennis player is? Do you know who the Vice President of Chrysler Corporation is? As you can see, success in America is no easy feat; only so many people can be No. 1. And if you are not, there is no one to blame but yourself, which is the second aspect of success in America./3

William Gavin, in an article in *Current,* June 1987, points out that "the pursuit of happiness implicity involves successfully concluding the pursuit. America does not guarantee success, but it provides for it." So if we fail, it's our own fault. Anyone can succeed in the land of opportunity, and if we don't it's because we didn't try hard enough, or work hard enough, or do the right thing—or maybe something is wrong with our very selves. This wouldn't be so bad except that in America, you don't get to set your own standards for success, which is the final way our society influences our attitudes about it./4

We are judged by what Carole Hyatt and Linda Gottlieb in their book, *When Smart People Fail,* call visible accomplishment—doing something rather than simply being something, and the judgment is delivered solely by others. W. Timothy Gallwey in his book, *The Inner Game of Tennis,* states that "Even before we received praise or blame for our first report card, we were loved or ignored for how well we performed our very first actions." These three aspects of the American perception of success are how we learn to fear failure. So let's turn our attention to a second and vital point to understand [:] how these factors contribute to a fear of failure./5

Hyatt and Gottlieb state that "Failure is a judgment about an event." Nothing more, nothing less. So why is failure so negative, so painful and for many of us so frightening? Because the judgment about the event is usually not our own objective judgment; it is colored and tainted by the cultural expectations we feel compelled to conform to. First of all, because success in America is so important, there is considerable pressure on us to succeed, or rather, considerable pressure not to fail. In a society where success is so admirable, failure is considered shameful. The tremendous pressure to succeed causes us to fear failure. Secondly, we live in the land of opportunity, so it seems we should be able to succeed. In her book, *Pathfinders*, Gail Sheehy states that "most people see a failed project as further evidence of their own inadequacies: if what I did was bad, I must be no good." We fear failure because of the statement it may make about ourselves, not just what we do. Finally, the third way our culture breeds a fear of failure is the standards by which it judges our successes and failures for us. As we have seen, the standards for success in America are rather stringent; whether in a competition, in the amount of money you make, or in your spot on the corporate ladder, being second is failure, only first is a success. We recognize how difficult, if not impossible this task may be, and we become afraid of the almost inevitable failure. As Gallwey states, "It is as if some believe that only by being the best, only be being a winner, will they be eligible for the love and respect they seek." The other problem is that we tend to believe that being first really is the standard for success, and we put personal successes aside as unimportant. Clearly then, a society can so greatly influence an attitude about success that we can learn to fear failure. Well now that I've probably only succeeded in reinforcing a fear of failure, I should point out that simply recognizing the influence of these societal attitudes will help us get a fresh perspective on failure./6

The key to diminishing a fear of failure is two-fold. Not only must we readjust how we perceive our own success, but also how we evaluate the successes of others. First, as students or competitors in anything, we need to set personal standards for success. Evaluate yourself with internal markers, not society's external ones. Rather than relying on a first place to determine our success, or our value, concentrate on achieving goals that mean something to us, that are a reflection of our own unique capabilities. Gallwey points out that "the score of a tennis match may be an indication of how well I performed, or how hard I tried, but it does not define my identity, nor give me cause to consider myself as something more or less than I was before the match." Sometimes the goal may be to just get through your speech— and I'm on my way there./7

Secondly, as teachers, coaches, even fellow competitors, we need to focus on the value of these personal goals rather than external achievements. Gallwey states that our anxiety over failure may be based on ". . . the mistaken assumption that one's sense of self-respect rides on how well he performs in relation to others." I experienced this myself when I returned from AFA Nationals a few weeks ago and had several people ask me how I did. Only when my English professor said to me, "How do you feel about Nationals?" was I able to share the successes and victories that meant the most to me; the ones that could never be measured by placement in a final round, the victories that would stay with me forever, long after the trophy was in a box in a basement somewhere. Today, when you leave this round, when you see your students and teammates, rather than asking them how they think they did, or how they placed, ask them how they feel about the round, what they learned, what made the round good for them. By doing this, we emphasize personal goals and achievements; whatever it may be is all over; only one person comes in first; but that does not erase the individual accomplishments of every other competitor./8

Today, after examining our societal attitudes about success, and then exploring how those attitudes generate a fear of failure, we are able to reassess how we view success and find that we don't need to fear failure after all. Well, I made it on the speech team, I made it to this tournament, and I've made it through this round. I am a success, regardless of my rank, because I am not measured by a trophy. I am measured by me./9

CHAPTER SUMMARY

Getting started is a matter of developing a rhetorical frame of mind that conditions you to think strategically about choices you have to make. That's planning. When planning and preparing your speech:

1. Select and narrow your subject, making it appropriate to you, your audience, the occasion, and time limits.

2. Determine your general and specific purposes, framing a dominant specific purpose to focus your thinking and wording the central idea or claim to guide your development of the key ideas.

3. Analyze your audience and the occasion so as to discover aspects of both that should affect what you say and how you say it.

4. Gather your material through self-inventory, library research, interviews, and the like.

5. Arrange and outline your points so as to package your ideas in clear and forceful ways.

6. Practice your speech aloud, working from outlines and then notecards, first alone and then with an audience.

7. Deliver the speech with all of the signs of self-confidence you can muster.

KEY TERMS

central idea (p. 49)
claim (p. 49)
general purposes (p. 47)

receiver orientation (p. 54)
specific purposes (p. 49)
thesis statement (p. 49)

SKILLBUILDING ACTIVITIES

1. Listed below are two groups of three statements about a single topic. Read all three statements in each group and write what you believe to be the claim of the group's message. Compare your phrasing of the claims with those of members of your class.
   a. Many prison facilities are inadequate.
   b. Low rates of pay result in frequent job turnovers in prisons.
   c. Prison employees need on-the-job training.

   a. There is a serious maldistribution of medical personnel and service.
   b. The present system of delivering medical service is excellent.
   c. Rural areas have a shortage of doctors.

2. Rewrite each of the following statements, making it into a clear and concise central idea for a speech:
   a. "Today I would like to try to get you to see the way in which the body can communicate a whole lot of information."
   b. "The topic for my speech has to do with the high amount of taxes people have to pay."
   c. "A college education might be a really important thing for some people, so my talk is on a college education."
   Now rewrite the last two statements (b, c) as claims. Be ready to present your versions in a class discussion.

3. Deliver your first regular speech. Your instructor will tell you about the general purpose and the type of talk he or she wants you to pursue. Some final words of advice: (a) Keep it simple. Avoid elaborate arguments, oratorical flourishes, complicated visual aids. Concentrate instead on coming up with a clear central idea or claim and easily organized developmental ideas. Use easy-to-follow illustrations or perhaps some expert testimony so that you get used to integrating two or more kinds of supporting materials. (b) Practice referring to and talking about the audience. Make sure they know you have them in mind by the way you approach them and adapt the content to them. (c) Work with a delivery pattern that's comfortable for you. Notecards usually work better than sheets of paper; stand up as comfortably as you can, even gesturing when you feel loose enough to do it; talk conversationally, looking at people when you make specific points. Good luck.

REFERENCES

1. It can be argued that all speeches are persuasive because, presumably, *any* change in a person's stock of knowledge, beliefs, attitudes, or behaviors is a kind of adjustment of the human mechanism that can be attributed to "persuasion." This view flows directly from a definition of persuasion by a mid-1960s author, Wallace Fotheringham, who defined persuasion as "that body of effects in receivers" that is caused by the speaker's message. Also attached to this position is another claim that says all persuasion ultimately is self-persuasion because a persuader can be successful only if he or she can call up ideas already accepted by audience members, attaching those ideas to some proposal being made. Both of these areas are ideas reviewed in

Charles U. Larson, *Persuasion: Reception and Responsibility,* 5th ed. (Belmont, Calif.: Wadsworth Publishing Company, 1989), 9–10. The opposing argument—that we ought to establish more careful boundaries around the idea of persuasion—and the concept of separation of informative and persuasive talk can be found in Herbert W. Simons, *Persuasion: Understanding, Practice, and Analysis,* 2nd ed. (New York: Random House, 1986), chap. 2, "What Is Persuasion?"

2.   University of Chicago Professor Wayne Booth was perplexed in the late 1960s and early 1970s by the failure of speakers—"futile babblers" (p. xi) he called them—who focused solely on their own beliefs and not upon the needs of audiences. His perplexity produced a moving book, *Modern Dogma and the Rhetoric of Assent* (Notre Dame, Ind.: University of Notre Dame Press, 1974). Also see David K. Berlo, *The Process of Communication* (New York: Holt, Rinehart & Winston, 1960), 52, 62.

3.   Diane M. Schleppi, "Looking Out for Number Two," *Winning Orations, 1989* (the Interstate Oratorical Association). Reprinted by permission of Larry Schnoor, Executive Secretary, Interstate Oratorical Association, Mankato State University, Mankato, Minn.

Planning and Preparing Your Speech

CHAPTER FOUR

Understanding Your Audience

"*L*adies and gentlemen of the jury," the defense lawyer said, "my client has had to work for a living all of his life. He started out, like some of you did, at the bottom of the ladder. He's never asked for any special breaks and he's always treated those of you who know him as a neighbor, fair and square. Why would he set fire to his own business—something he's worked so hard for? The night his building went up in smoke, so did half a lifetime's work and dreams—his and his family's. Arson is a serious crime and it deserves our prosecution to the limits of the law. That's our duty as citizens of this country! But let's not get carried away and accuse someone who's never even gotten a parking ticket! Let's go after the real criminals, not honest, law-abiding citizens like you and me."*

This defense lawyer knows that effective public speaking is *audience-centered*. By selecting his supporting materials, arranging the sequence of ideas, and choosing his appeals, he improves his chances of achieving the desired response—a verdict of *not guilty*—by tailoring his presentation to the individuals who collectively make up the jury.

As previous chapters have stressed, you need to interact with the people you are addressing. Selecting the subject, establishing your purpose, and narrowing the topic revolve around a consideration of your audience. The remaining steps in speech preparation—selecting supporting materials, arranging the sequence of ideas, and developing introductions and conclusions—likewise depend heavily upon audience analysis. Your effectiveness as a speaker depends upon adapting to your listeners.

Since it's impractical to consider each listener as an individual, you must analyze listeners as members of a group—your audience. You should look for common denominators that will help you to target your messages specifically to that group. Identifying the roles and physical characteristics of your listeners (demographic analysis) will help you to discover how they think (psychological profiling). One theme will be stressed throughout this chapter: the goal of audience analysis is to discover what facets of listeners' demographic and psychological characteristics are relevant to your speech purposes and ideas. This information will help you find ways to adapt your speech to your listeners.

ANALYZING YOUR AUDIENCE DEMOGRAPHICALLY

Demographic analysis is the statistical study of human populations, especially their size, density, distribution, and vital statistics. **Demographic variables** are physical characteristics, such as age, gender, education, group membership, and cultural and ethnic background. Since you can directly observe physical characteristics, it's often easier to begin your audience analysis with these demographic factors. In any audience you can identify traits that group members hold in common. When you begin your audience analysis, you will want to ask questions such as these:

1. *Age.* Are your listeners primarily young, middle-aged, or older? Does one age group seem to dominate a mixed audience? Is there a special relationship between age groups—parents and their children, for instance?
2. *Gender.* Is your audience predominantly male or female, or is the group made up of both genders?
3. *Education.* How much do your listeners already know about your subject? Do their educational or experiential backgrounds allow them to learn about this subject easily and quickly?
4. *Group Membership.* Do these people belong to groups that represent special attitudes or identifiable values?
5. *Cultural and Ethnic Background.* Are members of your audience predominantly from particular cultural groups? Do your listeners share a special heritage?

The importance of demographic analysis does not lie in simply finding answers to these and similar questions. Rather, the key is to decide if any of these demographic factors will affect your listeners' ability or willingness to understand and accept what you want to say. In other words, you must determine which factors are relevant to your audience and shape your message accordingly.

For example, if you're addressing a local kindergarten class, you must obviously take *age* and *education* into consideration. Here you will probably want to adapt to your young listeners by using a simpler vocabulary and by

Using Poll Data

Today, at least 2000 firms devote major portions of their work to public opinion polling, asking representative citizens what they think of everything from the president to a new brand of toothpaste. More than $4 billion is spent annually on polling. An analysis of front page campaign stories from October 9 to November 8, 1988, revealed 67 poll-related stories in the *Washington Post* and 42 such stories in *The New York Times* (Ratzan, page 457). We ended the 1988 presidential campaign by having more than one poll per day reported in our leading newspapers!

Poll data can be put to excellent use by speakers, as poll results are a kind of testimony of typical people. However, you must be careful to test polls before relying too heavily on them. Ask yourself questions such as the following:

1. *How big and representative was the sample?* Gallup and other leading polling agencies usually draw national samples of 1000–1800, and even then assume at least 5–7 percent error. Watch out for quick, small polls. In addition, if a sample is drawn by calling people during the day, all of the people with nine-to-five jobs are not represented. Read the fine print.

2. *How were the questions asked?* Suppose you're reading a poll on abortion laws. Consider two ways of asking whether people support abortion rights: "Should the state allow girls to kill their unborn children?" or "Should the state permit parents in consultation with physicians to terminate pregnancies in the first trimester in the event of rape, incest, or genetic malformation?" Both questions are asking whether abortion should be allowed, but each question asks in very, very different terms; wording can influence answers significantly.

3. *How big is the "undecided" or "no opinion" category?* It's one thing for politicians to have ten-point leads over their opponents when only 5 percent of the electorate is undecided, but it's something else entirely when 35 percent have not yet made up their minds. Examine the undecided middle.

Use polls after reading the fine print. In that way, you'll defend yourself from sloppy work.

For more information, see William Alonzo and Paul Starr, "A Nation of Numbers Watchers," *The Wilson Quarterly*, vol.9 (Summer 1985), 93–123; L. John Martin, preface to "Polling and the Democratic Consensus," in *The Annals of the American Academy of Political and Social Science*, vol. 472 (March 1984), 9; Scott C. Ratzan, "The Real Agenda Setters: Pollsters in the 1988 Presidential Campaign," *American Behavioral Scientist*, 32 (March-April 1989), 451–463.

every election; they tend to purchase the same kind of vehicles; they tend to perceive certain people and occupations as more respectable than others; and they tend not to change religions or places of worship. The demographic variable of age may indicate to you that your audience possesses many fixed beliefs.

Some fixed beliefs can even be called stereotypes. A **stereotype** is the perception that individuals who share one or a few common properties are the same in other ways as well. For example, we might say, "All police officers are honest" or "People who do things like that should be arrested!" or "Never trust a politician." The problem with stereotypes is that not all police officers are honest, some actions aren't criminal, and many politicians can be trusted. Stereotypes ignore individual differences and exceptions to rules.

In contrast, **variable beliefs** are less well anchored in our minds and experiences. You might enter college thinking you're well-suited by temperament and talent to be a chemist; however, after an instructor praises your abilities in a composition class, you may believe you are predestined to be a writer. Then, you take a marketing class and find out that you're very good at planning an advertising campaign. This self-discovery goes on and on as you experience one class after another until you finally select a major and a degree program. In this example, your beliefs about your talents and the ways that you can best use them change with your personal experiences. The information you've received from various authority figures has influenced these variable beliefs. And, since your beliefs are still not firmly fixed, they could change again as you encounter new experiences.

Before you speak, it's important to know which of your audience's beliefs are *fixed* (difficult to change) and which are *variable* (more easily altered) as well as which are held as fact or opinion. Assessing the nature of your audience's beliefs is important for three reasons:

1. *You can influence your audience's beliefs by repeating the pattern through which they normally accept beliefs.* For example, knowing that your audience accepts the statements of authorities as factual will encourage you to use the testimony of authorities to sway them.

2. *Establishing a psychological profile should help you outline some of the appeals you can make within your speech.* If your audience analysis shows that your listeners consider statistics to be factual, you can use scientific studies or numerical data in your speech. On the other hand, if your audience believes in the divine inspiration of certain religious documents, you can cite quotations or examples from these sources.

3. *A psychological profile also allows you to set realistic expectations as you plan your talk.* Not all audience beliefs are equally amenable to change through speeches. You should not try to accomplish impossible goals in a single speech. You may encounter resistance if you try to destroy too many beliefs, attitudes, or values.

Later in this chapter we'll discuss in more detail how to set speech goals. We'll also provide an extended example of an audience analysis.

Attitudes

The second task of psychological profiling is understanding audience attitudes. **Attitudes** may be defined as tendencies to respond positively or negatively to people, objects, or ideas. Attitudes are emotionally weighted responses. They express individual preferences and feelings, such as "Democracy is better than Communism," "Discrimination is wrong," "The Statue of Liberty is a beautiful monument," and "I like my public speaking class."

Because attitudinal statements express our preferences and feelings, they often control our behavior. We tend to do things that we like and avoid things that we dislike. As a speaker, you should consider the dominant attitudes of your audience. One dramatic example of the strength of attitudes occurred when the Coca-Cola® corporation introduced new *Coke*®, a refigured formula, with disastrous results. Although extensive blind taste tests indicated that people preferred *Coke's* new flavor, consumers reacted negatively because of their loyalty to the classic formula. Their attitudes controlled their purchasing behavior and the corporation was forced to "reintroduce" *Coca-Cola Classic*®. Before you speak, you must consider your audience's attitudes toward you, your subject, and your speech purpose.

The Audience's Attitudes Toward the Speaker

The attitudes of an audience toward you as a speaker will be based in part on your reputation and in part on your behavior during the speech. Two factors are especially important regarding your reputation: (a) the respect your listeners hold for you and your subject, and (b) their feelings of friendliness toward you.

You can do several things to encourage positive audience attitudes when you speak. You can enhance your audience's respect for you and your topic by (a) presenting evidence of your intelligence and expertise during the speech; (b) appearing to be fair, just, and sincere as you discuss the topic; and (c) providing clear, direct, and well-documented claims to support your proposition. You can strengthen your audience's friendliness toward you by (a) speaking energetically to suggest how important the topic is to you and should be to them; (b) appearing alert but comfortable in your role as a speaker; and (c) expressing your interest in them as listeners.

The Audience's Attitudes Toward the Subject

Sometimes people are interested in a subject and sometimes they are simply apathetic about it. In either case, the amount of interest they have can influence their response. Some researchers place **prior audience attitudes,** or existing predispositions in listeners, among the most crucial audience variables that determine speaking success.[2] If you try to convince people in your class that tuition should be doubled, your listeners will probably be hostile. They may refuse to listen or even walk out. They may conclude that you don't know what you're talking about, discrediting you as a speaker. They may fail to perceive your intent or your message accurately.

You can do several things as a speaker to minimize these potentially negative attitude reactions. You can stress common values such as the importance of a good education. You can use carefully selected supporting materials such as reliable statistics or examples familiar to your listeners. You can also minimize potentially negative listener reactions by arousing your audience's curiosity about some novel aspect of the subject.

On the other hand, if your audience analysis indicates that your listeners may be apathetic, you can stress ways the problem being discussed directly affects them. You must neutralize audience apathy by emphasizing the connections between your subject and your listeners' lives. When your listeners are apathetic, you need to make a special effort to gain their interest. You can use the nine factors of attention to accomplish this. (See pages 34–38.)

Interest, or lack of it, is only one aspect of an audience's attitude toward your subject. *Expectancy* is another. For example, as soon as you hear that a speech will be about the animal rights movement, you may begin to form favorable or unfavorable attitudes toward the speaker and the subject. As a general rule, the more your listeners know about your subject or the

Group expectations can vary dramatically from situation to situation. How might a speaker handle the expectations of this audience?

stronger their beliefs concerning it are, the more likely they are to have preconceived expectations. These expectations may be troublesome since frequently they operate as listening barriers or as filters that distort the meanings of your message. The introductory portion of your speech provides you with a special opportunity to create or to correct audience expectations. As you talk, you should bear in mind your listeners' expectations and adapt accordingly.

The Audience's Attitudes Toward the Speech Purpose

It may surprise you to learn that your audience holds attitudes toward your speech purpose even before you begin to speak. Parents may eagerly listen to your plan for a day-care center; future parents may be curious about your ideas; and listeners without children may resent having to listen and may be looking for an opportunity to argue. Since audience predisposition is seldom uniform, you need to determine through audience analysis what attitudes are predominant and then adapt your speech to those attitudes.

When the general purpose of your speech is to inform, your listeners' attitudes will be governed largely by their feelings and beliefs about the subject; that is, they will either be interested or apathetic. However, when the general purpose of your speech is to persuade, your listeners' attitudes will also be governed by their responses to the specific belief or action you urge. Your audience might best be described as one of the following:

- Favorable, but not aroused
- Apathetic
- Interested, but undecided about what to do or what to think
- Interested, but hostile to the proposed attitudes, beliefs, or actions
- Hostile to any change from the present state of affairs

Determining the predominant attitude of your audience toward your subject and purpose should guide you in selecting your arguments and developing the structure and content of your message. If your listeners are apathetic about the garbage glut, begin your speech by pointing out how many tons of waste each one of them contributes to the problem each year. Show them how they affect your subject and how your subject affects them. If they are hostile to recycling, you may wish to introduce the concept cautiously, emphasizing the economic advantages of reclaiming resources such as metals and paper. If they are interested but undecided, provide plenty of expert testimony and statistics showing that recycling works. If they are favorably disposed but not enthusiastic, motivate them by providing specific plans for creative or easy home recycling projects.

Audience analysis made prior to a speech is certain never to be fully correct. Audience attitudes may shift even while you are speaking.[3] The way listeners sit, their facial expressions, and their audible reactions—laughter, applause, fidgeting, whispering—can all be clues to their attitudes toward you, your subject, and your purpose. The conscientious communicator notices and adapts to these signs of audience feedback.[4]

Values

The third task of psychological profiling is understanding audience values. **Values** are the basic constructs organizing one's orientation to life. They provide standards for judging the worth of thoughts and actions. Values serve as the foundations for the beliefs and attitudes that cluster around them. (See Figure 4.1.)

Figure 4.1 Belief, Attitude, and Value Clusters
Beliefs, attitudes, and values are interdependent. They often form clusters that reinforce each other.

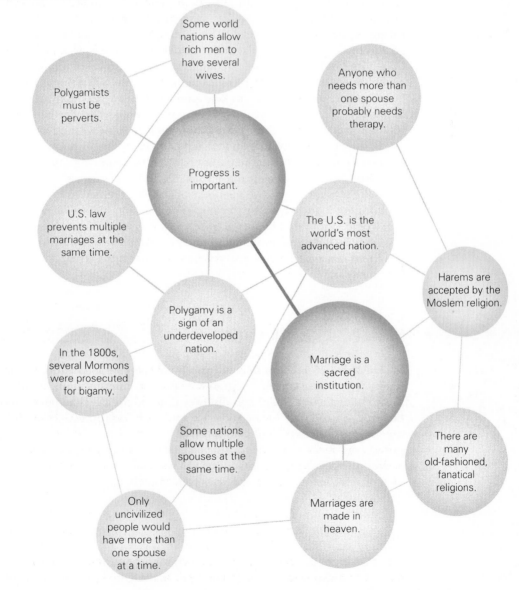

Beliefs, attitudes, and values are interdependent. That is, they tend to form consistent clusters that reinforce and repeat each other. Values are more basic than beliefs or attitudes because they represent broad categories that may motivate specific attitudes and beliefs. For example, a person may hold a certain value such as "Human life is sacred." That value can be expressed in multiple attitudes, including, "Abortion is wrong" or "Mercy killing is immoral." That value may also be expressed in beliefs such as "A fetus should be treated as a human being," "Most Americans are opposed to abortion rights legislation," or "Religious authority ought to be respected on questions of morality."

Values, then, underlie an individual's particular attitudes and beliefs. On an even broader scale, we can discuss **value orientations**—sometimes called *ideologies*—which are common views accepted by relatively large groups of people. Former President Ronald Reagan, regarded by many as "The Great Communicator," frequently appealed to value orientations in his public speeches. He often combined several values in a single sentence. In his 1980 acceptance speech, Reagan declared that people from all walks of life, regardless of political party, were bound together "in that community of shared values of family, work, neighborhood, peace, and freedom."[5]

Discovering what values audience members habitually bring to bear on issues is a critical part of audience analysis. These values organize and often influence the beliefs and attitudes your listeners also express. For example, if you are trying to persuade members of a student senate to allocate funds for bringing a guest speaker to campus, it will help you to know that they are strongly motivated by sociological (how the social life of the university will be affected) and pragmatic concerns (whether it is affordable). A search for *common ground*—shared values—represents a crucial step in audience analysis.

USING AUDIENCE ANALYSIS IN SPEECH PREPARATION

Identifying the demographic and psychological characteristics of your listeners is an important first step toward good communication. Identifying these characteristics helps you discover what might affect audience acceptance of you and your ideas. Audience analysis helps you search for clues to the way your listeners think and act. What you discover can help you better phrase your ideas, organize your speech, or determine your appeals. We will address the development and delivery of your speech in Chapters 9, 10, and 11. For now, let's focus on the ways your audience analysis helps you prepare to speak.

Audience Targeting: Setting Purposes Realistically

You should have little difficulty determining your general speech purposes—to inform, to entertain, or to persuade. Once you accomplish this, however, you need to realistically determine what you can expect to accomplish with your particular audience in the time you have available. As you think about targeting your audience, four considerations should arise: (a) your specific purpose, (b) the areas of audience interest, (c) the audience's capacity to act, and (d) the degree of change you can expect.

Your Specific Purpose

Suppose you have a part-time job with your college's Career Planning and Placement Office; you know enough about its operations and have enough personal interest in it to want to speak about career planning and placement to a variety of listeners. What you've discovered about different audiences should help you to determine appropriate specific purposes for each. If you were to talk to a group of incoming freshmen, for example, you would know that they probably

- know little about the functions of a career planning and placement office (have few beliefs in this area, none of which are fixed).
- are predisposed to look favorably on career planning and placement (have a positive attitude toward the subject).
- are more concerned with such pragmatic issues as getting an adviser, registering, and learning about basic degree requirements than they are with long-range matters such as finding postdegree placements (are motivated by pragmatic values).
- see you as an authoritative speaker and, consequently, are willing to listen to you (have a positive attitude toward speaker).

Given these audience considerations, you should probably keep your speech fairly general. Provide basic rather than detailed information about career planning and placement. You might phrase your specific purpose as follows: "To brief incoming freshmen on the range of services offered by the Career Planning and Placement Office." This orientation will include a brief description of each service and a general appeal to your audience to use these services to make some curricular decisions.

If you spoke to a group of graduating college seniors on the same subject, you would address the audience differently. You would discover that they

- are familiar with the Career Planning and Placement Office through roommates and friends who have used it (have beliefs that are fixed).
- have strong positive feelings about career planning and placement because they are hoping to utilize such services to find jobs when they graduate (have a positive attitude toward the subject).
- tend to think education has prepared them to "earn a decent living" (pragmatic value).
- may view you as an unqualified speaker on this subject, especially if you aren't a senior or aren't employed full-time (have a negative attitude toward speaker).

Given these factors, you should offer specific details in some areas. You should describe the special features of the office rather than simply outlining its general duties. Your listeners need to know "how"; they already know the "what." You should reassure them that the office successfully places many students and point out that it is more successful when students allow ample time for résumé development, job searching, and interviewing. You should demonstrate your expertise by talking about career possibilities across a variety of fields—especially if you know what fields are represented in the group you are addressing. You might phrase your specific purpose as follows: "To inform graduating seniors about Midstate University's philosophy of career planning and placement, about ways that the office can help students find employment, and about specific types of information and assistance the office provides students." Audience analysis will help you to shape your specific purposes and determine which are most appropriate to your listeners.

Areas of Audience Interest

You can use both demographic and psychological analyses to help you to determine what ideas will interest your listeners. Such analyses are critical in narrowing your choices and choosing specific ideas to develop. Suppose you know something about computer programming. An audience of industrial managers would probably be most interested in hearing how computers can save their companies money; a group of hospital administrators might want to learn how computers could enhance record-keeping and patient services; the Internal Revenue Service would appreciate a computer application to tax fraud discovery; and a general audience would be curious as to how computers might transform their everyday lives in the twenty-first century.

Sometimes, however, you'll want to stimulate a new set of interests in an audience. For example, assume that you want your classmates to recognize the value of hypnosis. You can stir their curiosity by tying the topic to existing interests. You might show how hypnosis can help develop concentration for more effective studying, reduce stress before examinations, and tap creative potential.

The Audience's Capacity to Act

As a speaker, don't ask your audience to accomplish the impossible. To demand that a group of striking workers place a tariff on imported goods is unrealistic. Asking them to picket the plant, however, is likely to get results.

You can often discover your listeners' potential for action through an audience analysis. Demographic factors will tell you about the channels of action available to your listeners. Voters can cast their ballots in elections, parents can teach their children, consumers can boycott products, and many people can contribute money. You can use the psychological factors that you discover through audience analysis to stimulate listeners' motivations to act.

You can also determine ranges of authority through an audience analysis, especially through analysis of demographic factors. In the case of a comparatively homogeneous audience (e.g., students), this analysis is relatively easy to perform. In the case of more heterogeneous groups, however, you may have to consider a broader range of listeners' capacities to act. For example, in speaking with a local school's PTA about instituting an after-school program of foreign language and culture instruction, you're addressing an audience comprised of school administrators (who can seek funding from the school board), teachers (who can volunteer instructional time), and parents (who can petition the school board, enroll their children, and volunteer to help with the program). So, you would include in your specific purposes goals for each of these subgroups of listeners.

Degrees of Change

Finally, as suggested earlier, you must be realistic in the degree of change you can expect from your listeners. How much information can you present for consideration? If you have a time limit or if your average listener's attention span is short, you need to limit your information. Demographic factors such as age and educational development will help you to reach these conclusions about your audience. Determining whether your information is new or is already known to your audience will influence how much material you can cover in a single speech as well.

How intensely can you motivate an audience to react to a topic? If your listeners are strongly opposed to downtown renovation, a single speech, no matter how eloquent, will probably not reverse their opinions. One attempt may only neutralize some of their objections. This is a more realistic goal for a single speech. How much action can you expect after your speech? If your prespeech analysis indicates that your listeners vehemently oppose nuclear power plants in your area, you can probably persuade many of them to work long hours on a variety of activities, such as picketing, lobbying, and participating in telephone marathons. However, if they are only moderately committed to opposing nuclear facilities, you might ask for a small monetary donation rather than an actual time commitment.

Audience analysis should help you to determine how you can phrase your specific purposes and central ideas for maximum effectiveness. It should also help you to set more realistic communication goals.

Audience Segmentation: Selecting Dominant Ideas and Appeals

So far, we've focused on how audience analysis helps you to target your audience as a group. Keep in mind, however, that no matter how closely people are seated in the room, they are still individuals. Your beliefs, attitudes, and values—while they are influenced by your culture and society—are ultimately yours. They are the unique products of your own experiences and your own thoughts.

It is often wise to divide your listeners into subgroups for specific appeals. What subgroups can you identify in this audience?

Ideally, then, approaching each listener individually would be most effective. Sometimes you can; however, such communication is time consuming and inefficient when you're dealing with matters of broad public concern. Imagine the impossibility of the president of the United States speaking to each of us individually. By means of a televised public speech, though, the president can talk to us in our own living rooms as if the speech were a personal conversation. You need to find a compromise between thinking of audiences as homogeneous masses and thinking of them as solitary individuals.

Advertisers use an approach called **audience segmentation** to divide a mass audience into a series of subgroups or "target populations." A typical college audience, for example, might be segmented by academic standing (freshmen through seniors), by academic major (art through zoology), by classroom performance (A+ to F), or even by extracurricular activity (ROTC, SADD, Young Republicans, Pi Kappa Delta). Specific appeals can then be directed to each of these subgroups.

Accurately Identifying Subgroups
Carefully identifying subgroups among your listeners allows you to better phrase your appeals and helps you to avoid unnecessarily irritating your listeners as well. A speaker who begins, "Because all of you girls are interested in cooking, I want to talk about four ways a food processor will save you time in the kitchen," will probably alienate most of the audience. Listeners might be angered by the stereotyped allusion to women as "girls" and might be offended that the speaker failed to consider that many men cook. The appeal would be better phrased, "Because everyone who cooks

is interested in saving time, . . ." Here, you're aiming at the proper audience segment—those who cook.

Similarly, you would not want to refer to *dumb jocks, artsy-craftsy theater majors,* or *computer nerds* in a speech to your class on the goals of college education. There will be occasions, however, when you should directly confront the beliefs, attitudes, and values of subgroups represented in your audience and when you won't say what people want to hear. But when you do, find ways that avoid stereotyped references to people and groups. Always cite ample and unbiased evidence when you challenge any group's beliefs, attitudes, and sacred values.

Selecting Relevant Psychological Statements

Audience segmentation should also help you to select statements of belief, attitudes, and values for inclusion in your speech. If you can identify the subgroups in your audience, you can include relevant psychological appeals to each in your speech. These appeals greatly increase the potential effectiveness of your message. Suppose you were to give a speech to members of a local community club, urging them to fund a scholarship. Your initial segmenting of the audience might tell you that the club is composed of medical professionals, social service personnel, educators, and business people. By thinking of the club as segmented into these subgroups, you should be in a position to offer each subgroup some reasons to support your proposal. You might outline the appeals this way:

I. *Proposition:* The membership of the Community Club should fund a college scholarship for a local student.
II. *Reasons*
  A. For doctors and hospital workers—well-educated people take better care of themselves. They are more likely to seek early treatment for serious health problems.
  B. For social service workers—the social-team concept means that working with everyone is necessary for the improvement of the community.
  C. For educators—by denying education to capable students, we neglect to tap into one of the most important resources of our community—young people.
  D. For community business people—well-educated citizens contribute more to the financial resources of the community as investors, property owners, and heads of households.

In an actual speech these basic appeals would each be expanded. From these examples, however, you can see how each appeal is based on beliefs and attitudes that you assume are important to segments of your audience. These appeals implicitly refer to the medical ethic of serving humankind; to the commitment of social services to helping people from all strata of life; to educators' beliefs and attitudes that youth are a national resource; and to business leaders' commitment to financial responsibility and success.

Audience analysis, in combination with audience segmentation, is a valuable tool for selecting your main lines of appeal and argument.

Choosing Among Valuative Appeals

Finally, audience segmentation will help you select valuative appeals for your speeches. **Valuative appeals** are composed of emotionally or ideologically weighted words or phrases chosen to stimulate a certain response. Even informative speeches, as we will discuss more fully in Chapter 12, need to contain appeals to audience interests. You can use a valuative vocabulary to motivate different segments of the audience to listen to and accept your information. For a demonstration speech, you might say, "Once you learn the three basic techniques of Southeast Asian cooking—cutting meats and vegetables, using spices, and quick-cooking your food in a wok—you'll expand your range of expertise in the kitchen (*personal value*); you'll save money on your food and energy bills (*economic value*); you'll create exquisite meals for your friends (*social value*); and you'll prepare more nutritious, healthful entrees for everyone (*pragmatic value*)." With this statement, you've given your audience four different reasons for listening. If four reasons aren't enough, you can say the meals will be beautiful, too, thereby adding an *aesthetic value.*

Valuative appeals are absolutely crucial for persuasive speaking because values are the foundations for people's beliefs, attitudes, and behaviors. Notice the variety of valuative appeals in the following example:

A speaker can use value appeals to motivate segments of an audience. What value appeals might work in this situation?

I. *Claim:* The United States should adopt immediate, severe economic sanctions against nations such as South Africa and the People's Republic of China that violate basic human rights.

II. *Valuative Appeals*

    A. *Political.* Getting tough with nations that consistently violate citizens' rights will increase international respect for the United States' commitment to supporting human rights. If successful, this approach may also give a voice to previously disenfranchised peoples or groups.

    B. *Pragmatic.* Economic sanctions are effective and nonviolent. Nations violating human rights are more likely to respond to economic sanctions than to verbal threats.

    C. *Psychological.* We will increase global dedication to basic human rights if we take these rights seriously enough to enforce them.

    D. *Cultural.* Equal and just treatment of groups of people may enhance their opportunity to contribute to the development of their nations. Nations are made richer by recognition of the heritage of all citizens.

    E. *Sociological.* We can promote a freer environment for political and social participation of citizens in government if nations abandon human rights violations.

    F. *Economical.* Individuals who have previously been denied access will have the opportunity to participate more fully in the resources of their nations.

While we have not used every conceivable value-term in this segmentation of appeals, the procedure should be clear: (a) think through in valuative terms why people might accept your claim; (b) then, use a valuative vocabulary in phrasing your actual appeals.

Understanding your audience is the most crucial step of speech preparation. The competent speaker must make many decisions about topic, specific purposes, and phrasing for central ideas, propositions, and dominant appeals; demographical and psychological analyses of audience members help the speaker make these decisions. To help yourself in carrying out these tasks, you'll want to (a) think through your personal experiences with identifiable groups in the audience; (b) talk with program chairpersons and others who can tell you who is in the audience and also tell you something about their interests; (c) ask speakers who have addressed this or similar audiences what you can expect; and (d) interview some of the people who will be in the audience to find out more about their beliefs, attitudes, and values.

These tasks are challenging, especially since most of us do not have the resources of public opinion polls and extensive social-psychological target group profiles. You may not be able to precisely identify all possible facets of your listeners' minds and habits. However, if you learn all you can about your listeners and use *relevant* considerations to make some key prespeech decisions, you'll improve your chances for success.

In this chapter we have surveyed an array of choices that you must make as you analyze your audience and occasion. If you work systematically, these choices will become clearer. One student prepared the following very comprehensive analysis of her audience as she prepared a speech to increase her audience's understanding of the disease known as Acquired Immune Deficiency Syndrome (AIDS).

UNDERSTANDING AIDS

I. Basic Speaking Situation
  A. *Title: The Great American Plague: AIDS.*
  B. *Subject:* What we should know about the coming crisis in American health—Acquired Immune Deficiency Syndrome.
  C. *General Purpose:* To persuade.
  D. *Specific Purpose:* To prove to members of a local political action caucus that AIDS poses a future national health threat.
  E. *Specific Audience:* The political action caucus is a community group whose function is to promote political consciousness and action in the community. It consists of varied membership, including local homemakers, business proprietors, the town mayor, the chair of the state Republican committee, and approximately one dozen interested listeners. A synopsis of the monthly meeting is broadcast over local radio stations and included on the editorial page of the local newspaper (reaching a secondary audience).
  F. *Proposition:* The caucus should be alerted to the pending crisis in national health.
II. Audience Analysis
  A. *Demographic Analysis*
    1. *Age:* Most of the individuals attending the meeting are between 30 and 65. The spectators are approximately 20–30. Except in cases of appeals to future events, age is probably not an important factor. The speaker is significantly younger than members of her audience (21). She will need to enhance her credibility as a speaker to compensate for her relative youth and inexperience.
    2. *Gender:* The caucus is a mixed group with slightly more women than men. Given the topic and proposition, the audience may initially have the attitude that AIDS is not a threat to them.
    3. *Education:* Approximately one-third of the listeners have completed B.A. degrees in varied fields, including political science, pharmacy, nursing, home economics, and accounting. All but four of the remaining members have finished high school; several have taken college courses. While several health profession-

als in the audience are familiar with disease history and control, most listeners are acquainted with the topic only through media coverage.

    4. *Group Membership:* All listeners are politically active and registered voters. Although they do not necessarily share party affiliation, they all agree that participation in the democratic process is vital.

    5. *Cultural and Ethnic Background:* Ethnic background is primarily European. Most consider AIDS to be a problem associated with minorities, including homosexual males, hemophiliacs, and intravenous drug users. All members of the caucus were either born or raised in this small, midwestern community that combines a rural economy and and a small-business economy.

B. *Psychological Analysis*

    1. *Beliefs*

        a. *Accepted Facts and Beliefs:* Anyone who contracts AIDS will die of it. There isn't anything that can currently be done to stop the disease. The incidence of AIDS is confined primarily to the East and West coasts. The only local resident to die from AIDS had visited New York—it is assumed that that is where he contracted the disease.

        b. *Fixed Beliefs:* The audience believes that drug use and homosexual behavior are morally wrong and should not be condoned. Only one or two members of the caucus would even consider hiring, renting to, or politically endorsing a person known to use drugs or to be homosexual. The medical profession has accounted for most breakthroughs in disease control and treatment.

        c. *Variable Beliefs:* Most probably believe that a degree of tolerance should be shown to members of unusual religious or political factions. Several would agree that the sexual revolution of the 1960s brought some advantages, such as greater openness, more individual responsibility, and better understanding of human sexuality. Several consider drug use to stem from socioeconomic causes rather than individual character flaws.

    2. *Attitudes*

        a. *Audience Attitude Toward Speaker:* The members of the caucus probably consider the speaker to be naive and idealistic. Her youthfulness severely undermines her credibility.

        b. *Audience Attitude Toward Subject:* The listeners are certainly hostile toward those they feel are guilty of spreading AIDS—anyone who is homosexual or dependent upon drugs. While they were surprised by the recent news of the AIDS death of a community resident, they are probably not very concerned because they don't consider themselves likely targets of the disease.

    c. *Audience Attitude Toward Purpose:* Most are basically apathetic. While they are curious about the disease, they don't really care about it since they think it won't touch their lives. Several members are hostile, given their strong personal religious attitudes toward drug use and homosexuality.

  3. *Values*

    a. *Predominant Values:* The political value of "majority rule" is strongly held by every listener. They are committed to the democratic process and take pride in community political involvement at the state and national levels. They see themselves as common people—"the heart of America"—fulfilling the American dream. Caucus members often point to community progress in civil rights issues, general educational reforms, and their high voter turnout during elections.

    b. *Relevant Value Orientation:* While caucus members voice democratic principles, they practice those ideals in a limited sphere. They promote fair treatment for some minority issues, such as equal rights, but they are unaware of or deny others. It would be counterproductive to point out this hypocrisy to the group since they take a great deal of pride in themselves and their local accomplishments.

III. Adaptive Strategies

  A. *Audience Targeting*

    1. *Specific Purpose:* To calm one set of suspicions and make it clear that this is not simply a moral issue. While recognizing the importance of traditional national values, also stress the practical importance of treating disease, regardless of moral issues. Emphasize that everyone's health may be affected if the disease is allowed through ignorance or neglect to spread unchecked.

    2. *Areas of Audience Interests:* Use the caucus members' fixed and anchored beliefs and values to advance the speech's goals. Stress audience commitment to the welfare of the community and nation, their belief in the democratic process, and their belief in the rights of citizens in minority factions. Encourage their feelings of pride in previous civic accomplishments and challenge them to face the coming AIDS crisis. In other words, show them that it is in their best interests to confront and discuss unpopular issues for the well-being of the entire community.

    3. *Audience's Capacity to Act:* The immediate goal is to increase their awareness of the AIDS crisis and to encourage them to discuss it in future meetings. Point out that other midwestern communities have debated the issues involved as they were faced with enrolling infected children in local schools and treating

AIDS patients in local hospitals. Stress predictions of future infection affecting broader populations. Overcome audience apathy and hostility by encouraging members to discuss the disease in other groups such as the local Parent-Teacher Organization, religious organizations, and community service groups.

4. *Degrees of Change:* Do not demand immediate commitments or political action. Push instead for an open forum for continued discussion on the issue.

B. *Audience Segmentation*

1. *Accurately Identifying Subgroups:* Emphasize the nature of the caucus' political rather than moral or personal involvements in community issues. Avoid stereotyping or judging religious or dogmatic individuals or groups. Deemphasize the moral aspects of the issue. While a moral emphasis might gratify the curious, it would strengthen the resistance of some listeners.

2. *Relevant Psychological Statements:* Recognize the group's excellent efforts at political reform in local projects. Remember that listeners have taken the time to attend and their commitment should be recognized. Stress the far-sightedness of the group on difficult issues such as this one. Point out that in a democracy, fair play requires that each side be given equal time and consideration before anyone reaches a final decision. Aim the bulk of the speech at gaining approval of open-minded discussions.

3. *Relevant Valuative Appeals:* Underscore the virtues of democratic process, freedom of expression, and equal rights for all American citizens. Encourage pride in previous caucus accomplishments and channel motivation toward achieving new goals. Highlight, too, the fundamental importance of both medical and political progress in achieving success.

With this prespeech audience analysis completed, the next steps in preparing the speech are clearer. The audience analysis points to the kinds of supporting materials needed. For instance, the speaker needs to supply accurate facts about the disease for listeners. She can also heighten their understanding of the disease through examples of individuals who have contracted AIDS. The speaker should do as follows:

1. Use the library computerized data base to investigate the history of AIDS in the United States.
2. Find out projected levels of AIDS infection for the future—this material should be available through the Center for Disease Control in Atlanta, Georgia, and AIDS awareness groups.
3. Identify the populations that are currently infected by AIDS—men, women, children.

4. Read local newspaper articles concerning the former community resident who died of AIDS.
5. If possible, interview community residents who knew the AIDS victim.
6. Search out examples of people who tested HIV positive, including school children in midwestern towns and medical personnel.
7. Develop a "typical" disease profile, detailing what occurs in the body and how the body copes with the disease.
8. Interview local medical authorities to discover the kinds of treatment currently used and the chances of AIDS infection occurring in the community.
9. Read expert opinions and discussions of the disease—especially those concerning the future rates of infection—and identify potential supporting materials, such as authoritative statements, statistics, explanations, and illustrations.
10. Prepare a list of other midwestern communities that have held community discussions or adopted measures regarding AIDS.
11. Anticipate and list potential questions and objections to the topic.
12. Check local and state medical codes and guidelines regarding infectious disease.

CHAPTER SUMMARY

1. Public speaking is *audience-centered*. The primary goal of audience analysis is to discover the facets of listeners' demographic and psychological backgrounds that are relevant to your speech's purposes and ideas.

2. Demographic analysis concentrates on describing audience characteristics such as *age, gender, education, group membership,* and *cultural* and *ethnic backgrounds.*

3. Psychological profiling seeks to identify the *beliefs, attitudes,* and *values* of audience members. Both demographic and psychological characteristics may affect your listeners' ability or willingness to accept and understand what you want to say.

4. Audience analysis allows you to set speech purposes realistically and to target audience subgroups through audience segmentation for more careful selection of ideas and appeals.

KEY TERMS

attitudes (p. 72)
audience segmentation (p. 80)
beliefs (p. 69)
demographic analysis (p. 67)
demographic variables (p. 67)
facts (p. 69)
fixed beliefs (p. 70)
opinion (p. 70)

prior audience attitudes (p. 72)
psychological profiling (p. 69)
stereotype (p. 71)
valuative appeals (p. 82)
value orientations (p. 76)
values (p. 75)
variable beliefs (p. 71)

SKILLBUILDING ACTIVITIES

1. Your instructor will divide the class into four-person groups to examine a contemporary speech. You might use a speech text from this textbook, from *Vital Speeches of the Day* (or an anthology of speeches), or from a newspaper, such as *The New York Times*. Identify the following in the speech:
   a. The general and specific purposes
   b. The organization of ideas or propositions
   c. The kinds of supporting materials
   d. The valuative appeals
   e. The audience segments addressed

   After discussing the speech with your group, try to suggest ways the speaker could have better adapted the message to the audience.

2. Gather some magazine advertisements and bring them to class. As a class or in groups, share your advertisements. Speculate about the audiences for which they were intended. To what attitudes are the advertisers trying to appeal? Are they trying to create beliefs? What tactics do they use? How effective do you think these tactics are?

3. In a group or individually, pretend you are the chief speech writer for each of the individuals listed below. Decide which audience subgroups you will need to address. What values, attitudes, and beliefs are they likely to hold? What can you say in your speech to engage their attention and support?
   a. The president of the United States addressing the nation on prime-time television concerning the latest international diplomatic development.
   b. The president of your student government welcoming the freshman students to campus at the beginning of the academic year.
   c. A defense lawyer conducting closing arguments in a jury trial for murder.
   d. A ninth-grade teacher cautioning a class about the use of illegal drugs.

REFERENCES

1. For more discussion, see Milton M. Rokeach, *Beliefs, Attitudes, and Values: A Theory of Organization and Change* (San Francisco: Jossey-Bass, 1968) and *The Nature of Human Values* (New York: Collier-Macmillan, Free Press, 1973).

2. See Muzafer Sherif and Carl L. Hovland, *Social Judgment* (New Haven: Yale University Press, 1961).

3. Such changes during the course of a speech are often dramatic. See Robert D. Brooks and Thomas Scheidel, "Speech as Process: A Case Study," *Speech Monographs*, 35 (1968), 1–7.

4. On adapting to feedback, see Paul D. Holtzman, *The Psychology of Speakers' Audiences* (Glenview, Ill.: ScottForesman, 1970), 33–36, 117.

5. See Henry Z. Scheele, "Ronald Reagan's 1980 Acceptance Address: A Focus on American Values," *Western Journal of Speech Communication*, 48 (1984), 51–61.

CHAPTER FIVE

Using Supporting Materials

> "*I can't believe he marked me down on supporting material!*" Angela was *distraught. "I worked well into the night in the library, running through government documents,* Statistical Abstracts, *and even some of the sources in CompuServe. My speech covered every base." "You missed the point,"* Jamie *replied. "You had plenty of material—it was just too much of a good thing. Your audience was drowning in statistics by the time you were done. The numbers came so fast we couldn't absorb them. You didn't use any illustrations or stories that we could remember. If your supporting material can't be absorbed by anyone, it's not really support, is it?"*

Effective public speaking demands more than an analysis of audience and occasion, more than a determination of what your general and specific purposes are, more even than the articulation of your central idea or claim. A speech travels on concrete materials. If your purpose is to provide information on ways to seek local employment, you need examples of employment opportunities in your own community for students with various interests and talents. If you wish to argue that, "Nuclear power plants are unsafe and must be shut down," you should be ready to authoritatively define "unsafe," to provide statistical and illustrative materials on the safety question, and to offer a plan for safely and practically shutting down existing facilities. On most topics and occasions, you're wasting listeners' time if you don't provide supporting materials.

Chapters 5 and 6 focus on finding and using supporting materials, which are the medium of exchange between your ideas and the audience. The functions of supporting materials are to *amplify, clarify,* or *justify* the beliefs, attitudes, and values that you are offering your listeners. They are the nutrients that bring ideas to life and sustain them once they've been implanted in the minds of others. First, we'll define and illustrate the various types of supporting materials. Then, we'll suggest some ways of finding, recording, and using these materials.

Before you assemble your speech you need to devote careful thought to finding and using supporting materials. That careful thought will pay off if you do it well. This chapter seeks to provide some of the critical thinking skills you need to use supporting materials to earn audience acceptance of your ideas. In the next chapter, we'll deal with the search process.

FORMS OF SUPPORTING MATERIALS

The verbal supporting materials used to clarify, amplify, or justify your central ideas or claims can be divided into six categories: (a) *explanation,* (b) *comparison and contrast,* (c) *illustration* (hypothetical or factual), (d) *specific instance,* (e) *statistics,* and (f) *testimony.* (See Figure 5.1.)

Explanation

An **explanation** is a description or expository passage that makes a term, concept, process, or proposal clear or acceptable. Explanations tell what, how, or why, and they are useful in showing the relationship between a whole and its parts. They also may give meaning to a difficult-to-envision concept. For example, Helen K. Sinclair, President of the Canadian Bankers' Association, wanted a lay audience to understand what banks are doing to stop the laundering of crime-related monies. She offered the following explanation of the approach used by banks to deal with what she called "suspicious transactions":

> *As part of this approach, bank employees ask customers making large or suspicious cash deposits to tell them where the money came from. If the customer refuses, the policy of our banks is to turn the business away.*
>
> *If the customer complies and makes a declaration as to the source of funds, the employee may accept the deposit—but he or she may also harbour some suspicions. When that's the case, the matter is referred to a more senior officer or to the bank's security people. Incidentally, we have 125 professional security people in the Canadian banking system—most of whom are former police officers—putting their considerable skills to this task.*
>
> *When notified by the staff, the security people in turn will conduct an investigation—if they are suspicious, they contact the police. Most of our banks also keep records of large or unusual cash transactions. And they review these to*

Figure 5.1 The Forms of Supporting Materials

The supporting materials used to clarify, amplify, or justify your central ideas or claims are comparison and contrast, testimony, statistics, illustration, explanation, and specific instance. What should you consider when you choose each of the six kinds of supporting materials?

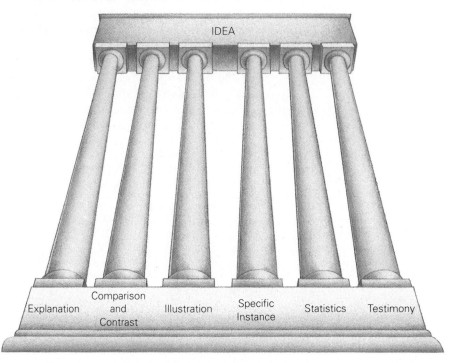

spot patterns of suspicious activity—identifying a customer who, perhaps, has accounts at a lot of different branches, and who is spreading unusual amounts among them.[1]

In this explanation you find most aspects of a clear presentation. Ms. Sinclair has explained (a) *how* suspicious transactions are processed, (b) *who* is involved at various stages, (c) *why* some acts are judged suspicious, and (d) *what* background various involved parties have. All of this is accomplished in easy-to-understand, everyday language.

Although explanations are good ways to clarify an idea, they shouldn't be too long or complicated and they shouldn't have to carry the weight of your argument. For example, Ms. Sinclair could be sure that some listeners would wonder about the propriety of tellers asking banking customers personal questions; surely some listeners would find the questions offensive. She needed to introduce additional materials that demonstrated that the suspicious transactions policy wouldn't drive away customers. Explanations clarify but seldom prove anything.

Comparison and Contrast

Comparisons point out similarities between something that is familiar to the audience and something that is not. *Contrasts,* on the other hand, clarify or support an idea by emphasizing differences.

Comparison

Comparisons are actually analogies connecting something already known or believed with an idea a speaker wishes to have understood or accepted. When, during the darkest days of the Civil War, critics attacked the administration's policies, Lincoln answered them by comparing the plight of the government with that of the famous tightrope walker Blondin, attempting to cross the Niagara Falls:

> *Gentlemen, I want you to suppose a case for a moment. Suppose that all the property you were worth was in gold, and you had put it in the hands of Blondin, the famous rope-walker, to carry across the Niagara Falls on a tightrope. Would you shake the rope while he was passing over it, or keep shouting to him, "Blondin, stoop a little more! Go a little faster!" No, I am sure you would not. You would hold your breath as well as your tongue, and keep your hands off until he was safely over. Now the government is in the same situation. It is carrying an immense weight across a stormy ocean. Untold treasures are in its hands. It is doing the best it can. Don't badger it! Just keep still, and it will get you safely over.*

Contrast

Contrasts help to clarify complex situations and processes by focusing on differences. A speaker explaining Australian football might want to contrast it with the rules governing United States football. To clarify Japanese Kabuki theater, a speaker may call on a theater system more familiar to the audience. Contrasts can be used not only to clarify unfamiliar or complex problems, but also to strengthen arguments that you wish to advance. Contrasts used as supporting material for claims often employ a string of examples, as in the case of a speech by John F. Copper of Rhodes College. Copper wanted to drive home the point that the United States has much to learn from the countries on the Pacific Rim. A series of contrasts helped him make his case:

> *In Japan the life expectancy is higher than in the U.S. The standard of health is better. Yet the health care system costs only a fraction of what it does in the U.S. Japan spends considerably less on education than America. Yet its students from K through 12 score better on both I.Q. and aptitude tests than U.S. students—at any age and on every part of these tests. How does Japan do it? Japan's city streets are safe. It has urbanized without increases in crime or mental illness. Is this magic; or is there something Americans could learn from [Japan]?*
>
> *We have viewed Asian countries as having a serious problem with corruption. Japan's government (which most Japanese feel is rife with corruption) pro-*

vides more services for less taxes collected from its citizens than the U.S. And low defense spending doesn't account for this; the difference is much bigger than that. Then where is the corruption? South Korea, Taiwan and a number of other Rim countries have governments which are much more cost-efficient than the U.S. government.

Japan is a model for environmental care—capitalist style. It has no drug problem. AIDS cases are few in number.

China and Hong Kong has—had a serious drug problem at one time— worse than the U.S. problem now. They solved it. Should we not ask how they did it?

Some Asian countries have race and ethnic problems. Some have solved them. How we might ask?[2]

Notice that Professor Copper didn't really develop the contrasts, as he was more interested in their cumulative effect than the proof force of any one of them; and he didn't even make both halves of the contrast— between a Rim country and the United States—explicit all of the time, relying instead upon the audience to finish the contrast for him. Getting an audience to reason along with you is an excellent strategy for getting them to accept your claims.

Comparison and Contrast Used in Combination

Finally, you can use comparisons and contrasts together so as to double your firepower. For example, former U.S. Secretary of Health, Education, and Welfare Joseph A. Califano, Jr., traveled the country, addressing audiences composed of both smokers and nonsmokers. By combining comparisons and contrasts, he warned the smokers about smoking and psychologically reinforced the abstention of everyone else in this fashion:

The tragic consequences of [smoking] are dramatically evident if we compare the later health consequences of smoking for two sixteen-year-olds: one who smokes a pack a day and one who does not. According to one estimate, the sixteen-year-old smoker has one chance in ten of developing a serious lung disease: lung cancer, emphysema, or chronic bronchitis, for example—providing he or she manages to avoid a crippling or killing heart attack. By contrast, the non-smoker will have one chance in one hundred of contracting a serious lung disease, and will have only half the risk of the smoker of suffering a heart attack.[3]

Whatever the form of comparison or contrast used, at least one of the items should be familiar to the audience and distinct enough from the other that the difference is clear.

Illustration

A detailed narrative example of the idea or statement you wish to support is called an **illustration.** Sometimes an illustration describes or exemplifies a concept, condition, or circumstance; sometimes it shows or demonstrates the results of adopting a plan or proposal. Always, however, an illustration is an *extended example* presented in narrative form that has a striking or memorable quality.

There are two principal types of illustration: the *hypothetical* and the *factual.* The first tells a story that could have happened or probably will occur; the second tells what actually happened.

Hypothetical Illustration

A **hypothetical illustration** is a story that describes a fictional situation or incident. Although imaginary, the story must seem believable to the audience; however, because it is hypothetical, it can exaggerate some details to make a point. Notice the details that Nicolas S. Martin, Executive Director of the Consumer Health Education Council, adds to drive home his argument about overregulation of the chemical fungicide EDB. After noting how little EDB the average consumer actually ingests, Martin creates a hypothetical illustration with its own antihero:

> *Nevertheless, Americans were bamboozled by what I call the Jim Bob Effect. My friend Jim Bob is an ardent environmentalist, he thinks we are doing ourselves in with all of our chemicals and technology. He wants to turn back the clock.*
>
> *Recently, Jim Bob bought a loaf of bread which, soon enough, was crawling with worms. Enraged, he wrote a letter to the manufacturer demanding to know why they would foist an infested loaf off on him. "I don't like my bread with worms," he barked. The Jim Bob Effect is when someone is so far removed, so ignorant, of food production, that he can—on the one hand—demand chemical free food, and on the other hand become addled at the size of a worm in his "preservative free" bread.*
>
> *I've seen the Jim Bob Effect many times in health food stores. These purveyors of chemical-free goods have turned back the clock and are constantly caught in the throes of a war against predators. I have seen a store so infested with maggots hatching from the food that it looked like a possum two days after being squashed on the roadway. I've seen the look on a chemical-free purist's face when the granola she just popped inside began to wiggle. Let me tell you, if she wasn't a victim of the Jim Bob Effect she would have begged for the fumigants and chemicals which would have prevented her distasteful experience.*
>
> *But most people think we can just do without EDB and the other chemicals. They don't understand that they would have to eat 400 tons per day of EDB-laced foods to equal the amount fed the rats used in tests, and that chemicals like EDB are all that stand between us and a mouthful of maggots.*[4]

Notice that Mr. Martin increased the emotional intensity of his speech through his choice of object (bread, the staff of life), bad effects (maggots, carriers of dirt and decay), and even visual images (the road-killed possum, the "mouthful of maggots"). He made the hypothetical illustration graphic and distasteful enough to make you think twice before demanding preservative-free, chemical-free food. He risked violating communication rules by using strong images. Some listeners might think his illustration backfired.

Factual Illustration

A **factual illustration** is a story that describes in detail a situation or incident that actually happened. The descriptions in a factual illustration can be vivid because the events actually happened. Vivid descriptions give the factual illustration a high persuasive value. So, when talking to the National Governors' Association about setting new educational goals for K–12 education, Ernest L. Boyer, President of the Carnegie Foundation, used vivid detail in a factual illustration to support his claim about the need to reduce school size:

> Recently at the Carnegie Foundation, we studied urban schools from Boston to Los Angeles. And going from place to place, I was struck by the bigness and the bleakness of these institutions. I was struck by the broken test tubes and by [B]unsen burners that wouldn't work. Above all, I was struck by the way most students in these schools moved facelessly from class to class—unconnected to adults. Finally, I was almost overwhelmed by the climate of anonymity I felt and concluded that many of today's teenagers drop out, simply because no one noticed that they had, in fact, dropped in.
>
> If I had just one wish for school reform I would break up every junior and senior high school into units of no more than 400 students each.[5]

Guidelines for Choosing Illustrations

Three considerations should be kept in mind when selecting illustrations, hypothetical or factual: (a) Is the illustration clearly related to the idea it's intended to support? If the connection is difficult to show, the illustration will not accomplish its goal. (b) Is it a fair example? An audience can be quick to notice unusual circumstances in an illustration; if you've focused on the exceptional case, your illustration will not be convincing. (c) Is it vivid and impressive in detail? If the illustration lacks vivid detail, its advantage will be lost. So, be sure your illustrations are pointed, fair, and vivid.

Specific Instance

A **specific instance** is an *undeveloped* illustration or example. Instead of describing a situation in detail, the specific instance merely mentions the person or event in question. Speakers use specific instances to clarify ideas. You might use a specific instance by saying, "You're all familiar with the pop machine that stands just inside this building's front door; half of you stop after class for a soda or can of juice. That pop machine suggests the topic of my speech today—the impact of machined fast food on the American diet." Or, you can use a series of specific instances to help establish a point. Notice how James K. Wellington demonstrates the seriousness of his claim that "Creative and imaginative students often are not recognized by their teachers":

> We should remember that the following persons were all identified as low achievers or misfits:

- *Einstein—four years old before he could speak; seven before he could read.*
- *Isaac Newton—was rated a poor elementary school student.*
- *Beethoven—music teacher said, "As a composer, he is hopeless."*
- *Thomas Edison—teacher told him he was too stupid to learn anything.*
- *F. W. Woolworth—worked in a dry goods store at 21; employers would not let him wait on customers; "didn't have enough sense."*
- *Walt Disney—fired by a newspaper editor; "no good ideas."*
- *Winston Churchill—failed 6th grade.[6]*

With these accumulated data, Wellington demonstrated to his listeners that there could be little doubt that teachers can err in their judgment of a child's ability.

Statistics

Statistics are numbers that show relationships between or among phenomena—relationships that can emphasize size or magnitude, describe subclasses or parts (segments), or establish trends. By reducing large masses of information into generalized categories, statistics clarify the nature of a situation and substantiate a potentially disputable claim.[7]

Magnitudes

We often use statistics to describe a situation or to sketch its scope or seriousness; that is, its size or **magnitude.** Especially if one statistical description of the size of a problem is piled upon others, the effect upon listeners can be strong. Notice how this piling-up technique was used by Joseph N. Hankin, President of Westchester Community College, in quantifying some of the failings of secondary education:

> *One-fourth of 17-year-olds do not know how many quarts are in a gallon; two-fifths cannot say what percent 30 is of 60; half cannot name one of their senators; 44 percent are unable to combine four short sentences into one longer one. Forty to fifty percent of urban children have "serious reading problems." Nearly 40 percent of 17-year-olds cannot draw inferences from written material; only 20 percent can write a persuasive essay; only a third can solve mathematics problems that require several steps. If you think these results are limited to 17-year-olds, you are mistaken. College students and even adults have been found to produce similar results.[8]*

Not all uses of magnitudes, of course, need such piling-up of instances. Simple, hard-hitting magnitudes sometimes work even better. For example, Brenda Theriault of the University of Maine, arguing that there is "very little nutritional value in a hamburger, chocolate shake, and fries," simply noted that "of the 1123 calories in this meal, there are 15 calories of carbohydrates, 35 calories of protein, and 1073 calories of fat."[9] These were all the numbers the audience needed in order to understand the nutrition in a typical fast-food meal.

Segments

Statistics can also be used to isolate the parts of a problem or to show aspects of a problem caused by separate factors; parts or aspects can be treated as statistical **segments.** In discussing the sources of income for a college or university, for example, you would probably segment the income by percentages coming from tuition and fees, state and federal money, gifts and contributions, special fees such as tickets, and miscellaneous sources. Then you'd be in a position to talk reasonably about next year's proposed tuition hike. Similarly, to drive home the point to his West German audience that the United States needs to "compete and learn" from the Pacific Rim countries, Professor Copper did a quick rundown of some segment numbers: eight of ten computers now sold in Europe are made in the United States; nine of ten VCRs are made in Japan. Europe has ten percent of the world's use of robots; the United States has 20 percent; Japan has 70 percent.

> *I have heard since I arrived in Europe that the unification of Germany will have a major impact on Europe's future and the world. I don't know why; the two Germanies combined will still be only one-half of Japan in the production of goods and services.*[10]

Professor Copper's segments were chosen carefully to arouse his audience in Kassel, West Germany. In mentioning computer and robotic technology, he was highlighting the two most important electronic and manufacturing technologies of today and tomorrow. In bringing up the unification of Germany, he suggested through segments that such a political move was not especially important economically. These few numbers were well selected for the audience and for Copper's claim that we must copy Pacific Rim countries to "compete and learn."

Trends

Statistics are often used to describe the direction in which a thing or process is heading across time. Statistical **trends** indicate where we have been and where we are going. (See Table 5.1.) An interesting use of a trend argument is found in Ronald K. Shelp's speech "A Crossroads in U.S. Trade Policy." As Vice-President of the Hoechst Celanese Corporation, Shelp worried about trade deficits and wanted to make sure his audience understood what had happened over the years:

> *Last year was the worst trade year in the history of our nation. One year ago we said exactly the same thing. And one year from now we will probably announce the same tragic news one more time.*
>
> *Only four years ago the trade deficit was 40 billion dollars. By the next year it was 60 billion dollars. It broke the 100 billion dollar mark in 1984. And it has been in free fall ever since.*
>
> *Everyone is aware of the painful havoc this wreaked on many manufacturing industries. The synonym for the industrial heartland has become the rustland, with 2.6 million manufacturing jobs lost between 1981 and 1986.*[11]

Table 5.1 Types of Statistics

In a speech to inform, a speaker might use three types of statistics to describe students at Central University. What other forms of supporting material could complement these numbers?

Magnitudes	*Segments*	*Trends*
"Three fourths of all Central University students come from the state."	"Sixty percent of all Central University students major in business; 25 percent are humanities majors; the remaining 15 percent are in fine arts."	"Since 1975, enrollment at Central University has increased by 20 percent every five years."

Notice Mr. Shelp's care in framing his argument. He first introduced it in ordinary language ("Last year was the worst . . . One year ago . . . And one year from now"). He then offered the numbers to make the point with "hard" evidence. Next, he drew conclusions. He included the lost jobs that he wanted his audience to believe were eliminated by the trade deficit. This, in fact, may have been the case, although, in this portion of the speech, he provided no proof. Nonetheless, his argument was generally convincing, thanks to his developmental approach to the trends argument: (a) state the trend, (b) provide evidence for it, and (c) indicate its implications.

When you use statistics to indicate magnitude, to divide phenomena into segments, or to describe trends, keep these cautions in mind:

1. *Translate difficult-to-comprehend numbers into more immediately understandable terms.* In a speech on the mounting problem of solid waste, Carl Hall illustrated the immensity of 130 million tons of garbage by explaining that trucks loaded with that amount would extend from coast to coast.[12]

2. *Do not be afraid to round off complicated numbers.* "Nearly 400,000" is easier for listeners to comprehend than "396,456"; "just over 33 percent" or, better yet, "approximately one-third" is preferable to "33.4 percent."

3. *Whenever possible, use visual materials to clarify complicated statistical trends or summaries.* Hand out a mimeographed or photocopied sheet of numbers; draw graphs on the chalkboard; prepare a chart in advance. Such aids will allow you to concentrate on explaining the significance of the numbers, rather than on making sure the audience hears and remembers them.

4. *Use statistics fairly.* Arguing that professional women's salaries increased 12.4 percent last year may sound impressive to listeners until they realize that women are still paid almost one-quarter less than men for equivalent work. In other words, provide fair contexts for your numerical data and comparisons.

The Numbers Game

The rise of science in this century has been accompanied by the rise of numerical data—and its public exhibition. By now you've been told by one poll that the public favors a liberalization of abortion laws two-to-one, but by another poll that the public favors tightening abortion laws by an equal percentage. You know that four out of five doctors surveyed recommend a particular brand of toothpaste. You've heard that one brand of cigarettes has the lowest levels of tar and nicotine. You've been informed that the U.S.S.R. has more missiles than the United States and that the United States has two times as many multiple warhead missiles as the U.S.S.R.

As both listener and speaker, you have to make some ethical calls when encountering such data:

1. Contradictory polls such as the ones on abortion usually result when polling agencies ask questions in biased ways. (See Chapter 4, In Pursuit of Excellence.) When you speak, are you morally obligated to reveal *who* conducted the poll and how they asked the questions? Can't you just cite the numbers?

2. Who were those "four out of five doctors surveyed"? Is it moral to cite statistics without reviewing how they were gathered and calculated?

3. If your favorite brand of cigarette is one of five brands that all have the same low tar and nicotine content, technically, of course, yours *has* the lowest—and so do the other four brands. Is it moral, however, to claim your brand is "the lowest," or must you say it is "one of the lowest"?

4. The missiles question might be settled if the arguers clarified what was being compared with what. It's one thing to compare numbers of rockets, regardless of their ages and sizes, but another to compare numbers in only one class of missiles—those carrying multiple warheads.

It's easy to fiddle with numbers—to round up or down, to compare only parts rather than wholes, and to ignore key situational details that would properly contextualize information for listeners. It's easy, but if you play fast and loose with numbers, you might get caught. Learn to play the numbers game honestly.

Testimony

When you cite the opinions or conclusions of others, you are using **testimony.** Sometimes testimony merely adds weight or impressiveness to an idea, as when you quote a witty saying from *Bartlett's Dictionary of Familiar Quotations*. At other times, it lends credibility to an assertion, especially when it comes from an expert witness. Georgia's Senator Sam Nunn used testimony to gird his argument that the United States military defense should rely more on the military reserves:

> *The third element in my strategy is greater utilization of the reserves. When we were facing a huge Warsaw Pact conventional threat and a short warning of an attack, most of the "tooth" of our combat capability was appropriately kept in the active components because we felt we had to be ready to go to war in a matter of days. To lower overall costs, much of the support or "tail" was put in*

reserve component units. Increased warning times now permit placing more of the "tooth" in the reserves as well.

The Assistant Secretary of Defense for Reserve Affairs, Mr. Stephen Duncan, recently summed it up well when he testified:

> *"I believe that for cost reasons alone, a rebuttable presumption should exist that missions should be considered for assignment to the Reserve forces unless there are sound and apparent military reasons for assigning the missions to the Active forces. If the presumption can't be easily rebutted, then a particular mission would seem to be a prime candidate for assignment to the Reserve forces."*[13]

All testimony should meet the twin tests of *pertinence* and *audience acceptability*. (See Figure 5.2.) When used to strengthen a statement, rather than merely to amplify or illustrate, testimony also should satisfy four more specific criteria:

1. The person quoted should be qualified, by training and experience, to speak on the topic being discussed.
2. Whenever possible, the authority's statement should be based on first-hand knowledge—an Iowa farmer is not an authority on a South Carolina drought unless he or she has personally observed the conditions.
3. The judgment expressed should not be unduly influenced by personal interest—asking a political opponent to comment on the current president's performance will likely yield a biased opinion.
4. The listeners should realize that the person quoted actually *is* an authority.

When citing testimony, do not use big names simply because they are well known. A TV star's opinion on the nutritional value of a breakfast cereal is less reliable than the opinion of a registered dietician. The best testimony comes from subject-matter experts whose qualifications your listeners recognize.

Finally, always acknowledge the source of an idea or particular phrasing. Avoid *plagiarism*—claiming someone else's ideas, information, or phraseology as your own. Plagiarism is stealing. Give your source credit for the material and give yourself credit for taking the time to find the sources. (See "Using Material Ethically" in Chapter 6.)

CRITICAL THINKING AND THE USE OF SUPPORTING MATERIALS

Most of us can, with effort, gather and create supporting materials; the hard part is using those supporting materials well. The effective use of supporting materials is an exercise in **critical thinking**—assessing the rational requirements for clarifying thoughts and proving something to someone else. As was suggested in the opening paragraph of this chapter, when you

the topic or when the subject matter is complex. Explanation, comparison, illustration, and magnitude and trend statistics can help the speaker amplify an idea, expanding on it so the audience can better examine the concept. These forms of support may be especially useful when the audience has only a slight knowledge of the concept. To strengthen or lend credibility to a point, a speaker can use factual illustration, specific instances, statistics, and testimony. These forms strengthen the idea by making it vivid and believable. These techniques are beneficial when the audience is hostile or when acceptance of a particular idea is critical to the overall purpose of the speech.

Be sure that the forms of support that you select support your ideas. If the materials used as supports do not clarify, amplify, or strengthen, they may not be applicable to the point you are trying to develop. Test the relevance of each supporting unit to be sure it contributes to the acceptance of the idea. Following are two outlines that illustrate how supporting material can be used.

Sample Outline for an Informative Speech

In the outline, note how the speaker has combined verbal and visual material to establish and develop the central idea. In this speech, the supportive material is used to amplify the idea.

HOW WE BREATHE

Central idea

Explanation

I. The human breathing mechanism may be likened to a bellows, which expands to admit air and contracts to expel it.
   A. When we inhale, two things happen.
      1. Muscles attached to the collarbone and shoulder bones pull upward and slightly outward.
      2. Muscles in the abdominal wall relax, allowing the diaphragm—a sheet of muscle and tendon lying immediately below the lungs—to fall.
   B. This permits the spongy, porous lungs to expand.
      1. A vacuum is created.
      2. Air rushes in.
   C. When we exhale, two things happen also.
      1. Gravity causes the rib cage to move downward.
      2. Muscles in the abdominal wall contract, squeezing the diaphragm upward.

D. The space available to the lungs is thus reduced.
   1. The lungs are squeezed.
   2. Air is emitted.

Comparison

E. The similarity between the breathing mechanism and a bellows is represented in this diagram:

Visual aid

[Show "How We Breathe" Diagram]

Restatement of central idea

II. In summary, then, to remember how the human breathing mechanism works, think of a bellows.
   A. Just as increasing the size of the bellows bag allows air to rush in, so increasing the space available to the lungs allows them to admit air.
   B. Just as squeezing the bellows bag forces air out, so contracting the space the lungs can occupy forces air to be emitted.

Sample Outline for a Persuasive speech

Study the following outline. Notice that the supporting material is used to strengthen each of the points in the speech. The audience would probably not accept these ideas without further development. Although the proof of a single point may not require the use of supportive materials as numerous or varied as those used in this outline, the variety of supportive materials shows how a number of different forms can be combined in a speech.

CABLE TELEVISION—AT YOUR SERVICE!

Claim

First supporting statement: hypothetical illustration

Specific instances within the illustration

I. Cable television soon will revolutionize your everyday life.
   A. Suppose, on a rainy day a few years from now, you decide to run your errands from your living room.
      1. You turn on your two-way communication unit and begin your round of errands:
         a. On Channel 37, your bank's computer verifies the amount of a recent withdrawal.
         b. On Channel 26, you ask the telephone company to review last month's long-distance charges.
         c. On Channel 94, a supermarket lets you scan products, prices, and home-delivery hours.
         d. On Channel 5, you study a list of proposed changes in the city charter.
            1. You can "call in" for further information.
            2. You can vote from your own home.

	e. On Channel 106, you have access to resource personnel at the public library.
Restatement of supporting statement	2. With "cable television at your service," you have accomplished your day's errands with minimum expenditure of time, gas, and parking-meter money.
Second supporting statement	B. These possibilities, once only dreams, are becoming actualities across the United States.
Specific instances	1. Most cities have public-access channels filled with local talent and ethnic programming.
	2. Ann Arbor, Michigan, and Columbus, Ohio, have been leasing channels to private firms and public utility companies.
Third supporting statement	C. Cable television soon will be available to virtually every household in the United States at a reasonable cost.
Comparison	1. Because the cost is shared by licensee and householder alike, no one bears an excessive burden.
Statistics	a. Commercial users find that leasing a channel costs little more than their computer-accounting systems and print/electronic advertising services.
	b. Studio facilities for the public-access channels are made available at cost in most cable television contracts—normally about $30 per hour.
	c. Current installation charges range from only $15 to $50.
	d. Monthly rental fees per household seldom exceed $25 for basic cable service.
Explanation combined with specific instances	2. The technical characteristics of cable television render it inexpensive.
	a. Some existent telephone lines and equipment can be used.
	b. The conversion box mounts easily on a regular television set.
	c. Studio costs are minimal.
	1. Relatively inexpensive one-half-inch videotape and broadcasting equipment can be used.
	2. Engineering and production personnel need minimal training for cable systems.
Restatement of claim	II. Given actual and potential uses, plus the positive cost-benefit ratio, cable television will revolutionize your daily life.
Comparison	A. Just as the wheel extended our legs and the computer our central nervous system, cable television will extend our communicative capabilities.
Testimony used as restatement of claim	B. In the words of Wendy Lee, communication consultant to new cable-television franchises, "We soon will be a nation wired fully for sight and sound. We will rid ourselves of the need for short shopping trips; we will cut the lines in doctors' offices; and we will put the consumer and the constituent into the front offices of his or her corporate suppliers and political servants. The telephone and the motor car will become obsolete."

CHAPTER SUMMARY

1. Supporting materials amplify, clarify, or justify the beliefs, attitudes, and values that speakers ask listeners to accept.

2. *Explanations* are descriptions or expository passages that make a term, concept, process, or proposal clear or acceptable.

3. *Comparisons* and *contrasts* point out similarities and differences between things that are familiar and things that are not.

4. *Illustrations* are detailed examples of ideas or statements you want listeners to accept. Some are *hypothetical* (fictional) and some *factual* ("real").

5. *Specific instances* are undeveloped illustrations, often used in groups or clusters to add power to ideas.

6. *Statistics* are numbers that show relationships between or among phenomena. Some emphasize size or *magnitude;* some describe subclasses or *segments;* and some establish *trends* or the directions in which matters are heading over time.

7. *Testimony* is made up of the opinions or conclusions of credible persons.

8. To effectively use these forms of support, you must learn *critical thinking skills* to: (a) assess the rational requirements for clarifying thoughts and proving those thoughts and (b) determine if audiences will accept those rational requirements.

KEY TERMS

comparison (p. 93)
contrast (p. 93)
critical thinking (p. 101)
explanation (p. 91)
factual illustration (p. 96)
hypothetical illustration (p. 95)
illustration (p. 94)

magnitude (p. 97)
segments (p. 98)
specific instance (p. 96)
statistics (p. 97)
testimony (p. 100)
trends (p. 98)

SKILLBUILDING ACTIVITIES

1. Read one of the speeches in this textbook. Identify its forms of supporting material. How effective are those materials in supporting the central idea or claim of the speech? How well do supporting materials seem to be adapted to the immediate audience? What else might the speaker have done to improve his or her use of supporting material?

2. Prepare an outline for a short speech that explains one point or idea clearly. State the central idea; amplify it with an explanation, a comparison/contrast, and an illustration; and restate the idea in other words. Turn the outline in to your instructor for evaluation. You may be asked to deliver the speech later.

3. Prepare an outline for a short speech proving one point or simple claim. State the claim; support the claim with statistical materials, a comparison/contrast, and an illustration; and restate the claim in other words. Turn the outline in to your instructor for evaluation. You may be asked to deliver the speech later.

REFERENCES

1. Helen K. Sinclair, "Dirty Business: Money Laundering and the War on Drugs," *Vital Speeches of the Day,* vol. LVI (April 15, 1990). Reprinted by permission of *Vital Speeches of the Day.*

2. John F. Copper, "U.S. Perspectives on the Pacific Rim: Compete and Learn," *Vital Speeches of the Day,* vol. LVI (June 1, 1990). Reprinted by permission of *Vital Speeches of the Day.*

3. Joseph A. Califano, Jr., "Adolescents: Their Needs and Problems," *Vital Speeches of the Day,* vol. XLIV (August 5, 1978). Reprinted by permission of *Vital Speeches of the Day.*

4. Nicolas S. Martin, "Environmental Myths and Hoaxes: The Evidence of Guilt Is Insufficient," *Vital Speeches of the Day,* vol. LVI (May 1, 1990). Reprinted by permission of *Vital Speeches of the Day.*

5. Ernest L. Boyer, "Education Goals: An Action Plan," *Vital Speeches of the Day,* vol. LVI (June 1, 1990). Reprinted by permission of *Vital Speeches of the Day.*

6. P. L. Smith, "Leadership in the Creative Process," *Vital Speeches of the Day,* vol. L (October 15, 1984). Reprinted by permission of *Vital Speeches of the Day.*

7. For a technical yet rewarding introduction to statistical analysis, see John Waite Bowers and John A. Courtright, *Communication Research Methods* (Glenview, Ill.: Scott-Foresman, 1984).

8. Joseph N. Hankin, "Where Were You 12 Years Ago?," *Vital Speeches of the Day* (March 1, 1988). Reprinted by permission of *Vital Speeches of the Day.*

9. Brenda Theriault, "Fast Foods," speech given at the University of Maine (Spring Term, 1982).

10. Copper, "U.S. Perspective on the Pacific Rim: Compete and Learn."

11. Ronald K. Shelp, "A Crossroads in U.S. Trade Policy," *Vital Speeches of the Day,* vol. LIII (August 1, 1987). Reprinted by permission of *Vital Speeches of the Day.*

12. Carl Hall, "A Heap of Trouble," *Winning Orations.* Reprinted by permission of Larry Schnoor, Executive Secretary, Interstate Oratorical Association, Mankato, Minn.

13. Sam Nunn, "Implementing a New Military Strategy: The Budget Decisions" from *Vital Speeches of the Day,* vol. LVI (May 15, 1990). Reprinted by permission of *Vital Speeches of the Day.*

CHAPTER SIX

Finding Supporting Materials

avid decided to search the Social Science/Humanities Index *data base for information relevant to a speech on TV news ratings. As one of his descriptors, he chose the word* television. *When he ran the search, the program came up with 32 single-spaced pages of references from the last eight years. Not only did the data search cost David almost $50, but it provided so much extraneous material that David asked to delay his speech a day so he could sort through his search. His was an expensive lesson.*

We live during the Communications Revolution. You have at your disposal the miracles that result from the harnessing of electricity: the computer chip, television, satellites, fax machines and electronic mail, and digital sound reproduction. Electronically, you can access and experience wildly diverse people, places, and events all over the world. You can now know almost everything about everything—only the deepest of political or personal secrets are unobtainable.

The thought of limitless knowledge is exhilarating but also dumbfounding. You're able to know everything, but, of course, you can't learn it all. You don't have the time or the resources for total knowledge. Rather, your interests are narrower: you want to learn some things that you're interested in and that pertain to the way you live your life. This chapter explores the challenge of limiting your search for materials—*how can you efficiently find and assemble only the materials relevant to your speeches, your audiences, and the occasions on which you're speaking?*

Finding supporting materials should be a purposive, targeted hunting process, not an aimless bibliographical spree in the library. You must develop some sense of the sorts of supporting materials relevant to a claim or subpoint, of the location of those materials and of efficient ways to search out those materials. In this short chapter we won't deal with these matters exhaustively because your own libraries will have their own ways of organizing and handling materials. We hope to get you off to a good start, however. We'll also deal with the ethics of using other individuals' materials.

DETERMINING THE KINDS OF SUPPORTING MATERIALS NEEDED

At the end of Chapter 5 we discussed the kinds of critical thinking needed to guide your choice of supporting materials. You need to consider (a) the rational requirements of the claim, (b) the range of available materials, (c) audience demands, and (d) the power-to-prove of various kinds of supporting materials.

These critical guidelines for selection should govern your search process. Suppose, for example, that you become interested in the rise in popularity of smokeless tobacco that has followed in the wake of antismoking campaigns. You want to give a speech on this topic to an audience of college students. What kinds of supporting materials do you need?

1. *Rational requirements.* Regardless of the specific claim you'll be advancing, certain sorts of supporting materials are reasonably required for speeches on this topic:
    a. Statistics on the number of people using smokeless tobacco and on growth in that number
    b. Statistics on the incidence of salivary cancer and other physical ailments associated with smokeless tobacco
    c. Testimony from people who use smokeless tobacco and from medical experts who study or treat its users
    d. Examples of typical users
    e. Detailed illustrations of the increase of the use of smokeless tobacco in various demographic groups
    f. Comparisons and contrasts between smokers and users of smokeless tobacco

The statistics provide a general picture; testimony, examples and illustrations, and comparisons and contrasts depict details.

2. *Available materials.* Do you have access to these kinds of materials? Your library might have the following materials:
    a. Governmental hearings on tobacco
    b. Medical journals with up-to-date research
    c. Pamphlets put out by special-interest groups such as the American Tobacco Institute
    d. General magazines with articles on smokeless tobacco
    e. Books on the history of tobacco use
    f. Computer access to special bibliographies on the topic

3. *Audience demand.* Your specific audience is probably most interested in the incidence of use of smokeless tobacco on campus. Images of lumberjacks and baseball players chewing and spitting might be interesting, but they will be irrelevant to your audience's experiences.

4. *Power-to-prove.* Opinions about tobacco use and its effects vary greatly possibly because the research conducted on the topic is believed by many people to be unsatisfactory. Medical experts, for example, believe that tobacco is harmful. They also tend to be strong supporters of correlational data in research—conclusions that are reached, not through experimentation, but through comparison of case histories of like or similar people. Medical research might compare the age and cause of death of users and nonusers of smokeless tobacco—people who seem to be similar in most other ways *except* for their use.

The American Tobacco Institute, however, points out that correlations between tobacco use and cause of death don't really "prove" anything, because many other factors besides tobacco use could be influencing an individual's health and mortality. The Institute also points out that the so-called "tobacco problem" is not only personal and medical, but also collective and agricultural; an attack on tobacco is an assault on the principal cash crop of four states and the government's system of crop subsidies. Other smokeless tobacco supporters might suggest that, while smokeless tobacco users occasionally run into medical problems, those problems are minuscule compared to the health consequences of lighted tobacco.

These two sets of experts make different assumptions and arrive at very different conclusions. Merely citing the findings of research is clearly not enough; you also have to test the authorities and their special interests in making and defending certain claims. You also have to ask, who are my listeners likely to believe?

Your review of initial considerations suggests the following search strategies for supporting materials:

I. *Topic:* Smokeless tobacco use among college students
II. *Sources*
   A. Background examples and illustrations from popular magazines
   B. Demographic studies of size of problem and medical studies of pathologies, morbidity, and mortality—from MEDLINE computerized search
   C. The opinions of experts from MEDLINE search, from pamphlets in the Vertical File Index—especially ones from the American Tobacco Institute—and from on-campus interviews with medical researchers if available
   D. Illustrations of use patterns from interviews with campus users—especially athletes
   E. Comparisons and contrasts from interviews with users who switched from cigarettes to smokeless tobacco

This kind of initial thinking-through of your topic (a) helps you figure out the claim you want to defend and (b) guides your search for the specific materials you'll want to examine and possibly include in your speech.

SOURCES OF SUPPORTING MATERIALS

Where and how do you find the kinds of supporting materials we've been discussing? Several sources are available to you: interviews with experts, letters and questionnaires, publications of many kinds, broadcasts, and, as we noted at the beginning of this chapter, computerized searches.

Interviews

When looking for material, many of us forget the easiest and most logical way to start—by asking questions. The goal of an **informational interview** is to obtain answers to specific questions. In interviewing someone, you seek answers that can be woven into the text of your speech. Interviews increase your understanding of a topic so that you avoid misinforming your audience, drawing incorrect inferences from information, and convoluting technical ideas. Your interviewee may be a content expert or someone who has had personal experience with the issues you wish to discuss. If you're addressing the topic of black holes, who is better qualified to help you than a physicist? If you're explaining the construction of a concrete boat, you might contact a local civil engineer for assistance. If you wish to discuss anorexia nervosa, you might interview a person who has suffered through the disorder. Interviews can provide compelling illustrations of human experiences.

You need to observe three general guidelines in planning an informational interview:

1. *Decide on your specific purpose.* What precise information do you hope to obtain during the interview? One caution: if you are interviewing a controversial figure, you may not be best served by engaging in an argument or by assuming a belligerent or self-righteous manner. Even if you disagree with the answers being given, your role is not that of Perry Mason, seeking to win a jury's vote by grilling the witness. However, your purpose can encompass tough questions or questions that seek further clarification of answers that seem "not right." Simply raise such questions without provoking an argument.

2. *Structure the interview in advance.* The beginning of an interview clarifies the purpose and sets limits on what will be covered during the session. You also can use this time to establish rapport with the person being interviewed. The middle of the interview comprises the substantive portion during which the information being sought is provided. Structure your questions in advance so that you have a rough idea of what to ask when. The

You might need to conduct an informational interview to gather information for a speech. You should carefully prepare your interview questions in advance in order to conduct an effective interview. What guidelines should you follow when preparing your interview questions?

interview may not follow your list exactly, but you'll have a convenient checkpoint to see whether all the information you need has been covered. You'll also find the list useful as you summarize your understanding of the major points, in order to avoid misinterpreting the meaning given to specific points by the person interviewed. What follows is an example of a format you might follow in an informational interview:

 I. Opening
    A. Mutual greeting
    B. Discussion of purposes
       1. Reason information is needed
       2. Kind of information wanted
 II. Informational Portion
    A. Question #1, with clarifying questions as needed
    B. Question #2, with clarifying questions as needed
    C. [and so on]
III. Closing
    A. Summary of main points
    B. Final courtesies

3. *Remember that interviews are interactive processes.* There is a definite pattern of "turn-taking" in interviews that allows both parties to concentrate

on one issue at a time and that assists in making the interview work for the benefit of both parties. The interactive pattern requires that both parties be careful listeners, since one person's comments will affect the next comment of the other. You'll need to remain flexible and free to deviate from your interview plan as you listen to the answers given to your questions. You'll also have to listen to what's said and almost simultaneously think ahead to the next item on your list of questions to decide if you should forge ahead or ask intervening questions that will clarify or elaborate on any previous responses.

From this discussion of interviewing, it should be clear that adept interviewers must have certain communicative skills.

1. *A good interviewer is a good listener.* Unless you listen carefully to what someone is saying and carefully interpret the significance of those comments, you may misunderstand. Because questioning and answering are alternated in an interview, there's plenty of opportunity to clarify remarks and opinions.

2. *A good interviewer is open.* Many of us are extremely wary of interviewers. We're cynical enough to believe that they have *hidden agenda*—unstated motives or purposes—that they're trying to pursue. Too often interviewers have claimed to only want a little information when actually they were selling magazine subscriptions or a religious ideal. If, as an interviewer, you're "caught" being less than honest, your chances for success are vastly diminished. Frankness and openness should govern all aspects of your interview communication.

3. *A good interviewer builds a sense of mutual respect and trust.* Feelings of trust and respect are created by revealing your own motivation, by getting the person to talk, and by expressing sympathy and understanding. To start with suspicion and distrust is to condemn the relationship without giving it a fair chance.

Printed Materials

The most common source of supporting materials is the printed word—newspapers, magazines, pamphlets, and books. Through the careful use of a library—and with the help of reference librarians—you can discover an almost overwhelming amount of materials relevant to your speech subject and purpose.

Newspapers
Newspapers are obviously a useful source of information about events of current interest. Moreover, their feature stories and accounts of unusual happenings provide a storehouse of interesting illustrations and examples. You must be careful, of course, not to accept as true everything printed in a newspaper, since the haste with which news sometimes must be gathered

makes complete accuracy difficult. Your school or city library undoubtedly keeps on file copies of one or two highly reliable papers, such as *The New York Times, The Observer, The Wall Street Journal,* or the *Christian Science Monitor,* and also a selection from among the leading newspapers of your state or region. If your library has *The New York Times* index, you can locate in the paper accounts of people and events from 1913 to the present. Another useful and well-indexed source of information on current happenings is *Facts on File,* issued weekly since 1940.

Magazines

An average-sized university library subscribes annually to hundreds of magazines and journals. Some, such as *Time, Newsweek,* and *U.S. News and World Report,* summarize weekly events. *Omni* and *Harper's* are representative of monthly publications that cover a wide range of subjects of both passing and permanent importance. *The Nation, Vital Speeches of the Day, Fortune, Washington Monthly,* and *New Republic,* among other magazines, contain comment on current political, social, and economic questions. More specialized magazines include *Popular Science, Scientific American, Sports Illustrated, Field and Stream, Ms., Better Homes and Gardens, Today's Health, National Geographic,* and *The Smithsonian.*

This list is, of course, merely suggestive of the wide range of periodicals available. To find a specific kind of information, use the *Readers' Guide to Periodical Literature,* which indexes most of the magazines you'll want to refer to in preparing a speech. Or, if you'd like more sophisticated material,

Libraries provide many forms of supporting materials including print and non-print media. What materials can you expect to find in your library? How would you conduct a systematic and efficient search for materials in your library?

consult the *Social Science Index* and the *Humanities Index,* now computerized in most libraries. Similar indexes are available for publications from technical fields and professional societies; a reference librarian can show you how to use them.

Yearbooks and Encyclopedias

The most reliable source of comprehensive data is the *Statistical Abstracts of the United States,* which covers a wide variety of subjects ranging from weather records and birth rates to steel production and election results. Information on Academy Award winners, world records in various areas, and the "bests" and "worsts" of almost anything can be found in the *World Almanac, The People's Almanac, The Guinness Book of World Records, The Book of Lists,* and *Information Please.* Encyclopedias, such as the *Encyclopaedia Britannica* and *Americana Encyclopedia,* attempt to cover the entire field of human knowledge and are valuable chiefly as initial reference sources or for background reading. Refer to them for important scientific, geographical, literary, or historical facts; for bibliographies of authoritative books on a subject; and for ideas you will not develop completely in your speech.

Documents and Reports

Various governmental agencies—state, national, and international—as well as many independent organizations publish reports on special subjects. The most frequently consulted governmental publications are the hearings and recommendations of congressional committees or of the United States Department of Health and Human Services and Department of Commerce. Reports on issues related to agriculture, business, government, engineering, and scientific experimentation are published by many state universities. Such endowed groups as the Carnegie, Rockefeller, and Ford Foundations and such special interest groups as the Foreign Policy Association, the Brookings Institution, the League of Women Voters, Common Cause, and the United States Chamber of Commerce also publish reports and pamphlets. Though by no means a complete list, *The Vertical File Index* serves as a guide to some of these materials.

Books

Most subjects suitable for a speech have been written about in books. As a guide to these books, use the subject-matter headings in the card catalog of your libraries. Generally, you will find authoritative books in your school library and more popularized treatments in your city's public library.

Biographies

The Dictionary of National Biography, the *Dictionary of American Biography, Who's Who, Who's Who in America, Current Biography,* and more specialized works organized by field contain biographical sketches especially useful in locating facts about famous people and in documenting the qualifications of authorities whose testimony you may quote.

Radio and Television Broadcasts

Lectures, discussions, and the formal public addresses of leaders in government, business, education, and religion are frequently broadcast over radio or television. Many of these talks are later mimeographed or printed by the stations or by the organizations that sponsor them. Usually, as in the case of CBS's *Meet the Press* or National Public Radio's *All Things Considered,* copies of broadcasts may be obtained for a small fee. Other broadcast content, such as national news broadcasts, is indexed by Vanderbilt University; your library may subscribe to that index, which is helpful in reconstructing a series of events. If no such manuscripts or transcripts are available, you'll have to audiotape the program—as long as you make no public use of the *tape* that you make—or take careful notes. Be exact! Just as you must quote printed sources accurately and honestly, so, too, are you morally obligated to respect someone's radio and television remarks and to give that person full credit.

Obviously, you won't have to investigate all of the foregoing sources of materials for every speech you make. Again, as in audience analysis, the key concept is *relevance:* go to the sources that will yield relevant materials. Historical statistics are more likely to be found in print materials than in a television program; a viewpoint on a local problem in an interview rather than a computer search. Use your head in selecting sources of materials to investigate and then carry out the search carefully. If you do, you'll minimize the time needed to find solid materials and yet make your speech authoritative and interesting.

RECORDING INFORMATION

When you find the information you've been looking for, either make a photocopy of it or take notes. Whether you keep your notes on 4 × 6 cards or in a notebook, it's helpful to have an accurate and legible record of the materials you wish to consider using in your speech. An incomplete source citation makes it difficult to find the information again, which can drive you crazy; hurried scribbles, too, are hard to decipher later. Many people find that notecards are easier to use than a notebook because they can be shuffled by topic area or type of support. If you do use a notebook, however, try to record each item on half of each page. There are two reasons to do this: since most of your information won't fill a page, you will save paper; and cutting the sheets in half will make it easier to sort your data or adopt a classification scheme and record information in accordance with particular themes or subpoints of your speech. When preparing notecards, place the appropriate subject headings at the top of the cards and the complete source citations at the bottom. This way, the cards can be classified by general subject (top right heading) and by specific information presented (top left heading). (See Figure 6.1.)

Computerized Searches

Your library undoubtedly subscribes to one or more computerized data bases. These work much like printed indexes—only much more quickly and thoroughly. Electronic data bases are usually updated regularly, making them much more timely than printed indexes. An average-sized university library probably has access to nearly 200 data files such as ERIC, BIOSIS, PsychInfo, AGRICOLA, Datrex, and MEDLINE. Computerized searches can be invaluable tools for research on speech topics if you run them intelligently.

1. *Pick the data base likely to have the information that you want.* With the help of a reference librarian and the descriptive material on the data bases, you'll know to go to ERIC, if you want scholarly and educational papers written by humanities professors, and to MEDLINE, if you can make use of psychological and scientific studies of diseases and other medical problems.

2. *Try some of the public data bases as well as library bases.* If you have access to a personal computer and modem, you can reach BRS/After Dark, CompuServe, The Source, Dow Jones News/Retrieval, and other general bases giving you a wealth of general information, news events, economic indicators, and the like.

3. *Be smart when picking key words for searches.* As the opening illustration in this chapter indicated, computerized searches can give you too much information if you select only broad categories such as "television." The more you're able to narrow and coordinate key words, the more likely you are to get usable material. So, if you're interested in television anchor people, coordinating the key words "television" and "news reporters" will get you what you want.

Searching library shelves for books can be rewarding; often you'll find an even more useful book beside the one you wanted. But, for sheer volume of information, nothing beats a computerized search.

Figure 6.1 A Sample Notecard

Notecards can be effective for recording information for later use. What essential information is important to enter on each notecard?

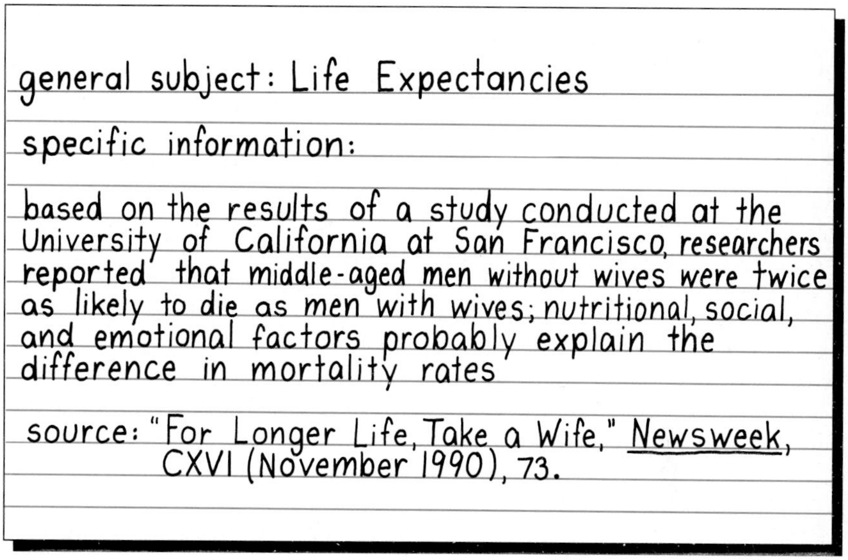

> general subject: Life Expectancies
>
> specific information:
>
> based on the results of a study conducted at the University of California at San Francisco, researchers reported that middle-aged men without wives were twice as likely to die as men with wives; nutritional, social, and emotional factors probably explain the difference in mortality rates
>
> source: "For Longer Life, Take a Wife," _Newsweek_, CXVI (November 1990), 73.

USING SOURCE MATERIAL ETHICALLY

Now that we've discussed locating and generating material for your speeches, we come to a major ethical issue—plagiarism. **Plagiarism** has been defined as "the unacknowledged inclusion of someone else's words, ideas, or data as one's own."[1] One of the saddest things an instructor has to do is cite a student for plagiarism. In speech classes, students occasionally quote material from _Reader's Digest, Newsweek, Time, Senior Scholastic,_ or other easy-to-obtain sources, not realizing how many speech teachers habitually scan the library periodicals section. Even if the teacher has not read the article, it soon becomes apparent that something is wrong—the wording differs from the way the person usually talks, the speech does not have a well-formulated introduction or conclusion, and the organizational pattern is not one normally used by speakers. Often, too, the person who plagiarizes an article reads it aloud badly, another sign that something is wrong.

Plagiarism is not, however, simply undocumented verbatim quotation. It also includes (a) undocumented paraphrases of others' ideas and (b) undocumented use of others' main ideas. For example, if you paraphrase a movie review from _Newsweek_ without acknowledging that staff critic David Ansen had those insights, or if you use the motivated sequence as a model for analyzing speeches without giving credit to Alan Monroe for developing it, you are guilty of plagiarism.

Suppose you ran across the following excerpt from Kenneth Clark's _Civilisation: A Personal View:_

It was the age of great country houses. In 1722 the most splendid of all had just been completed for Marlborough, the general who had been victorious over Voltaire's country: not the sort of idea that would have worried Voltaire in the least, as he thought of all war as a ridiculous waste of human life and effort. When Voltaire saw Blenheim Palace he said, "What a great heap of stone, without charm or taste," and I can see what he means. To anyone brought up on Mansart and Perrault, Blenheim must have seemed painfully lacking in order and propriety. . . . Perhaps this is because the architect, Sir John Vanbrugh, although a man of genius, was really an amateur. Moreover, he was a natural romantic, a castle-builder who didn't care a fig for good taste and decorum.[2]

Imagine that you decided to use the excerpt in a speech. The following examples illustrate what would constitute plagiarism and suggest ways that you could avoid it:

1. *Verbatim quotation of a passage* (read it aloud word for word). To avoid plagiarism: say, "Kenneth Clark, in his 1969 book *Civilisation: A Personal View,* said the following about the architecture of great country estates in eighteenth-century England: [then quote the paragraph]."

2. *Undocumented use of the main ideas:* "In eighteenth-century England there was a great flurry of building. Country estates were built essentially by amateurs, such as Sir John Vanbrugh, who built the splendid Blenheim Palace for General Marlborough. Voltaire didn't like war and he didn't like Blenheim, which he called a great heap of stone without charm or taste. He preferred the order and variety of houses designed by French architects Mansart and Perrault." To avoid plagiarism: say, "In his book *Civilisation: A Personal View,* Kenneth Clark makes the point that eighteenth-century English country houses were built essentially by amateurs. He uses as an example Sir John Vanbrugh, who designed Blenheim Palace for the Duke of Marlborough. Clark notes that, when Voltaire saw the house, he said, 'What a great heap of stone, without charm or taste.' Clark can understand that reaction from a Frenchman who was raised on the neoclassical designs of Mansart and Perrault. Clark explains English style arose from what he calls 'natural romanticism.' "

3. *Undocumented paraphrasing:* "The eighteenth century was the age of wonderful country houses. In 1722 the most beautiful one in England was built for Marlborough, the general who had won over France. When Voltaire saw the Marlborough house called Blenheim Palace, he said it was a great heap of stones." To avoid plagiarism: use the same kind of language noted under Example 2, giving Clark credit for his impressions.

Plagiarism is easy to avoid if you take reasonable care. Moreover, by citing such authorities as Clark, who are well educated and experienced, you add their credibility to yours. Avoid plagiarism to keep from being expelled from the class or even your school, and avoid it for positive reasons as well: improve your ethos by associating your thinking with that of experts.

CHAPTER SUMMARY

1. In searching for supporting materials, you're attempting to efficiently assemble not all information, but materials relevant to your speeches, your audiences, and the occasions on which you're speaking.

2. To determine the kinds of supporting materials needed before you search, you should consider (a) the rational requirements of the claim, (b) the range of available materials, (c) audience demands, and (d) the power-to-prove generally associated with various kinds of supporting materials.

3. In executing your searches, you'll want to know how to interview sources and to search through printed materials (newspapers, yearbooks and encyclopedias, documents and reports, books, and biographies) as well as radio and television broadcasts.

4. You need to record information carefully and in a form you can use easily.

5. You must also remember to use source material ethically, avoiding plagiarism.

KEY TERMS

informational interview (p. 112)   plagiarism (p. 119)

SKILLBUILDING ACTIVITIES

1. Your instructor will divide your class into groups. In the library, each group will locate the items in the left-hand column of the following list. First, determine which of the sources listed in the right-hand column contains the material you need. Next, find each source and write down the page numbers where the material can be found. On a later day, each group will turn in its reports, comparing its list with those of other groups.

Items	*Sources*
Weekly summary of current national news	*Book Review Digest*
	Congressional Record
Brief sketch of the accomplishments of Lee Iacocca	*Encyclopedia Americana*
	Facts on File
Description of a specific traffic accident	local newspaper
	The New York Times
Text of George Bush's 1989 inaugural address	*Oxford English Dictionary*
	Statistical Abstracts
Daily summary of stock prices	*Time*
Origin of the word "rhetoric"	*Vital Speeches of the Day*
Critical commentary on A. Bloom's	*Wall Street Journal*
The Closing of the American Mind	*Who's Who*
Current status of national legislation on educational reform	

2. Select a major problem, incident, or celebration that has appeared in the news recently. Examine a story or article written about it in each of the following: *The New York Times, Christian Science Monitor, USA Today, Time, Newsweek, New Republic,*

and either *The Wall Street Journal* or *Business Week.* In a column for each source, note specifically what major facts, people, incidents, and examples or illustrations are included and what conclusions are drawn. Be prepared to discuss the differences among the sources you consulted. How are their differences related to their readership? What does this exercise teach you about the biases or viewpoints of sources?

3. In your next speech, work at making your sources and their usefulness especially clear. When citing experts, mention their qualifications; when offering statistics or scientific studies, explicitly refer to reasons they ought to be judged acceptable; when listing examples or offering longer illustrations, indicate why you think they're typical of the problem you're discussing.

REFERENCES

1. Louisiana State University, "Academic Honesty and Dishonesty," adapted from *LSU's Code of Student Conduct,* 1981.

2. Kenneth Clark, *Civilisation: A Personal View* (New York: Harper & Row, 1969), 246.

CHAPTER SEVEN

Arranging and Outlining Your Speech

*B*ob had been his company's top sales representative for the past three years
and really knew his product thoroughly. One day he had to present his
company's product to the board of directors of a prospective client. Before beginning his presentation, Bob decided to loosen up the group a bit with some spontaneous introductory comments. He told the board about a fishing trip that he
had taken last summer and talked about teaching his daughter to bait a hook.
After what seemed like only five or ten minutes to Bob, the chair of the meeting
interrupted to say that the board was adjourning to another meeting. Bob was
shocked, but when he glanced at his watch he realized that he had rambled on
for over 20 minutes. Bob's firm lost the account.

As you can see, Bob's decision to ad lib was disastrous. Rather than preparing formal comments and sticking to them, Bob chose instead to begin his
speech by speaking in an impromptu or "off the cuff" manner. In doing so,
Bob ignored the five key criteria for communicating ideas to an audience:

 1.   *The plan of the speech must be easy for the audience to grasp and remember.*
Bob's listeners had difficulty understanding how his ideas fit together. The
ideas were not connected in ways that made immediate sense to them. As a
consequence, his listeners were frustrated in their attempts to untangle his
remarks. Their attention wandered, and the result was frustrating for both
Bob and his listeners.

2. *The organizational pattern must provide for full and balanced coverage of the material.* You must use a pattern that will complement your ideas and their supporting materials—one that will clarify your central idea or enhance your claim. It was difficult for Bob's listeners to figure out his claim because he talked about fishing instead of about his product.

3. *The structure of the speech should be appropriate to the occasion.* Bob's speech also failed because he underestimated the rigidity of the situation. Bob didn't satisfy his listeners' expectations nor did he adapt to the formality of the occasion. As you learned in Chapter 1, there are occasions when speakers are expected to observe group traditions. Presidential inaugural addresses, for example, tend to follow a particular format that has evolved from the addresses of our first presidents. Likewise, eulogies, speeches of introduction, Academy Awards acceptance speeches, and board meeting presentations normally evolve in an order that members of our culture have come to expect.

4. *The structure of the speech should be adapted to the audience's needs and level of knowledge.* When Bob rambled on about his personal life in a business meeting, he ignored his listeners' need to efficiently process information. He also insulted their intelligence by using informal language and by appearing to be unprepared. To avoid Bob's debacle, keep your audience in mind. Some organizational patterns described in this chapter are well suited to listeners who have little background on a subject. Other patterns work best when the audience is well informed and motivated to listen.

5. *The speech must move steadily forward toward a complete and satisfying finish.* Bob's listeners became increasingly frustrated because his speech didn't seem to be developing. They needed a sense of forward motion—of moving through a series of main points toward a clear destination. Repeated backtracking to pick up "lost" points will confuse your audience. Backtracking slows down the momentum of the speech, giving it a stop-and-start progression rather than a smooth forward flow. You also can enhance the sense of forward motion with internal summaries and forecasts, as well as transitions and physical movement to indicate progression.

TYPES OF ARRANGEMENT

Arrangement, as we use the term here, is the order or sequence of ideas in a pattern that suggests their relationship to each other. There are five general arrangement categories for speeches: (a) *chronological,* (b) *spatial,* (c) *causal,* (d) *topical,* and (e) *special patterns.*

Chronological Patterns

Chronological patterns trace the order of events in a time sequence. This arrangement of ideas is useful when your goal is to give listeners a strong sense of development or forward motion. When using the chronological sequence, you begin at a point in time and move systematically forward or backward. For example, you might describe the evolution of modern flight from the Wright brothers' first successful attempt to the Soviet cosmonauts' orbit of the earth; or you might trace the manufacture of an automobile by following the assembly line process from beginning to end. Here is an illustration of an outline using the chronological, or time, sequence:

Central Idea: The development of paper paralleled the development of technology.
  I. In A.D. 105, Chinese Emperor Ts'ai Lun conceived the idea of making paper from tree bark.
  II. In the period A.D. 618–907, the Chinese created transfer molds to make paper more efficiently.
  III. In 1694, the Bank of England printed money for the first time and built a machine for watermarking and engraving its bills.
  IV. In 1798, the first paper-making machine was invented by Nicholas-Louis Robert, finally moving the technology of papermaking into the modern era.

Spatial Patterns

In the **spatial pattern,** the major points of the speech are organized in terms of their physical proximity to or direction from each other. Descriptions of the migration patterns of Norwegian immigrants into the Midwest, for instance, would trace geographical movements into Iowa and Wisconsin, and from there into Minnesota, the Dakotas, and Montana. Consider another example of a spatial pattern:

Central Idea: Arranging your study space will help you make more efficient use of your study time.
  I. Clear the desk space directly in front of you so you have a place to work.
  II. Make sure that you have a bright light or lamp directly above the space you have cleared.
  III. Place a stack of blank paper for notes directly to the left of your cleared study space.
  IV. Keep sharpened pencils, pens, erasers, and other equipment in a desk drawer or pen holder to the right of your cleared study space.

Causal Patterns

As their name implies, **causal patterns** of speech organization move either (a) from an analysis of present causes to a prediction of future effects or (b) from present conditions to their apparent causes. Causal patterns give listeners a sense of physical coherence because ideas are developed in relationship to each other. Causal patterns assume that one event results from or causes another. (See page 292 for the tests of causality.) When using a *cause-effect pattern,* you might first point to the increasing number of closed college courses each semester and then show the result—it takes students longer to graduate. Or, using an *effect-cause pattern,* you could argue that delayed graduation is the result, at least in part, of the large number of closed courses. Compare the following outlines:

Central Idea: Acid rain [cause] is a rising problem because it threatens our health and economy [effect].

I. Factories across the United States emit harmful acid-forming sulfur dioxide and nitrogen oxide.

II. The effect of these emissions is to damage important ecological structures.
   A. Lakes and forests are threatened.
   B. The productivity of fertile soil is reduced.
   C. Acid particles in the air and drinking water cause 5–8 percent of all deaths in some regions of the United States.

Central Idea: Acid rain [effect] is primarily the result of modern technologies [causes].

I. If we are going to control acid rain, we must learn about and deal with its causes.

II. Human activities cause acid rain.
   A. One primary cause is air pollutants given off in the production of electrical energy.
   B. A second main cause is the emissions from motorized transportation.

Meaning is conveyed through patterns of organization. Which pattern of organization best fits this situation?

Notice that the first outline uses a cause-effect pattern; the second uses an effect-cause pattern. Adapt your speech to the situation by beginning with ideas that are better known to audience members; then proceed to the lesser known facets of the problem. You should use cause-effect if listeners are better acquainted with the cause; use effect-cause if the opposite is true.

Topical Patterns

Some speeches on familiar topics are best organized in terms of subject-matter divisions that have become standardized. Financial reports are customarily divided into assets and liabilities; discussions of government into legislative, executive, and judicial matters; and comparisons of kinds of telescopes into celestial and terrestrial models. **Topical patterns** are most useful for speeches that enumerate aspects of persons, places, things, or processes. Occasionally, a speaker tries to enumerate all aspects of the topic, as in a sermon on each of the Ten Commandments. More often, however, a partial enumeration of the primary or most interesting aspects is sufficient. For example, a speech on volleyball shots for an audience of beginners probably would concentrate only on the three main types of shots:

Central Idea: Knowing the three basic volleyball shots can increase the playing ability of amateur or backyard players.
  I. A *bump* is performed by bringing your shoulders together and clasping your hands under the ball.
 II. To *set* a ball, bring your hands above your head and hit the ball near your forehead using your fingers and keeping your palms open.
III. A *spike* is a quick power shot executed with one hand that drives the ball over the net and down into the opponent's court area.

Topical patterns are among the most popular and easiest to use. If you plan to enumerate only part of the topic, take care to explain your choices. You haven't made your choices seem coherent and logical if someone asks, "But why didn't you talk about scorekeeping in volleyball?"

The types of speech organization discussed so far—chronological, spatial, causal, and topical—are determined principally by the subject matter. While the audience is not ignored by the organization, it is the subject that usually suggests the pattern of organization. Some subjects, such as the historical development of a nation or a person's rise from obscurity to prominence, are clearly chronological. Subjects of a geographical nature—discussions of efficient kitchen design or a comet's orbit—fit more easily into the spatial structure. Still others—the reasons for inflation or recent rule changes in football—call for causal or topical patterns.

Special Patterns

At times, you may decide that rather than using any of the subject-oriented speech structures, it is more effective to use an audience-oriented, or

special pattern, for your material. These special patterns are often very successful because they are based upon the listener's needs. We want to call your attention to five special patterns of organization: (a) *familiarity-acceptance order,* (b) *inquiry order,* (c) *question-answer order,* (d) *problem-solution order,* and (e) *elimination order.*

Familiarity-Acceptance Order

Familiarity-acceptance order begins with what the audience knows or believes (the familiar) and moves on to new or challenging ideas (the unfamiliar). In an informative speech on quarks, you can begin with what the audience already knows about molecules and then introduce the new information on the subatomic particles called quarks. Similarly, if your aim is to persuade listeners to vote, you could begin with the facts or values about voting that your listeners already accept—that voting is a right guaranteed to all citizens. Then you could move on to provide new information about elections that were won by margins of several votes.

Relating new material to what is already known has long been recognized as one of the most effective methods of instruction. In fact, educational theorists have argued that all of our knowledge is derived analogically; that is, we learn not by adding unrelated bits of information to prior knowledge, but by comparing or contrasting new information with old.

Persuasive speeches based on accepted audience values are very well suited to skeptical or hostile audiences, especially when your reasoning is valid and your conclusions sound. When you meet these standards, your audience can't reject your claim without denying the underlying facts or values that they already accept. Here's an outline of a persuasive speech using familiarity-acceptance order:

Claim: Maria Campagna embodies the values our party stands for and, therefore, should be our nominee.
  I. We all agree, I am sure, that experience, ability, and integrity are prime requisites for a holder of high public office.
 II. Maria Campagna has these qualities.
    A. She has experience.
       1. She has served two terms as mayor of one of our largest cities.
       2. She has served in the state senate for twelve years.
    B. She has ability.
       1. She has successfully reorganized the cumbersome administrative machinery of our city government.
       2. She has become a recognized leader in the senate.
    C. She has integrity.
       1. She has never been suspected of any sort of corruption.
       2. Her word is as good as her bond.
III. Because Maria Campagna clearly has the qualities we demand of a holder of high public office, she deserves our support in her bid to be elected governor of this state.

Inquiry Order

Inquiry order develops the topic step-by-step in the same way you acquire the information or reach the conclusion. You may show listeners how to take prize-winning photographs by describing how the success and failure of your own experiments with film, lenses, and lighting eventually led to the conclusions you now offer. Or, if the purpose of your speech is to persuade, you may recount how you became aware of the need for new playground equipment, investigated possible choices, and searched for sources of funding until the solution you now advocate emerged as the best.

Inquiry order has a double advantage. First, it displays all facts and possibilities for the audience. Second, it enables listeners to judge accurately the worth of the information or policy being presented as it unfolds.

Question-Answer Order

Question-answer order raises and answers listeners' questions. First, you must determine which questions are most likely to arise in your listeners' minds. Then you need to develop your speech to answer each key question in a way that favors your conclusion. For example, after hearing about genetic engineering, people want to know how it may solve their own health problems or meet the needs of loved ones. When first learning about a new bond issue, listeners wonder how it will affect their taxes or social services. By structuring your speech to address these questions, you can maintain audience interest and involvement.

Problem-Solution Order

When you advocate changes in action or thought, your main points may fall naturally into a **problem-solution order.** (See Figure 7.1.) First, you establish that a problem exists. If your listeners are already aware of the problem, however, you might limit developing it too extensively. For example, if your listeners walk or ride bicycles to classes, they will be unaware that there aren't enough parking spaces on campus; but if they drive automobiles, they'll be quite familiar with the parking shortage. You also need to depict the problem in a way that will help your listeners perceive it the way you do. For example, listeners might be willing to put up with parking shortages if they accept the problem as a simple inconvenience of college life. You will need to show them that there is no reason to accept a parking shortage.

Once you've established that a problem exists, you must propose a solution to it. Your solution should be workable and practical. It would be silly to suggest that a multimillion dollar parking complex be built if financing isn't available or if the parking complex still wouldn't accommodate enough automobiles. However, a car-pooling or busing system is inexpensive and it limits the number of automobiles on campus.

Elimination Order

You may remember how you discovered the reason your car refused to start one time. You traced, step-by-step, the potential problems—dead battery,

Figure 7.1 Developing the Problem-Solution Pattern
Notice how the problems addressed help the speaker meet the intended purpose.

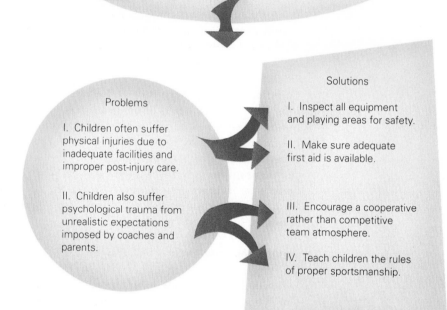

Purpose: To persuade my audience that concerned parents and coaches should act now to reduce the number of injuries in and traumatic effects of youth sports.

Problems

I. Children often suffer physical injuries due to inadequate facilities and improper post-injury care.

II. Children also suffer psychological trauma from unrealistic expectations imposed by coaches and parents.

Solutions

I. Inspect all equipment and playing areas for safety.

II. Make sure adequate first aid is available.

III. Encourage a cooperative rather than competitive team atmosphere.

IV. Teach children the rules of proper sportsmanship.

lack of gasoline, malfunctioning carburetor—and eliminated each one until you arrived at the correct cause: a blocked fuel line. With **elimination order,** you first survey all the available solutions and courses of action that could reasonably be pursued. Then, proceeding systematically, you eliminate each of the possibilities until one remains.

Elimination order is best suited to persuasive speeches. If you want student government to bring a special performer to campus, you might show that all other preferred entertainers are booked up, too expensive, or lack box office appeal. In this way, you lead the members of student government to agree with the choice you advocate.

To use elimination order effectively, you need to meet two requirements. First, you must make your survey of options all-inclusive. If you overlook obvious options, your listeners will not be obliged to accept the conclusion you desire. (See the discussion of "false division," page 293.) Second, you must make the options mutually exclusive; otherwise, your listeners might choose more than one. Consider this example in which only one alternative is best:

Claim: Building an outdoor volleyball/basketball court is the most practical plan for using our Student Council's recreation fund.

I. Three options have been proposed.
    A. A video arcade area
    B. A running/obstacle course
    C. An outdoor volleyball/basketball court
II. A video arcade area is impractical.
    A. Students would waste money.
    B. The cost of renting the machines is prohibitive.
III. A running/obstacle course is too expensive.
    A. The cost of the land cannot be met from our current treasury.
    B. We would also have to pay for maintenance.
IV. Therefore, an outdoor cement or asphalt court is the best choice.
    A. It is the least expensive.
    B. Its maintenance costs are minimal.

CONSISTENCY OF ARRANGEMENT

You may choose one method of arrangement for the main points of your speech and another for the subordinate ideas. You shouldn't, however, shift from one method to another during the presentation of the main points themselves—it will confuse your listeners and make you appear disorganized. The following outline illustrates how spatial, topical, and time patterns might be combined in a speech on the major cities of India:

Central Idea: The complexities of Indian culture are seen in India's cities.

I. The major cities of western India include Bombay and Ahmadabad.
    A. Bombay
        1. Early history
        2. Development under the British
        3. Conditions today
    B. Ahmadabad
        (Repeat chronological sequence under A above)
II. The major cities of central India include Delhi and Hyderabad.
    A. Delhi
        1. Early history
        2. Development under the British
        3. Conditions today
    B. Hyderabad
        (Repeat chronological sequence under A above)
III. The major cities of eastern India include Calcutta and Madras.
    A. Calcutta
        1. Early history
        2. Development under the British
        3. Conditions today
    B. Madras
        (Repeat chronological sequence under A above)

Perceptual Grouping: The Organization of Subordinate Points

What basic principles do we use to organize information into meaningful patterns? Gestalt psychologists have studied this question in detail for years. They believe that organization is basic to all mental activity and that it reflects the way the human brain functions. Although the assumptions of Gestalt psychology have less influence in the study of cognition and perception today than they did in the past, they provide us with some clues to patterns of thought.

As suggested in this chapter, psychologists have argued that human knowledge is derived analogically; that is, people learn by adding new bits of information to old constructs.

Table 7.1 Strategies for Organizing Speech Information

Organization Strategy	Main Construct	Explanation	Example
Parts of a Whole	Proximity	You help your audience perceive how the new information is all part of a whole.	"The grip, shaft, and head are the main parts of a golf club."
Lists of Functions	Continuity	You show your audience the connections between new information.	"The mission of a police department consists of meeting its responsibilities of traffic control, crime detection, and safety education."
Series of Causes or Results	Contiguity	You show your listeners the relationship between items of new information.	"The causes of high orange juice prices may be drought, frost, or blight in citrus-producing states."
Items of Logical Proof	Closure	You connect separate items of information along a coordinated line of reasoning.	"We need a new high school because our present building (a) is too small, (b) lacks modern laboratory and shop facilities, and (c) is inaccessible to handicapped students."
Illustrative Examples	Similarity	You help your audiences accept your main point by grouping specific cases or examples.	Cite the outcome of experiments to prove that adding fluoride to your community's water supply will help prevent tooth decay.

Although the information that we encounter changes, the constructs remain constant. There are several relatively static constructs that people use to group new bits of information:

1. *Proximity*—we group stimuli that are close together.
2. *Continuity*—we tend to simplify and to find similarities among things rather than differences.
3. *Contiguity*—we connect events that occur close together in time and space.
4. *Closure*—we complete figures by filling in the gaps or adding missing connections.
5. *Similarity*—we group items of similar shape, size, and color.

Methods for learning new vocabulary or for remembering people's names are often based on these simple constructs. For example, you use the principle of *proximity* when you remember the word *acerbic* (meaning sharp, bitter, or sour) because it resembles the word *acid*. When you stumble over the word *acerbic* in a sentence, you guess its meaning from its use and context by employing the principle of *closure*. You easily connect "acerbic" with "acerbity" because of the principle of *continuity*. When trying to remember someone's name, you might "flash back" to the first time you met that person, thus applying *contiguity*. Or, that person might remind you of another person with the same name because of their *similarity* in appearance.

You can adapt these constructs to organize the substructure of your speeches. When you do so,

you'll be providing your listeners with unfamiliar information in patterns of thinking that are familiar to them. Consider the constructs for organizing subordinate points shown in Table 7.1. Notice how these constructs are based upon the five constructs people use to make sense of new information.

These constructs also function as criteria against which your organizational coherence can be checked. Are your most important ideas *near*, or *proximate*, to each other? Do they advance a chain of thinking in a coherent manner implying *continuity*? Are they linked together or *contiguous*? Are they sufficiently comprehensive to permit accurate *closure*? Are they *similar* enough to suggest they belong together as main points?

As a public speaker, you can take advantage of the innate constructs by which the human brain organizes new information. You can use the constructs of proximity, continuity, contiguity, closure, and similarity to make your message more accessible to your listeners.

For elaboration of the constructs previously discussed, see Lyle E. Bourne, Jr., and Bruce R. Ekstrand, *Psychology: Its Principles and Meanings*, 4th ed. (New York: Holt, Rinehart & Winston, 1982), chap. 3; Dennis Coon, *Introduction to Psychology*, 3rd ed. (St. Paul: West, 1983), 104–124; Henry Gleitman, *Psychology* (New York: W. W. Norton, 1981), 228–253. For recent reviews of Gestalt psychology, see Rudolph Arnheim, "The Two Faces of Gestalt Psychology," *American Psychologist*, 41 (1986), 820–824; Ronald H. Forgus and Lawrence E. Melamed, *Perception: A Cognitive-Stage Approach*, 2nd ed. (New York: McGraw-Hill, 1976), 177–182; and Michael Kobovy and James R. Pomerantz, eds., *Perceptual Organization* (Hillsdale, N.J.: Lawrence Erlbaum Associates, 1980).

Note that spatial sequence is used for main points I, II, and III; topical sequence for subpoints A and B; and chronological sequence for sub-subpoints 1, 2, and 3. This pattern achieves psychological closure because listeners can anticipate the pattern once they understand it.

REQUIREMENTS OF GOOD OUTLINE FORM

The amount of detail that you include in an outline will depend on your subject, on the speaking situation, and on your previous experience in speech composition. New subject matter, unique speaking contexts, and limited prior speaking experience all indicate the need for a thorough outline. Under any circumstances, a good outline should meet the following four basic requirements:

1. *Each unit in the outline should contain one main idea.* If two or three ideas merge under one subpoint, the relationships they bear to one another and to the other ideas in the outline will not stand out clearly. Notice the difference in clarity between the following examples.

Wrong

I. You should ride a bicycle because bicycling is convenient.
   A. Bicycling is inexpensive.
   B. Bicycling is healthful.
      1. It is an excellent form of recreation.
      2. It is fun.

Right

I. You should ride a bicycle.
   A. Bicycling is an ideal form of transportation.
      1. It is convenient.
      2. It is inexpensive.
   B. Bicycling is also an excellent form of recreation.
      1. It is healthful.
      2. It is fun.

2. *Less important ideas in the outline should be subordinate to more important ones.* In an outline, subordinate ideas rank below main ideas in scope and importance since they directly support or amplify the main heading. Subordinate ideas are indented in an outline and they are marked with subordinate symbols. Study the following examples:

Wrong

I. The cost of medical care has skyrocketed.
   A. Operating room fees may be as much as $1000 or $1200.
      1. Hospital charges are high.
      2. A private room may cost as much as $800 a day.
   B. X rays and laboratory tests are extra expenses.

C. Complicated operations cost several thousand dollars.
   1. Doctors' charges constantly go up.
   2. Office calls usually cost between $25 and $60.
   3. Drugs are expensive.
   4. Most antibiotics cost at least $1.25 per dose.
D. The cost of nonprescription drugs has mounted.

Right

I. The cost of medical care has skyrocketed.
   A. Hospital charges are high.
      1. A private room may cost as much as $800 a day.
      2. Operating room fees may be as much as $1000 or $1200.
      3. X rays and laboratory tests are extra expenses.
   B. Doctors' charges constantly go up.
      1. Complicated operations cost several thousand dollars.
      2. Office calls usually cost between $25 and $60.
   C. Drugs are expensive.
      1. Most antibiotics cost at least $1.25 per dose.
      2. The cost of nonprescription drugs has mounted.

3. *The logical relationship between units of the outline should be shown by proper indentation.* Normally, you will place your main points nearest the left-hand margin of your outline because they're the most general and the most important statements. Place less important statements beneath and indent them to the right of the main points in order of increasing specificity. In your finished outline, the broadest and most central statements will be farthest to the left; the narrowest and most particular ones farthest to the right. If a statement is more than one line in length, the second line should be aligned with the first. Study the following example:

I. Main point
   A. Subpoint
   B. Subpoint
      1. Sub-subpoint
      2. Sub-subpoint
II. Main point
   A. Subpoint
      1. Sub-subpoint
      2. Sub-subpoint
   B. Subpoint

4. *A consistent set of symbols should be used throughout the outline.* Whatever system you use, be consistent. Items of the same importance should always be assigned the same type of symbol. Notice that throughout this book all main points are assigned roman numerals, all subpoints are assigned capital letters, and all sub-subpoints are assigned Arabic numerals. Most outlines follow the system used in this book.

All outlines should adhere to the four requirements just described. The final draft of a complete, formal outline, however, must adhere to one additional requirement: *all ideas in a formal outline should be written as full sentences.* As you prepare outlines for your classroom speeches, you'll find that phrasing each item as a full sentence will clarify its meaning and show its exact relationship to other points. You'll also find that a full statement of each point is a valuable aid as you elaborate that point when you speak.

PHRASING THE MAIN POINTS

You can help your listeners to understand your message better if you observe the rules of effective phrasing. (For further development of phrasing, see Chapter 9.) In order to achieve maximum effectiveness in the statement of your main points, keep in mind these four characteristics of good phrasing:

1. *Be concise.* State your main points as briefly as you can without distorting their meaning. Crisp, clear, straightforward statements are easier to grasp than rambling, vague, complex declarations. Say, "The Berlin Wall collapsed," not "The Berlin Wall, that symbol of postwar monolithic communism, crumbled symbolically and literally under the onslaught of political and economic change."

2. *Use vivid language.* Whenever possible, state your main points in evocative words and phrases. Drab, colorless statements are easily forgettable; punchy lines grab attention. Notice how much more vivid it is to say, "Have fun in the sun!" than it is to say, "Plan on spending your spring break in sunny Florida."

3. *Make your statements immediate.* Phrase your main points so they'll appeal directly to the concerns of your listeners. Instead of saying, "We should take immediate action to reduce the costs of education," say, "Cut tuition now!"

4. *Use parallel structure.* In a speech, your listeners have only one chance to catch what you're saying; parallelism in sentence structure helps them do so. Notice how the repetition of a key phrase aids the listener in remembering this series:

Ineffective
I. Weight lifters depend mainly on strength.
II. Cardiovascular endurance is important to distance runners.
III. When sailing, balance is a major factor.

Effective
I. Strength is most important to weight lifters.
II. Cardiovascular endurance is most important to distance runners.
III. Balance is most important to sailors.

Notice that in the effective series the phrase "is most important to" is repeated. Such parallelism will help your listeners grasp and remember the major ideas in your speech.

PREPARING AN OUTLINE

You should develop your outline, as well as the speech it represents, gradually through a series of stages. Your outlines will become increasingly complex as the ideas of your speech evolve and as you move it closer to its final form. There are three stages you will have to move your outline through, each of which has a specific function:

1. Develop a *rough outline* that establishes the topic of your speech, clarifies your purpose, and identifies a reasonable number of subtopics.
2. Prepare a *technical plot outline* of your speech in order to evaluate the strengths and weaknesses of your prospective presentation.
3. Finally, recast your material into a *speaking outline* that compresses your technical plot into key words or phrases that can be used to jog your memory when you deliver your speech.

Developing a Rough Outline

Suppose your instructor has assigned an informative speech on a subject that interests you. You decide to talk about drunk driving because a close friend was recently injured by an intoxicated driver. Your broad topic area is *drunk driving*.

In the six-to-eight minutes you have to speak, you obviously can't cover such a broad topic adequately. After considering your audience (see Chapter 4) and your time limit, you decide to focus your presentation on two organizations—Mothers Against Drunk Driving (MADD) and Students Against Drunk Driving (SADD).

As you think about narrowing your topic further, you jot down some possible ideas. You continue to narrow your list until your final ideas include the following:

1. Founders of MADD and SADD
2. Accomplishments of the two organizations
3. Reasons the organizations were deemed necessary
4. Goals of MADD and SADD
5. Action steps taken by MADD and SADD
6. Ways your listeners can help

You can help your listeners to follow your ideas by clustering similar ideas. Experiment with several possible clusters before you decide on the best way to arrange your ideas.

Your next step is to consider the best pattern of organization for these topics. A chronological pattern would enable you to organize the history of

MADD and SADD, but it would not allow you to discuss ways your listeners could help. Either cause-effect or effect-cause would work well if your primary purpose were to persuade. However, this is an informative speech, and you don't want to talk about the organizations as only the causes of the effect of reduced alcohol-related accidents. Of the special patterns, an inquiry order might work. You discard inquiry order, however, when you realize that you don't know enough about audience members' questions to use this organizational pattern effectively. After examining the alternatives, you finally settle on a topical pattern. A topical pattern allows you to present three clusters of information:

1. Background of MADD and SADD—information about the founders, why the organizations were founded
2. Description of MADD and SADD—goals, steps in action plans, results
3. Local work of MADD and SADD—how parents work with their teenagers and with local media to accomplish MADD and SADD goals

As you subdivide your three clusters of information, you develop the following general outline:

I. Background of MADD and SADD
   A. Information about the founders
   B. Reasons the organizations were founded
II. Description of the organizations
   A. Their goals
   B. The action steps they take
   C. Their accomplishments so far
III. Applications of their work on a local level
   A. "Project Graduation"
   B. Parent-student contracts
   C. Local public service announcements

A **rough outline** identifies your topic, provides a reasonable number of subtopics, and shows a method for organizing and developing your speech. Notice that you've arranged both the main points and subpoints topically. A word of warning: *you should make sure that the speech doesn't turn into a "string of beads" that fails to differentiate between one topic and the next.*

The next step in preparing an outline is to phrase your main headings more precisely. Then you can begin to develop each heading by adding subordinate ideas. As you develop your outline, you'll begin to see what kinds of information and supporting materials you need to find.

Developing a Technical Plot Outline

A **technical plot outline** is a diagnostic tool used to determine whether a speech is structurally sound. Use your technical plot outline to discover possible gaps or weaknesses in your speech. After completing your rough outline and learning more about your topic through background reading, you're now ready to assemble a technical plot outline.

Begin by examining your rough outline. Be flexible—if you discover that you must rearrange some topics or drop others to fit your time limits or audience's interests, then do so. Next, write each item of the outline as a complete sentence to convey your meaning clearly and precisely. Remember the requirements of good outline form discussed earlier. You should add to your outline a bibliography of the sources you consulted.

Lay the complete sentence outline beside a blank sheet of paper. On the blank sheet, opposite each outline unit, identify the corresponding supporting materials, types of motivational appeals, factors of attention, and other devices. For example, indicate on the blank sheet of paper wherever you have used statistics; you might also include a brief statement of the function of the statistics.

Then, examine the list of supporting materials, motivational appeals, factors of attention, and so on. Is there adequate supporting material for each point in the speech? Is the supporting material sufficiently varied? Do you use motivational appeals at key points in the speech? Do you attempt to engage your listeners' attention throughout the speech? Answering these questions with your technical plot outline can help you to determine whether your speech is structurally sound, whether there is adequate supporting material, whether you've overused any forms of support, and whether you have effectively adapted your appeals to the audience and content. Of course, many speeches don't need to be tested this thoroughly. Experienced speakers can often make an adequate analysis without drafting a complete technical plot outline. For the beginner, however, the technical plot outline is an effective way of checking the structure of a speech and the methods used to develop it.

Sample Technical Plot Outline

What follows is the complete content of an outline with its technical plot. For illustrative purposes, all items in the outline are stated as complete sentences. Such completeness of detail may be desirable if the occasion is especially important or if you have difficulty framing thoughts extemporaneously. Frequently, however, you will need to write out only the main ideas as complete sentences and state the subordinate ideas and supporting materials as key phrases. Check with your instructor if you have any doubt about how detailed to make your outline.

FRIENDS DON'T LET FRIENDS DRIVE DRUNK[1]

[The introduction and conclusion of this speech will be developed in detail in Chapter 8, Beginning and Ending Your Speech, pages 147–164.]

First topic: background on founders, helping create emotional identification

I. MADD and SADD were founded under tragic circumstances.
   A. MADD was founded in 1980 by Candy Lightner.
      1. One of her daughters was killed by a drunk driver.
      2. She wanted to protect other families from a similar tragedy.
   B. SADD was founded by Lightner's other daughter.
      1. The loss of her sister hurt her deeply.
      2. She knew the importance of peer pressure in stopping teenage drinking and driving.

Second topic: description
First subtopic: goals

II. You can understand MADD and SADD better if you know something about their goals, operations, and effectiveness.
   A. MADD and SADD were organized the way they were because the Lightners have specific goals they wish to achieve.
      1. They want the general public to carry out the agitation necessary to effect changes.

Specific instances

         a. Members of the public can put pressure on government officials.
         b. They can write letters-to-the-editor.
         c. They can campaign for state and local task forces.
         d. They can do all this for a minimal investment of money.
      2. They want to expose the deficiencies in current legislation and drunk driving control systems.

Statistics (segments)

         a. They want to toughen the laws on operating a motor vehicle when intoxicated [statistics on variations in state laws].

Specific instances

         b. They want to pressure judges to hand down maximum instead of minimum penalties [specific instances of light sentences].

Statistics (segments)

         c. They want to see more drunk driver arrests from city, county, and state law enforcement agents [statistics on arrest rates].
      3. They want to help the families of other victims.
         a. Most MADD and many SADD members have been victims themselves.

Testimony

         b. Families are taught to put their energy into getting something done [quotations from pamphlets] as well as into mourning.
      4. And finally, MADD and SADD want to educate the general public.
         a. They want to make people conscious of the tragedies of drunk driving.
         b. They want to focus media attention on the problem.

Second subtopic: action steps

   B. MADD's steps for action demonstrate the thoroughness with which the organization understands the processes of public persuasion.

Throughout, extended hypothetical illustration exemplifies the steps	1. First, a local chapter sets its goals.
	2. Second, it educates its organizers goal by goal so that everyone knows the reasons behind each step.
	3. Third, it sets research priorities.
	a. One group might check on local arrest records.
	b. Another might examine drunk driving conviction rates for various judges.
	c. A third might work with local media to find out how to secure time and space for a public service announcement on drunk driving.
	d. A fourth might talk with local schools and churches about safe prom nights.
	4. Fourth, once the research is complete, the local chapter can formulate its plans of action.
	5. Fifth, it can "go public" with action teams and task forces.
Testimony	6. This five-step process parallels the campaign model for public persuasion devised by Herbert W. Simons in his book *Understanding Persuasion*.
Third subtopic: results of MADD/SADD work	C. Although still young, organizations such as MADD and SADD already have had significant effects.
Statistics (magnitude)	1. By 1984, there were 320 MADD chapters across the country.
	2. About 600,000 volunteers are now working on MADD projects.
	3. State laws already are changing.
Specific instances	a. In 1982 alone, 25 different states enacted 30 pieces of drunk driving legislation as a result of MADD's lobbying.
	b. After petitions were submitted by the organizations, Congress raised the mandatory legal drinking age to 21.
	c. In Florida, convicted drunk drivers must have red bumper stickers on their cars reading, "CONVICTED DUI."
Statistics (trends)	4. Fatalities from drunk driving have decreased [quote pre-1980 and post-1980 statistics].
	5. MADD also takes credit for increasing the popularity of low-alcohol beer, wines, and wine coolers.
Third topic: local projects	III. You can work with MADD and SADD on local projects.
Explanation	A. Set up a workshop in local high schools for parent-child contracts.
	1. In such a contract (which has no legal status) the teen agrees to never drive drunk, calling on the parent for a ride instead, while the parent agrees to ask no questions and to impose no special penalties for the teen's intoxication.
	2. The contract reinforces the importance of not driving drunk and makes the commitment to safety a mutual commitment.
	B. Set up a SADD "Project Graduation."
Example	1. With the cooperation of the schools and, sometimes, local youth organizations or churches, a community can sponsor nonalcoholic postprom parties.

2. They allow prom-goers a chance to stay up late, have fun, and celebrate without alcohol.

C. Work with local media to use public service announcements to halt teen and adult drunk driving.

Specific instances

1. MADD chapters can order ads you may have seen on TV.
   a. Some oppose drunk driving.
   b. Some tell you to designate a non-drinking driver from among your group.
   c. Others urge hosts of parties to not let drunk guests drive.

Specific instance

2. SADD chapters also can order ads and school posters, nonalcoholic party kits, and the like [show sample items].

Developing a Speaking Outline

As you probably realize, a technical plot outline would be very difficult to use when you were actually delivering your speech on MADD and SADD. A technical outline is too detailed to manage from a lectern; you will probably be tempted to read it to your listeners because it includes so many details. If you read your outline, however, you'll lose your conversational tone.

Therefore, you need to compress your technical plot outline into a more useful form. A **speaking outline** is a short, practical form to use while delivering your speech. (See Figure 7.2.) This form consists primarily of

Speaking notes should be unobtrusive. When do they become distracting?

Figure 7.2 Sample Speaking Outline (on Notecards)

Notecards for a speech on MADD and SADD.

FRIENDS DON'T LET FRIENDS DRIVE DRUNK

I. Background
  A. MADD: 1980. Candy Lightner
  B. SADD: her other daughter for hi-school kids

II. Description
  A. Goals
    1. public agitation (gov't. officials, letters to editor, task forces, all for little money)
    2. expose deficiencies in current legis. & control
      a. tougher laws state by state (STATISTICS)
      b. pressure judges (JUDGE NORTON, SANDERS, HANKS)
      c. more arrests (STATISTICS)
    3. public education
      a. more conscious
      b. media attention

  B. MADD's action steps
    1. goals (what community needs most)
    2. educate organizers
    3. set research priorities (arrest records, conviction rates, PSA's, prom nights)
    4. formulate plans of action
    5. go public!
      (note on Simons's *Understanding Persuasion*)

  C. Results
    1. 320 MADD chapters by 1984
    2. 600,000 volunteers
    3. state laws changing
      a. 1982: 25 states, 30 pieces of legis.
      b. Congress: drinking age to 21
      c. Florida, red bumper-sticker, CONVICTED DUI
    4. fatalities down (statistics)
    5. popularity of low-alc beer: wines, coolers

III. Local projects
  A. contracts
  B. prom night (Operation Graduation)
  C. PSA's and publicity
    1. MADD TV ads
      a. after drunk driving
      b. sober group member
      c. host/guest—*Friends don't let friends d.d.*
    2. SADD projects
      a. school posters (SHOW POSTER)**
      b. non-alc party kits
      c. ads

summaries of the complete sentences in your technical outline. The actual method you use to create your speaking outline will depend on your personal preference; some people like to work with small pieces of paper, others with notecards. Whatever your choice, however, your speaking outline should serve several functions while you're addressing your audience: (a) it should provide you with reminders of the direction of your speech—main points, subordinate ideas, and so on; (b) it should record technical or detailed material such as statistics and quotations; and (c) it should be easy to read so that it does not detract from the delivery of your speech. Each notecard or piece of paper should contain only one main idea.

There are four main characteristics of properly prepared speaking outlines:

1. Most points are noted with only a key word or phrase—a word or two should be enough to trigger your memory, especially if you've practiced the speech adequately.
2. Ideas that must be stated precisely are written down fully, for example, "Friends don't let friends drive drunk."
3. Directions for delivery are included, such as "SHOW POSTER."
4. Emphasis is indicated in a number of ways—capital letters, underlining, indentation, dashes, and highlighting with colored markers (find methods of emphasis that will easily catch your eye, show the relationship of ideas, and jog your memory during your speech delivery).

CHAPTER SUMMARY

1. There are five characteristics of an effective speech: (a) *the plan of the speech is easy to grasp and remember,* (b) *the speech provides full and balanced coverage of the material,* (c) *the speech is appropriate for the occasion,* (d) *the speech adapts to the audience's needs and level of knowledge,* and (e) *the speech moves forward toward a complete and satisfying finish.*

2. Arrangement is the sequence of ideas in a pattern that suggests their relationship to each other. The five types of arrangement patterns are *chronological, spatial, causal* (effect-cause and cause-effect), *topical* (complete or partial enumeration), and *special.* Special arrangement patterns include familiarity-acceptance, inquiry, question-answer, problem-solution, and elimination order.

3. Be consistent when using arrangement patterns in combination. You may choose one method of arrangement for the main points of your speech and another method for the subordinate ideas. You shouldn't, however, shift from one method to another during the presentation of the main points themselves.

4. There are four requirements for good outline form: (a) *each unit should contain only one idea,* (b) *less important ideas should be subordinate to more important ones,* (c) *the logical relationship between units should be shown by proper indentation,* and (d) *a consistent set of symbols should be used throughout the outline.*

5. When phrasing main points, be *concise,* use *vivid* language, make your statements *immediate,* and use *parallel* structure.

6. In outlining a speech, first develop a *rough outline,* then prepare a *technical plot outline,* and finally recast your material into a *speaking outline.*

KEY TERMS

arrangement (p. 124)
causal pattern (p. 125)
chronological pattern (p. 124)
elimination order (p. 130)
familiarity-acceptance order (p. 128)
inquiry order (p. 129)
problem-solution order (p. 129)

question-answer order (p. 129)
rough outline (p. 138)
spatial pattern (p. 125)
speaking outline (p. 142)
special pattern (p. 128)
technical plot outline (p. 138)
topical pattern (p. 127)

SKILLBUILDING ACTIVITIES

1. For each of the following topics, suggest two ways that materials might be organized. Discuss which of the two would be most effective:
   a. Directions for driving in snow
   b. An explanation of television viewing habits of children
   c. A rationale for including women in a revised military draft system
   d. The effect that the influx of tourists from the West will have on the Soviet Union
   e. A description of the proposed route for a highway bypass

2. Bring a short magazine or newspaper article and a photocopy of it to class. Cut the photocopy into separate paragraphs or sentences. Ask a classmate to assemble the separated paragraphs or sentences into a coherent story. Compare your classmate's results to the original article.

3. For a speech entitled "The Investigator as a Resource"—discussing why a lawyer may want to hire a private detective on a case-by-case basis—rearrange the following points and subpoints in proper outline form:
   a. Investigative services can save the lawyer time.
   b. Investigative reports indicate areas the lawyer should concentrate on to build a case.
   c. It is advantageous for a lawyer to employ an investigator on a case-by-case basis.
   d. The investigator performs two basic services.
   e. Known witnesses must be interviewed and other witnesses identified.
   f. The detective examines reports from the FBI and other governmental and private agencies and evaluates them for reliability and to determine what has to be done.
   g. The investigator examines, collects, preserves, and analyzes physical evidence.
   h. The investigator compiles information in an effort to reconstruct an incident.
   i. Lawyers may need only occasional detective assistance on especially critical cases.
   j. Investigative reports can be used in out-of-court settlements.

REFERENCES

The material for this speech—including the statistics we have not included—was drawn from the following sources: "MADD from Hell," *Restaurant Hospitality* (April 1990); "One Less for the Road?" *Time* (May 20, 1985); "Razcal, MADD Party with High Schoolers," *Advertising Age* (November 20, 1989); "Glad to Be SADD," *Listen Magazine* (October 1982); "War Against Drunk Drivers," *Newsweek* (September 13, 1982); "They're Mad as Hell," *Time* (August 3, 1981); "How to Get Alcohol Off the Highway," *Time* (July 1, 1981); "Health Report," *Prevention Magazine* (June 1984); "Water Water Everywhere," *Time* (May 20, 1985); L. B. Taylor, *Driving High* (Watts, 1983); Sandy Golden, *Driving the Drunk Off the Road* (Washington, D.C.: Acropolis Books, 1983); and a pamphlet by the U.S. National Highway Traffic Safety Administration, *How to Save Lives and Reduce Injuries—A Citizen Activist Guide to Effectively Fight Drunk Driving* (Washington, D.C.: U.S. Government Printing Office, 1982).

CHAPTER EIGHT

Beginning and Ending Your Speech

"*T*hat was embarrassing," Yangsoo noted. "I was a little hurried this morning as I was finishing up my speech, and I figured I could wing the conclusion. I couldn't. I did manage to summarize the three main points, but then I still didn't know what to do. I can't believe I said, 'I guess I'm done now—I think I'll sit down.' " Yangsoo's teacher asked, "Did you notice that your audience was as embarrassed as you were? They felt sorry for you; they wanted you to have something to say at the end, to finish strong. Many of them actually dropped their heads so they wouldn't have to watch you suffer. Next time, don't just stop—conclude!"*

If you plunge headlong into a speech without thinking about a beginning, you'll probably succeed only in confusing the audience and making yourself miserable. And if you come to the end of your presentation without a prepared conclusion, you'll get flustered, both you and the audience will be embarrassed (as happened to Yangsoo), and the speech will end on a negative note. Just as aerobics instructors begin with warm-ups and end with cool-downs, so must you lead your audience into the environment of your speech systematically, and then take them back to their own worlds at the end. Well-prepared introductions and conclusions (a) allow you and your audience to enter into and then separate from a rhetorical relationship, (b) orient your audience to your purposes and ideas and then reinforce both at the end, and (c) signal clearly when your speech starts and ends so as to keep your audience as comfortable as possible.

Introductions and conclusions are not trivial aspects of public speaking; in most cultures they are governed by strict communication rules. If you disregard cultural norms, your credibility and, consequently, your effectiveness will suffer. If you meet expectations, you'll significantly improve your chances for rhetorical success. In this chapter, we'll review the purposes of introductions and conclusions, discuss and examine examples of various strategies for beginning and ending speeches, and explore ways to incorporate those strategies in an outline.

BEGINNING YOUR SPEECH

If the beginning of a speech is intended to complement the main idea or claim, the introduction must (a) *gain listeners' attention,* (b) *secure goodwill and respect for the speaker,* and (c) *prepare the audience for the discussion to follow.*

As a speaker you want your listeners to focus on all of your speech, but you must gain their attention first. You need to capture their attention during the first few moments of the speech; unless they're prepared to listen to what you say, your most interesting, useful information and most persuasive appeals will be wasted. By demonstrating the vitality of the topic and showing how important it may be for your audience, you can turn audience attention into a more developed interest. (You may want to review the factors of attention on pages 34–38.)

Your audience will probably have begun to form opinions about you and your topic even before you begin to speak. Obviously, you want those opinions to be favorable. You have an opportunity to enhance them during the first few moments of your speech. Your confidence in your topic and general presence on the platform should serve as nonverbal cues for your audience. In many situations, your own reputation or the chairperson's introduction will help generate goodwill. However, there may be times when your audience is opposed to you or your topic. In these instances, it's important to deal with opposition openly so that your topic will receive a fair hearing. By commenting on the differences between your views and those of your listeners, you can let them know that you're aware of differences but are seeking areas of consensus. When confronted by indifference, distrust, or skepticism, you must take steps to change these attitudes early in the speech so that your position will be received openly.

Finally, you should lead your listeners' thinking into the subject of your speech. You must prepare the audience by stating your purpose early; audiences that are forced to guess the purpose of a speech soon lose interest.

An introduction that secures your audience's attention and goodwill and prepares them to listen lays a solid foundation for acceptance of the central idea or proposition of your speech. There are a number of established means for tailoring your introduction to achieve these ends:

1. Referring to the subject or occasion
2. Using a personal reference or greeting

3. Asking a rhetorical question
4. Making a startling statement of fact or opinion
5. Using a quotation
6. Telling a humorous anecdote
7. Using an illustration

Referring to the Subject or Occasion

If your audience already has a vital interest in your subject, you need only to state that subject before presenting your first main point. The speed and directness of this approach suggest your alertness and eagerness to address your topic. Professor Russell J. Love used this approach when discussing rights for people with severe communication problems:

> *My talk tonight is concerned with the rights of the handicapped—particularly those people with severe communication disabilities. I will be presenting what I call a bill of rights for the severely communicatively disabled.*[1]

Although such brevity and forthrightness may strike exactly the right note on some occasions, you should not begin all speeches this way. To a skeptical audience, a direct beginning may sound immodest or tactless; to an apathetic audience, it may sound dull or uninteresting. When listeners are receptive and friendly, however, reference to the subject often produces a clear and businesslike opening.

Instead of referring to your subject, you may sometimes want to refer to the occasion that has brought you and your audience together. This is especially true of a special occasion, as when noted historian Arthur M. Schlesinger, Jr., appeared at a National Academy of Science gathering to honor the memory of a brilliant sponsor of the arts:

> *It is a high honor to be invited to inaugurate this series of annual lectures in memory of Nancy Hanks and in support of the cause she so nobly served—the sustenance and enrichment of the arts in America. And it is appropriate that this series should be sponsored by the American Council for the Arts, an organization that for 28 years has given the artistic condition of our diverse and combative society searching analysis and vigorous advocacy; all the more appropriate because Nancy Hanks was president of the ACA before she moved on to become the brilliantly effective leader of the National Endowment for the Arts.*[2]

Using a Personal Reference or Greeting

At times, a warm, personal greeting from a speaker or a remembrance of a previous visit to the audience or scene serves as an excellent starting point. Personal references are especially useful when a speaker is well known to the audience. Liz Carpenter—a veteran Washington reporter who served in the government under presidents Johnson, Ford, and Carter—took advantage of her reputation to open her speech to the National Press Club:

Dear old friends, colleagues of the press: How great thou art! How great it is to return after ten years and to find you are still here in the town where "try to remember" has become the national anthem. Like Rip Van Winkle, I rub my eyes in wonder at Washington today. Like George Bush, I wonder where I am and where I have been all this time. . . .

It seems like only ten years ago, the speed limit was 55. Today it's 65 and so am I. I'm observing the limit, but I warn you I'm accelerated. I am picking up speed, but at my age, that's about all. Well we are all into aging. That sex symbol, Paul Newman, is 62. Ben Bradlee [of the Washington Post*] is 66. Why am I so glad to know that?*

If I have any claim to this podium, it is because this National Press Building has been a big part of my life for forty years. . . [continued reminiscences].[3]

The way a personal reference introduction can be used to gain the attention of a hostile or skeptical audience is illustrated by a speech presented by Anson Mount, Manager of Public Affairs for *Playboy*, to the Christian Life Commission of the Southern Baptist Convention:

I am sure we are all aware of the seeming incongruity of a representative of Playboy *magazine speaking to an assemblage of representatives of the Southern Baptist Convention. I was intrigued by the invitation when it came last fall, though I was not surprised. I am grateful for your genuine and warm hospitality, and I am flattered (though again not surprised) by the implication that I would have something to say that could have meaning to you people. Both* Playboy *and the Baptists have indeed been considering many of the same issues and ethical problems; and even if we have not arrived at the same conclusions, I am impressed and gratified by your openness and willingness to listen to our views.*[4]

If a personal reference is sincere and appropriate, it will establish goodwill as well as gain attention. Avoid effusiveness and bubbly compliments, however, because listeners are quick to sense a lack of genuineness. At the other extreme, avoid apologizing. Don't say, "I don't know why I was picked to talk when others could have done it so much better" or, "Unaccustomed as I am to public speaking, ..." Apologetic beginnings suggest that your audience needn't waste time listening. Be cordial, sincere, and modest, but establish your authority and maintain control of the situation.

Asking a Rhetorical Question

Another way to open a speech is to ask a question or series of questions that get your audience to start thinking about your subject. For example, Nicholas Fynn of Ohio University opened a speech about free-burning of timberland as follows: "How many of you in this room have visited a National Park at one point in your life? Well, the majority of you are in good company."[5] Such a question introduces a topic gently and, with its direct reference to the audience, tends to engage your listeners.

Rhetorical questions are often used to forecast the development of the speech. Shannon Dyer of Southwest Baptist University in Missouri opened her speech by wondering out loud why whistleblowers didn't prevent the Challenger accident and the Union Carbide plant gas leak at Bhopal, India. She moved to the body of the speech with some rhetorical questions:

> *Thus, let's examine the dilemma of whistleblowers. First, who are whistleblowers? Then, what is the high personal price for their warnings? And finally, how can we protect these citizens—the watchdogs of our nation's safety?*[6]

Making a Startling Statement

On certain occasions, you may choose to open a speech with what is known as the "shock technique," making a startling statement of fact or opinion. This approach is especially useful when listeners are distracted, apathetic, or smug. For example, the Executive Director of the American Association for Retired Persons (AARP), after asking some rhetorical questions about health care, caught his listeners' attention with several startling statements:

> *Given what we're spending on health care, we should have the best system in the world.*
> *But the reality is that we don't.*
> *Thirty-seven million Americans have no health insurance protection whatsoever, and millions more are underinsured.*
> *We are twentieth—that's right, twentieth—among the nations of the world in infant mortality. The death rate for our black newborn children rivals that of Third World countries. And poor children in America, like their brothers and sisters in Third World nations, receive neither immunizations nor basic dental care.*
> *Those statistics give us a sense of the scope of the problem. What they don't adequately portray is the human factor—the pain and the suffering.*
> *While terminally ill patients may have their lives extended in intensive care units—at tremendous cost—middle-age minority women die of preventable and treatable cancer, hypertension and diabetes.*[7]

Avoid overusing shock techniques; your listeners will become very angry if you threaten them or attempt to disgust them. Don't let the technique backfire.

Using a Quotation

A quotation may be an excellent means of introducing a speech because it can prod listeners to think about something important, and it often captures an appropriate emotional tone. When Ronald W. Roskens was president of the University of Nebraska, he gave a speech on the topic of integrity to the Executive Club of Lincoln. Roskens opened his speech with a quotation:

Sir Harold Macmillan, the former British Prime Minister, once commented, "If you want to know the meaning of life . . . don't ask a politician."

[After discussing the then-current topic of Senator John Tower's troubles, Roskens continued.] *Excess, the traveling companion of moral malaise, has been tolerated, excused, ignored and otherwise buried for some time in our national life. The flotsam and jetsam of "It's OK, it doesn't matter" tends to collect layer upon layer until at last it bubbles to the surface at some inconvenient time, all toxic and sulphurous. Maybe it isn't any one act that is particularly poisonous—it is the layer upon layer that under pressure of its own weight, wells upward as a collective brew, malodorous and impossible to ignore.*[8]

Rosken's opening quotation made a strong statement about integrity, effectively piquing the interest of the audience and forcing listeners to react. Roskens could then proceed into a discussion of current examples of the national integrity crisis, confident that his audience was paying attention and pondering the topic of integrity.

Telling a Humorous Story

You can begin a speech by telling a funny story or relating a humorous experience. When doing so, however, observe three rules of communication:

1. *Be sure that the story is at least amusing,* if not absolutely funny; if it isn't, or if you tell it badly, you will embarrass yourself and your audience.
2. *Be sure that the story is relevant to your speech;* if its subject matter or punch line is not directly related to you, your topic, or at least your next couple of sentences, the story will appear to be a mere gimmick.
3. *Be sure that your story's in good taste;* in a public gathering, an off-color or doubtful story violates accepted standards of social behavior and can undermine an audience's respect for you (in general, you should avoid sexual, racist, antireligious, ageist, homophobic, and sexist humor).

All three of these rules were observed by George V. Grune, CEO of The Reader's Digest Association, Inc., as he delivered a commencement address to the Graduate School of Business at Rollins College:

This morning I'd like to talk about global marketing and the opportunities it offers American business today—and each of you individually. I understand international marketing was a favorite subject for many of you, and I suspect earning a living is uppermost on your minds, considering the occasion we celebrate today.

There is a story about a king who once called three wise men together and posed the same problem to each: "Our island is about to be inundated by a huge tidal wave. How would you advise the people?"

Humor can be used effectively in speech introductions. However, since humor can easily backfire, what three rules of communication should you observe whenever you use humor?

> *The first man thought long and hard and then said, "Sire I would lead the people to the highest spot on the island and then set up an all-night prayer vigil."*
>
> *The second said, "Master, I would advise the people to eat, drink and be merry for it would be their last opportunity to do so."*
>
> *The third wise man said, "Your majesty, if I were you, I would immediately advise the people to do their best to* learn how to live under water. *"*
>
> *As you progress in your business career, you'll face many challenges that will test your ability to in effect "learn how to live under water." Those who adapt and find new solutions to complex issues will be the most successful. And nowhere is that more true than in the global arena.*[9]

After relating his anecdote, Grune was ready to talk about the treacherous, difficult challenges facing students of international marketing.

Using an Illustration

A real-life incident, a passage from a novel or short story, or a hypothetical illustration can also get a speech off to a good start. As with a humorous story, an illustration should not only be interesting to the audience, but also relevant to your central idea or claim. Deanna Sellnow, a student at North

Dakota State University, used this technique to introduce a speech on private credit reporting bureaus:

> *John Pontier, of Boise, Idaho, was turned down for insurance because a reporting agency informed the company that he and his wife were addicted to narcotics, and his Taco Bell franchise had been closed down by the health board when dog food had been found mixed in with the tacos. There was only one small problem. The information was made up. His wife was a practicing Mormon who didn't touch a drink, much less drugs, and the restaurant had never been cited for a health violation.*[10]

Sometimes one of the seven approaches that we've discussed (see Figure 8.1) can be used alone; at other times, two or more of them can be combined. Whether used singly or in combination, however, the materials comprising your introduction should always be aimed at the same objective: arousing the attention and winning the goodwill and respect of your listeners. Moreover, those materials should be relevant to the purpose of your speech and should lead smoothly into the first of the major ideas that you wish to present; that is, your introduction should be an integral part of the speech. It should not be, for example, a "funny story" told merely to make an audience laugh, but it should be thematically and tonally tied to the body of the speech. Many speakers use a *forecast*—"In this speech, I will first ... and I will then ..."—in order to complete the task of orienting an audience before moving on to the substance of the discourse. A forecast is a relatively easy and yet effective way to make the transition from introductory notions to main concerns.

Figure 8.1 Types of Introductions and Conclusions

You can choose among different types of introductions and conclusions for your speeches. As you choose your introduction and conclusion, ask yourself if they orient your audience to your purposes and ideas and then summarize both at the end of the speech and if they signal clearly when your speech starts and ends.

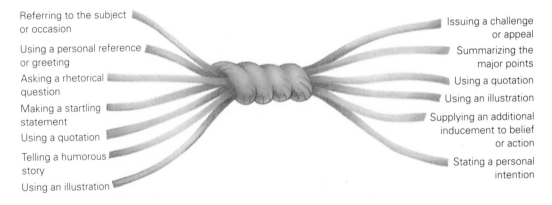

Referring to the subject or occasion

Using a personal reference or greeting

Asking a rhetorical question

Making a startling statement

Using a quotation

Telling a humorous story

Using an illustration

Issuing a challenge or appeal

Summarizing the major points

Using a quotation

Using an illustration

Supplying an additional inducement to belief or action

Stating a personal intention

Unacknowledged Hypothetical Illustrations

Most of us are suckers for a heart-rending human interest story. A speech against drunk driving might start with a gory story about the deaths resulting from teen drinking; a speech favoring euthanasia might begin with an account about a grandmother who dies a lingering, painful death; or a speech against deer hunting might begin with a reference to Bambi and his mother. It's easy to make up such stories or to find them in songs (e.g., "Teen Angel") or films (e.g., Madonna's redemptive death in *Dick Tracy*). The question is, should you ever make up stories but treat them as real?

In 1980, *Washington Post* reporter Janet Cooke won a Pulitzer Prize for a tear-jerking story about an 8-year-old homeless boy and heroin addict named "Jimmie." After Cooke received the award, someone accused her of making up the story. In response to the accusation, Cooke insisted that Jimmie was a composite character, based upon many addicts she had met. Even though Jimmie was fictitious, she insisted, his actions and most of his words were real. The Pulitzer Prize was taken away, although the committee acknowledged that writers often create such composite characters. Cooke's composite character, however, was just *too good* and she got caught.

You face the same dilemma Janet Cooke did. Suppose you're preparing a speech on reasons that students should join the Army or Navy reserve unit on campus. You want to stress the character-building effect of reserve experience, so, for your introduction and conclusion, you describe a fictitious student who, after joining the reserves, developed positive personal characteristics. If you acknowledge that she's a fictitious character, she'll lose her effectiveness as an example. Is it so wrong for you to pretend she's real? In general, what should be the limits to hypothetical illustrations?

When effective, your introductory remarks will both establish a common ground of interest and understanding as well as guide your audience toward the conclusion that you intend to reach.

ENDING YOUR SPEECH

Just as the introduction to the speech accomplishes specific purposes, so too does the ending, or conclusion. An effective conclusion should (a) *focus the attention of your audience,* (b) *establish a concluding mood,* and (c) *convey a sense of finality.*

The principal function of the conclusion of a speech is to focus your audience's attention on your central theme and purpose. If your speech has one dominant theme or idea, you will usually restate that point at the end in a manner that makes your meaning clear and forceful. If your speech is more complex, you may summarize its most important points or you may spell out the action or belief that these points suggest.

In addition to bringing the substance of the speech into final focus, your conclusion should aim at leaving the audience in the proper mood. If you want your listeners to express vigorous enthusiasm, you should stimulate that feeling in your closing remarks. If you want them to reflect thoughtfully on what you have said, you should encourage a calm, judicious attitude. Decide whether the response you seek is a mood of serious determination or lighthearted levity, of warm sympathy or utter disgust, of thoughtful consideration or vigorous action. Then, plan to end your speech in a way that will create that mood.

Finally, a good ending should convey a sense of completeness and finality. Listeners grow restless and annoyed when they are given reason to feel that the speaker has finished, only to hear him or her ramble on some more. Avoid false endings; tie the threads of thought together so that the pattern of your speech is brought clearly to completion:

1. Tell your listeners what you are going to say.
2. Say it.
3. Tell them what you said.
4. Sit down.

Speakers employ many strategies to convey a sense of closure to their speeches. Six conclusion techniques are used regularly:

1. Issuing a challenge or appeal
2. Summarizing
3. Using a quotation
4. Using an illustration
5. Supplying an additional inducement to belief or action
6. Stating a personal intention

Issuing a Challenge or Appeal

A speaker may conclude a speech by issuing a challenge or an appeal to the listeners, requesting support or action, or reminding the listeners of their responsibilities. Allen A. Schumer, Senior Vice President for Operations of the Miller Brewing Company, urged his audience to establish employee involvement programs in their companies and related some of his own company's experiences with such programs. He then issued a challenge:

> As I mentioned at the beginning, you are the people on the front lines of the Employee Involvement Revolution. If you win this battle of getting employee involvement accepted as a company concept, your company wins. And if your company or organization succeeds, we all succeed.
>
> It won't happen overnight, but next week may be too late in these days of economic and corporate uncertainty. Any journey, no matter how long, must begin with a first step. I encourage you to take that first step now! Believe me, it's a step you won't regret. I promise![11]

Summarizing the Major Points or Ideas

In an informative speech, a summary allows the audience to pull together the main strands of information and to evaluate the significance of the speech. In a persuasive speech, a summary gives you a final opportunity to present, in brief form, the major points of your argument. For example, Everette E. Dennis, Executive Director of the Gannett Center for Media Studies, tried in 1988 to persuade the Virginia Associated Press Newspaper Council to alter its methods of covering presidential campaigns. He gave many examples of reporting practices that lead to what he considers unfair reporting. To pull his ideas together, he used this summary:

> *To me fairness means:*
>
> 1. *Coherent presentation of the facts, of the basic elements and information required to know and understand the subject being reported.*
> 2. *A context and background that provides connections to the past and to concurrent issues, events and personalities.*
> 3. *More systematic information-gathering, making as efficient use as possible of many sources of information and in enough depth to enhance understanding. No critical stone should be left unturned or, if it is, the reader or viewer should be told.*
> 4. *Quality control of information. The role of the news media is to distinguish the important from the unimportant, reputable sources from unreliable ones. The media should make it clear whether information is being cited and quoted with approval or not.*
> 5. *More equitable sense-making and interpretation.*
>
> *There is a profound need for the reporter and editor to be a mapmaker, to offer a perspective on the many viewpoints and interests that shape the news and to render those voices with the right intensity and pitch.*
>
> *Finally, I think we need to reconcile our standards of news and the public's sense of fair play.*[12]

Using a Quotation

A quotation is often used to end a speech. Poetry may capture the essence of your message in uplifting language. Quoted prose, if the author is credible, can go further, gathering additional support for your central idea or claim. Notice how Tim Dolin of West Virginia's Marshall University was able to add the credibility of Senator John Glenn to his plea for public regulation of nuclear weapons waste and disposal:

> *After looking at the poor management within the nuclear weapons cycle, its impact on us and how the problem can be solved, it becomes obvious something must be done. As Senator John Glenn said, "The costs of cleaning up these sites will be extraordinarily high, but the costs of doing nothing will be higher. After all, what good does it do to protect ourselves from the Soviets by building nuclear weapons if we poison ourselves in the process."*[13]

Using an Illustration

Just as an illustration may be used to set the tone and direction of a speech, so too may it be used to conclude your conversation with an audience. Your illustration should be both *inclusive* and *conclusive*—inclusive of the main focus or thrust of your speech and conclusive in tone and impact. Sometimes the same illustration can be used to tie together a whole speech. This is what Michael Twitchell, a student in a speaking contest, did when talking about the causes and effects of depression:

Opening

Have you ever felt like you were the little Dutch boy who stuck his finger in the leaking dike? You waited and waited but the help never came. The leak became worse and the water rushed around you and swept you away. As you fought the flood, gasping and choking for air, you realized that the flood was inside yourself. You were drowning and dying in your own mind. According to the American Journal of Psychiatry, *as many as half the people in this room will be carried away by this devastating flood. What is this disaster? Mental depression.*

Closing

Let's go back to my illustration of the little Dutch boy. He was wise to take action and put his finger in the dike, preventing the flood. In the case of depression, each one of us must be like the little Dutch boy—willing to get involved and control the harmful effects of depression.[14]

Supplying an Additional Inducement to Belief or Action

Sometimes you may conclude a speech by quickly reviewing the leading ideas presented in the body and then supplying one or more additional reasons for endorsing the belief or taking the proposed action. In his speech, Michael Twitchell spoke at length about the devastating effects of depression. After proposing numerous reasons for people to get involved in the battle, Twitchell offered an additional inducement in the conclusion to his speech:

Why should you really care? Why is it important? The depressed person may be someone you know—it could be you. If you know what is happening, you can always help. I wish I had known what depression was in March of 1978. You see, when I said David Twitchell could be my father, I was making a statement of fact. David is my father. I am his son. My family wasn't saved; perhaps now yours can be.[15]

Stating a Personal Intention

Stating your own intention to adopt the action or attitude you recommend in your speech is particularly effective when your prestige with the audience is high, or when you have presented a concrete proposal needing immediate action. By professing your intention to take immediate action, you and your ideas gain credibility. Consider the following example of a conclusion in which a speaker states a personal intention to do what the speech urges listeners to do:

Today I have illustrated how important healthy blood is to human survival and how blood banks work to ensure the possibility and availability of blood for each of us. It is not a coincidence that I speak on this vital topic on the same day that the local Red Cross Bloodmobile is visiting campus. I want to urge each of you to ensure your future and mine by stopping at the Student Center today or tomorrow to make your donation. The few minutes that it takes may add up to a lifetime for a person in need. To illustrate how firmly I believe in this opportunity to help, I'm going to the Student Center to give my donation as soon as this class is over. I invite any of you who feel this strongly to join me.

Regardless of the means you choose for closing your speech, remember that your conclusion should focus the attention of your listeners on the central theme you've developed. In addition, a good conclusion should be consistent with the mood or tenor of your speech and should convey a sense of completeness and finality.

Speakers sometimes conclude their speeches by indicating their personal intentions to take action. This type of conclusion is especially effective when the speaker is highly regarded by listeners or when immediate actions are urged. Can you think of specific situations when this type of conclusion would work well?

FITTING THE BEGINNING AND ENDING TO THE BODY OF YOUR SPEECH

In Chapter 7 we considered various patterns for outlining and developing the body, or substance, of a speech. When the introduction and conclusion are added to the outline, the completed structure should look something like this:

Introduction

I. _____

II. _____

    A. _____

    B. _____

Body

I. _____

    A. _____

    B. _____

        1. _____

        2. _____

II. _____

III. _____

Conclusion

I. _____

II. _____

    A. _____

    B. _____

Sample Outline for an Introduction and a Conclusion

An introduction and conclusion for the classroom speech on MADD and SADD, outlined in Chapter 7 (pages 140–142), might take the following form. Notice that the speaker uses one of the factors of attention—suspense—in combination with startling statements to lead the audience into the subject and concludes by combining a final illustration with a statement of personal intention.

FRIENDS DON'T LET FRIENDS DRIVE DRUNK

Introduction

I. Many of you have seen the "Black Gash"—the Vietnam War memorial in Washington, D.C.
   A. It contains the names of more than 40,000 Americans who gave their lives in Southeast Asia between 1961 and 1973.
   B. We averaged over 3000 war dead a year during that anguishing period.

II. Today, another enemy stalks Americans.
   A. The enemy kills, not 3000 per year, but over 20,000 citizens every 12 months.
   B. The enemy is not hiding in jungles but can be found in every community in the country.
   C. The enemy kills, not with bayonets and bullets, but with bottles and bumpers.

III. Today, I want to talk about two organizations that are trying to contain and finally destroy the killer.
   A. Every TV station in this town carries a public service ad that says "Friends Don't Let Friends Drive Drunk."
   B. In response to the menace of the drunk driver, two national organizations—Mothers Against Drunk Driving and Students Against Drunk Driving—have been formed and are working even in this community to make the streets safe for you and me.
   C. [Central Idea] MADD and SADD are achieving their goals with your help.
   D. To help you understand what these familiar organizations do, first I'll tell you something about the founders of MADD and SADD; then, I'll describe their operations; finally, I'll mention some of the ways community members get involved with them.

[Body]

Conclusion

I. Today, I've talked briefly about the Lightners and their goals for MADD and SADD, their organizational techniques, and ways you can get involved.

II. The work of MADD and SADD volunteers—even on our campus, as I'm sure you've seen their posters in the Union—is being carried out to keep you alive.
   A. You may not think you need to be involved, but remember, after midnight one in every five or fewer drivers on the road is probably drunk, so you could be involved whether you want to be or not.

B. That certainly was the case with Julie Smeiser, a member of our sophomore class, who just last Friday was hit by a drunk driver when going home for the weekend.

III. If people don't take action, we could build a new "Black Gash"—this time for victims of drunks—every two years, and soon fill Washington, D.C., with monuments to needless suffering.

A. Such monuments would be grim reminders of our unwillingness to respond to enemies at home with the same intensity with which we attacked enemies abroad.

B. Better would be a positive response to groups such as MADD and SADD, who are attacking the enemy on several fronts at once in a war on motorized murder.

IV. If you're interested in learning more about SADD and MADD, stop by Room 324 in the Union tonight at 7:30 to hear the president of the local chapter of SADD talk about this year's activities—I'll be there; please join me.

CHAPTER SUMMARY

1. Introductions should gain attention, secure goodwill, and prepare an audience for what you will be saying.

2. Types of introductions include (a) referring to the subject or occasion, (b) using a personal reference or greeting, (c) asking a rhetorical question, (d) making a startling statement of fact or opinion, (e) using a quotation, (f) telling a humorous story, and (g) using an illustration.

3. In concluding your speech, you should attempt to focus the thoughts of your audience on your central theme, maintain the tenor of your speech, and convey a sense of finality.

4. Techniques for ending a speech include (a) issuing a challenge or appeal, (b) summarizing the major points or ideas, (c) using a quotation, (d) using an illustration, (e) supplying an additional inducement to belief or action, and (f) stating a personal intention.

5. Once you have prepared your introduction and conclusion, fit them to the body of your speech with appropriate transitions.

SKILLBUILDING ACTIVITIES

1. In class groups, devise *two* excellent introductory strategies for the following speakers to use in the situations noted:

Speaker	*Situation*
Phyllis Schlafly	Opening session of a Pro-Life conference
Roger Staubach	Banquet sponsored by Fellowship of Christian Athletes
Jimmy Carter	Seminar on achieving peace in the Middle East
Barbara Bush	Keynote for an international conference on literacy

2. To review the different ways to begin and end a speech, choose a topic and prepare two different one-minute introductions and conclusions. You will deliver these in an impromptu round of classroom speeches. The class will analyze the varying approaches and compare their strengths and weaknesses.

3. Participate in a class discussion on introductions and conclusions. One student will suggest a topic for a speech. A second student will suggest an appropriate introduction and conclusion and justify those choices. A third student will challenge those selections and propose alternative introductions and/or conclusions. Continue this discussion until everyone proposes and defends introductions and conclusions that could be appropriate to the speech topics discussed.

REFERENCES

1. From Russell J. Love, "The Barriers Come Tumbling Down," Harris-Hillman School Commencement, Nashville, Tenn. (May 21, 1981). Reprinted by permission.

2. Arthur M. Schlesinger, Jr., "America, the Arts and the Future," *Representative American Speeches 1987–88,* Owen Peterson, ed. (New York: H. W. Wilson Company, 1988), 60:127.

3. Liz Carpenter, "Reflections from the Grassroots," *Representative American Speeches 1987–88,* Owen Peterson, ed. (New York: H. W. Wilson Company, 1988), 60:181–182.

4. Anson Mount, Manger of Public Affairs for *Playboy* magazine, from speech presented to the Christian Life Commission of Southern Baptist Convention in *Contemporary American Speeches,* 5th ed., Wil A. Linkugel et al., eds. (Dubuque, Iowa: Kendall/Hunt, 1982).

5. Nicholas Fynn, "The Free Burn Fallacy," *Winning Orations 1989.* Reprinted by permission of Larry Schnoor, Executive Secretary, Interstate Oratorical Association, Mankato State University, Mankato, Minn.

6. Shannon Dyer, "The Dilemma of Whistleblowers," *Winning Orations 1989.* Reprinted by permission of Larry Schnoor, Executive Secretary, Interstate Oratorical Association, Mankato State University, Mankato, Minn.

7. From Horace B. Deets, "Health Care for a Caring America: We Must Develop a Better System," *Vital Speeches of the Day,* August 1, 1989. Reprinted by permission of the author.

8. Ronald W. Roskens, "Integrity: An Event Whose Time Has Come," *Vital Speeches of the Day,* vol. LV (June 1, 1989). Reprinted by permission of *Vital Speeches of the Day.*

9. George V. Grune, "Global Marketing: Global Opportunities," *Vital Speeches of the Day,* vol. LV (July 15, 1989). Reprinted by permission of *Vital Speeches of the Day.*

10. Deanna Sellnow, "Have You Checked Lately?," *Winning Orations.* Reprinted by permission of Larry Schnoor, Executive Secretary, Interstate Oratorical Association, Mankato State University, Mankato, Minn.

11. Allen A. Schumer, "Employee Involvement," *Vital Speeches of the Day,* vol. LIV (July 1, 1988). Reprinted by permission of *Vital Speeches of the Day.*

12. Everette E. Dennis, "Memo to the Press," *Vital Speeches of the Day,* vol. LIV (June 1, 1988). Reprinted by permission of *Vital Speeches of the Day.*

13. Tim Dolin, "The Hidden Legacy of the Arms Race," *Winning Orations 1989,* reprinted by permission of Larry Schnoor, Executive Secretary, Interstate Oratorical Association, Mankato State University, Mankato, Minn.

14. Michael A. Twitchell, "The Flood Gates of the Mind," *Winning Orations.* Reprinted by permission of Larry Schnoor, Executive Secretary, Interstate Oratorical Association, Mankato State University, Mankato, Minn.

15. Twitchell, "The Flood Gates of the Mind."

PART THREE

Presenting Your Speech

CHAPTER NINE

Wording Your Speech

*W*alter's family hosted Ricardo, a foreign exchange student from Honduras, for the academic year. Walter's family thought Ricardo's stay would be a good opportunity to learn Spanish. They were right. First, they began to associate Spanish words with objects and concepts—casa *with* house, dos *with* two, and blanca *with* white. But the family had a lot more to learn; knowing the Spanish equivalents of objects was not enough. They hadn't, for example, learned which nouns had masculine and which had feminine gender. In addition, the family was unaware of cultural implications of certain Spanish expressions such as "haciendo el oso," which literally means "playing the bear," but which refers to a traditional courtship ritual dictating that women must always be chaperoned. Walter's family learned a great deal about their own culture as well as Ricardo's when they tried to explain phrases such as "chill out" and "make a beeline" to Ricardo.

As Walter and his family discovered, language functions on multiple levels. Language is both a *referential* and a *relational* medium of communication. Through its direct, or denotative, aspects, language allows you to *refer* to persons, places, and things; through its indirect, or connotative, aspects, it signals relationships between you and your audience. **Denotative meaning** is the direct, literal meaning of words; **connotative meaning** is their indirect, emotional associations. It's not enough to know the words; you must also understand how language reflects your sense of reality—your culture and thinking.

In the next three chapters we'll turn our attention to the encoding or deciphering of these messages. **Encoding** occurs when you put ideas into words and actions. This includes your choice of language, use of visual aids, and even bodily and vocal behaviors. In this chapter, we'll focus on making effective word choices, selecting an appropriate style, and choosing among rhetorical strategies. To put your ideas into language is to stylize them. A **speaking style** is the message that results when a series of denotative word choices and their corresponding connotations are combined with verbal signals to establish a social-psychological relationship between the speaker and audience.

MAKING EFFECTIVE WORD CHOICES

Communicating with precision isn't easy. Yet, speakers can clarify their messages if they keep in mind five features of effective word choice: (a) *accuracy*, (b) *simplicity*, (c) *coherence*, (d) *language intensity*, and (e) *appropriateness*.

Accuracy

Careful word choice is an essential ingredient to effectively transmitting your meaning to an audience. If you tell a hardware store clerk, "I broke the dohickey on my hootenanny and I need a thingamajig to fix it," you had better have the hootenanny in your hand or the clerk won't understand. When you speak, your goal is precision. You should leave no doubt about your meaning.

Words are symbols that represent concepts or objects. Your listener may attach a meaning to your words that is quite different from the one you intended. This misinterpretation becomes more likely as your words become more abstract. *Democracy,* for example, doesn't mean the same thing to a citizen of the United States as it does to a citizen of the Soviet Union. In fact, *democracy* will probably elicit different meanings from Americans who belong to the Moral Majority than it will from those who belong to the Libertarian Party.

Students of general semantics, the study of words or symbols and their effect on human behavior, continually warn us that many errors in thinking and communication arise from treating words as if they were the actual conditions, processes, or objects. Words are not fixed and timeless in meaning.[1]

To avoid vagueness, choose words that express the exact shade of meaning you wish to communicate. You might say that an object shines, but the object might also *glow, glitter, glisten, gleam, flare, blaze, glare, shimmer, glimmer, flicker, sparkle, flash,* and *beam.* Which word allows you to more precisely describe the object?

Simplicity

"Speak," said Lincoln, "so that the most lowly can understand you, and the rest will have no difficulty." This advice is as relevant today as when Lincoln offered it. Because modern electronic media reach audiences more varied than any Lincoln imagined, we have even more reason to follow his advice today. Say *learn* rather than *ascertain, try* rather than *endeavor, use* rather than *utilize, help* rather than *facilitate*. Never use a longer or less familiar word when a simple one is just as clear. Billy Sunday, the famous evangelist, illustrated the effectiveness of familiar words in this example:

> *If a man were to take a piece of meat and smell it and look disgusted, and his little boy were to say, "What's the matter with it, Pop?" and he were to say, "It is undergoing a process of decomposition in the formation of new chemical compounds," the boy would be all in. But if the father were to say, "It's rotten," then the boy would understand and hold his nose. "Rotten" is a good Anglo-Saxon word, and you do not have to go to the dictionary to find out what it means.*[2]

Simplicity doesn't mean simplistic; no one is suggesting that you talk down to your audience. We are only suggesting that you consider how short, direct words convey precise, concrete meanings.

Coherence

People listening to you speak don't have the luxury of reviewing the points you make as they do when they are reading an essay that you wrote; nor are they able as you speak to perceive punctuation marks that might help them distinguish one idea from another. In order to be understood, oral communication requires **coherence,** or the logical connection of ideas. To achieve coherence, you must use **signposts** or words or phrases—such as *first, next,* or *as a result*—that help listeners follow the movement of your ideas. Signposts such as, "the history of this invention begins in . . . ," also provide clues to the overall message structure.

Summaries, just as signposts do, provide clues to the overall speech structure. Preliminary and final summaries are especially helpful in outlining the major topics of the speech. **Preliminary summaries** (also called *forecasts* or *previews*) precede the development of the body of the speech, usually forming part of the introduction; **final summaries** follow the body of the speech, usually forming part of the conclusion. Consider the following examples:

Preliminary Summaries
Today I am going to talk about three aspects of. . . .
There are four major points to be covered in. . . .

Final Summaries
I have talked about three aspects of. . . .
These four major points—[restate them]—are the. . . .

The history of the issue can be divided into two periods. . . .	The two periods just covered—[restate them]—represent the significant. . . .

In addition to these summarizing strategies, signposts may be **connectives,** or transitions—linking phrases that move an audience from one idea to another. The following are *connective* statements that you might use:

* *In the first place. . . . The second point is. . . .*
* *In addition to. . . , notice that. . . .*
* *Now look at it from a different angle: . . .*
* *You must keep these three things in mind in order to understand the importance of the fourth: . . .*
* *What was the result?*
* *Turning now to. . . .*

The preceding signposts are *neutral*—they tell an audience that another idea is coming, but don't indicate whether it is similar, different, or more important. You can improve the coherence of your message by indicating the precise relationships among ideas. Those relationships include *parallel/hierarchical, similar/different,* and *coordinate/subordinate* relationships. Here are some examples:

* Parallel: *Not only . . . but also. . . .*
* Hierarchical: *More important than these. . . .*
* Different: *In contrast. . . .*
* Similar: *Similar to this. . . .*
* Coordinated: *One must consider X, Y, and Z. . . .*
* Subordinated: *On the next level is. . . .*

Preliminary or final summaries and signposts are important to your audience. The summaries give listeners an overall sense of your entire message; if listeners can easily see the structure, they'll better understand and remember your speech. The signposts lead your listeners step-by-step through the speech, signaling specific relationships between ideas.

Language Intensity

As a speaker, you can communicate your feelings about ideas and objects through your word choices. That is, you can communicate your *attitude* toward your subject by choosing words that show how you feel. For example, consider these attitudinally weighted terms:

Highly Positive	*Relatively Neutral*	*Highly Negative*
savior	G.I.	enemy
patriot	soldier	baby-killer
freedom fighter	combatant	foreign devil

Doublespeak

Advertisers and politicians are often accused of using words that deceive or mislead. Some do use trigger words or labels designed to solicit knee-jerk reactions from consumers and voters. Think of any recent advertising or political campaign. You can probably identify several key terms designed to capture public sentiments. *Political liberal,* for instance, was once a positive label. In the 1988 national presidential campaign, *political liberal* became associated with negative attributes. *Liberal* connoted the big spender—someone who wasted public energy and tax dollars on unrealistic schemes.

You can probably identify hundreds of words or phrases used to disguise facts. The Reagan administration didn't raise taxes, but did pursue *revenue enhancement* through *user fees.* People below the poverty line are *fiscal underachievers.* Nuclear weapons are labeled *radiation enhancement devices* and *peacekeepers.* Departments of defense are actually devoted to conducting war. And, the 1984 invasion of Grenada was officially a *pre-dawn vertical insertion.* Some language usage makes the unpleasant seem good and the positive appear negative. Language can shield us from the reality it represents.

Such namecalling is by no means limited to politicians. Advertisers market "new" and "improved" products. We're tantalized with *real faux pearls* and *genuine imitation leather.* Advertisers exploit our health consciousness with *low cholesterol* and *high fiber* ingredients. Now everything from breakfast cereals to beer is made with oat bran—at least until the next food fad hits the supermarket shelves.

The potential for exploiting language is a part of the persuasive process. Take a few moments and think about the following uses of language:

1. Suppose that you notice biased language in an article you're reading as you research a speech topic. Should you cite the article as supporting material in your speech?

2. You genuinely believe in your recommendations for a solution to the problems you outline in a speech and want to convince your listeners that they need to sign a petition for change. Should you state your action step in language that is highly distorted?

3. Should you ever use racy, obscene, or questionable language during a speech? Does it affect the relationship you establish with your listeners?

4. Is it ever fair to call someone who is not present a *crook* or attach a similar label to them?

5. Do you think language can obscure our understanding of reality? Under what circumstances do you think this happens? Should anything be done to make language more honest? What can be done to accomplish this?

These nine terms are organized by their intensity, ranging from the highly positive *savior* to the highly negative *foreign devil.* Notice the religious connotations present in these extreme examples of language intensity.

How intense should your language be? Communication scholar John Waite Bowers has suggested a useful rule of thumb: let your language be, roughly, one step more intense than the position or attitude held by your audience.[3] For example, if your audience is already committed to your negative position on tax reform, then you can choose intensely negative words, such as *regressive* and *stifling*. If your audience is uncommitted, you should opt for comparatively neutral words, such as *deficits* and *brackets*. And, if your audience is in favor of tax changes, you can use positive words, such as *progressive* and *stimulating*. Intense language can generate intense reactions, but only if you match your word choices to your listeners' attitudes.

Appropriateness

Besides being accurate, clear, coherent, and properly intense, your language should be appropriate to the speech topic and situation. Solemn occasions call for language that is restrained and dignified; joyful occasions call for word choices that are informal and lively. You wouldn't use slang in a speech at a memorial service and you shouldn't present a humorous after-dinner speech in a somber style, unless you're trying to be ironic. Suit your language to the tone of the occasion.

You must also make sure that your language is appropriate to your audience. Before you use informal language, check to see who is listening. Informal language, including slang, quickly goes out of style. *Gee whiz, wow, good grief, far out, awesome,* and *radical* became popular at different times. *Far out* would sound silly in a speech to your peers and *radical* would sound ridiculous to an audience of senior citizens.

SELECTING AN APPROPRIATE STYLE: STRATEGIC DECISIONS

We've discussed the general qualities of effective word choice—simplicity, coherence, language intensity, and appropriateness. Next, we'll consider the aspects of speaking style that control audience members' impressions of you as a person, the nature of your message, and even the occasion itself. The combination of these aspects of oral communication is generally called *tone*. **Tone** is the predominant effect or character of the speech. (See the discussion of contextual rules, page 13.)

While tone is an elusive quality of speech, you may, nevertheless, identify some of its primary features. We'll pay special attention to four dimensions of tone: *written vs. oral style, serious vs. humorous atmosphere, gendered vs. gender-neutral language,* and *propositional vs. narrative form.*

Written vs. Oral Style

Generally, spoken language is uncomplicated; it has to be since we use it every day—at the grocery store, over the back fence, around the supper table, and in the street. But some spoken language is complicated and formal; this is the type of language many people use when giving a speech. There are two types of language: *oral style* and *written style*. While **oral style** is informal and imprecise (typical of conversation), **written style** is formal and precise (typical of written works). Consider the following examples of written and oral style:

Written Style	Oral Style
Remit the requested amount forthwith.	Hand over the cash.
Will you be having anything else?	Whutkinahgitcha?

Most of us compose speeches in a written, rather than an oral, style. This is more likely if we write out the whole speech before giving it. The result is stilted and stiff, and is likely to read as follows:

> *I am most pleased that you could come this morning. I would like to use this opportunity to discuss with you a subject of inestimable importance to us all—the impact of inflationary spirals on students enrolled in institutions of higher education.*

Translated into an oral style, this speech excerpt would run as follows:

> *Thanks for coming. I'd like to talk today about a problem for all of us—the rising cost of going to college.*

Notice how much more natural the second version sounds. The first is wordy—filled with prepositional phrases, complex words, and formal sentences. The second contains shorter sentences and simpler vocabulary, and it addresses the audience directly.

For most speech occasions, you should cultivate an oral style. On rare, highly ceremonial occasions, you may decide to read from a prepared text. However, even then, you should strive for oral style.[4]

Serious vs. Humorous Atmosphere

You cultivate the atmosphere of the speaking occasion largely through your speaking style. In a graduation speech or an awards banquet address, you want to encourage the personal reflection of your listeners. But, at a fraternity gathering or holiday celebration, you want to create a social, interactive atmosphere.

Sometimes the atmosphere of the occasion dictates what speaking style should be used. You don't expect a light, humorous speaking style during a funeral. Even so, sometimes a minister, priest, or rabbi will tell a heartwarming story about the deceased. Yet, the overall tone of a funeral eulogy is somber. In contrast, a speech after a football victory, election win, or successful fund drive is seldom solemn. Victory speeches are times for celebration and unity.

Keep in mind that humorous speeches can have serious goals. As we will note in Chapter 15, even speeches designed to entertain have worthy purposes. These speeches can be persuasive and they can be given in grave

Getting someone to see your point of view often depends on strategic rhetorical decisions. What choices could be involved here?

earnestness. The political satirist who throws humorous but barbed comments at pompous, silly, or corrupt politicians aims at amusing the audience as well as at achieving political reform.

The speaking **atmosphere** is the mind-set or mental attitude that you attempt to create in your audience. A serious speaker urging future doctors to remember the things that are most important in life might say, "Rank your values and live by them." That same idea expressed by actor Alan Alda sounded more humorous:

> *We live in a time that seems to be split about its values. In fact it seems to be schizophrenic.*
>
> *For instance, if you pick up a magazine like* Psychology Today, *you're liable to see an article like "White Collar Crime: It's More Widespread Than You Think." Then in the back of the magazine they'll print an advertisement that says, "We'll write your doctoral thesis for 25 bucks." You see how values are eroding? I mean a doctoral thesis ought to go for at least a C-note.* [5]

Which atmosphere is preferable? Your answer depends on the speaking situation, your speech purpose, and your listeners' expectations.

Gendered vs. Gender-Neutral Nouns and Pronouns

While words themselves are not intrinsically good or bad, they can communicate values or attitudes to your listeners. One word may have a positive connotation; another may have a negative connotation. Gender-linked words, particularly nouns and pronouns, require special attention. **Gender-linked words** are those that directly or indirectly identify males or females—*policeman, washerwoman, poet,* and *poetess.* Pronouns such as *he* and *she* and adjectives such as *his* and *her* are also obviously gender-linked words. **Gender-neutral words** do not directly or indirectly denote males or females—*chairperson, police officer,* or *firefighter.*

Since the 1960s and the advent of the women's liberation movement, consciousness of gendered language has gradually surfaced. The question of whether language use affects culture and socialization is still being debated. However, as a speaker you must be careful to not alienate your audience or to unconsciously propagate stereotypes through your use of language. As a speaker there are three troublesome issues that affect you:

1. *Inaccurately excluding members of one sex.* Some uses of gendered pronouns inaccurately reflect social-occupational conditions in the world—"A nurse sees *her* patients eight hours a day, but a doctor sees *his* for only ten minutes." Many women are doctors and many men are nurses. Most audience members are aware of this and may be displeased if they feel that you're stereotyping roles in the medical profession.

2. *Stereotyping male and female psychological or social characteristics.* Real men never cry. A woman's place is in the home. The Marines are looking for a few good men. Sugar 'n spice 'n everything nice—that's what little girls are made of. Falling back on these stereotypes gets speakers into trouble with audiences, both male and female. In these days of raised consciousness, audiences are insulted to hear such misinformed assertions. In addition, these stereotypes stop you from seeing potential in individuals whose talents are not limited by their gender.

3. *Using gendered nouns inappropriately.* Many occupation-related nouns—*mailman, stewardess, policeman*—came into parlance when one gender dominated such positions. The *-ess* ending—Jewess, mistress of ceremonies, actress, and poetess—is a carryover from times when gender inflections were a part of our language. Many roles in the past had gender associated with them as well; *chairman* is an obvious example. If you use gender inflections, listeners may accuse you of social insensitivity. They may be sidetracked by your reluctance to say *mail carrier* or *chairperson* instead of listening to the point you're making.

These three problem areas demand your attention. A speaker who habitually uses sexist language is guilty of ignoring important speaking conventions that have taken shape over the last several decades.

How can you avoid sexist language? Here are four easy ways:

1. *Speak in the plural.* Say, "Bankers are often. . . . *They* face. . . ."
This tactic is often sufficient to make your languge gender-neutral.

2. *Say* he or she *when you must use a singular subject.* Say, "A student majoring in business is required to sign up for an internship. *He or she* can. . . ." This strategy works well as long as you don't overdo it. If you find yourself cluttering sentences with "he or she," switch to the plural.

3. *Remove gender inflections.* It's painless to say *firefighter* instead of *fireman, chair* or *chairperson* instead of *chairman,* and *tailor* instead of *seamstress.* Gender inflections can usually be removed without affecting your speech.

4. *Use gender-specific pronouns for gender-specific processes, people, or activities.* It is acceptable to talk about a mother as *her* or a current or former president of the United States as *him.* Men do not naturally bear children and women have not yet been elected to the White House.

Ultimately, the search for gender-neutral idioms is an affirmation of mutual respect and a recognition of equal worth and the essential dignity of individuals. Gender differences are important in many aspects of life, but when they dominate public talk, they're ideologically oppressive. Be gender neutral in public talk to remove barriers to effective communication.[6]

Propositional vs. Narrative Form

Finally, speaking styles can differ greatly in another important way: some styles are highly *propositional,* while other styles are highly *narrative.* When using a **propositional form** of speaking, the speaker offers a series of claims and supports each one with evidence. When using a **narrative form,** the speaker offers a story that contains a compelling message or moral.

Suppose that you wished to persuade your classmates to make regular appointments to see their academic advisers. Such a speech, in propositional form, might resemble this:

I. You ought to see your adviser regularly because he or she can check on your graduation requirements.
   A. Advisers have been trained to understand this school's requirements.
   B. Advisers also probably helped write the departmental requirements for your major.
II. You ought to see your adviser regularly because he or she usually can tell you something about careers in your field.
   A. Most faculty members at this school regularly attend professional meetings and find out what kinds of schools and companies are hiring in your field.
   B. Most faculty here have been around a long time and have seen what kinds of academic backgrounds get their advisees good jobs after graduation.
III. You ought to see your adviser regularly so that you can check out your own hopes and fears with someone.

A. Good advisers help you to decide whether you want to continue with your major.

B. And, if you do decide to change majors, your adviser will often help you to find another adviser in another department.

This same speech, cast into narrative form, evolves as a story:

I. I thought I could handle my own advising around this school, and that attitude really got me into trouble.
   A. I could read, and I thought I knew what I wanted to take.
   B. I decided to steer my own course, and here's what happened.
II. At first, I was happy, taking any old course I wanted to.
   A. I skipped the regular laboratory sciences (Chemistry, Biology, Physics) and took "Science and Society" instead.
   B. I didn't take Statistics to meet my math requirement but instead slipped into Remedial Algebra.
   C. I piled up the hours in physical education so that I could have a nice grade-point average to show my parents.
III. But when I was half done with my program I realized a few things.
   A. I hadn't met about half of the general education graduation requirements.
   B. I wanted to go into Nursing.
IV. So, last year I had to go back to freshman- and sophomore-level courses even though I was technically a junior.
   A. I was back taking the basic science and math courses.
   B. I was still trying to complete the social science and humanities requirements.
V. In all, I'm now in my fifth year of college, with at least one more term to go.
   A. My classmates who used advisers have graduated.
   B. I suggest you follow their examples rather than mine if you want to save time and money.

Most of the time, you'll rely on propositional forms of speaking; most audiences expect it. But, in some situations, a story will allow you to make your points equally well—if not better. If you're a good storyteller, you can enchant your listeners and make it easier for them to remember your ideas.

Selecting an appropriate style is a matter of assessing yourself, your audience, the situation or context, and your speaking purposes. A thorough assessment of these variables will help you to select an appropriate style—written or oral, serious or humorous, gendered or gender-neutral, and propositional or narrative.

CHOOSING RHETORICAL STRATEGIES

The general atmosphere of the speech is one facet of an appropriate speaking style. Your speaking style also depends, in part, on rhetorical strategies.

Rhetorical strategies are word and phrase choices intended to control the impact of the speech. There are countless rhetorical strategies available to you. We will focus on four of the most common: (a) *definitions*, (b) *restatement*, (c) *imagery*, and (d) *metaphor*.

Definitions

Audience members need to understand the fundamental concepts of your speech. You can't expect them to understand your ideas if your language is unfamiliar. Eight types of definitions are useful to speakers.

Defining from Dictionaries

A dictionary or *reportive* definition categorizes an object or concept and specifies its characteristics: "An orange is a *fruit* (category) that is *round, orange* in color, and a member of the *citrus family* (characteristics)." A dictionary definition indicates how people in general use a word.

Dictionary definitions sometimes help you to learn an unfamiliar word. Normally, dictionary definitions must be followed by other kinds of definitions that more precisely clarify a concept. You certainly would not depend on *Webster's Third International Dictionary* to define *foreclosure* or *liability* for a presentation on real estate law. For this technical application, sources such as *Black's Law Dictionary* or *Guide to American Law* are more highly respected.

Defining in Your Own Words

Occasionally, a word has so many meanings that you have to choose one. If that is the case, you must use a *stipulative definition* to orient your listeners

Definitions help you grasp concepts. What kinds of definitions are probably being used in this situation?

to your subject matter. A stipulative definition designates the way a word will be used in a certain context. You might say, "By liberal arts education I mean. . ." or you might use an expert's stipulative definition or *authoritative definition* such as, "Harriet Smith, president of this university, defines a liberal arts education as one in which students are taught not merely technical operations and job-related skills but also ways of thinking and reasoning. Today, I want to explore that definition and what it means to you in your four years here."

Defining Negatively

You can further clarify a term or concept by telling your audience how you are *not* going to use the term or concept—by defining negatively. Following the stipulative definition of liberal arts, you could have said, "By liberal arts I do not mean simply courses in the humanities, fine arts, and sciences." Defining negatively can clear away possible misconceptions. Using a negative definition along with a stipulative definition allows you to treat a familiar concept in a different way.

Defining from Origins

Sometimes you can reinforce an idea by telling your listeners where a word came from:

> Sincere *comes from two Latin words*—sine *meaning* without *and* ceres, *meaning* wax. *In early Rome, a superior statue was one that had no flaws that had to be filled with wax. A superior statue was thus said to be* sine ceres— without wax. *Today, the phrase* a sincere person *carries some of that same meaning.*

This is an *etymological definition*. An etymological definition is the derivation of a single word. A genetic definition is the history of a word or idea. You could, for instance, explain the American concept of freedom of speech by examining important discussions of that idea in eighteenth-century England and by showing how the American doctrine took its shape from British experiences. Defining words or ideas from original sources gives an audience a sense of continuity. At times, it explains nuances of meaning that we cannot reveal in any other way.

Defining by Examples

One of the best ways to define is by an *exemplar definition*, especially if the concept is unfamiliar or technical. Exemplar definitions are familiar examples. You might tell your listeners, "Each day, most of you stroll past Old Capitol on your way to classes. That building is a perfect example of what I want to talk about today—Georgian architecture." Be careful to use in your definition only those examples that are familiar to your audience members.

Defining by Context

You can also define a word or concept by putting it in its usual context through a *contextual definition*. A contextual definition uses an example to define a word. For example, the difference between *imply* and *infer* is shown in this way: "When she spoke to Jack, Jennifer implied that she liked him; Jack inferred from Jennifer's comments that she liked him."

A contextual definition can also point to an actual context; for example, "While there are many possible meanings of the word *revolution*, today I want to use it to describe the events that produced the democracy movement in China." Then, you would specify those events.

Defining by Analogy

Still another means of making technical or abstract notions easier to understand is the *analogical definition*. An analogy compares a process or event that is unknown with those that are known, as in, "Hospitals and labs use cryogenic tanks, which work much like large thermos bottles, to freeze tissue samples, blood, and other organic matter."

By referring to what is familiar, the analogical definition can make the unfamiliar much easier to grasp. Just make sure that the analogy fits.

Defining by Describing Operations

Some words or concepts are best defined by explaining how they work—by offering an *operational definition*. Operational definitions describe how an idea is measured. Scientists often use operational definitions to translate abstract concepts into concrete concepts. Thus, a social scientist might define *intelligence* as follows: "An intelligence quotient is a person's performance on the Wechsler-Bellevue Intelligence Test compared with the performance of other members of the population."

Restatement

If accuracy and simplicity were your only criteria as a speaker, your messages might resemble a famous World War II bulletin: "Sighted sub, sank same." But, because words literally disappear into the atmosphere as soon as they're spoken, you don't have the writer's advantage when transmitting ideas to others. Instead, you must rely heavily on rephrasing and reiteration or *restatement*. **Restatement** is (a) the *rephrasing* of ideas or concepts in different words or sentences and (b) the *reiteration* of ideas or concepts from more than one point of view.

Rephrasing

Skillful rephrasing can clarify a message and make it more specific. These effects can be seen in the following passage from John F. Kennedy's inaugural address:

> *Let the word go forth from this time and place, to friend and foe alike, that the torch has been passed to a new generation of Americans—born in this century, tempered by war, disciplined by a hard and bitter peace, proud of our ancient heritage, and unwilling to witness or permit the slow undoing of those human rights to which this nation has always been committed, and to which we are committed today at home and around the world.*

Let every nation know, whether it wishes us well or ill, that we shall pay any price, bear any burden, meet any hardship, support any friend, oppose any foe to assume the survival and the success of liberty.[7]

Notice how Kennedy used different words to rephrase "a new generation of Americans" and to list the sacrifices that the new generation of Americans was willing to make to ensure liberty.

Reiteration

Reiterating an idea from a number of perspectives usually involves listing its components or redefining the basic concept. You can see this principle of reiteration at work in the following excerpt from a student speech. Note how the speaker looks at *political image* from a variety of perspectives:

A "politician's image" is really a set of characteristics attributed to that politician by an electorate [formal perspective]. *A political image, similar to an image from a mirror, is made up of attributes that reflect the audience's concerns* [metaphorical perspective]. *An image is composed of bits and pieces of information and feelings that an audience brings to a politician* [psychological perspective], *and, therefore, it represents judgments made by the electorate based on verbal and nonverbal acts the politician has engaged in* [sociological perspective]. *Therefore, if you think of a political image only in terms of manipulation, you are looking only at the mirror. Step back and examine the beholder, too, and you will find ways of discovering what a "good" image is for a politician.*

Restatement—rephrasing or reiteration—can help your listeners remember your ideas more readily. However, be careful of mindless repetition; too many restatements, especially of simple ideas, can be boring.

Imagery

Your listeners grasp their world through the sensations of sight, smell, hearing, taste, and touch. To intensify your listeners' experience, you can appeal to these senses. But, of course, the primary senses through which you can reach your listeners *directly* are the visual and the auditory. Listeners can see you, your facial expressions, your movements, and your visual aids, and they can hear what you say. (See Figure 9.1.)

You can stimulate your listeners' senses *indirectly* by using language to recall images they have previously experienced. Through the use of vivid words you can create sensory pictures. **Imagery** consists of illusions created in the imagination through language. The language of imagery is divided into seven types, each related to the particular sensation that it seeks to trigger: (a) *visual* (sight), (b) *auditory* (hearing), (c) *gustatory* (taste), (d) *olfactory* (smell), (e) *tactual* (touch), (f) *kinesthetic* (muscle strain), and (g) *organic* (internal sensations).

Figure 9.1 The Types of Imagery

Speakers can stimulate their listeners' senses indirectly through language which triggers sensations.

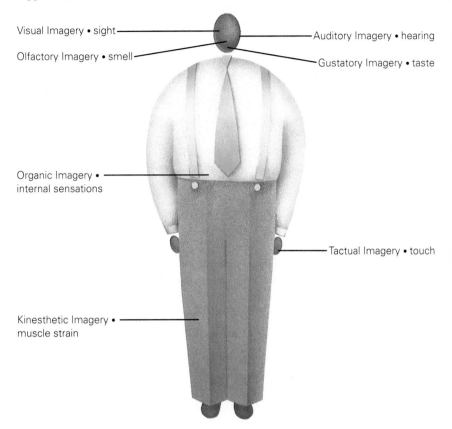

Visual Imagery • sight

Olfactory Imagery • smell

Auditory Imagery • hearing

Gustatory Imagery • taste

Organic Imagery • internal sensations

Tactual Imagery • touch

Kinesthetic Imagery • muscle strain

Visual Imagery

Visual imagery describes optical stimuli. Try to make your audience "see" the objects or situations that you're describing. Mention *size, shape, color,* and *movement*. Recount events in vivid visual language. For example, during cold war tension between the United States and the Soviet Union, General Douglas MacArthur had to prepare the cadets of the United States Military Academy for their uncertain future. To give his theme of "duty, honor, and country" intensity, MacArthur relied on visual images constructed through language. Note particularly the stress on images of size, shape, color, and movement as MacArthur talks about the American soldier:

> *In twenty campaigns, on a hundred battlefields, around a thousand campfires, I have witnessed that enduring fortitude, that patriotic self-abnegation, and that invincible determination which have carved his statue in the hearts of his people.*

From one end of the world to the other, he has drained deep the chalice of courage. As I listened to those songs in memory's eye I could see those staggering columns of the First World War, bending under soggy pack on many a weary march, from dripping dusk to drizzly dawn, slogging ankle deep through mire of shell-pocked roads; to form grimly for the attack, blue-lipped, covered with sludge and mud, chilled by the wind and rain, driving home to their objective, and for many, to the judgment seat of God. [. . .]

Always for them: Duty, honor, country. Always their blood, and sweat and tears, as they saw the way and the light. And twenty years after, on the other side of the globe, again the filth of dirty foxholes, the stench of ghostly trenches, the slime of dripping dugouts, those boiling suns of relentless heat, those torrential rains of devastating storms, the loneliness and utter desolation of jungle trails, the bitterness of long separation of those they loved and cherished, the deadly pestilence of tropical disease, the horror of stricken areas of war.

Their resolute and determined defense, their swift and sure attack, their indomitable purpose, their complete and decisive victory, always through the bloody haze of their last reverberating shot, the vision of gaunt, ghastly men, reverently following your password of duty, honor, country.[8]

Auditory Imagery

To create *auditory imagery,* use words that help your listeners "hear" what you're describing. Auditory imagery can project an audience into a scene. Author Tom Wolfe described a demolition derby by recounting the chant of the crowd as it joined in the countdown, the explosion of sound as two dozen cars started off in second gear, and finally "the unmistakable tympany of automobiles colliding and cheap-gauge sheet metal buckling."[9]

Gustatory Imagery

Gustatory imagery depicts sensations of taste. Sometimes you may even be able to help your audience "taste" what you're describing. Mention its saltiness, sweetness, sourness, or spiciness. Remember that foods have texture as well as taste. While demonstrating how to make popcorn, you might mention the crispness of the kernels, the oily sweetness of melted butter, and the grittiness of salt. Such descriptions allow your listeners to participate in the experience through their imaginations.

Olfactory Imagery

Olfactory imagery relates sensations of smell. Help your audience "smell" the odors connected with the situation you describe. Smell is a powerful sense because it normally triggers a flood of associated images. You can stimulate this process by describing the odor or by comparing the odor with more familiar ones. Elspeth Huxley remembers her childhood trek to Kenya at the turn of the century by recalling its smells:

It was the smell of travel in those days, in fact the smell of Africa—dry, peppery yet rich and deep, with an undertone of native body smeared with fat and red ochre and giving out a ripe, partly rancid odour which nauseated some

Europeans when they first encountered it but which I, for one, grew to enjoy. This was the smell of the Kikuyu, who were mainly vegetarian. The smell of tribes from the Victoria Nyanza basin, who were meat-eaters and sometimes cannibals, was quite different; much stronger and more musky, almost acrid, and, to me, much less pleasant. No doubt we smelt just as strong and odd to Africans, but of course we were fewer in numbers, and more spread out.[10]

Tactual Imagery

Tactual imagery is based on the sensations that come to us through physical contact with external objects. In particular, tactual imagery gives sensations of texture and shape, pressure, and heat or cold. Let your audience "feel" how rough or smooth, dry or wet, or slimy or sticky modeling clay is (*texture and shape*). Let them sense the pressure of physical force on their bodies, the weight of a heavy laundry bag, the pinch of jogging shoes, the blast of a high wind on their faces (*pressure*).

Sensations of heat or cold are aroused by *thermal imagery*. Review the excerpt from Douglas MacArthur's speech for some vivid examples of each type of tactual imagery.

Kinesthetic Imagery

Kinesthetic imagery describes the sensations associated with muscle strain and neuromuscular movement. Let your listeners experience for themselves the agonies and joys of marathon racing—the muscle cramps, the constricted chest, the struggle for air—and the magical serenity of getting a second wind and gliding effortlessly towards the finish line.

Organic Imagery

Hunger, dizziness, nausea—these are organic images. *Organic imagery* captures internal feelings or sensations. There are times when an experience is not complete without the description of inner feelings. The sensation of dizziness as you struggled through the rarified mountain air to reach the summit is one example. Another is the way the bottom dropped out of your stomach when the small plane tipped sharply, then righted itself. Since such imagery is powerful, you shouldn't offend your audience by overdoing it. Develop the rhetorical sensitivity required to create vividness without making the resultant image gruesome, disgusting, or grotesque.

The seven types of imagery we have considered—*visual, auditory, gustatory, olfactory, tactual, kinesthetic,* and *organic*—may be referred to as "doorways to the mind."[11] They open new levels of awareness that help listeners experience your message. Different people respond to different kinds of imagery, so you should insert several types of perceptual "doorways."

In the following example, note how the speaker combines various sensory appeals to arouse listener interest and reaction:

The strangler struck in Donora, Pennsylvania, in October of 1948. A thick fog billowed through the streets enveloping everything in thick sheets of dirty moisture and a greasy black coating. As Tuesday faded into Saturday, the fumes

You can re-create experiences for others through image-evoking language. How would you describe this scene to someone?

from the big steel mills shrouded the outlines of the landscape. One could barely see across the narrow streets. Traffic stopped. Men lost their way returning from the mills. Walking through the streets, even for a few moments, caused eyes to water and burn. The thick fumes grabbed at the throat and created a choking sensation. The air acquired a sickening bittersweet smell, nearly a taste. Death was in the air.[12]

In this example, college student Charles Schaillol uses vivid, descriptive phrases to affect the senses of his listeners—*visual:* "thick sheets of dirty moisture"; *organic:* "eyes to water and burn"; and *olfactory, gustatory:* "sickening bittersweet smell, nearly a taste."

To be effective, such illustrations must appear plausible. The language must convey a realistic impression—that it could happen. The speaker who describes the strangler that struck Donora offers a plausible account of the event. More importantly, he does so in a fashion that arouses feelings. His listeners wouldn't have shared the experience if he had simply said, "Air pollution was the cause of death in Donora."

Metaphor

The images created by appealing to the senses are often the result of using metaphors. A **metaphor** is the comparison of two dissimilar things. Charles Schaillol's description of fog as "thick sheets of dirty moisture" is one example. Scholar Michael Osborn notes that the metaphor should "result in an intuitive flash of recognition that surprises or fascinates the hearer."[13] Furthermore, good metaphors should extend our knowledge or increase our awareness of a person, object, or event. When they are fresh or vivid, metaphors can be powerful aids in evoking feelings. For example, referring to a table's "legs" is a metaphor, but it's boring. It's much more interesting to say, "Balanced on four obese toothpicks, the antique table swayed under its heavy burden."

Metaphors drawn from everyday experiences provide wide audience appeal. In the following speech, Martin Luther King, Jr., relied on our experiences of light and darkness:

> *With this faith in the future, with this determined struggle, we will be able to emerge from the bleak and desolate midnight of man's inhumanity to man, into the bright and glittering daybreak of freedom and justice.*[14]

This basic light-dark metaphor was important because it allowed King to suggest (a) sharp contrasts between inhumanity and freedom and (b) the inevitability of social progress (as "daybreak" follows "midnight"). In other words, the metaphor worked—it communicated King's beliefs about justice and injustice and urged others to action.

Words are not neutral conduits for thought. Words not only reflect the "real" world outside your mind, but also, as critic Kenneth Burke suggests, help *shape* our perceptions of people, events, and social contexts. Language has a potent effect on people's willingness to believe, to feel, and to act.

Sample Speech

William Faulkner (1897–1962) presented the following speech on December 10, 1950, as he accepted the Nobel Prize for Literature. His listeners might have expected a speech filled with the kind of pessimism so characteristic of his novels. Instead, he greeted them with a stirring challenge to improve humankind.

Notice in particular Faulkner's use of language. Although known for the tortured sentences of his novels, he expresses his ideas clearly and simply in his speech. His style is written, yet his use of organic imagery and powerful metaphors keep the speech alive. The atmosphere is generally serious, befitting the occasion. You might expect a Nobel Prize-winner to talk about himself, but Faulkner did just the opposite. He stressed his craft—writing—and the commitment necessary to practice that craft; this material emphasis lead naturally to an essentially propositional rather than narrative form. More than 40 years ago, William Faulkner offered a speech that is as relevant today as it was in 1950.

ON ACCEPTING THE NOBEL PRIZE FOR LITERATURE[15]
William Faulkner

I feel that this award was not made to me as a man, but to my work—a life's work in the agony and sweat of the human spirit, not for glory and least of all for profit, but to create out of the materials of the human spirit something which did not exist before. So this award is only mine in trust. It will not be difficult to find a dedication for the money part of it commensurate with the purpose and significance of its origin. But I would like to do the same with the acclaim too, by using this moment as a pinnacle from which I might be listened to by the young men and women already dedicated to the same anguish and travail, among whom is already that one who will some day stand here where I am standing. . . . /1

Our tragedy today is a general and universal physical fear so long sustained by now that we can even bear it. There are no longer problems of the spirit. There is only the question: When will I be blown up? Because of this, the young man or woman writing today has forgotten the problems of the human heart in conflict with itself which alone can make good writing because only that is worth writing about, worth the agony and the sweat. . . . /2

He must learn them again. He must teach himself that the basest of all things is to be afraid; and, teaching himself that, forget it forever, leaving no room in his workshop for anything but the old verities and truths of the heart, the old universal truths lacking which any story is ephemeral and doomed—love and honor and pity and pride and compassion and sacrifice. Until he does so, he labors under a curse. He writes not of love but of lust, of defeats in which nobody loses anything of value, of victories without hope and, worst of all, without pity or compassion. His griefs grieve on no universal bones, leaving no scars. He writes not of the heart but of the glands. . . . /3

Until he relearns these things, he will write as though he stood among and watched the end of man. I decline to accept the end of man. It is easy enough to say that man is immortal simply because he will endure: that when the last ding-dong of doom has clanged and faded from the last worthless rock hanging tideless in the last red and dying evening, that even then there will still be one more sound: that of his puny inexhaustible voice, still talking. I refuse to accept this. I believe that man will not merely endure: he will prevail. He is immortal, not because he alone among creatures has an inexhaustible voice, but because he has a soul, a spirit capable of compassion and sacrifice and endurance. The poet's, the writer's, duty is to write about these things. It is his privilege to help man endure by lifting his heart, by reminding him of the courage and honor and hope and pride and compassion and pity and sacrifice which have been the glory of his past. The poet's voice need not merely be the record of man, it can be one of the props, the pillars to help him endure and prevail. . . . /4

CHAPTER SUMMARY

1. Successful speeches generally are characterized by *accurate, simple, coherent, properly intense,* and *appropriate* language choices.

2. In selecting an appropriate speaking style, you must make decisions about *written vs. oral language,* a *serious vs. humorous atmosphere, gendered vs. gender-neutral language,* and *propositional vs. narrative forms* of presentation.

3. *Rhetorical strategies* are word and phrase choices intended to control the impact of the speech. Four of the most common are *definition, restatement, imagery,* and *metaphor.*

4. You can define in eight ways: *from dictionaries, in your own words, negatively, from original sources, by example, by context, by analogy,* and *by describing operations.*

5. *Restatement* is the intentional repetition of ideas or concepts through rephrasing or reiteration.

6. *Imagery* is illusions created in the imagination through language. There are seven types of images: *visual, auditory, gustatory, olfactory, tactual, kinesthetic,* and *organic sensations.*

KEY TERMS

atmosphere (p. 173)
coherence (p. 168)
connectives (p. 169)
connotative meaning (p. 166)
denotative meaning (p. 166)
encoding (p. 167)
final summaries (p. 168)
gender-linked words (p. 174)
gender-neutral words (p. 174)
imagery (p. 180)
metaphor (p. 184)

narrative form (p. 175)
oral style (p. 171)
preliminary summaries (p. 168)
propositional form (p. 175)
restatement (p. 179)
rhetorical strategy (p. 177)
signposts (p. 168)
speaking style (p. 167)
tone (p. 171)
written style (p. 172)

SKILLBUILDING ACTIVITIES

1. Choose one of the items listed below and describe it using the seven kinds of imagery to create an involving portrait for your listeners.
    a. an extinct animal
    b. a tropical plant
    c. a breakfast food
    d. a complicated machine
    e. a historic building

2. As a take-home assignment, rewrite a complicated message (e.g. an insurance policy, agreement for a credit card or loan, income tax instructions, or difficult

passage from a textbook) in simple yet still-accurate language. Present the material as a short speech in your class. Turn it in for your instructor's comments.

3. Read one of the sample speeches in this textbook. Identify the methods the speaker uses to make the language effective. Were the speaker's word choices effective? Did the speaker choose an appropriate style? What rhetorical strategies can you discover in the speech?

REFERENCES

1. For more on this subject, see Doris B. Garey, *Putting Words in Their Places* (Glenview, Ill.: ScottForesman, 1957) and Roger Brown, *Words and Things* (Glenview, Ill.: ScottForesman, 1968).

2. Quoted in John R. Pelsma, *Essentials of Speech* (New York: Crowell, Collier, and Macmillan, 1934), 193.

3. John Waite Bowers, "Language and Argument," in *Perspectives on Argumentation,* G. R. Miller and T. R. Nilsen, eds. (Glenview, Ill.: ScottForesman, 1966), esp. 168–172.

4. For a summary of several technical studies distinguishing between oral and written styles and for a discussion of 16 characteristics of oral style, see John F. Wilson and Carrroll C. Arnold, *Public Speaking as a Liberal Art,* 5th ed. (Boston: Allyn and Bacon, 1983), 227–229.

5. Alan Alda, "A Reel Doctor's Advice to Some Real Doctors," in Stephen E. Lucas, *The Art of Public Speaking* (New York: Random House, 1983), 364.

6. Studies of gender and communication have recently exploded. For extensive background, see Barbara and Gene Eakins, *Sex Differences in Human Communication* (Boston: Houghton Mifflin Co., 1978); Barrie Thorne and Nancy Henley, eds., *Language and Sex: Difference and Dominance* (Rawley, Mass.: Newbury House, 1975); and Robin Lakoff, *Language and Women's Place* (New York: Harper & Row, 1975). For more current overviews, see H. M. Hacker, "Blabbermouths and Clams: Sex Differences in Self-Disclosure in Same-Sex and Cross-Sex Friendship Dyads," *Psychology of Women Quarterly,* 5 (1981), 385–401; Judith C. Pearson, *Gender and Communication* (Dubuque, Iowa: Wm. C Brown, 1985); Barbara Bate, *Communication and the Sexes* (New York: Harper & Row, 1987); Lea P. Stewart, Pamela J. Cooper, and Sheryl A. Friedly, *Communication Between the Sexes: Sex Differences and Sex-Role Stereotypes* (Scottsdale, Ariz.: Gorsuch Scarisbrick, 1986); and Carole Spitzack and Kathryn Carter, "Women in Communication Studies: A Typology of Revision," *Quarterly Journal of Speech,* 73 (November 1987), 401–423.

7. From *Public Papers of the Presidents of the United States: John F. Kennedy* (Washington, D.C.: U.S. Government Printing Office, 1961).

8. Excerpts from Douglas MacArthur, "Duty, Honor and Country," *The Dolphin Book of Speeches,* George W. Hibbit, ed. (George W. Hibbit, 1965). Reprinted by permission of Doubleday & Company, Inc.

9. A selection from Tom Wolfe, *The Kandy-Kolored Tangerine-Flake Streamline Baby* (Thomas K. Wolfe, Jr., 1965). Reprinted by permission of Farrar, Straus and Giroux, Inc. and International Creative Management.

10.   Elspeth Huxley, *The Flame Trees of Thika: Memories of an African Childhood* (London: Chatto & Windus, 1959), 4.

11.   Victor Alvin Ketcham, "The Seven Doorways to the Mind," *Business Speeches by Business Men,* William P. Sandford and W. Hayes Yeager, eds. (New York: McGraw-Hill Book Company, 1930).

12.   From Charles Schaillol, "The Strangler," *Winning Orations.* Reprinted by permission of Larry Schnoor, Executive Secretary, Interstate Oratorical Association, Mankato State College, Mankato, Minn.

13.   Michael Osborn, *Orientations to Rhetorical Style* (Chicago: Science Research Associates, 1976), 10.

14.   From Martin Luther King, Jr., "Love, Law and Civil Disobedience" (Martin Luther King, Jr., 1963). Reprinted by permission of Joan Daves.

15.   William Faulkner, "On Accepting the Nobel Prize for Literature," *The Faulkner Reader* (New York: Random House, Inc., 1954).

CHAPTER TEN

Using Visual Aids

*D*amon decided to save a little time and money on visual aids for his speech by ordering an opaque projector, which projects pages of a book directly onto a screen. His problems began almost as soon as he arrived at the classroom. First, he nearly herniated himself carrying the projector into the room; he had no idea how heavy it would be. Then, when he turned the projector on, he could barely make himself heard over its noisy cooling fan. And, as he showed the first graphic, his classmates broke into laughter—the image was upside down. Finally, Damon discovered that the magnification on an opaque projector is so minimal that the people in the back row could not even read the graph. After that experience, Damon and his classmates decided to leave opaque projectors alone and stick to other, easier-to-see visual aids for their speeches.

From the time you participated in "show and tell" as a second grader to the times when you and your family watched the slides of your vacation, you've included visual aids in your communication efforts. Like Damon, you still are communicating visually as a public speaker. Your physical presence in front of an audience makes a powerful visual statement, and your use of visual aids can make visual communication an essential part of the speech transaction. For these reasons, it's important for you to learn more about visual aids.

Your world is filled with visual communication. Television, film, transparencies, VCRs and videotape, overhead projections, billboards, banners trailing from airplanes, and sidewalk tables with store bargains surround you and demand your attention. You live in one of the most visually oriented societies in the world today. Thousands of companies—from major television and film studios to small-town graphics production shops in neighborhood basements—thrive on your interest in superior visual communication.

Research on visual media, learning, and attitude change has given us a lot of information about the impact of visual aids on audiences.[1] Experienced speakers have offered additional advice. In this chapter, we'll combine what we've learned from social-scientific research with wisdom from old pros. First, we'll focus on the functions of visual aids; then we'll examine the various types of visual aids and explore ways to use them effectively.

THE FUNCTIONS OF VISUAL AIDS

Visual aids are those materials that rely primarily upon sight. Visual materials enhance your presentation in two ways: (a) they aid listener comprehension and memory and (b) they add persuasive impact to your message.

Comprehension and Memory

The truth of the old saying "A picture's worth a thousand words" depends on whether the picture adds information that's easily understood visually. Research has demonstrated that bar graphs are especially effective at making statistical information more accessible to listeners. Charts and human interest visuals, such as photographs, have proven to help listeners process and retain data.[2] Even simple pictures have had significant effects on children's recall and comprehension during storytelling.[3] Visuals can be immensely valuable if your purpose is to inform or teach an audience.

Persuasion

In addition to enhancing comprehension and memory, visuals can heighten the persuasive impact of your ideas because they engage listeners actively in the communicative exchange. Lawyers, for example, aware of the dramatic persuasive effects of visuals, often include visual evidence of injuries or crimes in their cases in order to sway the opinions of juries. Some lawyers have even experimented with the use of video technology to create dramatic portrayals of events in order to influence jury decisions, such as the dangerous condition of an intersection in an involuntary manslaughter case or anatomy drawings showing fatal wounds in a homicide case.

Undeniably, your credibility and your persuasiveness are enhanced by good visuals.[4] Visual materials satisfy the "show-me" attitude prevalent in listeners; in this way, they provide a crucial means of meeting listener expectations.[5]

TYPES OF VISUAL SUPPORT

Visual materials can be divided into two broad categories: (a) *actual objects* and (b) *symbolic representations of actual objects*. As we discuss each group, we'll examine specific approaches to using the visual materials to supplement your oral presentations.

Actual Objects

The objects that you bring to a presentation, including your own body, can be categorized under two headings: (a) *animate* (living) objects and (b) *inanimate* (nonliving) objects.

Animate Objects

Live animals or plants can, under some circumstances, be used to enhance your speeches. If your speech explores the care and feeding of laboratory mice, you can reinforce your ideas by bringing to the speech one or two mice in a properly equipped cage. Describing the differences between two varieties of plants may be easier if you demonstrate the differences with real plants. Discretion and common sense about what's possible and in good taste will help make such visuals work for you rather than against you. You might be stretching your luck, for example, by bringing a real horse into the classroom to show how one is saddled or by bringing in an untrained puppy to show how one is paper trained.

You want to use the actual object to focus audience attention on your speech, not to distract the audience with the object. A registered Persian cat may seem to be a perfect visual aid for a speech about what judges look for in cat shows until the cat gets loose in the classroom or causes allergic reactions; then your message may be lost in the process.

Speakers who demonstrate the yoga positions, warm-up exercises, ballet steps, or tennis strokes they discuss in their speeches add concreteness and vitality to their presentations. For example, a senior nursing major might add credibility by wearing a uniform when demonstrating CPR.

Remember to control the experience. Make sure that members in the back rows can see you. Demonstrate a yoga position from a sturdy table top rather than from the floor. Slow the tempo of a tennis stroke so that the audience can see any intricate action and subtle movements. One advantage of properly controlled visual action is that with it you can control the audience's attention to your demonstration.

Inanimate Objects

Demonstrations are often enhanced by showing the actual object under discussion. A speech about stringing a tennis racket is enhanced by a demonstration of the process with an actual racket. A speech about the best way to repair rust holes in an automobile fender is clarified by samples of the work in stages. Cooking or house remodeling demonstrations are enlivened with samples prepared before the presentation, since the presenter usually doesn't have time to complete the actual work during the presentation.

Most importantly, you want to keep audience attention focused on the message of your speech. To do this, place the object between you and the audience as much as possible. If you stand in front of the object or to the side, you risk blocking the audience's view, disrupting their focused attention, and frustrating them.

Symbolic Representations

When you can't use actual objects or your own physical movement to clarify your message, you can resort to using **symbolic representations** or objects, tokens, or images that represent the content of your speech. These representations may be relatively *concrete*—such as photographs, slides, films, or videotapes—or *abstract* drawings—such as graphs, charts, and models.

Concrete Representations
Concrete representations closely resemble the content of the speech. *Photographs* can give the audience a visual sense of your topic. With photographs you can illustrate flood damage to ravaged homes or depict the beauty of a wooded area threatened by a new shopping mall. One problem with photographs, however, is that audiences may not be able to see details from a distance. You can compensate for this shortcoming by enlarging photos so that people can see them more easily. Avoid passing small photos through the audience because such activity is noisy and disruptive. The purpose of a visual aid is to draw the attention of all members of the audience simultaneously.

Slides (35 mm transparencies) allow you to depict color, shape, texture, and relationships. If you're presenting a travelogue, you need slides to show your audience the buildings and landscape of the region. If you're giving a speech on the history of the steam engine, you need slides to show various steam engines in operation. If you're speaking against the construction of a dam, you can enhance your persuasiveness by showing slides of the white water that will be disrupted by the dam. If you're discussing stylistic differences among famous artists, you need to show slides of art works from the Baroque and Neoclassical periods.

Using slides requires familiarity with projection equipment. It also requires some forethought about the setup of the presentation. Attention to small, seemingly inconsequential details will make a major difference in how smoothly the presentation goes. Do you know how to change the projection lamp? Did you bring along a spare bulb just in case? Will you need an extension cord? Do you know how to remove a jammed slide? If you operate on the assumption that whatever can go wrong will, you'll be prepared for most problematic circumstances.

Videotapes and *films* can also be useful in illustrating your points. Videotaped segments from several current situation comedies can dramatically

Symbolic representations convey information in various ways. For instance, a photograph of a sailboat (left) gives an audience a realistic but complicated view of the object, whereas an abstract representation, such as a diagram (bottom), strips away unnecessary details to illustrate the object more clearly. Also abstract, yet highly visible, a model (right) provides a three-dimensional image of the object, allowing a speaker to point out its parts and discuss their functions.

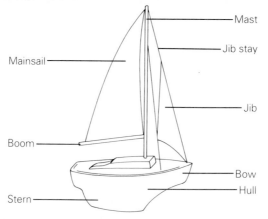

Mast

Jib stay

Mainsail

Jib

Boom

Bow

Hull

Stern

reinforce your claim that minorities are underrepresented in daytime television. Two or three videotaped political ads can help you illustrate methods for packaging a candidate. Again, familiarity with the operation of a videocassette recorder or film projector ensures a smooth presentation. Too often, speakers assume that the equipment will be provided and a skilled technician will be available, only to find that no one can get the machine running properly. Such delays increase your nervousness and detract from your presentation.

Abstract Representations

If you need to illustrate the growth of inflation or show how social security revenues will be spent in the next six months, you'll find yourself resorting to more abstract representations than those previously discussed. **Abstract representations** show ideas symbolically, often in numbers. The form of the representation—drawings, charts, graphs—will depend on the formality of the situation. If you're brainstorming building renovation ideas with a prospective client, quick sketches may suffice. However, if you're meeting with the client's board of directors, the same rough drawings will be inadequate. The board will expect a polished presentation, complete with a professionally prepared prospectus. Similarly, chalkboard drawings may be sufficient to explain cell division to a group of classmates, but when presenting the same information as part of a Science Fair project, you need refined visual support materials. The care with which you prepare these visuals will convey either an attitude of indifference or concern to your audience.

Chalkboard drawings are especially valuable when you want to present an idea step by step. By drawing each stage as you discuss it, you can control the audience's attention to your major points. Coaches often use this approach when showing players how to execute a particular play. Time lines and size comparison diagrams can also be sketched on a chalkboard. To visually represent the history of the civil rights movement in the United States, you can create a time line that illustrates key events, such as the arrival of the first slaves in Jamestown, the Emancipation Proclamation, and the 1965 Voting Rights Act.

Speakers can use *overhead projectors* just as they would use chalkboards—illustrating their points as they talk. However, overhead projectors offer some advantages over chalkboards. One advantage of an overhead projector is that you can turn it off when you've made your point, thus removing any distraction from your message. Another advantage is that you can uncover one part of a transparency at a time, keeping the remainder covered so as to control the flow of information. Finally, you can prepare transparencies before the speech, giving them a more professional appearance than chalkboard drawings. During the speech you can point to the transparency or add to it to emphasize your claims.

When you're using either a chalkboard or an overhead projector, be aware of your technique. First, make your drawings large enough so that the audience can see them. Second, if you continue to talk to the audience as you draw, be brief; your audience's attention will wander if you talk to the board or to the light source for more than a minute or two. Third,

Figure 10.1 Bar Graph
Bar graphs illustrate relationships.

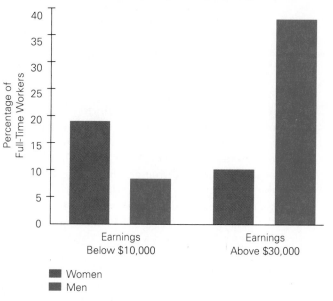

The Gender Gap of Income Inequality

■ Women
■ Men

Source: U.S. Bureau of the Census, 1986.

Figure 10.2 Line Graph
Line graphs can reveal relationships, but they can also deceive the unwary. These graphs show the same data but use different spacing along the axes to change the visual image.

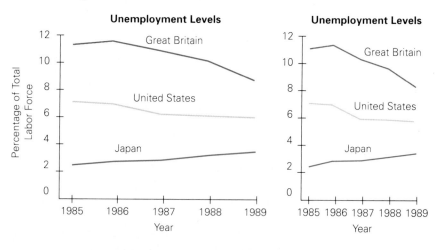

Source: Data Resources, 1989.

Figure 10.3 Pie Graph
Pie graphs dramatize relationships among a limited number of segments. Ideally,
a pie graph should have from two to five segments. A pie graph should never
have more than eight segments.

Ratings of Overall Quality of U.S. Airlines Service

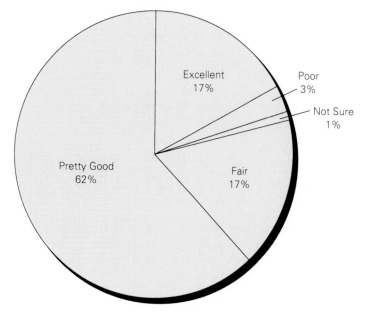

Business Week/Harris Poll conducted December 12-16, 1988.

consider the visual field while you draw—where should you stand to avoid
blocking the audience's view of your visuals? Fourth, when you're through
talking about the illustration, erase it or turn off the projector.

   Graphs show relationships among various parts of a whole or between
variables across time. There are several types of graphs:

1.   **Bar graphs** show the relationships between two or more sets of figures.
(See Figure 10.1.) If you were illustrating the difference between lawyers'
and doctors' incomes or between male lawyers' and female lawyers'
incomes, you would probably use a bar graph.

2.   **Line graphs** show relationships between two or more variables, usually
over time. (See Figure 10.2.) If you were trying to explain a complex economic correlation between supply and demand, you would use a line graph.

3.   **Pie graphs** show percentages by dividing a circle into the proportions
being represented. (See Figure 10.3.) A charitable organization could use
a pie graph to show how much of its income was spent on administration,

Figure 10.4 Pictograph
Speakers with artistic skills can create interesting visual aids, such as this graphic representation of U.S. wine exports.

U.S. Wine Exports

1985

1986

1987

1988

= one million gallons

research, and fund-raising campaigns. Town governments use pie graphs to show citizens what proportion of their tax dollars go to municipal services, administration, education, recreation, and law enforcement.

4. **Pictographs** represent size and number with symbols. (See Figure 10.4.) A representation of U.S. and Soviet exports of grain might use a miniature drawing of a wheat shock or ear of corn to represent 100,000 bushels; this representation would allow a viewer to see at a glance the disparity between the exports of two countries.

Your choice of bar, line, pie, or pictorial graphs will depend on the subject and the nature of the relationship you wish to convey. A pie graph, for example, can't easily illustrate discrepancies between two groups; nor can it show effects of change over time.

Regardless of the type of graph you choose, when you are preparing a graph, you must be very careful to not distort your information. A bar graph can create a misleading impression of the difference between two items if one bar is short and wide while the other is long and narrow. Line graphs can portray very different effects of change if the units of measurement are not the same for each time period. You can avoid misrepresenting information by using consistent measurements in your graphs and by using a computer to generate your graphs (see page 202).

Charts and **tables** condense large blocks of information into a single representation. If you want to discuss what products are imported and exported by Japan, you can break down imports and exports on a table. If you want to show the channels of communication or the lines of authority in a large company, your presentation will be much easier to follow if your listeners have an organizational chart for reference.

There are two special types of charts: **flipcharts** unveil ideas one at a time on separate sheets; **flowcharts** show the chronological stages of a process on a single sheet. Both flipcharts and flowcharts may include drawings or photos. If you present successive ideas with a flipchart you'll focus audience attention on specific parts of your speech. If you present successive ideas with a complete chart, however, the audience may stray from your order of explanation to read the entire chart. You can use a flowchart to indicate what actions might be taken across time—for example, a flowchart will allow audiences to visualize the stages of a fundraising campaign.

As long as the information is not too complex or lengthy, tables and charts may be used to indicate changes over time and to rank or list items and their costs, frequency of use, or relative importance. Tables and charts should be designed so that they can be seen and so that they convey data simply and clearly. Too much information will force the audience to concentrate more on the visual support than on your oral explanation. For example, a dense chart showing all the major and minor offices of a company may simply overwhelm listeners as they try to follow your explanation. If the organization is too complex, you may want to develop a series of charts, each one focusing on a smaller unit of information.

Models can dramatize your explanations. **Models** are reduced or enlarged scale replicas of real objects. Architects construct models of new projects to show clients. Developers of shopping malls, condominiums, and business offices use models when persuading zoning boards to grant needed rights-of-way or variances. You can use models of genes to accompany your explanation of gene splicing. As with other visual aids, models need to be manageable and visible to the audience. If you are using a model that comes apart so that different pieces can be examined, practice removing and replacing the parts beforehand.

STRATEGIES FOR SELECTING AND USING VISUAL AIDS

Your decision about which visual aids will work best for you should be based on four considerations: (a) the characteristics of the audience and occasion, (b) the communicative potential of various visual materials, (c) your ability to integrate verbal and visual materials effectively, and (d) the potential of computer-generated visual materials.

Consider the Audience and Occasion

Before you choose your visual aids, common sense will tell you to consider what your listeners already know about your subject. Do you need to bring a map of the United States to an audience of college students when discussing the westward movement of the population in this country? Of, if you're going to discuss a football team's offensive and defensive formations, should you provide diagrams of the formations for your listeners? Can you expect an audience to understand the administrative structure of the federal bureaucracy without providing an organizational chart?

How readily an audience can comprehend *aurally* what you have to say is another more difficult question to consider. It may be quite difficult, for example, to decide what your classmates know about governmental structures or what Rotary Club members know about football plays. Probably the best thing you can do is to check out your speculations by speaking with several of your potential listeners well ahead of your speech. In other words, before making any final decisions about visual supporting materials, do as much audience research as you possibly can.

As part of your preparation for using visuals, take into account the nature of the speaking occasion. Certain kinds of occasions demand certain types of visual support materials. The corporate executive who presents a report of projected future profits to the board of directors without a printed handout or diagram will probably find his or her credibility questioned. The military adviser who calls for governmental expenditures for new weapons without offering pictures or drawings of the proposed weapons and printed technical data on their operation is not likely to be a convincing advocate. An athletic coach without a chalkboard at halftime may succeed only in confusing team members. In short, if you speak in situations that demand certain kinds of visual media, plan ahead to supply those kinds of visual media. If the speech occasion doesn't appear to require certain visual supports, analyze the occasion further for different visual possibilities. Use your imagination. Be innovative. Don't overlook opportunities to make your speech more meaningful, more exciting, and more interesting for your listeners.

Consider the Communicative Potential of Various Visual Aids

Keep in mind that each type of visual aid is best at communicating a particular kind of information. Each type also must blend with your spoken presentation as well as with your audience. In general, pictorial or photographic visuals can make an audience *feel* the way you do. For example, you can use slides, movies, sketches, or photographs of your travels in Indonesia to accompany a travelogue. Such visual aids stimulate in your audience the kinds of feelings that you experienced in another place, situation, or time.

Visuals containing descriptive or written materials, on the other hand, can help an audience *think* the way you do. For example, models, diagrams, charts, and graphs about the population and economy of Indonesia may persuade your listeners to conclude that the United States should send more foreign aid to Indonesia.

Integrate Verbal and Visual Materials Effectively

To be effective, visual aids should complement your spoken message. Visuals should save time, enhance the impact of your speech, clarify complex relations, or generally enliven your presentation. Consider the following suggestions for getting the maximum benefit from your visuals:

1. *Design abstract symbolic representations with care.* Use contrasting colors (red on white, black on yellow) to highlight different information in an organizational chart or table or to differentiate segments of a pie graph or bars in a bar graph. As a rule, color commands attention better than black and white do.

2. *Keep charts and other graphic aids clear and simple.* Research has demonstrated that plain bar graphs are the most effective method for displaying statistical comparisons.[6] The reason may be that bar graphs represent numbers in a visual form. Make sure that your bar graphs work for you—make essential information stand out clearly from the background. Let simplicity guide your preparation.

3. *Make your visuals large enough to be seen clearly and easily.* Listeners get frustrated when they must lean forward and squint in order to see detail in a visual aid. Make your figures and lettering large enough so that everyone can see them. Follow the example of John Hancock who, when signing the Declaration of Independence in 1776, wrote his name large enough to "be seen by the King of England without his glasses."

4. *Make your visuals neat.* Draw neatly, spell correctly, make lines proportional, and make letters symmetrical. Such advice may seem unnecessary, but too often beginning speakers throw together visual materials at the last minute. They forget that their visual aids also contribute to audience assessment of their credibility. Misspelled words and sloppy graphs will lower listeners' estimation of your competence.

5. *Decide how to handle your visual aids in advance.* Decide on a visual aid and practice with it well in advance, especially for demonstration speeches. Suppose you want to demonstrate tombstone dabbing or making paper casts of old tombstone faces. Tombstones are heavy. Do you bring one to class? Tombstone dabbing takes time and is very messy. How much of the process do you show? You could discuss in detail the chemicals used for cleaning stone surfaces, the different kinds of paper, various dabbing techniques, and locations of the most interesting tombstones. How detailed should you get? Unless you think through such questions in advance, you may find yourself making poor decisions during the speech.

6. *Be prepared to compensate orally for any distraction your visual aid may create.* Remember that you must compete with your visual aid for your listeners' attention. Listeners may find the visual aid so intriguing that they miss part of your message. You can partially compensate for any potential distraction by building reiteration into your speech. By repeating your main ideas you can be reasonably certain that your listeners will follow your thoughts. As added insurance, you might also keep your visual aid out of sight until you need to use it.

7. *Be prepared to coordinate slides, films, overhead projections, or videotapes with your verbal message.* Mechanical or electronic messages can easily distract your listeners. If your audience concentrates harder on the moving images than on your words, however, you defeat your own purpose. You need to talk louder and move more vigorously when using a machine to communicate, or you need to refuse to compete with the machine at all; that is, show the film or slides either *before* or *after* you comment on their content. Whatever strategy you choose, make sure that your visual materials are well integrated into your oral presentation.

8. *Hand your listeners a copy of the materials you wish them to reflect on after your speech.* If you're making recommendations to a student council, you should provide copies of your proposal for the council's subsequent action. Or, if you're reporting the results of a survey, your listeners will better digest the most pertinent statistics if you give each listener a copy of them. Few people can recall the seven warning signs of cancer, but they might keep a wallet-sized list handy if you provided them with it. Of course, you would not duplicate your entire speech for everyone—select only those items with lasting value.

These suggestions should enable you to take advantage of the communicative potential of visual media. Good visual aids don't detract from your message. Instead, they fit your ideas and leave the audience with a feeling of completeness.

Evaluate Computer-generated Visual Materials

You can tap into the expanding world of computer graphics as well in considering visual aids. While you may not be able to produce results similar to those on the latest televised football game, you can still use readily available computer-generated visual materials. Here are some suggestions for ways to use such materials:

1. *Use computer graphics to create an atmosphere.* It's easy to make computer banners with block lettering and pictures. Hang a banner in the front of the room to set a mood or establish a theme. For example, a student urging her classmates to get involved in a United Way fundraising drive created a

Well-prepared computer-generated visual aids can enhance your credibility by giving your presentation a professional quality. What are the drawbacks of computer-generated visual aids?

banner with the campaign slogan, "Thanks to you, it works, for all of us." Initially, the banner captured attention; during the speech the banner reinforced the theme.

2. *Enlarge small computer-generated diagrams.* Most computer diagrams are too small to be seen easily by an audience. You can use a photo duplicating machine that enlarges images sometimes 140 to 200 percent of the original size to make a more visible diagram.

3. *Consider enhancing the computer-generated image in other ways.* Use markers to color in pie graphs or to darken the lines of a line graph. Use press-on letters to make headings for your graphs. Convert computer-generated images into slide transparencies for projection during your speech. Mixing media in such ways can give your presentations a professional look. If you have access to the right technology, you can create three-dimensional images of buildings, machines, or the human body.

4. *Know the limitations of computer technology.* Remember that you're the lead actor and your visuals are props. Choose the visuals that fit your purpose, physical setting, and audience needs. Computers are most effective when processing numerical data and converting them into bar, line, and pie graphs.

CHAPTER SUMMARY

1. *Visual aids* as a discrete mode, or channel, of communication can *aid listener comprehension and memory* and *add persuasive impact* to a speech.

2. There are two main types of visual aids—*actual objects* and *symbolic representations.*

3. Actual objects include both *animate objects* (living plants, animals, and even the speaker) and *inanimate objects* (nonliving things).

4. Symbolic representations include *concrete representations* (*chalkboard drawings, graphs, charts* and *tables, models,* and *computer-generated materials*) as well as *abstract representations.*

5. In selecting and using visual aids, *consider the audience and occasion, consider the communicative potential of various visual aids,* and *find ways to integrate verbal and visual materials effectively.*

KEY TERMS

abstract representations (p. 195)
bar graphs (p. 197)
charts (p. 199)
concrete representations (p. 193)
flipcharts (p. 199)
flowcharts (p. 199)
graphs (p. 197)

line graphs (p. 197)
models (p. 199)
pictographs (p. 198)
pie graphs (p. 197)
symbolic representations (p. 193)
tables (p. 199)
visual aids (p. 191)

SKILLBUILDING ACTIVITIES

1. Plan a short speech explaining or demonstrating a complex process. Choose two different types of visual aids and ask the class to evaluate their effectiveness.

2. Work in small groups to develop at least three different types of visual aids for three of the following topics. A representative of each group will report to the class as a whole, telling about or showing the proposed visual aids.
   a. How to play a musical instrument
   b. How to splint a broken arm or leg
   c. How to assemble a disassembled product
   d. How to do the Australian crawl
   e. How to cut your utility bill

3. Videotape a television demonstration show and play the videotape in class. Evaluate the use of visual aids in the show. Were they easily seen? Did they demand attention? Did the speaker use the visual aids effectively? What would have made the use of visual aids more effective?

4. Evaluate the effectiveness of the visual aids used in your textbooks. What types of visual aids do the textbooks use? How are the visual aids used—to reinforce information, to clarify ideas, or to support theories? Which subjects seem to require more visual support?

REFERENCES

1.   The general theories of Gestalt psychology are reviewed in Ernest R. Hilgard, *Theories of Learning* (New York: Appleton-Century-Crofts, 1956). Their applications in areas of visual communication can be found in Rudolph Arnheim, *Visual Thinking* (Berkeley: University of California Press, 1969); John M. Kennedy, *A Psychology of Picture Perception* (San Francisco: Jossey-Bass, 1974); Sol Worth, "Pictures Can't Say Ain't," *Versus,* 12 (December 1975), 85–108; Leonard Zusne, *Visual Perception of Form* (New York: Academic Press, 1976); and John Morgan and Peter Welton, *See What I Mean: An Introduction to Visual Communication* (London: Edward Arnold, Publishers, Ltd., 1986). For discussions of research on media and learning, see Gavriel Salomon, *Interaction of Media, Cognition, and Learning* (San Francisco: Jossey-Bass, 1979); and E. Heidt, *Instructional Media and the Individual Learner* (New York: Nichols, 1976).

2.   William J. Seiler, "The Effects of Visual Materials on Attitudes, Credibility, and Retention," *Speech Monographs,* 38 (November 1971), 331–334.

3.   Joel R. Levin and Alan M. Lesgold, "On Pictures in Prose," *Educational Communication and Technology Journal,* 26 (1978), 233–244. See Marilyn J. Haring and Maurine A. Fry, "Effect of Pictures on Children's Comprehension of Written Text," *Educational Communication and Technology Journal,* 27 (1979), 185–190.

4.   For more specific conclusions about the effects of various sorts of visual materials, see Virginia Johnson, "Picture-Perfect Presentations," *Training & Development Journal,* 43 (1989), 45; F. M. Dwyer, "Exploratory Studies in the Effectiveness of Visual Illustrations," *AV Communication Review,* 18 (1970), 235–244; G. D. Feliciano, R. D. Powers, and B. E. Kearle, "The Presentation of Statistical Information," *AV Communication Review,* 11 (1963), 32–39; M. D. Vernon, "Presenting Information in Diagrams," *AV Communication Review,* 1 (1953), 147–158; and L. V. Peterson and Wilbur Schramm, "How Accurately Are Different Kinds of Graphs Read?," *AV Communication Review,* 2 (1955), 178–189.

5.   For a clear exploration of the relationships between ideas and visuals, see Edgar B. Wycoff, "Why Visuals?" *AV Communications,* 11 (1977), 39, 59.

6.   See Feliciano et al., "The Presentation of Statistical Information"; Vernon, "Presenting Information in Diagrams"; and Peterson and Schramm, "How Accurately Are Different Kinds of Graphs Read?"

CHAPTER ELEVEN

Delivering
Your Speech

*N*ikolai moaned, *"I just don't understand why I blanked out like that. I'm really embarrassed. How can I ever give another speech?" Professor Ramirez smiled. "Why do you think you had memory lapses during your speech?" "Oh, I don't know. I just couldn't remember which words came next." "How did you prepare to give this speech?" Nikolai's professor asked. "Did you write it out?" "Sure. I always write them out, then memorize them. Then I make notecards and my outline to hand in. But I never had trouble remembering a speech before." "Nikolai, maybe you've been using the wrong approach. What do you think would happen if you made a detailed outline first and didn't write out the speech word-for-word at all?" Nikolai considered his professor's suggestion. "Well, I suppose I could, but what if I couldn't remember the exact words I wanted to use?" "That's where the outline would be helpful. It would jog your memory and you wouldn't be tied to your notes as much. I'll bet your eye contact and responsiveness to your audience would improve, too."*

Similar to the student in this conversation, you may be struggling with the physical aspects of delivering your speeches. You're in good company—history records that many famous speakers had to overcome severe delivery problems before becoming effective speakers. Abraham Lincoln suffered from extreme speech fright; Eleanor Roosevelt was awkward and clumsy; John F. Kennedy had to overcome a strong dialect and repetitive gestures. Each of these famous speakers, as well as others, realized that the success of a speech depends not only on careful planning before the speech but also on the presentation of ideas during the speech. The oral presentation of the speech can add to or detract from the impact of the ideas.

As you speak, you must be aware that you communicate with your entire body—your face, your gestures, your voice, and your posture. Your voice and bodily movements—the *aural and visual channels of communication*—help to transmit your feelings and attitudes about yourself, your audience, and your topic. You may see speakers who reluctantly approach the platform, dragging their feet and fussing with their notes. Their feelings and attitudes are abundantly clear even before they utter their first words. Unwittingly, these speakers establish audience predispositions that work against them. Even if their ideas are important, those ideas are overshadowed by their distracting nonverbal communication.

If you've heard a recording or seen a video of Martin Luther King, Jr. giving his "I Have a Dream" speech, you can't fail to recognize the dramatic difference between hearing him speak and reading a copy of the speech. The same is true of Jesse Jackson, Margaret Thatcher, Ronald Reagan, and Barbara Jordan, among others. Their delivery adds impact to their ideas. It's clear that oral presentation adds to the impact of the message. Sometimes, *how* something is said is more memorable than *what* is said.

Your speech will gain strength and vitality if it's presented well. To help you achieve this objective, we'll discuss three important aspects of presentation: selecting the method of presentation, using your voice to communicate, and using your body to communicate.

SELECTING THE METHOD OF PRESENTATION

What method should you use when presenting your speech? Your choice will be based on several criteria, including *the type of speaking occasion, the purpose of your speech, your audience analysis,* and *your own strengths and weaknesses as a speaker.* Attention to these considerations will help you to decide whether your method of presentation should be (a) *impromptu,* (b) *memorized,* (c) read from a *manuscript,* or (d) *extemporized.*

The Impromptu Speech

The ability to speak off the cuff is useful in an emergency, but you should avoid impromptu speeches in other situations because they produce unpredictable outcomes. An **impromptu speech** is delivered on the spur of the moment without preparation. In an impromptu speech you must rely entirely on previous knowledge and skill. You might be asked in the middle of a fraternity meeting, for example, to give a progress report on your fraternity pledge committee. For best results when speaking extemporaneously, try to focus on a single idea, such as plans for the annual pledge-week open house, carefully relating all details connected to that idea. This strategy will keep you from rambling incoherently.

The Memorized Speech

On rare occasions, you may write out your speech and commit it to memory. When notecards or a TelePrompTer cannot be used, it may be acceptable for you to give a **memorized speech.** When making a toast at your parents' twenty-fifth wedding anniversary, for example, you probably wouldn't want to speak from notecards. Some speakers, such as comedians, deliver their remarks from memory to free their hands for special gestures.

Speakers who use memorized presentations are usually most effective when they write their speeches to sound like informal and conversational speech rather than formal, written essays. Keep in mind that when you are using a memorized speech, you will have difficulty responding to audience feedback. Since the words of the speech are predetermined, you can't easily adjust them as the speech progresses.

The Manuscript Speech

A **manuscript speech** is a speech that the speaker writes out beforehand and then reads from a manuscript or teleprompter. By using TelePrompTers, speakers can appear to be looking at television viewers while they're really reading their manuscripts projected onto clear sheets of Plexiglas. When extremely careful wording is required, the manuscript speech is appropriate. When the president addresses Congress, for example, a slip of the tongue could undermine domestic or foreign policies. Many radio and television speeches are read from a manuscript because of the strict time limits imposed by broadcasting schedules.

Speakers must choose among several methods of presentation. Which method is used here? What are other options?

The Extemporaneous Speech

With few exceptions, the speeches you deliver will be extemporaneous. For this reason, most of the advice in this textbook pertains to extemporaneous speaking. Extemporaneous speeches are nearly as polished as memorized ones, but they are more vigorous, flexible, and spontaneous.

Before giving an **extemporaneous speech** you must plan carefully and prepare a detailed outline and speaking notecards. Then, working from the notecards, you must practice the speech aloud, using your own words to communicate the ideas. Your expressions may differ somewhat each time you deliver the speech. Your notecards, however, will regulate the order of ideas. With this approach you gain control of the material and also preserve spontaneity of expression. Be sure to adequately prepare your extemporaneous speech with careful planning and practice. Otherwise, your speech may resemble an impromptu speech—in fact, the terms *impromptu* and *extemporaneous* are often confused.

USING YOUR VOICE TO COMMUNICATE

Your voice is an instrument that helps convey the meaning of language—it affects how listeners perceive and interpret your message.[1] Although you have been speaking for years, you probably have not tapped the potential of your voice. You will need to take time to practice to achieve your vocal potential just as you would to master any instrument. The suggestions in this section will help you to get started.

You communicate your enthusiasm to your listeners through your voice. By learning about the characteristics of vocal quality, you can make your ideas more interesting. Listen to a stock market reporter rattle off the daily industrial averages. Every word might be intelligible, but the reporter's vocal expression may be so repetitive and monotonous that the ideas seem unexciting. Then, listen to Al Michael giving a play-by-play account of a football game or Dick Vitale covering a basketball game. The vividness of their broadcasts depends largely upon the way they use their voices.

Our culture prizes one essential vocal quality above all others—a sense of "conversationality."[2] The most successful speakers of our time have cultivated the ability to make their listeners feel that they are being addressed personally. Even speakers who talk to millions via the mass media on afternoon talk shows or evening newscasts speak as though they are engaging each listener in a personal conversation. Speakers who have developed a conversational quality have recognized that, when giving a speech, they are talking "with," not "at," an audience.

The Effective Speaking Voice

Successful speakers use their voices to emotionally color their messages. Several vocal attributes contribute to the meanings public speakers convey

The most successful speakers of our time possess the quality of conversationality. What is conversationality?

to audiences. A flexible speaking voice has *intelligibility, variety,* and *understandable stress patterns.*

Intelligibility

Intelligibility is dependent upon loudness, rate, enunciation, and pronunciation. Most of the time, inadequate articulation, a rapid speaking rate, or soft volume is acceptable because you know the people you're talking with and because you're probably only 3–5 feet from them. In public speaking, however, you may be addressing people you don't know, often from 25 feet or more away. In such situations, to ensure maximum intelligibility, you must consider four independent but related factors: (a) *your vocal volume,* (b) *the rate at which you speak,* (c) *the care with which you enunciate important words,* and (d) *the standard of pronunciation that you observe.*

Adjust Your Volume. Probably the most important single factor in intelligibility is the volume at which you speak. Volume is related to the *distance* between you and your listeners and the amount of *noise* that is present.[3] You must realize that your own voice sounds louder to you than it does to your listeners. Obviously, you need to project your voice by increasing your volume if you're speaking in an auditorium filled with several hundred people. However, you shouldn't forget that a corresponding reduction in volume is also required when your listeners are only a few feet away.

In addition to distance, the amount of surrounding noise with which you must compete has an effect on your volume. Even in normal circumstances, some noise is always present. For example, the noise level of rustling leaves 6 feet away (10 decibels) is louder than a whisper. The noise in an empty theatre averages 25 decibels, but when the theater is filled with a "quiet" audience the level rises to 42. In a factory, a constant noise level of about 80 decibels is typical—about the same level as very loud speaking at close range. (See Figure 11.1.)

How can you determine the proper vocal volume for a particular speech situation? You can always use indirect feedback. Look to see if your listeners—even those people at the back of the room—appear to be hearing you. Or, better yet, use direct feedback. Ask your listeners if they can hear you. Ask your instructor or your friends about the loudness of your voice. You'll soon learn to adapt your volume to various situations.

Control Your Rate. **Rate** is the number of words spoken per minute. In animated conversation, you may jabber along at 200–250 words per minute. This rate is typical of people raised in the North, Midwest, or West. As words tumble out of your mouth in informal conversations, they're usually intelligible because they don't have to travel far. In large auditoriums or outdoors, though, rapid delivery can impede intelligibility. Echoes sometimes distort or destroy sounds in rooms; ventilation fans interfere with sound. In outdoor situations, words seem to drift and vanish into the open air.

When addressing larger audiences, you should slow down to an average of 120–150 words per minute. Obviously you don't go around timing your speaking rate, but you can remind yourself of potential rate problems as you prepare to speak. Get feedback from your instructors and classmates regarding your speaking rate.

Of course, we aren't saying that you should never speak rapidly. There are times when variety in rate will help you to stir and intensify the emotions of your listeners. But if you speed up, compensate by adjusting your volume and enunciating more carefully.

Enunciate Clearly. **Enunciation** refers to the crispness and precision with which you form words. Good enunciation is the clear and distinct utterance of syllables and words. Most of us are "lip lazy" in normal conversation. We slur sounds, drop syllables, and skip over the beginnings and endings of words. This "laziness" may not inhibit communication between friends, but it can seriously undermine a speaker's intelligibility.

Figure 11.1 Loudness Levels

As you can see, noise varies considerably. How could you adjust your volume if you were speaking to a "quiet" audience? What if you were competing with a lawnmower outside the building?

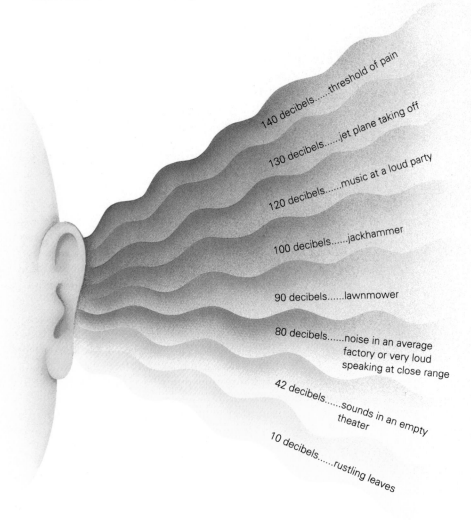

140 decibels......threshold of pain

130 decibels......jet plane taking off

120 decibels......music at a loud party

100 decibels......jackhammer

90 decibels......lawnmower

80 decibels......noise in an average factory or very loud speaking at close range

42 decibels......sounds in an empty theater

10 decibels......rustling leaves

When speaking publicly, force yourself to say *going* instead of *go-in, just* instead of *jist,* and *government* instead of *guvment.* You will need to open your mouth more widely and force your lips and tongue to form the consonants firmly. If you're having trouble enunciating clearly, ask your instructor for some exercises to improve your performance.

Meet Standards of Pronunciation. To be intelligible, you must form sounds carefully and meet audience expectations regarding acceptable pronunciation. If your words can't be understood because they are slurred, garbled, or otherwise inarticulate, your listeners won't be able to grasp what you say. Even if your words are recognizable, any peculiarity of pronunciation is sure to be noticed by some listeners. Your different pronunciation may distract your listeners and may undermine your credibility as a speaker.

Standards of pronunciation differ between geographic regions and cultural groups. A **dialect** is language use—including vocabulary, grammar, and pronunciation—unique to a particular group or region. Your pronunciation and grammatical or syntactical arrangement of words determine your dialect. You may have a "foreign accent," a white southern or black northern dialect, a New England "twang," or a Hispanic trill.

Since dialects have different rules for vocabulary, grammar, and pronunciation, a clash of dialects can result in confusion and frustration for both speaker and listener. Occasionally an audience may make negative judgments about the speaker's credibility—that is, the speaker's education, reliability, responsibility, and capacity for leadership—based solely on the speaker's dialect.[4] Paralinguists call these judgments based on dialect "vocal stereotypes."[5] Many news anchors for national networks, wary of the effect of "vocal stereotypes," have adopted a midwestern American dialect, a manner of speaking that is widely accepted across the country. Many speakers become "bilingual," using their own dialects when facing local audiences, but switching to midwestern American when addressing more varied audiences. When you speak, you'll have to decide whether you should use the grammar, vocabulary, and vocal patterns of middle America.

Variety

As you move from conversations with friends to the enlarged context of public speaking, you may discover that listeners accuse you of monotony of pitch or rate. When speaking in a large public setting, you should compensate for the greater distance that sounds will have to travel by varying certain characteristics of your voice. Variety is produced by changes in *rate, pitch,* and *force,* and by *pauses.*

Vary Your Rate. Earlier, we discussed the rate at which we normally speak. Consider ways to alter your speaking rate to match your ideas. Slow down to emphasize your own thoughtfulness or quicken the pace when your ideas are emotionally charged. Observe, for example, how a sports announcer varies speaking rate from play to play or how an evangelist changes pace regularly. A varied rate keeps an audience's attention riveted to the speech.

Change Your Pitch. **Pitch** is the frequency of sound waves in a particular sound. Three aspects of pitch—level, range, and variation—are relevant to effective vocal communication. Your everyday **pitch level**—whether it is habitually in the soprano, alto, tenor, baritone, or bass range—is adequate for most of your daily communication needs.

However, when you speak in public, you should employ a broader **pitch range.** In normal conversation, you may use only a few notes, sometimes even less than an octave. But such a limited range may seem monotonous during a speech. Given the distances sounds must travel between speaker and audience and the length of time speakers talk, you have to exaggerate your range of sounds during a speech. Your pitch "highs" must become higher and your "lows" should be lower. Usually, the more emotionally charged your ideas, the more you should vary your pitch range. Obviously, you can get carried away. Just as a narrow pitch range communicates boredom, an extremely wide pitch range can communicate artificiality or uncontrolled excitement or fear.

The key to successful control of pitch ultimately depends on understanding the importance of **pitch variation.** As a general rule, use higher pitches to communicate excitement and lower pitches to create a sense of control or solemnity. Adjust the pitch to fit the emotion.

As a second rule, let the sense of the sentence control your pitch variations. For example, move your voice up at the end of a question. Such an abrupt change in pitch is called a **step**. A more gradual or continuous pitch inflection is termed a **slide.** Television announcer Ed McMahon uses both of these techniques in his famous introduction of Johnny Carson. (See Figure 11.2) Ed slides his voice up until he reaches a high pitch level at the end of the word *Here's*; then, he steps down the scale on the word *Johnny*. Such vocal slides and steps add emphasis to words. By mastering their use, you'll be able to call attention to your word choices, making your meaning clearer and more precise.

Figure 11.2 Ed McMahon's Pitch Variation
Notice how Ed McMahon uses both a slide and a step in his well-known opening to the "Tonight Show."

The Gender Gap of Income Inequality

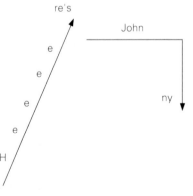

Stress

A third aspect of vocal behavior is stress. **Stress** is the way in which sounds, syllables, and words are accented. Without vocal stress, everything in a speech would sound the same. The resulting message would be both incomprehensible and emotionless. Without vocal stress, you'd sound like a computer. Vocal stress is achieved in two ways—through *vocal emphasis* and through the *judicious use of pauses*.

Use Vocal Emphasis. **Emphasis** is the way that you accent or attack words. You create emphasis principally through increased volume, changes in pitch, or variations in rate.

Emphasis can affect the meanings of your sentences. Notice how the meaning of "Tom's taking Jane out for pizza tonight" varies with changes in word emphasis:

1. "TOM's taking Jane out for pizza tonight." (Tom and *not* John or Bob is taking Jane out.)
2. "Tom's taking JANE out for pizza tonight." (He's not taking out Sue.)
3. "Tom's taking Jane OUT for pizza tonight." (They're not staying home as usual.)
4. "Tom's taking Jane out for PIZZA tonight." (They're not having seafood or hamburgers.)
5. "Tom's taking Jane out for pizza TONIGHT." (They're going out tonight—not tomorrow or next weekend.)

Without careful control of vocal force, a speaker's messages will be subject to a great many interpretations. A lack of vocal stress not only gives the impression that you are bored, but also causes needless misunderstandings of your meaning. Changes in rate can also be used to add emphasis. Relatively simple changes can emphasize where you are in an outline—"My s-e-c-o-n-d point is. . . ." Several changes in rate can indicate the relationship among ideas. Consider the following example:

> *We are a country faced with* . . . [moderate rate] *financial deficits, racial tensions, an energy crunch, a crisis of morality, environmental depletion, government waste* . . . [fast rate] *and-a-stif-ling-na-tion-al-debt* [slow rate].

The ideas pick up speed through the accelerating list of problems but then come to an emphatic halt with the speaker's main concern—the national debt. Such variations in rate emphasize for an audience what is and what isn't especially important to the speech.

Use Helpful Pauses. Pauses are the intervals of silence between or within words, phrases, or sentences. Pauses punctuate thought by separating groups of spoken words into meaningful units. When placed immediately before a key idea or the climax of a story, they can create suspense—"And the winner is [pause]." When placed after a major point, pauses can add emphasis. Inserted at the proper moment, a dramatic pause can express feelings more forcefully than words. Clearly, silence can be a highly effective communicative tool if used intelligently and sparingly, and if not embarrassingly prolonged.

Sometimes, speakers fill silences in their discourse with sounds—*ums, ahs, ers, well-ahs, you-knows,* and other meaningless fillers. No doubt, you have heard speakers say, "Today, ah, er, I would like, you know, to speak to you, um, about a pressing, well-uh, like, a pressing problem facing this, uh, campus." Such vocal intrusions convey feelings of hesitancy and lack of confidence. You should make a concerted effort to remove these intrusions from your speech. Also, avoid too many pauses, and those that seem artificial, because they can make you appear manipulative or overrehearsed.

On the other hand, don't be afraid of silences. Pauses allow you to stress important ideas, such as when the audience waits for the punch line in a story or argument. Pauses also intensify the involvement of listeners in emotional situations, such as when Barbara Walters or William F. Buckley, Jr., pause for reflection during an interview.

Controlling the Emotional Quality

A listener's judgment of a speaker's personality and emotional commitment often centers on that speaker's vocal quality—the fullness or thinness of the tones and whether the sound is harsh, husky, mellow, nasal, breathy, or resonant. Depending on your vocal quality, an audience may judge you as being angry, happy, confident, fearful, sincere, or sad.

Fundamental to a listener's reaction to vocal quality are **emotional characterizers**—cues about a speaker's emotional state. These cues include laughing, crying, whispering, inhaling, or exhaling.[6] Emotional characterizers combine with your words to communicate subtle shades of meanings. Consider for a moment, a few of the many ways you can say, "I can't believe I ate the whole thing." You might say it as though you were reporting a fact, as if you can't believe you ate it *all,* or as though eating the entire thing were an impossible achievement. Finally, you might say it as though you were expressing doubts about whether you did actually eat the whole thing. As you say the sentence to express these different meanings, you might laugh or inhale sharply, altering your emotional characterizers. Such changes are important cues to meaning for listeners.

Your vocal qualities are of prime importance in determining the impression you make on an audience. While you can't completely control your vocal qualities, you can be alert to their effects on your listeners. Keep your repertoire of vocal qualities in mind as you decide how to express key ideas for an audience.

Practicing Vocal Control

Do not assume that you'll be able to master in a day all of the vocal skills that have been described. Take the time to review and digest the ideas

Effective vocal delivery can be important in many contexts. Can you think of other ways to employ the characteristics of effective vocal delivery?

presented. Above all, *practice* out loud. Record yourself on tape and then listen to the way you are conveying ideas. Ask your instructor to provide exercises designed to make your vocal instrument more flexible. When you're able to control your voice and make it respond to your desires, you'll have a great deal more control over your effect on listeners. Before any vocal skill can be natural and effective with listeners, it must become so automatic that it will work with little conscious effort. Once your voice responds flexibly in the enlarged context of public speaking, you'll be able to achieve the sense of conversationality so highly valued in our society.

USING YOUR BODY TO COMMUNICATE

Just as your voice gives meaning to your message through the aural channel, your physical behavior carries meaning through the visual channel. While your listeners are trying to grasp your ideas aurally, they are simultaneously trying to clarify their understanding of your messages visually. You can use the aural and visual channels to create a better understanding of your presentation.[7] To help you explore the ways of enhancing your use of the visual channel, we'll examine the speaker's physical behavior.

Dimensions of Nonverbal Communication

In recent years, research has reemphasized the important role of physical, or nonverbal, behaviors in effective oral communication.[8] Basically, three generalizations about nonverbal communication should occupy your attention when you are a speaker:

1. *Speakers reveal and reflect their emotional states through their nonverbal behaviors.* Your listeners read your feelings toward yourself, your topic, and your audience from your facial expressions. Consider the contrast between a speaker who walks to the front of the room briskly, head held high, and one who shuffles, head bowed and arms hanging limply. Communications scholar Dale G. Leathers summarized a good deal of research into nonverbal communication processes: "Feelings and emotions are more accurately exchanged by nonverbal than verbal means. . . . The nonverbal portion of communication conveys meanings and intentions that are relatively free from deception, distortion, and confusion."[9]

2. *The speaker's nonverbal cues enrich or elaborate the message that comes through words.* A solemn face can reinforce the dignity of a funeral eulogy. The words, "Either do this or do that," can be illustrated with appropriate arm-and-hand gestures. Taking a few steps to one side tells an audience that you are moving from one argument to another. A smile enhances a lighter moment in your speech.

3. *Nonverbal messages form a reciprocal interaction between speaker and listener.* Listeners frown, smile, shift nervously in their seats, and engage in many types of nonverbal behavior already noted in Chapter 2. In this chapter, we will concentrate on the speaker's control of physical behavior. There are four areas of nonverbal communication that concern every speaker: (a) *proxemics,* (b) *movement and stance,* (c) *facial expressions,* and (d) *gestures.*

Proxemics
Proxemics is the use of space by human beings. Two components of proxemics are especially relevant to public speakers:

1. *Physical arrangements*—the layout of the room in which you are speaking, including the presence or absence of a lectern, the seating plan, the location of chalkboards and similar aids, and any physical barriers between you and your audience.
2. *Distance*—the extent or degree of separation between you and your audience.[10]

Both of these components have a bearing on the message you communicate publicly. Typical speaking situations involve a speaker facing a seated audience. Objects in the physical space—the lectern, a table, several flags—tend to set the speaker apart from the listeners. This "setting apart," you must remember, is both *physical* and *psychological.* Literally, as well as figuratively, objects can stand in the way of open communication. If you're trying to create a more informal atmosphere, you should reduce the physical barriers in the setting. You might stand beside or in front of the lectern

Figure 11.3 Classification of Interhuman Distance
Anthropologist Edward T. Hall has identified typical distances for various human interactions. Can you provide an example of communication that might occur at each of the four distances?

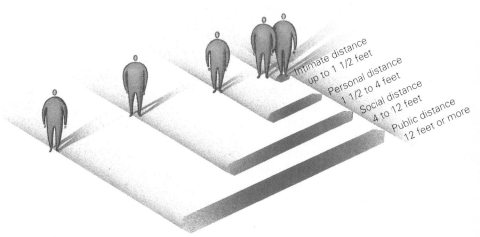

instead of behind it. In very informal settings, you might even sit on the front edge of a table while talking.

There are several factors that determine how you will use space:

1. The *formality* of the occasion—the more solemn or formal the occasion is, the more barriers will be required (on highly formal occasions, speakers may speak from an elevated platform or stage).
2. The *nature of the material*—extensive quoted material or statistical evidence may require you to use a lectern; the use of visual aids often demands that special equipment such as an easel, table, or overhead projector be included in the room.
3. Your *personal preference*—you may feel more at ease speaking from behind rather than in front of the lectern.

The distance component of proxemics adds a second set of considerations. In most situations, you'll be talking at what anthropologist Edward T. Hall has termed a "public distance"—12 feet or more from your listeners.[11] (See Figure 11.3.) To communicate with people at that distance, you obviously can't rely on your normal speaking voice or subtle changes in posture or movement. Instead, you must compensate for the distance by using larger gestures, broader shifts of your body, and increased vocal energy. By contrast, you should lower your vocal volume and restrict the breadth of your gestures when addressing a few individuals at a closer distance.

Movement and Stance
How you move and stand provides a second set of nonverbal cues for your audience. **Movement** includes physical shifts from place to place; **posture**

refers to the relative relaxation or rigidity and vertical position of the body. Movements and posture can communicate ideas about yourself to an audience. The speaker who stands stiffly and erectly may, without uttering a word, be saying, "This is a formal occasion" or "I am tense, even afraid, of this audience." The speaker who leans forward, physically reaching out to the audience, could be saying silently but eloquently, "I am interested in you. I want you to understand and accept my ideas." The speaker who sits casually on the front edge of a table and assumes a relaxed posture may suggest informality and readiness to engage in a dialogue with listeners.

Movements and postural adjustments regulate communication. As a public speaker, you can, for instance, move from one end of a table to the other to indicate a change in topic. Or, you can accomplish the same purpose by changing your posture. At other times, you can move toward your audience when making an especially important point. In each case, you're using your body to reinforce transitions in your subject or to emphasize a matter of special concern.

An equally important point to remember is that your posture and movements can also work against you. Aimless and continuous pacing is distracting. Nervous bouncing or swaying makes listeners uneasy, and if you adopt an excessively erect stance, you may increase tension in your audience. Your movements should be purposive, and they should enhance the meaning of your words. Only then will stance and movement help your communicative effort and produce the impression of self-assurance and control that you want to exhibit.[12]

Facial Expressions

Your face is another important channel of nonverbal messages. When you speak, your facial expressions function in a number of ways. First, they communicate much about yourself and your feelings. What researchers Paul Ekman and Wallace V. Friesen call affect displays are communicated to an audience through the face. **Affect displays** are facial signs of emotion that an audience perceives when scanning your face to see how you feel about yourself and how you feel about them.[13]

Second, facial changes provide listeners with cues that help them interpret the contents of your message. Are you being ironic or satirical? Are you sure of your conclusions? Is this a harsh or pleasant message? Researchers tell us that a high percentage of the information conveyed in a typical message is communicated nonverbally. Psychologist Albert Mehrabian has devised a formula to account for the emotional impact of the different components of a speaker's message. Words, he says, contribute 7 percent, vocal elements 38 percent, and facial expression 55 percent.[14]

Third, the "display" elements of your face—your eyes, especially— establish a visual bonding between you and your listeners. Our culture values eye-to-eye contact. The speaker who looks people "square in the eye" is perceived as earnest, sincere, forthright, and self-assured. In other words, regular eye contact with your listeners helps establish your credibility. The speaker who looks at the floor, who reads from notes, or who delivers a speech to the back wall severs visual bonding and loses credibility.[15]

Of course, you can't control your face completely, which is probably why listeners search it so carefully for clues to your feelings. You can, however, make sure that your facial messages don't belie your verbal ones—when you're uttering angry words, your face should be communicating anger; when you're pleading with your listeners, your eyes should be engaging them intently. In short, use your face to your advantage.

Gestures

Gestures are purposive movements of the head, shoulders, arms, hands, and other areas of the body that support and illustrate the ideas you're expressing. Fidgeting with your clothing and notecards or clutching the sides of the lectern aren't purposive gestures and they distract from the ideas you're communicating. The effective public speaker commonly uses three kinds of gestures:

1. *Conventional gestures* are physical movements that are symbols with specific meanings assigned by custom or convention. These gestures *condense* ideas: they are shorthand expressions of things or ideas that would require you to take many words to describe fully. The raised-hand "stop" gesture of the traffic officer, the manual sign language of hearing impaired persons, and the arm signals of football referees are all conventional gestures.

2. *Descriptive gestures* are physical movements that describe the idea to be communicated. Speakers often depict the size, shape, or location of an object by movements of the hands and arms; that is, they "draw pictures" for listeners. A speaker might use the thumb and index finger to describe the "O" rings of a space shuttle, for example, or raise an arm to indicate the height of a stranger.

3. *Indicators* are movements of the hands, arms, or other parts of the body that express feelings. Speakers may throw up their arms when disgusted, pound the lectern when angry, shrug their shoulders when puzzled, or point a threatening finger when issuing a warning. Such gestures arouse listeners' feelings. They communicate emotions to your listeners and encourage similar responses in them. Your facial expressions and other body cues usually reinforce such gestures.[16]

Once you understand their purposes, your gestures can be perfected through practice. As you practice, you'll obtain better results if you keep in mind three factors that influence the effectiveness of gestures: (a) *relaxation,* (b) *vigor and definiteness,* and (c) *proper timing.*

First, if your muscles are tense, your movements will be stiff and your gestures awkward. You should make a conscious effort to relax your muscles before you start to speak. You might "warm up" by taking a few steps, shrugging your shoulders, flexing your muscles, or breathing deeply.

Second, good gestures are natural and animated. They communicate the dynamism associated with speaker credibility. You should put enough force into your gestures to show your conviction and enthusiasm. Avoid exaggerated or repetitive gestures such as pounding the table or chopping the air to emphasize minor ideas in your speech. Vary the nature of your gestures as the ideas in your speech demand.

Third, timing is crucial to effective gestures. The *stroke* of a gesture—that is, the shake of the fist or the movement of the finger—should fall on, or slightly precede, the point the gesture emphasizes. Try making a gesture after the word or phrase it was intended to reinforce has already been spoken and notice how ridiculous it seems. Practice making gestures until they're habitual and then use them spontaneously as the impulse arises.

Adapting Nonverbal Behavior to Your Presentations

Although you may never completely control your physical behavior, you can gain skill in orchestrating your gestures and other movements. You can consciously make some decisions about how you will use your body together with the other channels of communication to communicate effectively. As we conclude this chapter, let's review some of these choices.

1. *Plan a proxemic relationship with your audience that reflects your own needs and attitudes toward your subject and your listeners.* If you feel comfortable behind a lectern, use it, but keep in mind that it places a barrier between you and your listeners. If you want your whole body to be visible to the audience, yet you feel the need to have your notes at eye level, stand beside the lectern and arrange your notecards on it. If you want to relax your body, sit behind a table or desk—be sure you can compensate for the resulting loss of action by increasing your vocal volume. If you feel physically relaxed and want to be "open" to your audience, stand in front of a table or desk. Start with yourself and learn to work publicly as the person you really are.

Also take into account the needs of your listeners. The farther you are from your listeners, the more important it is for them to have a clear view of you, the harder you must work to project your words, and the broader your physical movements must be. The speaker who crouches behind a lectern in an auditorium of 300 people soon loses contact with the audience. Think of the large lecture classes you've attended or outdoor political rallies you've witnessed. Recall the delivery patterns of speakers who worked effectively in such situations. Put them to work for you.

2. *Adapt the physical setting to your communicative needs.* If you're going to use visual aids—such as a chalkboard, flipchart, or working model—remove the tables, chairs, and other objects that might obstruct your audience's view. Increase intimacy by arranging chairs in a small circle or stress formality by using a lectern.

3. *Adapt the size of your gestures and amount of your movement to the size of the audience.* Keeping in mind what anthropologist Edward Hall noted about public distance in communication, you should realize that subtle changes

of facial expression or small hand movements can't be seen clearly in large rooms or auditoriums. Although many auditoriums have a raised platform and slanted floor to allow a speaker to be seen more clearly, you should adjust to the distance between you and your audience by making your movements and gestures larger.

4. *Continuously scan your audience from side to side and from front to back, looking specific individuals in the eye.* Your head should not be in constant motion; "continuously" does not imply rhythmical, nonstop bobbing. Rather, you should interact with the entire group in front of you. Take them all into your field of vision periodically; establish firm visual bonds with individuals occasionally. Such bonds enhance your credibility and keep your auditors' attention riveted on you.

5. *Use your body to communicate your feelings about what you're saying.* When you're angry, don't be afraid to gesture vigorously. When you're expressing tenderness, let that message come across your relaxed face. In other words, when you communicate publicly, use the same emotional indicators as you do when you talk to individuals on a one-to-one basis.

6. *Use your body to regulate the pace of your presentation and to control transitions.* Shift your weight from one idea to another. Move more when you're speaking more rapidly. Reduce bodily action and gestures accordingly when you're slowing down to emphasize particular ideas.

7. *Finally, use your full repertoire of gestures while talking publicly.* You probably do this in everyday conversation without even thinking about it; recreate that behavior when addressing an audience. Physical readiness is the key. Keep your hands and arms free and loose so that you can call them into action easily, quickly, and naturally. Let your hands rest comfortably at your sides, relaxed but ready. Then, as you unfold the ideas of your speech, use descriptive gestures to indicate size, shape, or relationships, making sure the movements are large enough to be seen in the back row. Use conventional gestures also to give visual dimension to your spoken ideas. Keep in mind that there is no "right" number of gestures to use. However, as you practice, think of the kinds of bodily and gestural actions that complement your message and purpose.

Selecting the appropriate method of presentation and using your voice and body productively will enhance your chances of gaining support for your ideas. *Practice* is the key to the effective use of these nonverbal elements. Through practice, you'll have an opportunity to see how your voice and body complement or detract from your ideas. The more you prepare and practice, the more confident you'll feel about presenting the speech, and, so, the more comfortable you'll be. Remember that the nonverbal channel of communication creates meaning for your audience.

CHAPTER SUMMARY

1. Every speaker should effectively use the *aural* and *visual channels* of communication.

2. Begin with an appropriate method of presentation—*impromptu, memorized, manuscript,* or *extemporaneous* delivery. Your choice will be based on the type of speaking occasion, the seriousness and purpose of your speech, your audience analysis, and your own strengths and weaknesses as a speaker.

3. Regardless of the method of presentation, a good voice enables a speaker to make a message clearer. A flexible speaking voice has *intelligibility, variety,* and *understandable stress patterns.*

4. *Volume, rate, enunciation,* and *pronunciation* interact to affect intelligibility.

5. Different standards of pronunciation create regional differences known as *dialects.*

6. Changes in *rate, pitch,* and *stress* and *pauses* create variety in presentation and help eliminate monotonous delivery.

7. *Emotional characterizers* communicate subtle shades of meaning to listeners.

8. Three generalizations about nonverbal communication demand your attention: (a) *speakers reveal and reflect their emotional states through their nonverbal behaviors;* (b) *nonverbal cues enrich or elaborate the speaker's message;* and (c) *nonverbal messages form an interaction between speaker and listener.*

9. Speakers knowledgeable about the effects of *proxemics* can use space to create physical and psychological intimacy or distance. A speaker's *movement* and *posture* regulate communication.

10. *Facial expressions* communicate feelings, provide important cues to meaning, establish visual bonding with listeners, and establish speaker credibility.

11. *Gestures* enhance listener responses to messages if the gestures are relaxed, definite, and properly timed.

12. Speakers commonly use *conventional gestures, descriptive gestures,* and *indicators.*

KEY TERMS

affect displays (p. 220)
dialect (p. 213)
emotional characterizers (p. 216)
emphasis (p. 215)
enunciation (p. 211)
extemporaneous speech (p. 209)
gesture (p. 221)
impromptu speech (p. 207)
manuscript speech (p. 208)
memorized speech (p. 208)
movement (p. 219)

pitch (p. 213)
pitch level (p. 214)
pitch range (p. 214)
pitch variation (p. 214)
posture (p. 219)
proxemics (p. 218)
rate (p. 211)
slide (p. 214)
step (p. 214)
stress (p. 215)

SKILLBUILDING ACTIVITIES

1. Divide the class into teams and play charades. For rules, see David Jauner, "Charades as a Teaching Device," *Speech Teacher,* 20 (November 1971), 302. A game of charades will not only loosen you up psychologically but should help sensitize you to the variety of small but perceptible cues you "read" when interpreting messages.

2. Form small task groups. Appoint a member of the group to record ideas and then think of as many situations as possible when each of the four methods of speaking would be used. Choose a reporter to convey the group's examples to the class.

3. Choose a selection from a poetry anthology and practice reading it aloud. As you read, change your volume, rate, pitch, and emphasis and use pauses. Practice reading the poem in several ways to heighten different emotions or to emphasize different interpretations. Record the poem with a tape recorder and evaluate it when you play it back or ask a friend to listen and offer suggestions.

REFERENCES

1. R. Geiselman and John Crawley, "Incidental Processing of Speaker Characteristics: Voice as Connotative Information," *Journal of Verbal Learning and Verbal Behavior,* 22 (1983), 15–23.

2. W. Barnett Pearce and Bernard J. Brommel, "Vocalic Communication in Persuasion," *Quarterly Journal of Speech,* 58 (1972), 298–306.

3. The term *loudness* is used synonymously with *intensity* here because the former term is clearer to most people. Technically, of course, loudness—a distinct function in the science of acoustics—is not strictly synonymous with intensity. To explain the exact relationship between the two terms is beyond the scope of this book because the explanation involves many complicated psychophysical relationships. For a full discussion of these relationships, see Giles W. Gray and Claude M. Wise, *The Bases of Speech,* 3rd ed. (New York: Harper & Row, 1959), chap. 3.

4. Mark L. Knapp, *Essentials of Nonverbal Communication* (New York: Holt, 1980).

5. Klaus R. Scherer, H. London, and Garret Wolf, "The Voice of Competence: Paralinguistic Cues and Audience Evaluation," *Journal of Research in Personality,* 7 (1973), 31–44; Jitendra Thakerer and Howard Giles, "They Are—So They Spoke: Noncontent Speech Stereotypes," *Language and Communication,* 1 (1981), 255–261.

6. Bruce L. Brown, William J. Strong, and Alvin C. Rencher, "Perceptions of Personality from Speech: Effects of Manipulations of Acoustical Parameters," *Journal of the Acoustical Society of America,* 54 (1973), 29–35.

7. Haig Bosmajian, ed., *The Rhetoric of Nonverbal Communication* (Glenview, Ill.: ScottForesman, 1971).

8. Much of this research is summarized in Mark L. Knapp, *Nonverbal Communication in Human Interaction,* 2nd ed. (New York: Holt, 1978).

9. Dale G. Leathers, *Nonverbal Communication Systems* (Boston: Allyn & Bacon, 1975), 4–5.

10. For a fuller discussion of each of these components, see Leathers, *Nonverbal Communication Systems,* 52–59.

11. Hall divides interhuman communication distances into four segments: *Intimate Distance*—up to 1 1/2 feet apart; *Personal Distance*—1 1/2–4 feet; *Social Distance*—4–12 feet; and *Public Distance*—12 feet or more. On the basis of these distinctions he has carefully noted how people's eye contact, tone of voice, and ability to touch and observe change from one distance to another. See Edward T. Hall, "Distances in Man," *The Hidden Dimension* (New York: Doubleday, 1969), chap. X.

12. Albert E. Scheflen, "The Significance of Posture in Communication Systems," *Psychiatry,* 27 (1964), 321.

13. Paul Ekman, Wallace V. Friesen, and P. Ellsworth, *Emotion in the Human Face: Guidelines for Research and an Integration of Findings* (New York: Pergamon, 1972).

14. Robert Rivlin and Karen Gravelle, *Deciphering the Senses: The Expanding World of Human Perception* (New York: Simon and Schuster, 1984), 98.

15. For a difficult but rewarding essay on the management of demeanor, see Erving Goffman, "On Face Work," *Interaction Ritual: Essays on Face-to-Face Behavior* (New York: Doubleday, 1967), 5–46.

16. For a more complete system of classifying gestures, see Paul Ekman and Wallace V. Friesen, "Hand Movements," *Journal of Communication,* 22 (December 1972), 360.

Types of Public Speaking

CHAPTER TWELVE

Speeches to Inform

"*H*ow on earth can I make this speech interesting and relevant to my class?" Cherif asked his instructor, Ms. McGee. He knew a great deal about the Vietnam War and he wanted his class to know more about its causes and its effects on American life. "Well," his instructor replied, "first think about what really interests your classmates." "Bar hopping, sports, movies, dances, and television," replied Cherif. "Then that's your key," Ms. McGee answered. "Bar hopping's my key?" "No, no," she said, "mass media are the keys! Think of all the television programs and films focusing on Vietnam. For movies, we've had* Coming Home, Apocalypse Now, The Deer Hunter, Full Metal Jacket, Platoon, Born on the Fourth of July, *and all the* Rambo *movies. On television we've had docudramas such as HBO's* Vietnam War Stories *as well as prime time TV series such as* Magnum P.I., Hill Street Blues, Tour of Duty, *and* China Beach. *Some have touched on Vietnam and others have featured it. Use those movies and TV programs as ways to reach your audience.*"

Our society almost worships facts. A staggering amount of information is available to us, particularly because of such technological developments as electronic media, photostatic printing, miniaturized circuitry, image transmission via phones (fax machines), and computerized data storage and retrieval systems. Mere information, however, does nothing and tells us nothing. Information is simply there until human beings shape, interpret, and act on it. That's why public speakers are called upon to assemble, package, and present information to other human beings.

One theme will be sounded again and again in this chapter: *"mere information" is useless until someone puts it together in ways that make it clear and relevant to others.* Informative speeches are needed to clarify and make data and ideas relevant to audiences. Without clarification or interpretation and relevance, information is meaningless; the informative speaker's job is to adapt data and ideas to human needs. In this chapter, we'll discuss various types of informative speeches, outline the essential features of all informative talks, and then review some of the usual ways of structuring each type of informative speech.

TYPES OF INFORMATIVE SPEECHES

Informative speeches take many forms depending on the situation, the level of knowledge possessed by listeners, and your own abilities as a presenter of data. Four of these forms—(a) *speeches of definition,* (b) *instructions and demonstrations,* (c) *oral reports,* and (d) *lectures*—occur so frequently, however, that they merit special attention. They represent four common ways in which people package or integrate information to meet the needs of others.

Speeches of Definition

"Mommy, what's a 'tattletail'?" "Professor Martinez, what's the difference between RAM and ROM?" "Joanne, before we can decide whether to buy this house, you're going to have to answer a dumb question for us—what are 'covenants'?" You've been asking questions like these all of your life. A speech of definition does not merely offer a definition of an idea or concept; you could refer people to a dictionary if that were all that was involved. Rather, a **speech of definition** seeks to define concepts or processes in ways that make them relevant to a situation or problem that listeners face. Once five-year-old Sarah knows what a tattletale is, she'll know she has a human relations problem; once you know the differences between RAM and ROM, you'll make a great leap forward in your introduction to computing class; and once you know that covenants are binding agreements that may restrict land use, you'll explore them very carefully before purchasing property.

Instructions and Demonstrations

Throughout your life, classroom instructions, job instructions, and instructions for the performance of special tasks have played vital roles. Not only have you gone through many "tell" sessions, but you've also had people "show" you how to execute actions—how to sort various kinds of plastic jugs for recycling, how to manage a voter registration table, how to grow and replenish a yogurt culture. Generally, **instructions** are verbal communications that explain complex processes, while **demonstrations** are verbal and nonverbal messages explaining and illustrating those processes. Both involve the serial presentation of information, usually in steps or phases, and both require clarity, simply because your listeners are expected to repeat or reproduce these steps themselves after you've spoken.

Oral Reports

An **oral report** is a speech that assembles, arranges, and interprets information gathered in response to a request made or a goal set by a group. Academic reports, committee reports, and executive reports are examples of oral reports. Scientists and other scholars announce their research findings in oral reports at professional conventions. Committees in business, industry, and government carry out special research or advisory tasks and then present oral reports to their parent organizations or constituencies. Board chairpersons present oral reports annually to the stockholders on the past year's activities.

Lectures

Lectures increase the audience's understanding or appreciation of a particular field of knowledge or activity. They usually involve some sort of *explanation*. Lecturers define unclear or new concepts but also indicate how a

Classroom lectures are probably the first type of informative speeches that come to your mind. What are the characteristics of the most effective classroom lectures you've heard?

certain situation arose or point out the implications of an old or new policy. For instance, a business executive might not only define "management by objectives" but also go on to show how such management can modernize even a small business; a historian might tell a group of students what social-cultural forces converged to create the American Revolution; and a social worker could lecture an audience of government officials on the local impact of the Gramm-Rudman Act and tax reform. Characteristic types of lectures include talks on travel and public affairs; classroom lectures; and talks at club meetings, study conferences, and institutes.

ESSENTIAL QUALITIES OF INFORMATIVE SPEECHES

Five qualities should characterize any speech to inform: (a) *clarity*, (b) *the association of new ideas with familiar ones*, (c) *packaging or clustering ideas*, (d) *coherence*, and (e) *motivational appeal*.

Clarity

The quality of clarity is largely the result of effective organization and the careful selection of words. Informative speeches achieve maximum clarity when listeners can follow and understand what the speaker is saying.

In organizing your speech, observe the following rules:

1. *Don't try to cover too many points.* Confine your speech to three or four principal ideas, grouping whatever facts or ideas you wish to consider under your four headings. Even if you know a tremendous amount about your subject matter, remember that you can't make everyone an expert with a single speech.

2. *Clarify the relationship between your main points by observing the principles of coordination.* Word your transitions carefully—"*Second,* you must prepare the chair for caning by cleaning out the groove and cane holes"; "The Stamp Act Crisis was *followed by* an *even more important* event—The Townshend Duties"; "To test *these* hypotheses, we set up the *following* experiment." Such transitions allow auditors to follow you from point to point.

3. *Keep your speech moving forward according to a well-developed plan.* Don't jump back and forth between ideas, charging ahead and then backtracking; that approach creates more smoke than light.

In selecting your words, follow the advice we offered in Chapter 8:

1. *Use a precise, accurate vocabulary without getting too technical.* In telling someone how to finish off a basement room, you might be tempted to say, "Next, take one of these long sticks and cut it off in this funny-looking

gizmo with a saw in it and try to make the corners match." An accurate vocabulary will help your listeners remember what supplies and tools to get when they approach the same project: "This is a ceiling molding; it goes around the room between the wall and the ceiling to cover the seams between the paneling and the ceiling tiles. You make the corners of the molding match by using a mitre box, which has grooves that allow you to cut 45-degree angles. Here's how you do it."

2. *Simplify when possible, including only as much technical vocabulary as you need.* Don't make a speech on the operation of a two-cycle internal combustion engine sound as if it came out of a lawn mower mechanic's operational manual. An audience bogged down in unnecessary detail and complex vocabulary can become confused and bored.

3. *Use reiteration when it clarifies complex ideas, but avoid simply repeating the same words.* Instead, rephrase to help solidify ideas for those who had trouble getting them the first time: "Unlike a terrestrial telescope, a celestial telescope is used for looking at moons, planets, and stars; that is, its mirrors and lens are ground and arranged in such a way that it focuses on objects thousands of miles, not hundreds of feet, away from the observer."

Associating New Ideas with Familiar Ones

Audiences grasp new facts and ideas more readily when they can associate them with what they already know. In a speech to inform, try to connect the new with the old. (See Figure 12.1.) To do this, you need to have done enough solid audience analysis so that you know what experiences, images, analogies, and metaphors to use in your speech.

Sometimes the associations you ought to make are obvious. A college dean talking to an audience of manufacturers on the problems of higher education presented his ideas under the headings of raw material, casting, machining, polishing, and assembling. He translated his central ideas into an analogy that his audience, given their vocations, would be sure to understand and appreciate. If you cannot think of any obvious associations, you may have to rely on common experiences or images. For instance, you might explain the operation of the human eye pupil by comparing it to the operation of a camera lens aperture.

Packaging or Clustering Ideas

Another way that you can help listeners make sense out of your speech is by providing them with a well-organized package of tightly clustered ideas. Classic research on memory and organization demonstrated that the "magic number" of items we can remember is seven, plus or minus two; more recent research has suggested that the number is probably five, again

Figure 12.1 Association of New Ideas with Familiar Ones
Audiences grasp new concepts more quickly when those concepts are compared to things they already know. What familiar concepts could you use to explain molecules? Bronze casting? Foreign trade deficits?

plus or minus two.[1] This research suggests that you ought to group items of information under three, five, or seven headings or in three, five, or seven clusters. You might, for example, organize a lecture on the history of the Vietnam war into three clusters—the 1950s, the 1960s, and the 1970s—rather than breaking it down year by year. College registration may be presented to freshmen as a five-step process: (a) secure registration materials, (b) review course offerings, (c) see an advisor, (d) fill out the registration materials, and (e) enter the information into the school's computer system. The American Cancer Society has organized the most common symptoms of cancer into seven categories to help you remember them.

Mnemonic devices in your outline also can help. CPR instructors teach the ABC of cardiopulmonary resuscitation: (a) clear the airwaves, (b) check the breathing, and (c) initiate chest compressions. A speaker giving a talk on the Great Lakes can show listeners how to remember the names of the lakes by thinking of HOMES: Huron, Ontario, Michigan, Erie, and Superior. These memory devices also help speakers remember the main points in their outlines. Information forgotten is information lost; package your data and ideas in memorable but not silly ways.

Coherence

Solid informative speeches must not only be packaged well; they also must be coherent. Some people see coherence as a quality that must be inherent

Packaging with Gestalt Psychology

Packaging or clustering items of information according to Gestalt psychology is often useful for speakers. Gestalt psychologists throughout this century have been interested in discovering why things appear the way they do to us. Five principles of perception and cognition are still current in the literature:

1. *Proximity* suggests that elements close together seem to organize into units of perception; you see pairs made up of a ball and a block, not sets of blocks and sets of balls.

2. *Similarity* suggests that like objects are usually grouped together; you see three columns rather than three rows of items.

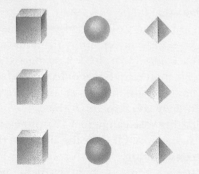

3. *Good continuation* identifies properties that appear to be logical extensions of each other; you see the curved line and the jagged line as separate figures even though they intersect.

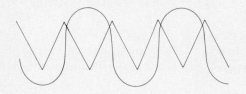

4. *Closure* is the tendency to complete suggested shapes; you see the figure of a tiger even though the lines are not joined.

5. *Symmetry* suggests that balanced objects are more pleasing to perceive than unbalanced ones.

These five principles suggest ways you can package or cluster items in your speeches: (a) Put your most important ideas close together so they can play off each other. (b) Construct your main points in similar ways grammatically to make the structure stand out. (c) Put in the logical words—*because of, similarly, not only but also,* etc.—to provide good continuation. (d) Offer enough typical examples to allow for closure. (e) And balance your treatments of the main ideas to give a sense of symmetry; for example, use parallel sentences.

Gestalt principles are not the be-alls and end-alls for organizing informative speeches, but they can help.

For more information, see John R. Anderson, *Cognitive Psychology and Its Implications* (New York: W. H. Freeman & Co., 1980), 53–56; Ronald H. Forgus and Lawrence E. Melamed, *Perception: A Cognitive-Stage Approach,* 2nd ed. (New York: McGraw-Hill Book Co., 1976), 177–182; and Michael Kobovy and James R. Pomerantz, eds., *Perceptual Organization* (Hillsdale, N.J.: Lawrence Erlbaum Associates, 1980).

in a speech, just as every note in a great musical composition magically seems to belong. Coherence, however, is also a matter of organization—of creating a pattern that knits your subtopics together in a meaningful manner. Sometimes, it's easy to create a coherent pattern; when giving a speech on the structure of the federal government, you can interrelate the three branches easily.

At other times, especially when you're not covering all the components of a subject in your speech, you have to manufacture coherence. Occasionally, you might even have to force some of your ideas into a pattern. Suppose you decide to give a speech on the Nielsen television program rating system. You might decide to discuss only three aspects of the subject—the definition of the system, the way the system works, and the way network executives use the system to determine which programs to continue the next season and which to drop. To give the speech coherence, you could use a question-answer organizational pattern and begin the body of your speech in this fashion: "People who worry about the effect of the Nielsen ratings on what they watch usually ask three questions: 'What *is* a Nielsen rating, anyway?,' 'How is the rating done?,' and 'Why do the networks rely on it for making decisions on shows?' To answer these common questions, and to explain the 'what,' 'how,' and 'why' of television ratings, today I first will. . . ." Notice that the speaker has taken a common trio of words—*what, how, why*—and used them as an organizing principle to give coherence to this explanatory speech. The audience will be able to follow along easily, looking for these three words to signal shifts in the speech.

Motivating Your Audience

Finally, and perhaps most important, you must be able to motivate your audience to listen. Unfortunately, many people ignore this essential feature of good informative speeches. Many of us blithely assume that because *we* are interested in something, our audience also will want to hear about it. To you, stamp collecting may be an interesting, relaxing, and profitable hobby, but until your listeners are likewise convinced, they will yawn through your speech on American commemoratives.

Keep in mind what we've said about attention and motivation when preparing informative speeches: *(a)* use the factors of attention to engage the members of your audience and to draw them into your speech, and *(b)* once you've captured your listeners initially, be sure to build motivational appeals into your speech—reasons why your listeners should want to know what you're about to tell them. If you indicate that your talk will increase their interpersonal effectiveness, provide them with additional income, and reduce their confusion about important matters, you'll be making your speech relevant and compelling, and your listeners will certainly want to listen.

STRUCTURING INFORMATIVE SPEECHES

Now that we've described the various types of informative speeches and examined their essential features, it's time to examine ways to structure each of those types. Of course, it's possible to use any of the organizational patterns we've described earlier, but some patterns are better suited to particular types than others.

Speeches of Definition

Because one of your primary jobs in speeches of definition is to bring coherence and focus to information or concepts, structuring such speeches is a crucial activity.

Introduction

Because speeches of definition treat either unfamiliar or familiar concepts in a new light, their introductions must create *curiosity* and establish *need* in listeners. Creating curiosity is a special challenge in speeches on unfamiliar concepts, as we're all tempted to say, "Well, if I've made it this far through life without knowing anything about black holes or carcinogens or trap blocking, why should I bother with learning more about these ideas now?" Somehow, you need to make people wonder about the unknown. Arousing a desire-to-listen is crucial.

Speeches of definition must also be attentive to the needs or wants of the listeners. In other words, their introductions should include motivational materials—explicit statements that indicate how the information can affect the audience such as, "Understanding the dynamics of trap blocking will help you better appreciate line play in football and therefore increase your enjoyment of the game every Saturday afternoon in our stadium."

Body

Most speeches of definition use a topical pattern because such speeches usually describe various aspects of an object or idea. It seems natural, for example, to use a topical pattern for a speech on computer programming careers, organizing the body of the speech around such topics as "the duties of a computer programmer," "skills needed by a computer programmer," and "training you will need to become a computer programmer."

There are occasions when other patterns may serve your specific purpose even better than topical patterns. You might use an effect-cause pattern, for example, when preparing an informative speech on the laws of supply and demand. You could enumerate a series of effects with which people are already familiar—soaring prices coupled with seemingly fantastic sales and interest rates that apparently change every other week—and then discuss the laws of supply and demand that account for such confusing fiscal patterns.

A speech defining and illustrating organic lawn care could be outlined in a topical pattern as follows:

WHAT IS ORGANIC LAWN CARE?

Introduction

Appeal to curiosity

  I. A common sight in most city and suburban neighborhoods these days is a group of little green people driving up in green vehicles, surrounding houses with hoses and small green machines, spraying foul-smelling liquids on all sides of those houses, and leaving behind only illegible signs with dire warnings about poisons.

  II. No, these are not Martians; they're lawn care specialists in green shirts spraying fertilizers, herbicides, and pesticides on lawns, cutting the grass down to the length of golf course greens, and hauling lawn clippings away to the local landfill.

Fact

      A. With an estimated 20 million acres of lawn and 600 trillion grass plants in the United States, lawn care is big business.

Tie to the public

      B. Americans have come to believe that professional chemical lawn care is a way to show personal and civic pride.

  III. These practices are potentially ruinous to the environment.

Financial appeal

      A. Lawn clippings account for nearly 20 percent of landfill congestion during spring and summer months, raising your garbage pickup costs.

Financial appeal

      B. Overwatering lawns is responsible for about one-eighth of the average homeowner's water use—about 50 gallons per week, increasing your monthly water bill.

Health appeal

      C. If even ten percent of America's lawnowners used organic pesticides, we could remove 2.5 to 5 million pounds of toxic chemicals from the environment every year.

Financial appeal and appeal to sympathy

      D. Furthermore, we could save you some veterinarian expenses, as untotaled animals each year get sick from the residues left in their backyards.

Body

  I. Let me review some of the main practices that can make you an "organic lawnowner."

Definition

      A. "Organic" usually refers to the use of weed and pest control procedures already present in nature.

      B. In the case of "organic lawn care," however, we usually talk not only about getting rid of artificial chemical treatments, but also about ways of using water and grass itself for the betterment of the lawn and garden area in general.

  II. Three lawn care practices comprise "organic lawn care":

Topic 1

      A. You have to reeducate yourself about lawn mowing.

          1. You were taught to set mower blades low to make your lawn look like a golf course, but if you set the blades high, your grass

develops healthier roots and provides natural shade for the ground, allowing it to retain moisture better.

2. "Cut it high and let it lie" is the key for dry periods, as the grass clippings help retain moisture and work as a natural fertilizer.

3. In normal periods, lawn clippings should be picked up and composted into fertilizer rather than jammed into landfills.

Topic 2

B. You can become smarter about watering your lawn.

1. Most lawns need about one inch of water once a week, applied slowly to prevent runoff, rather than a little every night.

2. To slow evaporation, water in the cool of the morning rather than in the heat of the afternoon.

3. If your grass turns brown during a drought, leave it alone as it's dormant; it will return to normal when regular rainfall begins again.

Topic 3

C. Wean yourself from the use of chemical herbicides and pesticides.

1. Natural grass mulching is an excellent fertilizer.

2. Dandelions and crab grass can often be dug out more easily than sprayed away, and handweeding won't kill the worms songbirds eat.

3. Healthy grass will choke out many weeds.

4. Various border flowers help keep away some of the more irksome varieties of bugs.

Conclusion

Summary

"Organic lawn care," therefore, is not simply a matter of chemical-free gardening but, rather, a total approach to the care, feeding, and use of your lawn and lawn products.[2]

Notice several features of this speech: (a) An attempt to engage listeners' curiosity and a review of listeners' personal needs are offered early to draw listeners in to the topic. Environmental themes, of course, are particularly good for this kind of speech. (b) Listeners' usual understanding of *organic*—nonchemical or nonartificial—is mentioned early and adjusted so that the audience knows the speech will deal with more than chemistry. (c) Three dimensions or topics are developed in the body of the speech to engage three aspects of listeners' thinking. (d) After offering a summary of the central idea, the speaker is ready to launch into a conclusion.

Conclusion

Conclusions for speeches of definition have two characteristics: (a) they usually include a summary of the main points and (b) they often stress the ways that people can apply the ideas they have been presented. For example, the speaker discussing organic lawn care could conclude by offering listeners the names of some pertinent books (such as those in footnote 2 of this chapter), the meeting time and place of your town's organic gardening club, or even the addresses of some local examples of lawns cared for with organic procedures.

Instructions and Demonstrations

Your overall strategy with instructions and demonstrations should be to isolate and group a series of steps that can be fully understood and visualized by your audience. Furthermore, you need to construct introductions, bodies, and conclusions carefully so as to engage and enlighten your audience.

Introduction

In some speaking situations, such as presentations in speech communication classrooms, listener attendance may not be voluntary. On these occasions, you'll have to pay attention to motivational matters. However, in most instances your audience will have invited you to speak or will be attending your talk voluntarily, so you can assume listener interest. When giving instructions or offering a demonstration, you'll usually need to spend only a little time generating curiosity or motivating people to listen. After all, if you're instructing listeners in a new office procedure or giving a workshop on how to build an ice boat, they already have the prerequisite interest and motivation; otherwise they wouldn't have come. When your audience is already motivated to listen, you can concentrate your introduction on two other tasks.

In speeches of instruction and demonstration, you will often encounter rate, scale, and coordination problems of verbal and visual materials. What suggestions should you consider to solve these problems?

1. *Preview your speech.* If you're going to take your listeners through the steps involved in making a good tombstone rubbing, give them an overall picture of the process before you start detailing each operation.

2. *Encourage listeners to follow along,* even through some of the more difficult steps. A process such as tombstone rubbing, for example, looks easier than it is: many people are tempted to quit listening and give up somewhere along the way. If, however, they are forewarned and are promised special help with the difficult techniques, they are more likely to bear with you.

Body

As we suggested earlier, you will package most speeches of demonstration and instruction in a chronological and/or spatial pattern simply because a nonsequential organizational pattern would be very confusing. Consequently, speakers usually have little trouble organizing the body of a speech of demonstration or instruction. Their problems are more likely technical:

1. *The problem of rate.* If the glue on a project needs to set before you can go on to the next step, what do you do? You can't just stand there and wait for it to dry. You need to have preplanned some material for filling the time—perhaps additional background or a brief discussion of what problems one can run into at this stage. Preplan your remarks carefully for those junctures; otherwise, you're likely to lose your audience.

2. *The problem of scale.* How can you show various embroidery stitches to an audience of 25? When dealing with minute operations, you often must increase the scale of operation. In this example, you could use a large piece of poster board or even a 3′ by 4′ piece of cloth stretched over a wooden frame. By using an oversized needle, yarn instead of thread, and stitches measured in inches instead of millimeters, you could easily make your techniques visible to all audience members. At the other extreme, in a speech on how to make a homemade solar heat collector, you probably would want to work with a scaled-down model.

3. *The coordination of verbal and visual methods.* Both instructions and demonstrations usually demand that speakers "show" while "telling." To keep yourself from becoming flustered or confused, be sure to practice doing while talking—demonstrating your material while explaining aloud what you're doing. Decide where you'll stand when showing a slide so that the audience can see both you and the image; practice talking about your aerobic exercise positions while you're actually doing them; work a dough press in practice sessions as you tell your mythical audience how to form professional-looking cookies. If you don't, you'll inevitably get yourself into trouble in front of your real audience.

Thinking through procedural and technical problems that you might face might lead to a speaking outline such as the following one:

HOW TO PLANT TOMATOES

Coordinate verbal and visual materials

I. First, you must select a variety of tomato seed that's suited to various geographical, climatological, agricultural, and personal factors. [*Display chart, showing varieties in columns along with their characteristics.*]
   A. Some tomatoes grow better in hard soils; some in loose soils.
   B. Some varieties handle shade well; some in direct sunlight.
   C. Some are well suited to short growing seasons; others to long seasons.
   D. Each variety tends to resist certain diseases, such as blight, better than others.

II. Once you have selected a variety (or maybe even two, so that they mature at different times) you must start the seeds.

Coordinate verbal and visual materials

   A. Prepare a mixture of black dirt, peat moss, and vermiculite as I am doing. [*Do it, indicating proportions.*]
   B. Fill germination trays, pots, or cut-off milk cartons with the germination soil, and insert seeds. [*Do it.*]

Reduce time delay (rate)

   C. With water, sunlight, and patience, your plants will grow. I can't show you that growth here today, but I can use these seedlings to illustrate their care along the way. [*Bring out half-grown and fully grown seedlings.*]

Coordinate verbal and behavioral actions

   1. When the seedlings are about an inch or two tall, thin them. [*Demonstrate.*]
   2. At about six inches [*show them*], you can transplant them safely.
   3. But, you'll know more about which plants are strong if you wait until they are ten to twelve inches tall. [*Show them plants of different strengths.*]

   D. Now you are ready to transplant the seedlings to your garden.
   1. Carefully unpot the seedlings, being sure not to damage the root network. [*Demonstrate.*]

Coordinate visual and verbal materials; enlarge materials

   2. Put each seedling in a hole already prepared in your plot; this diagram shows you how to do that. [*Show an enlarged drawing that illustrates hole size and depth, a mixture of peat moss and vermiculite in the bottom, and spacing of plants.*]
   3. Pack the garden soil firmly but not so hard as to crush the roots.
   4. Water it almost every day for the first week.

Coordinate verbal and visual materials; reduce size of materials

   5. Put some sort of mulching material—grass clippings, hay, black sheets of plastic—between the rows if weeds are a problem. [*Another drawing or picture.*]

   E. Once you know your plants are growing, cage or stake each plant. [*Show sketches of various styles of cages or stakes and discuss the advantages of each.*]

Conclusion

Conclusions for demonstration speeches usually have three parts:

1. First, *summaries are offered.* Most audiences need this review, which reminds them to question procedures or ideas they don't understand.

2. Second, some *bolstering has to take place.* People trying their hands at new processes or procedures usually get in trouble the first few times and need to be reassured that this is natural and can be overcome.

3. Finally, *help should be offered.* What sounded so simple in your talk can be much more complicated in execution. If possible, make yourself available for assistance: "As you fill out your registration form, just raise your hand if you're unsure of anything and I'll be happy to help you." Or point to other sources of further information and assistance: "Here's the address of the U.S. Government Printing Office whose pamphlet X1234 is available for only a dollar; it will give you more details"; "If you run into a filing problem I haven't covered in this short orientation to your job, just go over to Mary McFerson's desk, right over here. Mary's experienced in these matters and is always willing to help." Such statements not only offer help, but assure your audience members that they won't be labeled as dull-witted if they actually have to ask for it.

Oral Reports

Your principal strategy in an oral report must be to meet the audience's expectations with the information and the recommendations you present.

Introduction

Oral reports are requested by a group, committee, or class; the audience, consequently, generally knows what it expects and why. As a result, in introducing oral reports, you need not spend much time motivating your listeners. Instead, you should concentrate on (a) reminding your audience of what they requested; (b) describing carefully the procedures you used in gathering your information; (c) forecasting the development of various subtopics so your audience can follow you easily; and (d) pointing ahead to any action that your listeners are expected to take in light of your information. The key to a good introduction for an oral report is *orientation*— reviewing the past (your listeners' expectations and your preparations), the present (your goal now), and the future (your listeners' responsibilities once you are done). Remember that you're giving your report to your audience for a purpose.

Body

The principle for organizing the body of an oral report can be stated simply: *select the organizational pattern best suited to your audience's needs.* Have you been asked to provide your listeners with a history of a group or problem? Use a chronological pattern. Do they want to know how a particular state of affairs came to be? Try a cause-effect format. Have you been asked to discuss an organizational structure for the group? A topical pattern will allow you to review the constitutional responsibilities of each officer. If you were asked to examine the pros and cons of various proposals and to recommend one to the group, you would probably choose the elimination pattern, as illustrated in the following example:

Sample Outline for an Oral Report

REPORT FROM THE FINAL EXAMINATION COMMITTEE

I. My committee was asked to compare and contrast various ways of structuring a final examination in this speech class and to recommend a procedure to you. [*The reporter's "charge."*]
    A. First, we interviewed each one of you.
    B. Then, we discussed the pedagogical virtues of various exam procedures with our instructor.
    C. Next, we deliberated as a group, coming to the following conclusions. [*Orientation completed.*]
II. At first we agreed with many students that we should recommend a take-home essay examination as the "easiest" way out.
    A. But, we decided our wonderful textbook is filled with so much detailed and scattered advice that it would be almost impossible for any of us to answer essay-type questions without many, many hours of worry, work, and sweat.
    B. We also wondered why a course that stresses oral performance should test our abilities to write essays.
III. So, we reviewed the option of a standard, short-answer, in-class final.
    A. Although such a test would allow us to concentrate on the main ideas and central vocabulary—which has been developed in lectures, readings, and discussion—it would require a fair amount of memorization.
    B. And, we came back to the notion that merely understanding communication concepts will not be enough when we start giving speeches outside this classroom.
IV. Thus, we recommend that you urge our instructor to give us an oral examination this term.
    A. Each of us could be given an impromptu speech topic, some resource material, and ten minutes to prepare a speech.
    B. We could be graded, in this way, on both substantive and communicative decisions we make in preparing and delivering the speech.
    C. Most important, such a test would be consistent with this course's primary goal and could be completed quickly and almost painlessly.

Conclusion

Most oral reports end with a conclusion that mirrors the introduction. Your report's purpose is mentioned again; its main points are reviewed; committee members (if there are any) are thanked publicly; and then either a motion to accept the committee recommendations (if there are any) is offered or, in the case of more straightforwardly informative reports, questions from the audience are requested. Conclusions to reports—when done well—are quick, firm, efficient, and pointed.

Lectures

You'll find it's often difficult to engage an audience fully in a lecture—to get them interested in the topic and tuned in to the point of view you're taking. This problem should guide the way you structure the introductions, bodies, and conclusions of lectures.

Introduction

Introductions and conclusions can give you your greatest challenges when structuring lectures. Particularly important in lectures is raising curiosity: how many of your classmates are wondering about the causes of the Vietnam War at ten o'clock in the morning? As was suggested in this chapter's opening vignette, you can earn your listeners' attention by relating your topic to something with which they are familiar or that interests them—in the case of the speech on Vietnam, the mass media. If the lecture will be complex, you must also include in your introduction a forecast of the lecture's structure.

Body

Most lectures fit well into causal or topical organizational patterns. The body of your Vietnam War lecture could be divided into causes and effects; or it could be set up topically were you to discuss the social, economic, political, and moral dimensions of the war. A straightforward problem-solution format also works well with the right subject matter; for example, a speech on the problem of bringing the North and South Vietnamese to the negotiating table could be built around the military, political, and sociocultural steps the U.S. took to force direct negotiation between them.

Conclusion

Typically, the conclusion of a good lecture suggests additional implications or calls for particular actions. (See Figure 12.3.) For example, if you have explained in a lecture how contagious diseases spread through geographical areas, you should probably conclude by discussing actions that listeners can take to break the contagion cycle. Or if you have explained the concept of children's rights to a parent-teacher organization, you might close by asking your listeners to consider what these rights *should* mean to them—

Figure 12.3 Checklist for Introductions and Conclusions to Informative
Speeches

Speeches of Definition

_____ 1. Does my introduction create curiosity or entice my audience to listen?
_____ 2. Does my introduction include an explicit statement that shows my
listeners how the information in my speech will affect them?
_____ 3. Does my conclusion summarize my main ideas?
_____ 4. Does my conclusion stress ways my listeners can apply the ideas I've
discussed?

Instructions and Demonstrations

_____ 1. Does my introduction encourage everyone to listen?
_____ 2. Does my introduction pique listener curiosity?
_____ 3. Do I preview my main points in my introduction?
_____ 4. Do I summarize my main points in my conclusion?
_____ 5. Do I encourage listeners to try new procedures even though they may
experience initial difficulty?
_____ 6. Do I tell my listeners where they can find help or information in the
future?

Oral Reports

_____ 1. Do I remind my listeners of their request for information?
_____ 2. Do I describe the procedures I used for gathering information for this
report?
_____ 3. Does my introduction include a forecast of subtopics?
_____ 4. Does my introduction suggest the action which will be recommended
in the report?
_____ 5. Does my conclusion mention the main purpose of the report?
_____ 6. Does my conclusion review the main points of the report?
_____ 7. Do I recognize and thank committee members for their contributions?
_____ 8. Do I call for action on a motion or questions from my listeners?

Lectures

_____ 1. Does my introduction raise listeners' curiosity?
_____ 2. Do I forecast my main topics in my introduction?
_____ 3. Does my conclusion suggest implications of the information listeners
have received or call for listeners' action?

how they should change their thinking and their behavior toward six-year-olds.

Suppose you're a theatre buff and you decide to give a lecture on Shakespeare's Globe Theatre. Consider the following outline as an illustration of how some of this advice about lectures can work for you.

has applications reaching far beyond the music industry into education, professional job training, home maintenance, and health care, just to name a few. This is Compact Disc Interactive, the technology that Phillips, Sony, Hitachi, Toshiba, and a number of other companies which are difficult to pronounce, are calling "the next electronic revolution." In fact, according to a phone interview with President of International Consumer Technologies Robert Kotick: When CDI hits the market in the fall of 1988, it will change everything—from the way we learn and work to the way we buy our clothes and see our physician. So this new technology is going to have a profound effect on our lives. Perhaps we should learn more about it. /1

We'll first examine what CDI is, including what is meant by that "I" for interactive, explore some of the applications of this new electronic revolution, and evaluate the concerns of the future acceptance of compact disc interactive. /2

In order to understand what CDI is, we need to first have a working knowledge of the technology behind it, or what I like to call the ABC's of CD's. A compact disc, CD audio, or CDI, is a type of laser disc which just means that the information on it is read by a laser, or a type of light beam. The programming of a compact disc involves embedding the disc with a series of pits. For example, one disc might contain Encyclopedia Britannica's A through L; another, duplicate film footage of the Wright Brother's first flight; and a third, the Air Force theme song. So when you type "History of Airplanes" into a personal computer, amazing things happen. The laser beam passes over the pits, the screen becomes a movie screen, as you watch Wilbur and Orville give it one more shot. A recorded human voice describes the scene, and provides you with historical information while the background music of the Air Force theme song can be heard through state-of-the-art CD technology. But with Compact Disc interactive, what you see is only the beginning of what you get. It's the interactive, in Compact Disc Interactive, that makes this technology so revolutionary. Interaction means you can move and see and change anything on the screen, in the music, or in the narration. You can even put yourself on the screen. And the image you will be viewing is more than the cheap computer graphics we are so used to seeing. This image was taken from one of the latest Macintosh programs; and this is a CDI image, comparable to a high-quality Hollywood film. As stated in the March 29th, 1988 edition of the *Wall Street Journal,* "The time has come when people have a choice of watching 'Raiders of the Lost Ark' or being in 'Raiders of the Lost Ark.'" /3

Now that we have a basic understanding of CDI technology, let's briefly consider the technology required to use it. One of the key considerations in the development of CDI was its ability to piggyback on previous technology like television sets and CD players. The result is a remarkably flexible system. CDI disks can be played three different ways: by plugging a CDI disk player into your television set; by plugging one into your personal computer; or on a full-fledged CDI system which includes a keyboard, a disk drive, and a touch sensitive screen. /4

But, adaptable or not, a technology without application does bring us right back to, uh—interesting. In a speech presented at the 1987 IEEE Convention of the Institute of Electrical and Electronic Engineers, Inc., Gordon Stober, President of Polygram Corporation, said that CDI presently has over ninety applications. For our purposes we will narrow these to three areas. CDI's role in entertaining, in healing, and in living day-to-day. /5

CDI has created an entirely new form of entertainment—interactive movies. The August 1987 edition of *CDI News* discussed two movies: "Exposed" (an adult film which the article did not cover extensively, and so neither shall we) and "Danger in Dreamland." This film was originally produced by a Chicago comedy troop called Firesign Theatre, and follows the antics of Nick Danger. Antics—which you determine. For example, Nick would approach a door, hear a blood-curdling scream from the other side, so he'd step away from the door, and the frame freezes. You, the viewer, are asked, "Should Nick go through the door?" You respond, and the film continues until the next decision. /6

In the medical profession, CDI has both preventive and curative applications. One form of prevention is training, and Phillips International Media Corporation has recently introduced a CPR dummy that uses CDI technology. A narrative explanation and a video familiarize the student with this procedure, and then the dummy is hooked up to the machine. And the dummy is actually pretty bright. It talks, saying "your hand's in the wrong place," "the pressure's uneven," or "you're doing just fine." CDI has curative abilities, in that you can maintain records of not only medical charts and graphs, but also film footage of your surgery and your recovery process. This will allow physicians to draw more accurate diagnoses, and better serve your needs. /7

But it is CDI's role in our day-to-day lives that's most fascinating. CDI's function on the home front ranges from mundane bookkeeping to do-it-yourself disks. Reynolds and Reynolds Computer Systems of Dayton, Ohio, has introduced their latest idea at the 1987 IEEE Convention. They are producing do-it-yourself auto maintenance disks which are interactive. Now the disk essentially contains a movie of engine repair, except you can stop the movie at any time, pick parts up, turn them around, ask questions, look at the engine from a different angle, anything that would make it easier and more fun for you to do it yourself. /8

If you'd like to leave the car to the mechanics, but would stay home to do your shopping, Phillips is working the bugs out of a system that would essentially serve as a visual mail order catalog. One of the most intriguing parts of this system is that a portion of the disk has been left blank so that when you purchase it, visual images of you and your family members can be programmed onto the disk allowing you to try things on before buying. /9

Now this disk itself is going to run anywhere between fifteen and thirty-five dollars, whereas the full-fledged CDI system according to the August 1987 edition of *CDI News* is going to cost between $500 and $1,000. Now the attractiveness of these costs to the general consumer is just one of the many concerns over the future acceptance of CDI. /10

There seems to be some question over whether America wants to inter-act, as Gary Kilgo, President of Knowledge Set, stated in an April interview. Let's take the average person out there. Are they really going to buy a CD player and hook it up to their TV set? Most people are just interested in pop-ping a beer and watching a game. And there's nothing wrong with that. It is responses like this that have sparked CDI producers to work all the harder on programs that might appeal to the general public, and understandably, because that appeal is very important. /11

But the greatest concern over the effect of CDI is what impact it might have on our younger society. Will the child that learns how to interact with the computer, whether at home or at school, also be able to interact with people? This is a significant concern, and consequently educators, programmers, and parents alike are keeping a close eye on CDI, and under-standably. Compact Disk Interactive is estimated to hit the market in under six months. Consumer and computer experts concur as to both the negative and the positive potential of CDI. /12

Now having acquired a basic understanding of CDI technology, its appli-cations in a number of areas, and some of the concerns over its future accep-tance, you should be able to draw your own conclusions about participating in this interesting evolution, because you'll soon be encountering the grand-child of this odd little disc, this miracle music technology. Compact Disk Interactive (CDI)—it's the next electronic revolution. /13

CHAPTER SUMMARY

1. Speeches to inform include talks that seek to assemble, package, and interpret raw data, information, or ideas.

2. The four types of informative speeches are (a) *speeches of definition,* (b) *instruc-tions* and *demonstrations,* (c) *oral reports,* and (d) *lectures.*

3. No matter what type of informative speech you're preparing, you should strive for five qualities: (a) *clarity,* (b) *ways to associate new ideas with familiar ones,* (c) *methods for packaging or clustering ideas to aid memory and comprehension,* (d) *coher-ence,* and (e) *methods of motivating your audience.*

4. Each type of informative speech can be structured into introductions, bodies, and conclusions that maximize your ability to reach your audiences.

KEY TERMS

demonstrations (p. 229)
instructions (p. 229)
lectures (p. 230)

oral reports (p. 230)
speeches of definition (p. 229)

SKILLBUILDING ACTIVITIES

1. In a concise written report, indicate and defend the type of arrangement (chronological sequence, spatial sequence, and so on) you think would be most suitable for an informative speech on at least five of the following subjects.
   a. The campus parking situation
   b. Recent developments in the women's rights movement
   c. Indian jewelry of the Southwest
   d. Saving our environment
   e. How the stock market works
   f. Censorship of the arts
   g. Wonder drugs of the 1980s and 1990s
   h. The fraternity tradition
   i. Space stations: living in a weightless world
   j. What life will be like in the year 2010

2. Plan a two- to four-minute speech in which you will give instructions. For instance, you might explain how to calculate your life insurance needs, how to canvass for a political candidate, or how to make a group flight reservation. This exercise is basically descriptive, so limit yourself to using a single visual aid.

3. Describe a unique place you have visited on a vacation—for example, a church in a foreign city or a historical site. Deliver a four- or five-minute speech to the class in which you describe this place as accurately and vividly as possible. Then ask the class to take a moment to envision this place. If possible, show them a picture of what you have described. How accurately were they able to picture this place? How might you have ensured a more accurate description? What restrictions did you feel without the use of visual aids?

REFERENCES

1. For background on information packaging, see G. Mandler, "Organization and Memory," *Human Memory: Basic Processes,* Gordon Bower, ed. (New York: Academic Press, 1977), 310–354; Mandler's articles in C. R. Puff, ed., *Memory Organization and Structure* (New York: Academic Press, 1976); and G. A. Miller, "The Magic Number Seven, Plus or Minus Two: Some Limits on Our Capacity for Processing Information," *Psychological Review,* 63 (1956), 81–97.

2. Information for this outline taken from Warren Schultz, *The Chemical-Free Lawn* (New York: Rodale Press, 1989) and The Earth Works Group, *50 Simple Things You Can Do to Save the Earth* (Berkeley, Calif.: Earthworks Press, 1989).

3. Material for this outline drawn from Stanley Wells, *Shakespeare* (London: Kaye & Ward Ltd., 1978) and John Russell Brown, *Shakespeare and His Theatre* (New York: Lothrop, Lee & Shepard Books, 1982).

4. Barbara Seidl, speech given at the 1988 National Individual Events Tournament at Bradley University, Peoria, Ill. (April 9–11, 1988). Reprinted with permission.

CHAPTER THIRTEEN

Speeches to Persuade and Actuate

*F or as long as she can remember, Joan has been a baseball fan. As a child, she
played in Little League, and now she attends major league games to cheer on
the home team. Sitting in the bleachers, she sometimes notices the billboards
along the outfield fences for City Loan Bank, Swede's Auto Repair, the local
burger franchise, and smokeless tobacco products. Some of her favorite players
endorse soft drinks and sports equipment on television. And no game is complete without a ballpark hot dog sold by a roving vendor. Joan even has arguments with her co-workers about the merits of various players and about coach-
ing decisions.*

The thoughts and actions Joan takes—buying season tickets, drinking the
soft drink her favorite player endorses, and patronizing merchants who
advertise at the park—are the results of effective persuasion. Similar to
Joan, most of us are subject to persuasion every day, even when we don't
realize it. Public speaking for the purpose of persuasion shares many of the
same features of other kinds of persuasion, such as advertising, that we
experience all the time.

The general purpose of persuasion is to change or reinforce attitudes
or behaviors. The speaker who persuades makes a very different demand
on the audience than the speaker who informs. The informative speaker
is satisfied when listeners understand what has been said. However, the
persuader attempts to influence the listener's thoughts or actions. The

We are bombarded with competing persuasive messages every day. What messages vie for your attention here?

persuader may even demand that the audience agree with or act on the speech. Occasionally persuaders seek to reinforce ideas or actions that already exist in listeners. They may defend the status quo or urge the rejection of proposed changes. Whatever the specific purpose, the general purpose of persuasion is to convince audiences.

Think back to our discussion of specific speaking purposes. The specific speaking purpose helps you to determine what kind of speech you need to give. If your purpose was to help your audience understand the American two-party political system, you could offer an informative speech tracing the development of that system through various periods of American history. But, if your general speaking purpose is to convince people that one party is better than the other, that a particular election has been misinterpreted by some historians, or that voting is a fundamental democratic right, you would choose to change your audience's attitudes with a persuasive speech.

To persuade audiences successfully, you must make them *want* to believe or act. When people are forced to accept beliefs, they may soon abandon them. Actions done unwillingly are usually done inefficiently and without any sense of reward or accomplishment. For this reason, two subsidiary purposes of persuasive speaking must be kept in mind: (a) *to provide the audience with motives for believing by appealing to their basic needs or desires* and (b) *to convince them that your recommendation will satisfy these desires.*

We'll begin this chapter with a discussion of *motive needs* and the *motivational appeals* that speakers can use to tap those needs. Then, we'll examine the *motivated sequence,* an organizational pattern that helps you to successfully incorporate motivational appeals in your speeches.

ANALYZING THE NEEDS AND DESIRES OF LISTENERS

As we have said, a speech must appeal to listeners' needs and desires. It's helpful to think of these needs and desires as *motive needs.*

The Concept of Motive Needs

A **motive need** is an impulse to satisfy a psychological-social want or a biological urge. Such needs may arise from physiological considerations—pain, lack of food, or a room that is too hot or cold—and they may come about for sociocultural reasons, such as when you feel left out of a group or wonder whether your peers like you. If you feel the need deeply, your feelings may compel you to do something about your situation. You might eat, adjust the thermostat, or join a group. In each situation, you will have been motivated to act.

Using Maslow's Hierarchy of Motive Needs

Psychologist Abraham H. Maslow studied the needs that impel human beings to think, act, and respond as they do. He developed the following classification of those needs:[1]

1. *Physiological Needs*—for food, drink, air, sleep, and sex.
2. *Safety Needs*—for security, stability, protection from harm or injury, structure, order, law, predictability, and freedom from fear and chaos.
3. *Belongingness and Love Needs*—for warm affection with spouse, children, parents, and close friends; for feeling a part of social groups; and for acceptance and approval.
4. *Esteem Needs*—for self-esteem based on personal achievement, mastery, competence, confidence, freedom, and independence; and for the esteem of others (reputation, prestige, recognition, status).
5. *Self-Actualization Needs*—for self-fulfillment, becoming what you potentially can be; for actualizing your capabilities; for being true to your essential nature (what you *can* be you *must* be).[2]

These needs, according to Maslow, function in a **hierarchy;** that is, lower-level needs must be met before higher-level needs are met. Persons caught up in the daily struggle to find food and shelter (first-level needs) have little time and energy left to strive for the esteem of others or self-actualization (fourth- and fifth-level needs). Once the basic requirements of living are satisfied, however, higher-level drives take over. But the progression is not irreversible—you can move upward or downward from one level to another as your life changes. (See Figure 13.1.) Sometimes, higher-level needs will overpower lower-level needs. For example, you may feel dizzy from hunger, yet, because of higher-level social needs, you will continue to diet. In this case, the need for social approval is strong and may control the way you satisfy your physiological needs. Although there are some exceptions to the hierarchical nature of Maslow's categories, his classification of needs is useful in conceptualizing human motivation.

Developing Motivational Appeals in Public Speaking

Once you recognize the power of motive needs to propel human action, you may ask, "How can I identify and satisfy these needs in a speech? How can I use these basic needs, wants, and desires as the basis for effective public communication?" The answer to both of these questions is, "With the use of motivational appeals." A **motivational appeal** is either (a) a visualization of a desire and a method for satisfying it or (b) an assertion that an entity, idea, or course of action holds the key to fulfilling a particular motive need.

Suppose that you want to borrow a friend's car. How do you prepare to ask? Usually, you create scenarios in your head. In these scenarios, you try out various motivation appeals: "Should I mention how far it is to walk? What about a reminder of the time I loaned something? Should I ease my friend's fears by stressing my safe driving record?" By examining the alternatives, you assemble a group of motivational appeals and organize them into arguments.

Figure 13.1 Maslow's Hierarchy of Needs
Abraham Maslow arranged fundamental human needs in a hierarchy in which lower-level needs must be met before higher-level needs operate. Can you think of several examples of each need?

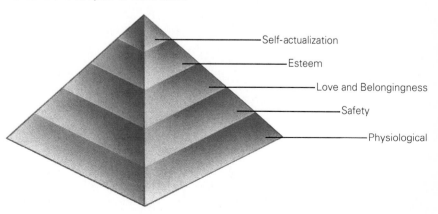

- Self-actualization
- Esteem
- Love and Belongingness
- Safety
- Physiological

At other times, you may create motivational appeals through verbal labeling or **attribution**.[3] Suppose that you avoid going to church because you think of churches as conformist, authoritarian, dominating, repressive, and destructive institutions. One night, however, you attend a religious meeting where the preacher talks about the adventure of living a God-based life, the beauty of God's creation, the reverence one feels in living a spiritual life, and the endurance one must call upon to overcome doubts. On reflection, you decide that you have misconstrued the church's motivation. You become a devout churchgoer.

What happened? You changed the attributes of *church* in your own mind. Instead of attributing negative terms, such as conformity, authority, and dominance, to *church,* you began to attribute to it positive terms, such as adventure, beauty, and reverence. Your behavior eventually changed because you had begun to use different terms to label things. Motivational appeals may use language to activate desires in people.

Some Common Motivational Appeals

If you attempted to list the potential motivational appeals for every audience, you might never finish; the task is endless. Rather than trying to list each individual appeal, consider the general thrust of each *motive cluster.* A **motive cluster** is the group of individual appeals that are grounded in the same fundamental human motivation. Table 13.1 on page 257 shows the three motive clusters—affiliation, achievement, and power—as well as the motivational appeals within each cluster.[4] **Affiliation motives** include the desire to belong to a group or to be well liked or accepted. This cluster also includes love, conformity, dependence upon others, sympathy toward others, and loyalty. **Achievement motives** are related to the intrinsic or extrinsic desire for success, adventure, creativity, and personal enjoyment. **Power motives** concern primarily the desire to exert influence over others.[5]

If you begin with this list, you will be in a better position to choose those motivational appeals with the greatest relevance to your topic and audience. Remember this guideline as you make your choices: *motivational appeals work best when they have value for your listeners.* Analyze your audience and then choose your motivation appeals based on what you've learned about it.

The Affiliation Cluster

Affiliation motives are dominated by a desire for acceptance or approval. They refer to a greater concern for promoting interpersonal bonds than for achieving personal success or individual power. A social desire to be part of a group is an affiliation motive. What follows are some examples of appeals to listeners' affiliation desires:

1. *Companionship and Affiliation.* We all need others—their presence, their touch, and their acceptance of who we are. That's why we respond to appeals such as, "We care about you," "Join our group and find fellowship

Table 13.1 Motive Clusters

Individual motivational appeals fall into clusters that share a common theme. Think of a current television advertisement and identify the motive clusters in it.

Affiliation	Achievement	Power
Companionship	Acquisition/saving	Aggression
Conformity	Success/display	Authority/dominance
Deference/dependence	Prestige	Defense
Sympathy/generosity	Pride	Fear
Loyalty	Adventure/change	Autonomy/independence
Tradition	Perseverance	
Reverence/worship	Creativity	
Sexual attraction	Curiosity	
	Personal enjoyment	

with kindred souls," and "You're one of a select group to receive this special offer."

2. *Conformity.* At times, people's sense of belonging becomes so strong that they feel psychological pressure to be "one of the crowd." Commercials stressing what "the prudent homeowner does," what "the successful businesswoman wears," and what "all Americans believe" contain appeals to conformity.

3. *Deference/Dependence.* We defer to wisdom, experience, or expertise that surpasses our own. Testimony of experts to whom listeners might defer is a successful form of supporting material.

4. *Sympathy/Generosity.* Regardless of the belief of many people that human beings are basically selfish, on many occasions people can be shamed or prompted to sacrifice for others. All appeals to giving, to the support of others, and to self-sacrifice in the name of the "common good" assume that your **social self**—the part of you that bonds to others—will overcome your **private self**—the self-centered part of you. "Reach out and touch someone," "Give that others might live," and "There but for the grace of God go I" are appeals that form the heart of many actuative speeches.

5. *Loyalty.* Periodically, we all want to celebrate our membership in groups and societies. In times of crisis, this feeling can become overwhelming. At these times, you can call for extraordinary actions that demonstrate individuals' adherence to the group. You can ask listeners to be loyal to family, friends, organizations, states, geographical regions, or their nation.

6. *Tradition.* We are all sensitive to our own mortality and to our place among those who preceded us. This sensitivity increases our susceptibility to appeals to family, group, and social traditions as (a) entities for which we have responsibility and (b) guides to our behavior.

7. *Reverence or Worship.* Many times in our lives we recognize our own inferiority to others, to institutions, to nature, and to deities which humble us in their magnitude and eternity. Reverence can take three forms: *hero worship, reverence for institutions,* and *divine worship.* As a speaker, you have relatively little power to influence your listeners to revere you or your words. But, you can appeal to the reverence your listeners have for objects, people, or institutions.

8. *Sexual Attraction.* Sex appeal is used to advertise everything from automobiles and toothpaste to vacations and zippers. Sex sells. As our consciousness of gender roles has been raised, we may find blatantly sexual appeals objectionable. However, when you scrutinize sexual appeals, you'll notice that at the core they are appealing to people's desire to be attractive. And, although we may object to blatantly sexual appeals, we may respond to messages that promise to enhance our personal physical and psychological attractiveness and well-being.

The Achievement Cluster

Achievement motives concern an individual's desire to attain goals, to excel in certain behaviors or activities, or to obtain prestige or success. The following appeals to achievement motives can pull a person toward the accomplishment of a particular goal:

1. *Acquisition/Saving.* Our society is more and more concerned with personal material success as evidenced by the growth of assertiveness training workshops, investment clubs, and get-rich-quick schemes, so appeals to personal financial reward are potent. By describing material rewards in social, spiritual, or personal terms, you can also appeal to other motives at the same time as you appeal to achievement motives.

2. *Success/Display.* "The successful executive knows. . . ." "To make maximum use of your talents, act today. . . ." Appeals such as these depend on people's interest in making a mark and in developing or actualizing themselves.

3. *Prestige.* Ads for luxury automobiles and designer clothes make use of this appeal to our sense of worth—to our "place" in a community or within a power structure. Ownership of material goods gives us status. An appeal to listeners' desire for prestige should take into account their desire for affiliation. For example, driving an expensive foreign car identifies one as a member of an elite group.

4. *Pride.* Appeals to pride—a sense of our own or our group's worth—can drive us to collective or individual achievement. Such appeals tighten our loyalties to groups and, when coupled with appeals to adventure, creativity, or independence, move us to greater personal exertion.

5. *Adventure/Change.* "Taste the High Country!" says the beer advertiser. "Join the Navy and see the world," says the local recruiter. The human soul yearns for release; the human body tingles at the prospect of risk. Participating in adventure is a way that people validate their own worth.

6. *Perseverance.* Sometimes we must be patient, yet persistent, in seeking our goals. Change is often slow, but certainly worth the wait. Visualizing what the future will bring is an effective strategy in motivating people to persevere. "We shall overcome" and "For a better tomorrow" appeal to perseverance.

7. *Creativity.* As Maslow noted, the height of self-actualization is a sense of well-developed abilities and talents. The ads that say, "Draw me," urging you to draw a duck in order to earn a scholarship to a correspondence art course and cookbooks that promise you'll become a gourmet chef appeal to your need to be creative.

8. *Curiosity.* Children open alarm clocks to find out where the tick is and adults crowd the sidewalks to gaze at a celebrity. Appeals to curiosity launch exploration, scholarship, and experimentation.

9. *Personal Enjoyment.* Like appeals to creativity, curiosity, and independence, appeals to personal enjoyment depend on selfish instincts. As many times as we act as group members, we act as individuals, responding to the promise of personal comfort and luxury, esthetic enjoyment, recreation and rest, relief from home and work restraints, and just plain fun.

The Power Cluster

Humans seek to dominate and control others, either physically or symbolically; appeals to *power motives* are often the most potent of all appeals. Although people can use power to manipulate others, not all uses of power are negative. By appealing to people's sense of social and moral responsibility, as well as to the following power motives, you can urge people to use power in positive ways:

1. *Aggression.* Humans tend to form territorial or hierarchical groups and societies. The human urge to claim rights and territory is the foundation for appeals to personal and social competition. No one wants to lose. That's why advertisers tell you to "get ahead of the crowd" or "Beat your competition to the punch."

2. *Authority/Dominance.* Aggressive people can win in competition. But people with power and authority not only *win;* they *control* objects, situations, or other people. Even McGruff, the crime-fighting dog featured in public service announcements who says, "Take a bite out of crime," appeals to your desire to dominate.

3. *Defense.* In spite of the fact that aggression is considered natural, we sometimes attempt to curtail or control it. A socially acceptable way to raise people's fighting spirit for a public cause is to appeal to the need for common or mutual defense—to the sense of survival that is a basic need in Maslow's hierarchy. Most declarations of war are phrased as declarations of self-defense.

4. *Fear.* People have many fears—of failure, of death, of speechmaking, of inadequacy. Fear is a powerful motivation and it can be used to inspire people to good and evil. Fear can drive people to achievement and bravery or to hatred and butchery. Use fear appeals cautiously.

5. *Autonomy/Independence.* You frequently hear, "Be your own person; don't follow the crowd." Appeals to "be yourself" and "stand on your own two feet"—similar to the appeal to adventure—draw their force from our struggles to stand apart from one another.

You may have noticed that some of the appeals we've just described seem to contradict each other. For example, fear seems to oppose adventure; sympathy and generosity seem to work against independence. Remember that human beings are rather changeable creatures who, at different times, may pursue quite different goals.

There are an endless number of human wants, needs, and motives, and of combinations of the three. We have, however, discussed some of the basic motives to which expert speakers often appeal in order to motivate their listeners.[6]

Using Motivational Appeals

In practice, motivational appeals are seldom used alone; speakers usually combine them. Suppose you were selecting a new car. What factors would influence your decision? One would be price (*saving*); another would be comfort and appearance (*personal enjoyment*); a third might be European styling (*imitation*) or, conversely, uniqueness (*independence*). These factors combined would add up to *pride* of ownership.

Some of these influences, of course, would be stronger than others; some might conflict. But all of them would probably affect your choice. You would base your decision to buy the car on the strongest appeals.

Because motivational appeals are interdependent, it's a good idea to coordinate them. You should select three or four appeals that are related

Using Fear Appeals

Among the most potent appeals to audiences are fear appeals. Research suggests that fear appeals are so powerful that they actually can interfere with a listener's ability to process information critically. However, research indicates that fear appeals retain their effectiveness over extended periods of time.

Sometimes fear appeals are used for laudable goals such as the Juvenile Awareness program at New Jersey's Rahway State Prison (the basis of the 1977 television special "Scared Straight"). In this program, delinquent youths are introduced to convicts who describe the horrors of prison life. Results suggest that the program helps deter youths from further delinquent activity.

However, fear appeals are always accompanied by the potential for misuse. The possibility of misuse raises a number of ethical considerations. Think about the following applications to your classroom speaking. Evaluate the ethics of each situation. What would you do if you were the speaker? Why?

1. You are planning a persuasive speech to convince your audience that war is morally wrong. You are totally committed to peace and believe that anything you can do to maintain peace in this world is your moral obligation, so you exaggerate some of the facts about recent world conflicts to frighten your audience about the results of war.

2. You give a speech on the increase of date rape on college campuses. In order to convince your audience that date rape is wrong and extremely common, you create scenarios that appeal to the fears of your listeners. Your scenarios are so vivid that several of your listeners, who are rape survivors, are visibly overcome with emotion. One of the listeners is so upset that she must leave the classroom during your speech. Everyone in the audience sees her leave.

3. Knowing that the arousal of fear impedes the ability to think critically, you decide to arouse fears in your listeners so that they fail to perceive that your argument is unsound. You feel that it is your listeners' responsibility to listen critically and if they are willing to accept unsound arguments, they're fools.

4. You feel very strongly that the college president is wrong to continue investing college money in countries where torture and imprisonment without trial are legal. You present a very persuasive speech about your feelings. In your speech, you appeal to your audience's fears by suggesting that the college president is actually propagating torture and corrupting the values of U.S. citizens to the point that someday torture and imprisonment without trial might be legal in the United States. Your listeners become so incensed, as a result of your speech, that they march to the president's house and set his car on fire.

5. You are preparing to give a speech on hate crimes in the United States. You want to make sure that you have your audience's attention before you begin, so you decide to present the details of a series of grisly murders committed in your town by a psychopath—even though these murders were not motivated by hate but by mental illness, and so they aren't examples of hate crimes.

Product advertisers rely on motivational appeals to influence the buying behaviors of target audiences. Which motivational appeals can you identify in these advertisements?

and that target segments of your audience. When you cluster appeals, you tap multiple dimensions of your listeners' lives.

Review your appeals for their pertinence and consistency. After all, you don't want to describe the *adventure* of spelunking, or cave exploration, so vividly that you create a sense of *fear*. Conflicting appeals are counterproductive.

Examine the following series of main headings for a speech given by a tourist agency representative urging students to take a summer trip to Europe:

Acquisition and savings	I. The three-week tour is being offered for the low price of $2000.
Independence	II. There will be a minimum of supervision and regimentation.
Companionship	III. You'll be traveling with friends and fellow students.

In the complete presentation, this representative also emphasized the educational value of the experience (*self-advancement*) and said that a special mountain-climbing expedition would be arranged (*adventure*). Notice how the speaker avoided conflicting appeals and targeted student audiences.

One final piece of general advice: inconspicuous appeals work best. Avoid saying, "I want you to *imitate* Jones, the successful banker" or "If you give to the anti-apartheid fund, we'll print your name in the newspapers so that your *reputation* as a caring person will be known to everybody." People rarely admit, even to themselves, that they act on the basis of self-centered motivations—greed, imitation, personal pride, and fear. Be subtle when using these appeals. For example, you might encourage listeners to imitate the actions of well-known people by saying, "Habitat for Humanity counts among its volunteers former President and First Lady Jimmy and Rosalyn Carter."

ORGANIZING THE SPEECH: THE MOTIVATED SEQUENCE

Now it's time to think about organizing your appeals. As we've been suggesting, a very important consideration in structuring appeals is your listeners' psychological tendencies—ways in which individuals' own motivations and circumstances favor certain ways of structuring ideas. Basically, people move from motives to action by following one of two perceptual paths: (a) *world or problem orientation* and (b) *self-centered or motivation-centered orientation*.

Early in this century, the American philosopher John Dewey recognized the human tendency toward a *world* or *problem orientation* when he devised his *psychologic*—a pattern for thought that he called "reflective thinking." In Dewey's view, we tend to follow a systematic procedure for solving problems. First, Dewey said, we become aware of a specific need—a situation with which we are, for one reason or another, dissatisfied. Second, we examine this situation to determine its nature, scope, causes, and implications. Third, we search for new orientations or operations to solve the problem or satisfy the need. Fourth, we compare and evaluate the possible solutions. And, fifth, we select the solution that, on the basis of reflection, seems most likely to handle the real-world dimensions of the problem.[7] In essence, Dewey adapted the *scientific method* to individual and group problem solving.

In the 1920s, salespersons and advertisers began recognizing the human tendency to be more *self-centered* and more *motivation-centered*. They realized that a person buys an automobile not simply to get around, but also to convey a certain image. We buy certain clothes to identify ourselves with others who wear that style. We buy furniture that is both functional and decorative. In other words, our personal motivations often control our decisions and actions.

Alan Monroe (1903–1975), the original author of this textbook, trained sales personnel in the 1920s and was familiar with Dewey's ideas. As he thought about Dewey's psychologic and about the various sales techniques that he had taught people to use, Monroe discovered that he could unite both sets of approaches to behavior—one based on the personalized scientific method and the other rooted in an understanding of human motivation—to form a highly useful organization pattern. Since 1935, this structure has been called **Monroe's Motivated Sequence** (see Figure 13.2).[8] We will devote the rest of this chapter to it.

The motivated sequence ties problems and solutions to human motives. In terms of our preceding discussion, the motivated sequence is simultaneously *problem-oriented* and *motivation-centered*.

The motivated sequence for the presentation of verbal materials is composed of five basic steps:

1. *Attention.* Create interest and desire.
2. *Need.* Develop the problem by analyzing things wrong in the world and by relating those wrongs to the individual's interests, wants, or desires.
3. *Satisfaction.* Propose a plan of action that will alleviate the problem and satisfy the individual's interests, wants, or desires.
4. *Visualization.* Depict the world as it will look if the plan is put into action.
5. *Action.* Call for personal commitments and deeds.

Using the Motivated Sequence to Structure Persuasive Speeches

Sometimes your purpose is to change listeners' thinking rather than stimulate any overt action. In such cases, you can adapt the basic pattern of the motivated sequence and either end with the visualization step or ask for belief in the action step. The motivated sequence for a persuasive speech might resemble the following:

1. *Getting attention:* capture the attention and interest of the audience.
2. *Showing the need:* make it clear that a judgment concerning the worth of the person, practice, or institution is needed; do this by showing why a judgment is important to your listeners personally or why it is important to their community, state, nation, or world.
3. *Satisfying the need:* explain the criteria on which an intelligent judgment is based; advance what you believe to be the correct judgment and show how it meets the criteria.
4. *Visualizing the results:* picture the advantages that come from the judgment you endorse or the evils that will result from failing to support it.
5. *Requesting action or approval:* appeal for the acceptance of the proposed judgment.

Figure 13.2 The Motivated Sequence
Notice how the audience will respond to each step of the motivated sequence.

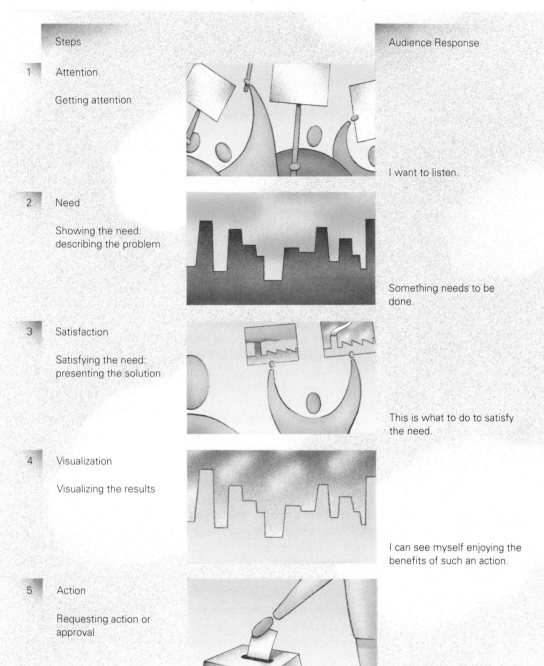

Steps		Audience Response
1	Attention Getting attention	I want to listen.
2	Need Showing the need: describing the problem	Something needs to be done.
3	Satisfaction Satisfying the need: presenting the solution	This is what to do to satisfy the need.
4	Visualization Visualizing the results	I can see myself enjoying the benefits of such an action.
5	Action Requesting action or approval	I will do this.

Sample Outline for a Persuasive Speech

Each of the five steps of the motivated sequence, adapted as we have suggested, is illustrated in the following speech outline:

ARE LOTTERIES THE ANSWER?[9]

Specific purpose: To persuade listeners to reject the hidden costs of state-wide lotteries.

Attention step (hypothetical illustration)

I. Yesterday, thousands of men and women in our state stepped up to the cashier at their local convenience stores and purchased lottery tickets. Many of these men and women, such as Eldon Washington and Carmen Ruiz, went home with a chance on a dream instead of the basic necessities of life. Tomorrow, they'll go back to purchase another lottery ticket. It's time we reconsidered this form of institutionalized gambling—our state lottery.

Need step

II. The costs of the state lottery must be addressed.
   A. The state lottery has two hidden costs.
      1. It encourages gambling.
         a. The percentage of people playing the lottery has risen dramatically in states such as California and Ohio.
         b. The number of people being treated for compulsive gambling disorders has risen in the same proportions.
         c. With few exceptions, states do not have sufficient treatment programs for compulsive gamblers.
      2. The lottery is a regressive tax on the poor.
         a. People earning under $10,000 per year are more likely to buy lottery tickets than any other group.
         b. The poor spend a higher percentage of their incomes on lottery tickets.
   B. Unless we reconsider the hidden costs of our state lotteries, they will continue to encourage gambling and exploit the poor.

Satisfaction step

III. What can be done to offset the negative impacts of the state lottery?
   A. More states should be encouraged to follow the example of New Jersey, one of the few states to fund a program to help compulsive gamblers.
      1. New Jersey spends less than .0007% of total lottery revenues for its treatment program.
      2. Studies indicate that treatment of compulsive gambling is highly successful.
   B. Limits should be placed on advertising for lottery ticket sales.
      1. Total advertising budgets should be fixed.

2. Advertisements should be discontinued during the peak family television viewing hours.

C. Limits should be placed on the amount of tickets purchased by one individual.

Visualization step

IV. If government were to act more responsibly in its promotion of the state lottery, imagine the benefits that would accrue.

A. An increased number of compulsive gamblers could be identified and treated.

1. Treatment programs could be built and staffed with a minimal amount of lottery revenues.

2. The focus on treatment probably would encourage further research into addictive behaviors.

B. The media mania accompanying large jackpots could be curbed.

C. The propensity of some individuals to spend beyond their means would be stopped.

D. The revenue produced by the lottery would remain relatively unaffected.

Action step

V. We need to understand the true costs of our state lotteries.

A. Consider those who are most affected by lottery ticket purchases—compulsive gamblers and the poor.

B. When given the opportunity, voice your opinion for treatment programs and limiting advertisements—we need responsible government.

Using the Motivated Sequence to Structure Actuative Speeches

The motivated sequence provides an ideal blueprint for urging an audience to take action. Let's look first at some ways that you might use Monroe's sequence to structure actuative speeches.

Step 1: Getting Attention

You must challenge audience apathy at the very beginning of your speech if you hope to persuade your listeners to adopt a belief or to act. A review of pages 148–154 will remind you how startling statements, illustrations, questions, and other supporting materials can focus attention on your message. You can't persuade an audience unless you have its attention.

Step 2: Showing the Need: Describing the Problem

When you've captured the attention of your listeners, you're ready to clarify why your policy is needed. To do this, you must show that a definite problem exists. You must point out, through facts and figures, just how bad the present situation is: "Last month our Littleton plant produced only 200 carburetors rather than the 300 scheduled. If we don't increase production, we'll have to shut down our main assembly line at Denver. That will cost the company over $800,000 and put 150 people out of work."

In its full form, a need or problem step has four parts:

1. *Statement:* give a definite, concise statement of the problem.
2. *Illustration:* give one or more examples explaining and clarifying the problem.
3. *Ramification:* offer additional examples, statistical data, testimony, and other forms of support showing the extent and seriousness of the problem.
4. *Pointing:* offer an explanation of how the problem directly affects the listener.

The *statement* and *pointing* should always be present, but the inclusion of *illustration* and *ramification* will depend on the amount of detail required to convince the audience. Whether you use the complete development or only part of it, the need step is critical in your speech. Here your subject is first tied to the needs and desires of your listeners.

Step 3: Satisfying the Need: Presenting the Solution

The solution or satisfaction step urges the adoption of a policy. Its goal is to get your listeners to agree that the program you propose is the correct one. Therefore, this step consists of presenting your proposed solution to the problem and proving that this solution is practical and desirable.

Five items are usually contained in a fully developed satisfaction step:

1. *Statement:* state the attitude, belief, or action you wish the audience to adopt. This is a statement of action: "We need to adopt a quota system for our Littleton carburetor plant."

2. *Explanation:* make sure that your proposal is understood. Visual aids such as charts and diagrams can be very useful here. In our example, you would define the quota system: "By quota system, I mean that workers at the Littleton plant should be paid by the actual number of carburetors completed rather than the hours worked."

3. *Theoretical demonstration:* show how your proposed solution meets the need. For example, you could say, "Worker productivity will rise because workers are paid, not just for putting in time, but for completing carburetors."

4. *Reference to practical experience:* supply examples to prove that the proposal has worked effectively where it has been tried. Facts, figures, and the testimony of experts support your contention: "Production at our New Albany plant increased by 50 percent after we instituted this salary schedule."

5.   *Meeting objections:* forestall opposition by answering any objections that might be raised against the proposal. You might counter the objections of the labor union by arguing, "Increased plant productivity will allow us to expand the medical benefits for plant workers."

Just as certain phases can sometimes be omitted from the need step, one or more of these phases can be left out of the satisfaction step. Also, the foregoing order does not always have to be followed exactly. Occasionally, you can best meet objections by answering them as they arise. In other situations, the theoretical demonstration and reference to practical experience can be combined. If the satisfaction step is developed properly, at its conclusion the audience will say, "Yes, you are right; this is a practical and desirable solution to the problem you identified."

Step 4: Visualizing the Results

The function of the visualization step is to intensify desire. It should picture for the audience how conditions will be in the future if your proposal (a) is adopted or (b) is not adopted. Because it projects the audience into the future, this step might also be called the *projection step*.

This projection can be accomplished in one of three ways: by (a) the *positive* method, (b) the *negative* method, or (c) the method of *contrast:*

1.   *The positive method.* Describe how conditions will improve under your proposal. Make such a description vivid and concrete. Select a situation that you are quite sure will arise. Then, picture your listeners actually enjoying the conditions your proposal will produce. For example, if plant productivity allows better medical benefits, describe the advantages for everyone—lower deductibles, dental care, free eye examinations, and hospice services.

2.   *The negative method.* Describe conditions as they will be in the future if your proposal is *not* carried out. Picture for your audience the evils that will arise from failure to follow your advice. Select the most undesirable conditions and show how they will be aggravated if your proposal is rejected. You might describe plant employees losing their jobs and pension plan and the trauma of locating new jobs in a tight job market.

3.   *The method of contrast.* Combine the two preceding methods. Use the negative approach first and then use the positive approach. In this way, the benefits of the proposal are contrasted with the disadvantages of the present system. The following excerpt illustrates how a speaker urging you to carefully think about all four years of college before you start your freshman year might develop a visualization step by the method of contrast:

> *Suppose that you enter the university, as nearly a quarter of our students do, with little sense of educational interests and goals. In your first two semesters, you simply take a few required courses and pass your writing and speaking skills tests. In your second year, you start experimenting with some electives on the basis of friends' recommendations—"Take Speech 101 because it's easy,"*

"Take Photography 102 because it's cool," "Take Art 103 because it's pretty," "Take History 104 because I'm taking it," "Take Astronomy 105 because the professor is neat." Now comes your junior year. You're nowhere near a major and you're getting close to the three-quarter pole in your education. Your adviser nags you, your parents nag you, your friends nag you—even you get down on yourself. In your senior year, you sample some social work courses, finally discovering something you really like. Only then do you realize it will take three or four more semesters—if you're lucky—to complete a B.S.W. degree.

In contrast, suppose you're one of another quarter of our entering students—those who seek career and personal advising early. You enroll for the no-credit "Careers and Vocational Choices" seminar your first semester. While meeting your liberal arts requirements, you take classes in as many different departments as possible so as to get a broad sampling. Near the end of your sophomore year, you talk with people in both Career Planning and personal counseling, all the while trying courses in areas of possible interest. By your junior year, you get departmental advisers in two majors, find out you don't really like one as much as you thought, and then go only to the second after midyear. You then complete that major, taking a correspondence class to catch up because you were a little behind, but still you graduate with other freshmen who entered the year you did.

Careful planning, reasoning through choices, and rigorously analyzing your own interests and talents—these are the actions that separate the completers from the complainers at the end of your years here. So. . . . [Move into the action step at this point.]

Whichever method you use—positive, negative, or contrast—remember that the visualization step must stand the test of reality. The conditions you picture must be realistic and vivid. Let your listeners actually see themselves enjoying the advantages or suffering the evils you describe. The more realistically you depict the situation, the more strongly your listeners will react.

Step 5: Requesting Action

The function of the action step is to call for explicit action. You can call for action with a challenge or appeal, a special inducement, or a statement of personal intention. Review the conclusions discussed in Chapter 8 for examples.

Your request for action should be short to take advantage of your audience's motivational intensity. Finish your speech firmly and sit down.

Remember that the motivated sequence is flexible. You can adapt it to various situations once you are familiar with its basic pattern. Similar to cooks who alter good recipes to their personal tastes, you can adjust the formula for particular occasions—changing the number of main points from section to section, sometimes omitting restatement from the attention step, sometimes omitting the positive or negative projections from the visualization step. *Similar to any recipe, the motivated sequence is designed to give you a formula that fits many different situations.* It gives you an excellent pattern, but it does not remove the human element; you still must think about your choices. Consider the choices made in the following example.

NUMBERS THAT CAN SAVE YOUR LIFE[10]

Attention step

Specific purpose: To urge students to begin checking their blood pressure even while in school.

I. Americans live in a maze of numbers:
   A. Your student ID number identifies you on the campus.
   B. Your telephone number lets others reach you.
   C. Your social security number follows you from near birth to death and after.

Need step

II. A number most of you ignore, however, could kill you—your blood pressure.

(Statistics)
   A. According to the Department of Health and Human Services, this year 310,000 Americans will die from illnesses where the major factor is hypertension.

(Statistics)
   B. Two million will suffer strokes, heart attacks, and kidney failure as a direct result of hypertension.

(Testimony)
   C. According to Dr. Theodore Cooper, Director of the Heart and Lung Institute, "Hypertension can be brought under control through proven treatment which is neither unduly hazardous, complicated or expensive."

(Explanation)
   D. You must understand what high blood pressure does to your body before this will sink in.
      1. When your blood pressure becomes too great for the arterial walls, it can tear a muscle, and if the artery breaks, you can die.
      2. High pressure can also result from fatty tissues, salts, and fluid build-ups that cause the arteries to narrow and the heart to work harder, until it can't.

(Testimony)
   E. Even worse, according to the National High Blood Pressure Council, "Half of those who have high blood pressure don't even know that they do. Of those who do, only half are being treated; only half again of those have their blood pressure under control. Patients and physicians alike just don't seem to take this condition seriously."

Satisfaction step

III. Thus, the public needs to be aware of these problems, health care must be improved, and hypertensives must learn that self-control is life.
   A. Public service ads can keep the issue before the public.
   B. Community- and business-supported hypertension clinics must be established at little or no cost to clients.
   C. Individuals simply must monitor their own blood pressure regularly.

Visualization step

IV. The future of a significant proportion of our population depends on these programs.

(Negative)
   A. Given the American diet, general lack of exercise, and tense lifestyles, without these programs heart attacks will claim more and more victims annually.

B. With such programs, our collective health will improve measurably.
   1. Drs. Andrea Foote and John Erfurt have established a Worker Health Program, which was tested at four different sites and which allowed 92 percent of the hypertensives at those jobs to control their blood pressure.
   2. The Hypertensive Education Program in Michigan and Connecticut is cutting the insurance rates in those states.
   3. In 1970, Savannah, Georgia, had the infamous title of "Stroke Capital of the World," but today, with 14 permanent blood pressure reading stations and special clinics, the stroke rate has been cut in half.

V. Even now, in your prime, it's time for you to develop good health maintenance habits.
   A. You could be one of America's 11 million people with high blood pressure and not even know it.
   B. Even if you're not, you should monitor yourself, safe in the knowledge that your pressure is in the normal—90/70 to 140/90—range.
   C. Get your blood pressure checked today, free of charge, at the Student Health Center and save a life—your own.

Sample Speech to Actuate Using the Motivated Sequence

The following speech, delivered to a joint session of Congress on December 8, 1941, by President Franklin Delano Roosevelt requested a declaration of war against Japan. Round-the-clock negotiations with Japan had been suddenly disrupted when, on Sunday morning, December 7, the Japanese launched a massive surprise attack on Pearl Harbor, Hawaii, sinking eight American battleships and other smaller craft and leveling planes and airfields.

The nation was numbed, Congress was indignant, and the president moved quickly. The joint session was held in the House chamber. The galleries were overflowing, and the speech was broadcast worldwide.

Notice that this message contains only a short attention step because the surprise attack created all of the necessary attention, a longer need step (paragraphs 2–11) that details the situation in the Pacific, and a short satisfaction step (paragraph 12) that only hints at American military strategy. The visualization step (paragraphs 13–17) attempts to steel the nation for war, and it is followed by a concise, sharply drawn action step. The president's strategies seem clear. The fact that the need and visualization steps receive detailed development shows his concern for (a) providing an informational base for the action and (b) offering a psychological orientation to wartime thinking.

FOR A DECLARATION OF WAR AGAINST JAPAN[11]
Franklin Delano Roosevelt

Attention step

TO THE CONGRESS OF THE UNITED STATES: Yesterday, December 7, 1941—a date which will live in infamy—the United States of America was suddenly and deliberately attacked by naval and air forces of the Empire of Japan. /1

Need step

The United States was at peace with that nation and, at the solicitation of Japan, was still in conversation with its government and its Emperor, looking toward the maintenance of peace in the Pacific. Indeed, one hour after Japanese air squadrons had commenced bombing in Oahu, the Japanese Ambassador to the United States and his colleague delivered to the Secretary of State a formal reply to a recent American message. While this reply stated that it seemed useless to continue the existing diplomatic negotiations, it contained no threat or hint of war or armed attack. /2

It will be recorded that the distance of Hawaii from Japan makes it obvious that the attack was deliberately planned many days or even weeks ago. During the intervening time the Japanese government had deliberately sought to deceive the United States by false statements and expressions of hope for continued peace. /3

The attack yesterday on the Hawaiian Islands has caused severe damage to American naval and military forces. Very many American lives have been lost. In addition, American ships have been reported torpedoed on the high seas between San Francisco and Honolulu. /4

Yesterday the Japanese government also launched an attack against Malaya. /5

Last night Japanese forces attacked Hong Kong. /6

Last night Japanese forces attacked Guam. /7

Last night Japanese forces attacked the Philippine Islands. /8

Last night the Japanese attacked Wake Island. /9

This morning the Japanese attacked Midway Island. /10

Japan has, therefore, undertaken a surprise offensive extending throughout the Pacific area. The facts of yesterday speak for themselves. The people of the United States have already formed their opinions and well understand the implications to the very life and safety of our nation. /11

Satisfaction step

As Commander-in-Chief of the Army and Navy I have directed that all measures be taken for our defense. /12

Visualization step

Always will we remember the character of the onslaught against us. /13

No matter how long it may take us to overcome this premeditated invasion, the American people in their righteous might will win through to absolute victory. /14

Action step

> I believe I interpret the will of the Congress and of the people when I assert that we will not only defend ourselves to the uttermost but will make very certain that this form of treachery shall never endanger us again. /15
>
> Hostilities exist. There is no blinking at the fact that our people, our territory, and our interests are in grave danger. /16
>
> With confidence in our armed forces—with the unbounded determination of our people—we will gain the inevitable triumph—so help us God. /17
>
> I ask that the Congress declare that since the unprovoked and dastardly attack by Japan on Sunday, December 7, a state of war has existed between the United States and the Japanese Empire. /18

CHAPTER SUMMARY

1. Speeches to persuade and actuate have *psychological or behavioral change* as their primary goal.

2. Because we seek to satisfy basic needs before higher-level needs, according to Maslow, the concept of *motive need* is central to an understanding of persuasion and actuation.

3. There are five categories of motive needs: (a) *physiological needs*, (b) *safety needs*, (c) *belongingness and love needs*, (d) *esteem needs*, and (e) *self-actualization needs*.

4. Keys to the achievement of persuasion are *motivational appeals*, which are verbally created *visualizations* or *assertions* that link an idea, entity, or course of action to a *motive*.

5. Occasionally motivational appeals are attached directly to other concepts in a verbal process known as *attribution*.

6. Commonly used motivational appeals can be grouped into three clusters: *affiliation, achievement*, and *power*.

7. *Monroe's Motivated Sequence* is an organizational pattern for actuative and persuasive speeches based on people's natural psychological tendencies.

8. The five steps in the motivated sequence are *attention, need, satisfaction, visualization*, and *action*. Each step can be developed by using appropriate rhetorical devices.

KEY TERMS

achievement motives (p. 256)
affiliation motives (p. 256)
attribution (p. 256)
hierarchy (p. 254)
Monroe's Motivated Sequence (p. 264)
motive cluster (p. 256)

motive need (p. 254)
motivational appeal (p. 255)
power motives (p. 256)
private self (p. 257)
social self (p. 257)

SKILLBUILDING ACTIVITIES

1. Present a five- to eight-minute actuative speech in which your primary goal is to get class members to *actually* do something—sign a petition, write a letter to an official, attend a meeting, give blood, or take some other personal action. Use the motivated sequence to create attention, lay out needs, propose a solution, visualize the results, and call for action. On a future "Actuative Speech Check-Up Day," find out how many took the actions you suggested. How successful were you? Why?

2. In a brief persuasive speech, attempt to alter your classmates' impression or understanding of a particular concept. Analyze their current attitudes toward it and then prepare a speech reversing those attitudes. Sample topics might include: pesticides, recycling, compulsory health insurance, public regulation of the medical profession, animal rights, or genetic counseling for prospective parents.

3. What relevant motivational appeals might you use in addressing each of the following audiences? Be ready to discuss your choices in class.
   a. A group of farmers protesting federal agricultural policy.
   b. A meeting of pre-business majors concerned about jobs.
   c. Women at a seminar on nontraditional employment opportunities.
   d. A meeting of local elementary and secondary classroom teachers seeking smaller classes.
   e. A group gathered for an old-fashioned 4th of July picnic.

REFERENCES

1. Abraham H. Maslow, *Motivation and Personality* (New York: Harper & Row, 1954).

2. In the 1970 revision of his book, *Motivation and Personality,* Maslow identified two additional needs—the cognitive and esthetic needs—as higher need states that frequently operate as part of self-actualization.

3. For a fuller discussion of *attribution,* see Philip G. Zimbardo, *Psychology and Life,* 11th ed. (Glenview, Ill.: ScottForesman, 1985), 576–579.

4. For a fuller discussion of these and other motivational appeals, see Bruce E. Gronbeck, Ray E. McKerrow, Douglas Ehninger, and Alan H. Monroe, *Principles and Types of Speech Communication,* 11th ed. (Glenview, Ill.: ScottForesman, 1990), Chapter 6.

5. Katharine Blick Hoyenga and Kermit T. Hoyenga, *Motivational Explanations of Behavior: Evolutionary, Physiological, and Cognitive Ideas* (Monterey, Calif.: Brooks/Cole Publishing Co., 1984), chap. 1; Joseph Veroff, "Contextualism and Human Motives," *Frontiers of Motivational Psychology: Essays in Honor of John W. Atkinson,* Donald R. Brown and Joseph Veroff, eds. (New York: Springer-Verlag, 1986), 132–145; Abigail J. Stewart, ed., *Motivation and Society: A Volume in Honor of David C. McClelland* (San Francisco, Calif.: Jossey-Bass, Inc., Pubs., 1982); Janet T. Spence, ed., *Achievement and Achievement Motives* (San Francisco, Calif.: W.H. Freeman & Co., 1983).

6. See David C. McClelland, *Power: The Inner Experience* (New York: Irvington Pubs., 1975); David C. McClelland, *Human Motivation* (Glenview, Ill.: ScottForesman, 1985).

7. John Dewey, "Analysis of Reflective Thinking," *How We Think* (Boston: D.C. Heath & Company, 1910), 72.

8. Anyone interested in how Alan Monroe conceived of and used the motivated sequence should see the first edition of this textbook: Alan H. Monroe, *Principles and Types of Speech* (Chicago, Ill.: ScottForesman, 1935), vii–x.

9. We have omitted the supporting materials, but most can be found in Tim Schreiner, "The West: Who Plays California's Lottery?" *American Demographics,* 8 (June 1986), 526; John Mikesell and Maureen A. Pirog-Good, "State Lotteries and Crime: The Regressive Revenue Producer is Linked With a Crime Rate Higher by 3 Percent," *American Journal of Economics and Sociology,* 49 (January 1990), 7, 13; William H. Willemen, "Lottery Losers," *The Christian Century,* 107 (January 1990), 48.

10. The outline is based on Todd Ambs, "The Silent Killer"; his materials were formed into an outline by special arrangement with Larry Schnoor, Executive Secretary, Interstate Oratorical Association, Mankato State University, Mankato, Minn.

11. Originally published in the *Congressional Record,* 77th Congress, 1st Session, vol. 87, pt. 9 (December 8, 1941), 9504–9505.

CHAPTER FOURTEEN

Argumentation and Critical Thinking

"*Turrell Baker for President! We need a strong class president, and Turrell has proven he can lead through his active participation in school sports. Turrell holds the school record for passes completed, and he was instrumental in winning our last two home games this year. Turrell's versatile, too. He participated in track and field as a middle distance runner, and was a key player on an intramural volleyball team. We need effective decisionmakers in student government. Turrell's just the person to do the job right!" Ms. Caligari looked up from the flyer she had been reading. "So," she asked her public speaking class, "would this message convince you to vote for Turrell?" The students murmured, but no one said much. Ms. Caligari smiled. "You're having trouble making up your minds here because of relevance: are Turrell's athletic experiences and achievements relevant to the claim that he'd make a great class president? If the reasons don't fit the claim, the argument's dead."*

The ability to think critically is central to your participation in the social world. You're constantly bombarded with requests, appeals, and pleas to change your beliefs or adopt new ways of doing things. Sorting through all those appeals to determine which are justified and whether you should alter your thoughts or actions requires analysis and evaluation skills. Before committing yourself, you've got to be able to analyze appeals, such as those given for Turrell Baker, to determine if the reasons fit the claim being made. If you don't do that, you'll follow every new piper who comes along playing catchy tunes, regardless of where that person is leading you.

You need to develop what's called a *critical spirit*—the ability to analyze others' ideas and requests.[1] Criticism isn't a matter of putting someone down; it's a process of careful assessment, evaluation, and judgment of ideas and motives. It's also a matter of supporting your assessment, evaluation, and judgment with reasons. As you engage in critical evaluation, assessing reasons or offering counterreasons for accepting or rejecting claims, you become an *arguer.* You also become an arguer when you advance a claim and then offer reasons why others ought to accept it. The critical spirit has two applications to public speaking:

1. Through *argumentation,* a speaker offers reasons giving support and force to particular claims.
2. Through *critical thinking,* a listener evaluates such claims and their supporting arguments prior to accepting or rejecting them.

Argumentation and critical thinking, thus, are both social processes, whereby people exchange views, and psychological processes, whereby people evaluate reasoning. In this chapter, we'll examine both the social and psychological aspects of argumentation. We'll begin by examining the social process, then discuss the formal structure or machinery of arguments, then offer ways that you can critically evaluate the arguments of others, and finish with some tips to help you argue effectively.

ARGUMENTATION AS A SOCIAL PROCESS

Argumentation is a process of advancing propositions or claims supported by good reasons, and allowing others to examine those claims and reasons in order to test them or to offer counterarguments. Through argumentation, people hope to come to reasonable conclusions about factual, valuative, and policy matters. Argumentation is distinct from other types of public speaking because it is so thoroughly *rule governed.* A major difference between argumentation and mere fighting is that argumentation proceeds according to social conventions and informal rules of logic. And, while argumentation is usually considered a kind of persuasion, changing the beliefs, attitudes, values, and behaviors of others, it also is a form of mutual truth-testing, helping participants arrive at conclusions together via prescribed forms of talk. The act of arguing does not consist merely of offering an opinion or just stating information; it commits you to communication according to certain rules. Four major social conventions or agreements apply to argumentation: (a) bilaterality, (b) self-risk, (c) fairness, and (d) rationality.

Convention of Bilaterality

Argumentation is inherently bilateral: it requires at least two people or two competing messages. The arguer, whether he or she says so explicitly, is presenting a message that is open for others to examine and evaluate. When you engage in argumentation, you understand that others may differ and present opposing messages. The seller of new cars seldom wishes to engage in this kind of critical exchange; Ford, General Motors, and Chrysler are hoping to persuade, not argue with, you. However, when candidates for political office present campaign platforms, they expect counteranalysis or counterarguments from opposing candidates. Usually, candidates invite reasoned responses to their ideas. Often, formalized public debates ensue.

Convention of Self-Risk

When you engage in argumentation and open up your ideas to critique and counterproposals, you assume certain risks. There's always a chance that your ideas will fail, but you face that risk any time you voice them in public. More important, in argumentation there is a risk that you'll be proven wrong. For example, when you argue that all federal employees should be subjected to mandatory drug testing to detect the use of illegal chemical substances, you face the possibility that people who oppose this action will convince your audience that such a proposal is not only expensive but impractical. Public scrutiny can expose your own or your opponent's weaknesses. This risk is potent enough to make many people avoid public argumentation. With some understanding of argumentation and a little practice, you can develop the skill and confidence to engage in the public exchange of ideas.

The Fairness Doctrine

Arguers also commit themselves to a version of what the broadcast industry calls the "fairness doctrine." The Federal Communication Commission's fairness doctrine maintains that every viewpoint must be given equal access to the airwaves. In the same way, arguers say, in effect, "I have the right to be heard. You may reject my claims and reasons, but first you must hear me out." For this reason, most legislative bodies are reluctant to cut off debate. They are committed to upholding First Amendment rights of expression through the fairness doctrine. While we may not agree with a point of view, we must uphold another's right to express it.

Commitment to Rationality

Arguers commit themselves to proceed reasonably. Reasonable argument depends upon two conditions being met: (a) the arguer must provide good

Lawyers are professional advocates who work within a framework of rule-governed argumentation. How do the conventions of bilaterality, self-risk, fairness, and the commitment to rationality influence the process of legal argument?

reasons for every claim made and (b) each arguer has the right to question each proposition asserted. Argumentation is a rational form of communication in which all parties believe there are good reasons for the acceptance of their claims. Arguers are obligated to provide these reasons rather than simply voicing unsupported personal opinions or feelings. The arguer meets the commitment to rationality by advancing relevant reasons to defend a claim.

In argument all four of these social conventions or agreements must be observed. If you argue, for instance, that international peace is best achieved through military preparedness, you have an obligation to show how military preparedness maintains peace and why it is the best way to maintain peace (commitment to rationality). As you speak, you must anticipate that someone may prove you wrong (convention of self-risk). You also must recognize that another person has the right to disagree with you (the fairness doctrine). That person may assert that military preparedness actually encourages rather than curtails aggression (the convention of bilaterality). No matter what the proposition, each arguer has the right to ask, "Why do you believe that?" (the convention of rationality).

In some cases, arguers are committed not only to generalized conventions or accepted bases of argumentation, but also to formalized procedures or technical strictures. Among the most common of these technical rules is *parliamentary procedure*, as set forth in *Robert's Rules of Order* and similar systems. When speaking within a system of parliamentary procedure, you're expected to frame ideas in *motions,* to adjust the ideas of others via *amendments,* and to get parliamentary procedures explained with motions of *personal privilege.* In many formal meetings, such systems of rules are used to enhance efficiency and fairness. Because such technical rules are important and you'll undoubtedly encounter them, we've included a brief section on parliamentary procedure for meetings in Chapter 16.

From looking at these four conventions that you must accept every time you argue, it's clear that the word *argument* can mean at least three different things. Those different meanings represent three levels of thought and action, ranging from the whole process of exchange to the actual construction of pieces of speeches:

Level 1: The Argumentative Process
Level 1 consists of the overall process of arguing, with proponents and opponents taking turns addressing each other. Initial speeches given by each side are often called **constructive speeches,** when each side is offering a different course of action, or **refutative speeches,** when someone is arguing against an opponent. Each person or side may continue the argument through a series of *rebuttals* until a decision is reached by voting or consensus.

Level 2: The Argumentative Speech
An argumentative speech includes (a) an introduction that sets out a position or claim and suggests criteria for assessing it; (b) a body organized around a series of reasons that support the claim; and (c) a conclusion that summarizes the position and indicates why your position is superior to your opponent's.

Level 3: The Argumentative Unit
Each point made in an argument consists of three building blocks: (a) the *claim,* (b) the *evidence,* and (c) the *reasoning pattern.* (See Figure 14.1.) Taking apart such argumentative units will be our next task. Argumentation thus is social process, communicative product, and rational structure. You need to operate well on all three levels to be the complete arguer.

THE MACHINERY OF ARGUMENTATION

Every argumentative unit is like a piece of machinery, and all of its parts must work together for the argument to compel assent from an audience. Just as a machine is built out of belts and pulleys that transform power sources into some kind of work, so an argument is built out of three essential elements that must work together to compel belief in another person: (a) the claim or proposition being defended, (b) the relevant evidence that you provide in support of that claim, and (c) the reasoning pattern (sometimes called the *inference*) that you use to connect the evidence with the claim.

Figure 14.1 The Levels of Argumentation
Why are all three steps necessary in the argumentative speech?

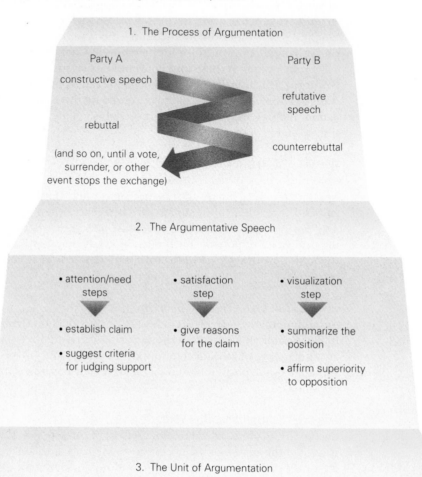

1. The Process of Argumentation

Party A
constructive speech

rebuttal

(and so on, until a vote, surrender, or other event stops the exchange)

Party B

refutative speech

counterrebuttal

2. The Argumentative Speech

- attention/need steps
- establish claim
- suggest criteria for judging support

- satisfaction step
- give reasons for the claim

- visualization step
- summarize the position
- affirm superiority to opposition

3. The Unit of Argumentation

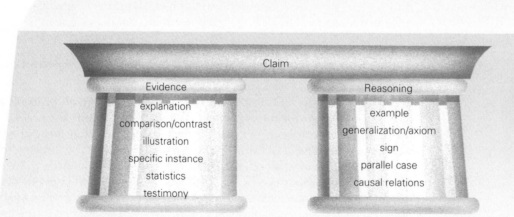

Claim

Evidence
explanation
comparison/contrast
illustration
specific instance
statistics
testimony

Reasoning
example
generalization/axiom
sign
parallel case
causal relations

Types of Claims

Most argumentative speeches assert that (a) something is or is not the case; (b) something is desirable or undesirable; or (c) something should or should not be done. Such judgments or assessments are the speaker's **claims** or propositions. Your first task as an arguer or listener is to determine the type of claim being argued.

Claims of Fact

A **claim of fact** asserts that something is or is not the case. If you're trying to convince listeners that "Price controls on raw agricultural products will result in food shortages," you're presenting a factual claim—asserting that a given state of affairs exists. When confronted with this sort of claim, two questions can occur to the critically aware listener:

1. *By what criteria, or standards of judgment, should the truth or accuracy of the claim be measured?* If you're asked to determine someone's height, you immediately look for a yardstick or other measuring tool. Similarly, listeners look for a standard by which to measure the appropriateness of a factual claim. Before agreeing that price controls result in shortages, discriminating listeners will want to know what you mean by *shortages*. Would you define *shortages* as "the disappearance, for all practical purposes, of a given kind of food" or merely as "less of that food than everyone might desire?" Against what standard, precisely, is the accuracy of the claim to be judged? As a speaker, you need to build those judgments into your speeches.

2. *Do the facts of the situation fit the criteria?* Does the actual amount of produce presently on supermarket shelves fall within the limits set by your definition of *shortages*? First get listeners to agree to certain standards of judgment and then present evidence that a given state of affairs meets those standards. In these ways, you work to compel the assent of listeners to your factual claims.

Claims of Value

When your claim goes one step further, asserting that something is good or bad, desirable or undesirable, justified or unjustified, you're advancing a **claim of value**—a claim about the intrinsic worth of the belief or action in question. Here, too, it is always appropriate to ask (a) *by what standards is something to be judged?* and (b) *how well does the item in question measure up to the standards specified?* For example, we can measure the quality of a college by the distinction of its faculty (*intellectual value*), the excellence of its physical plant (*material value*), the success of its graduates (*practical value*), the size of its endowment (*monetary value*), or the reputation that it enjoys according to surveys of educational excellence (*educational value*). You then can assess the worth of a particular college by each of these criteria to come up with the sorts of scores you find in books that rate colleges. In other words, value judgments are *not* more assertions of personal preference—"I like Miami of Ohio." Rather, they must be argued for, as if someone else is going to examine or challenge them.

Claims of Policy

A **claim of policy** recommends a course of action that you want the audience to approve. Typical examples are: "Federal expenditures for pollution control *should be* substantially increased"; "The student senate *should have* the authority to expel students who cheat." In both instances, you're asking your audience to endorse a proposed policy or course of action. When analyzing a policy claim, four questions are relevant:

1. *Is there a need for such a policy or course of action?* If your listeners don't believe that a change is called for, they're not likely to approve your proposal.

2. *Is the proposal practicable?* Can we afford the expense it would entail? Would it really solve the problem or remove the evil it is designed to correct? Does such a policy stand a reasonable chance of being adopted? If you can't show that your proposal meets these and similar tests, you can hardly expect it to be endorsed.

3. *Are the benefits your proposal will bring greater than its disadvantages?* People are reluctant to approve a proposal that promises to create conditions worse than the ones it is designed to correct. Burning a barn to the ground may be a highly efficient way to get rid of rats, but it's hardly a desirable one. The benefits and disadvantages that will result from a plan of action must always be carefully weighed along with considerations of its basic workability.

4. *Is the offered proposal superior to any other plan or policy?* Listeners are hesitant to approve a policy if they have reason to believe that an alternative course of action is more practicable or more beneficial.

As you've seen, then, different types of claims make varying demands on you as an arguer. (See Table 14.1.) And, too, *it's essential that arguers tell audiences how to assess their claims.* Articulating criteria or standards for judgment is essential for the person who tries to win an argument. If you think tuition increases should be tied to the Consumer Price Index while your opponent believes tuition should be tied to rises and falls in state tax revenue, you have a serious disagreement over what standards to apply. Rather than haggling about increases and decreases in tuition, you and your opponent have to stop and see whose standard for judgment will be accepted by your listeners. When criteria are agreed upon, you and your opponent can return to claims concerning increases or decreases in tuition.

Unless there are sound reasons for delay, you should announce your claim early in your speech. If listeners don't see precisely where you're going in your argument, your strongest arguments may be lost on them.

Table 14.1 Types of Claims

Notice how each type of claim can be analyzed.

Claim	Description	Analysis
CLAIM OF FACT	assertion of truth or that something exists	1. By what criteria is the truth or accuracy of the claim measured? 2. Do the facts of the situation fit the criteria?
CLAIM OF VALUE	assertion that something is good or bad; desirable or undesirable; justified or unjustified	1. By what standards is something to be judged? 2. How well does the thing measure up?
CLAIM OF POLICY	recommendation of a course of action	1. Is there a need for this policy or course of action? 2. Is the proposal practicable? 3. Are the benefits of the proposal greater than its disadvantages? 4. Is the proposal better than other courses of action?

Take time to say something such as this: "Today, I want to convince you that increases and decreases in student tuition should be coupled with the Consumer Price Index. If the Board of Regents takes this action, the cost of education will be more fairly distributed between the state and the students."[2]

Types of Evidence

As you discovered in Chapter 5, supporting materials are the items that you use to clarify, amplify, and strengthen the ideas in your speech. They provide evidence for the acceptance of your central idea and its supporting points. Evidence is a crucial part of developing a clear, compelling argument. It can be presented in any of the forms of supporting materials with which you are already familiar: explanations, comparisons and contrasts, illustrations, specific instances, statistics, and testimony.

You've already engaged in the process of research required to find the supporting materials necessary to reinforce your ideas. The selection of relevant evidence is particularly important in constructing good arguments. There is no single or easy rule for selecting relevant evidence. Supporting

Careful audience analysis will help you to determine what kind of evidence will work best for your listeners. In order to choose the best evidence, what questions should you ask about your listeners?

material that is relevant to one claim may not be relevant to another, or it may be relevant as logical proof but not as a compelling reason for action. You should consider both the *rational* and the *motivational* characteristics of evidence during selection.

Rationally Relevant Evidence

The type of evidence you choose should reflect the type of claim you advocate. For example, if you're defending the claim that censorship violates the First Amendment guarantee of freedom of speech, you'll probably choose testimony by noted authorities or definitions of terms to advance your claim. On the other hand, examples, illustrations, and statistics work better for showing that a problem exists or a change is needed. If you present statistics that show that nine out of ten Americans believe that removing adult literature from public library shelves is a violation of their rights, you'll be showing that there is popular support for a change. As you can see, the claim you present requires a logically relevant type of evidence. As you plan your arguments, you should ask yourself, "What type of evidence is logically relevant in support of my claim?"

Motivationally Relevant Evidence

If you hope to convince listeners to adopt your attitudes or actions, your claim must be supported by more than logically relevant evidence. Your

Using Evidence in Argumentation

As we noted in the Ethical Moments in Chapter 3, many ethical decisions confront the arguer in public debate. Some of these decisions have to do with how you treat your opponent, how you use the time you're sharing with another speaker, and how you play to the audience. Some decisions center on how you use evidence. Consider the following ethical dilemmas:

1. Should you suppress evidence that contradicts a point you're making? If your opponent doesn't know about it, should you bring it up?

2. What about those qualifiers? Should you leave in all of the "maybe's" and "perhaps's" when you read a quotation? After all, if you turn in a speech outline, you can always use ellipses (those three little dots that indicate something's been left out) to honestly report what you did.

3. Does it make any difference if you overqualify a source? Perhaps you've discovered an article by a staff researcher at the National Institute of Health that supports your position. Will it hurt if you pretend that the researcher is an Under-Secretary of Health? After all, it'll add to the force of your argument. Should you care?

4. What difference does it make if a poll was conducted by the National Right-to-Life Committee or Planned Parenthood's Pro-Choice Committee? What if each organization asks polling questions in such a way as to encourage a particular response? Can you just say that "a recent national poll found that 75 percent of our citizens favor abortion rights?" You haven't really lied in suppressing the polling agency or the actual questions, have you? Is this acceptable?

---

evidence must also create in listeners a desire to become involved. That is, it must be motivationally relevant to them. In order to best determine what evidence works for specific audiences, you should ask two questions:

1. *What type of evidence will this audience demand?* Whenever Congress proposes a new form of taxation, taxpayers usually demand that it also supply statistical evidence, financial reports, an explanation of underlying key concepts, testimony from experts in economics, examples of the ways the new laws will affect them, and comparisons and contrasts with other potential tax legislation. Mere examples or illustrations are not compelling enough to garner public support for higher taxes. On the other hand, if you're reviewing a recent film for a group of friends, an example from the plot, a figurative analogy, or an illustration of dialogue would be more forceful as proof than statistical counts of words, box office receipts, or testimony from published movie critics. Careful audience analysis will help you determine what type of evidence is needed to move your particular group of listeners psychologically.

2. *To which specific pieces of evidence will your listeners be most responsive?* This is a question that you should pose once you've determined the type of evidence required by your argument. For example, if you've decided to use expert testimony to support your argument, whom should you quote? Or, if you're using an illustration, should you use a factual example or develop one of your own? Will listeners be more moved by a personalized story or a general illustration?

To answer these and similar questions about your listeners, you need to analyze them. A homogeneous audience may be suspicious of outsiders. They might react best to local experts or illustrations from their community or range of experience. A heterogeneous audience, on the other hand, will require more generally recognized authorities and geographically varied examples because it does not share experience and background. While you can't always tailor your evidence to listeners' demographic or psychological characteristics, you can attempt to consider what those characteristics are.

Overall, it's one thing to accidentally discover supporting materials in the library, but quite another to shrewdly search for supporting material. In selecting evidence, keep in mind both your claim and its requirements as well as your listeners and their needs.

Forms of Reasoning

The third element of a unit of argumentation is that which "connects" the evidence with the claim. This element is called **reasoning** or *inference*. Reasoning is a process of connecting something that is known or believed (evidence) to a concept or idea (claim) you wish others to accept. **Patterns of reasoning** are habitual ways in which a culture or society uses inferences to connect what is accepted to what they are being urged to accept. There are five reasoning patterns: (a) from *examples*, (b) from *generalization or axiom*, (c) from *sign*, (d) from *parallel case*, and (e) from *causal relation*.

Reasoning from Examples
Often called *inductive* reasoning, **reasoning from examples** is a matter of examining a series of examples of known occurrences (evidence) and drawing a general conclusion (claim). The inference of this reasoning pattern is that what is true of particular cases is true of the whole class. This inference represents a kind of mental inductive leap from specifics to generalities. For example, the National Cancer Institute has studied hundreds of individual case histories and discovered that people whose diets are high in fiber are less prone to contract cancers of the digestive tract. With an inductive leap, the Institute then moved to the factual claim, "High fiber diets prevent certain types of cancer." Commuters use a similar pattern of reasoning every time they drive during rush hour. After trial and error, they decide that a residential street is the best route to take home between 5:00 and 5:30 P.M. and the expressway between 5:30 and 6:00 P.M. In other words, after experiencing enough instances, they arrive at a generalization and act on it.

Reasoning from Generalization or Axiom

Reasoning from generalization or axiom or applying a general truth to a specific situation, sometimes called *deduction,* is essentially the reverse of reasoning from examples which is called *induction.* In high school consumer education class you may have learned that buying goods in large quantities saves money (the generalization). Now, you may shop at discount stores because they purchase goods in quantity, thereby saving money and passing that savings on to you (the claim deduced from the evidence). Or, you may believe that getting a college education is the key to a better future (the generalization). Therefore, if you get a college degree, you will get a better job (claim). This inference gathers power because of *experience* (you learned it through observation) or by *definition* (one of the characteristics of education is self-improvement). You ultimately accept this inference because of the uniformities you believe exist in the world.

Reasoning from Sign

Reasoning from sign uses an observable mark, or sign, as proof of the existence of a state of affairs. You reason from sign when you note a rash or spots on your skin (the evidence) and decide you have measles (the claim). The rash does not cause measles; rather, it's a sign of the disease. Detectives, of course, are experts at reasoning from sign. When they discover that a particular suspect had motive, access, and a weapon in his possession (the signs), they make the claim that he might be the murderer. Your doctor works the same way every time she examines your tongue and your throat for signs of trouble. Reasoning from sign works well with natural occurrences (ice on the pond is always a sign that the temperature has been below 32°F). However, reasoning from sign can be troublesome in the world of human beings (as when some people take skin color as a sign of laziness or dishonesty). Signs, of course, are circumstantial evidence—and could be wrong. Just ask detectives and doctors. The inference that evidence is a sign of a particular conclusion is not always true. Yet, we often must use signs as indicators; otherwise, we couldn't project our economy, predict our weather, or forecast the rise and fall of political candidates.

Reasoning from Parallel Case

Another common reasoning pattern, **reasoning from parallel case,** involves thinking solely in terms of similar things and events. Your college or university, for example, probably designed its curriculum by examining the curricula of similar colleges or universities. These curricula functioned as evidence; the claim was that similar courses should be offered at your university. The inference that linked the evidence and the claim was probably something such as this: "What worked at Eastern University will work here at Western University because they are similar institutions." Your instructors might use parallel reasoning every time they tell you, "Study hard for this exam. The last exam was difficult; this one will be too." Obviously this is not a generalization, since every exam will probably not be the same. However, your instructors are asserting that the upcoming examination and past examinations are similar cases—they have enough features in common to increase the likelihood that careful study habits will benefit you.

Reasoning from Causal Relation

Finally, **reasoning from causal relation** is an important vehicle for reaching conclusions; it's even used as a basic pattern for organizing entire speeches. The underlying assumption of causal reasoning is that events occur in a predictable, routine manner, with causes that account for occurrences. Reasoning from causal relation involves associating events that come before (antecedents) with events that follow (consequents). (See Table 14.2.) When substance abuse appears to be increasing across the country, people scramble to identify causes: the existence of international drug cartels, corrupt foreign governments, organized crime inside our own borders, lower moral standards, the break-up of the nuclear family, and lax school discipline. The trick for the arguer is to assert causes that might reasonably be expected to produce the effects; you need to be able to point to material connections between, for example, foreign governments' actual policies and the presence of drugs in Chicago or other American cities. Overall, the inference in causal reasoning is simple and constant: every effect has a cause.

Table 14.2 Kinds of Reasoning

Try to think of additional examples for each kind of reasoning.

Reasoning	Description	Examples
REASONING FROM EXAMPLES (Inductive Reasoning)	drawing a general conclusion from instances or examples	"Jan, Miyoshi, and Vernon all passed that class. I probably will too."
REASONING FROM GENERALIZATION OR AXIOM (Deductive Reasoning)	applying a general conclusion to a specific example	"America has always supported liberty and democracy, so it should now, too."
REASONING FROM SIGN	using an observable mark or symptom as proof of a state of affairs	"The sky is getting dark in the West. It's probably going to storm."
REASONING FROM PARALLEL CASE	asserting that two things or events share similar characteristics or patterns	"Sofia is quick tempered, so I'll bet her brother is too."
REASONING FROM CAUSAL RELATION	concluding that an event that occurs first is responsible for a later event	"Inflation is triggered by failing consumer confidence in fiscal policies."

People in this culture judge these five forms of reasoning to be logical or rational. You can rely primarily on these forms to connect evidence with claims.

EVALUATING ARGUMENTS

The reasoning process is the pulley around which the machine of argument runs. As both speaker and critical listener, you must test reasoning in order to protect yourself from embarrassment when you're arguing and from faulty decisions when you're listening to others. For each kind of reasoning there are special tests or questions that help you determine the soundness of arguments.

Tests for Reasoning

Consider the following questions as you construct arguments and evaluate those of others:

Reasoning from Examples

1. *Have you looked at enough instances to warrant generalizing?* You don't assume spring has arrived after experiencing one warm day in February.

2. *Are the instances fairly chosen?* You certainly hope your neighbors don't think you have a rotten kid just because she picked one of their flowers; you want them to judge your daughter only after seeing her in many different situations.

3. *Are there important exceptions to the generalization or claim that must be considered?* While it is generally true from presidential election studies that "As Maine goes, so goes the nation," there've been enough exceptions to that rule to keep presidential candidates who lose in Maine campaigning hard even after the primary.

Reasoning from Generalization or Axiom

1. *Is the generalization true?* Remember that sailors set certain courses on the assumption that the world was flat and that for years parents in this country accepted as gospel Benjamin Spock's generalizations about child rearing.

2. *Does the generalization apply to this particular case?* Usually, discount stores have lower prices, but if a small neighborhood store has a sale, it may well offer better prices than discount houses. While the old saying "Birds of a feather flock together" certainly applies to birds, it may not apply to human beings.

Reasoning from Sign

Is the sign fallible? As we have noted, many signs are merely circumstantial. Be extremely careful not to confuse sign reasoning with causal reasoning. If sign reasoning were infallible, your weather forecaster would never be wrong.

Reasoning from Parallel Case

1. *Are there more similarities than differences between the two cases?* City A and City B may have many features in common—size, location, and so on—yet they probably also have many different features, perhaps in the subgroups that make up their populations and the degree of industrial development. Too many differences between two cases rationally destroy the parallel.

2. *Are the similarities you have pointed out the relevant and important ones?* There are two children in your neighborhood who are the same age, go to the same school, and wear the same kinds of clothes; are you therefore able to assume that one is well-behaved simply because the other is? Probably not, because more relevant similarities than their clothing and age would include their home lives, their relationships with siblings, and so forth. Comparisons must be based on relevant and important similarities.

Reasoning from Causal Relation

1. *Can you separate causes and effects?* We often have a difficult time doing this. Do higher wages cause higher prices, or is the reverse true? Does a strained home life make a child misbehave, or is it the other way around?

2. *Are the causes strong enough to have produced the effect?* Did Ronald Reagan's winning smile really give him the election, or was that an insufficient cause? There probably were much stronger and more important causes.

3. *Did intervening events or persons prevent a cause from having its normal effect?* If a gun is not loaded, you cannot shoot anything, no matter how hard you pull the trigger. Even if droughts normally drive up food prices, that might not happen if food has been stockpiled, if spring rains left enough moisture in the soil, or if plenty of cheap imported food is available.

4. *Could any other cause have produced the effect?* Although crime often increases when neighborhoods deteriorate, increased crime rates can be caused by any number of other changes—alterations in crime reporting methods, increased reporting of crimes that have been going on for years, or closings of major industries. We rationally must sort through all of the possible causes before championing one.

Detecting Fallacies in Reasoning

As we've been stressing, your primary job as a critical listener and arguer is to evaluate the claims, evidence, and reasoning of others. On one level, you're looking for ways that the ideas and reasonings of others are important to your own thinking, and, on another level, you're examining the logical soundness of their thinking. A **fallacy** is a flaw in the rational properties of an argument or inference. Fallacies can be divided into three categories: (a) *fallacies in evidence,* (b) *fallacies in reasoning,* and (c) *fallacies in language.*

Fallacies in Evidence

As the label suggests, **fallacies in evidence** occur in the way we use supporting material to reach our claims. Three types of these fallacies stand out: (a) hasty generalization, (b) false division, and (c) genetic fallacy.

1.   *Hasty generalization (faulty "inductive leap").* A **hasty generalization** is a claim made on the basis of too little evidence. You should ask, "Has the arguer really examined enough typical cases to make a claim?" If the answer is no, then a flaw in reasoning has occurred. Urging the ban of aspirin because several people have died of allergic reactions to it or the closure of a highway because of a traffic fatality are examples of hasty generalization.

2.   *False division.* A **false division** occurs when someone argues that there's only one way to divide a process or idea. In fact, there may be many ways to view the process or idea. Be on the lookout when someone argues that the only ways to treat the mentally handicapped are to confine them to institutions or to place them with guardians. *Only* often signals a false division; there may well be other options worth our attention.

3.   *Genetic fallacy.* A **genetic fallacy** occurs when someone assumes that the only "true" understanding of some idea, practice, or event is to be found in its origins—in its "genes," literally or metaphorically. People sometimes assume that if an idea has been around for a long time, it must be true. Many people who defended slavery in the nineteenth century referred to the Biblical practices of slavery and to those of the early American settlers to support their claim. Genetic study can help us understand a concept, but it's hardly proof of present correctness or justice.

Fallacies in Reasoning

Logical flaws often occur in the thought process itself. Five **fallacies in reasoning** should be mentioned.

1.   *Appeal to ignorance (argumentum ad ignoratiam).* People sometimes **appeal to ignorance** by arguing with double negatives: "You *can't* prove it

won't work!" They may even attack an idea because information about it is incomplete. "We can't use radio beams to signal UFOs and extraterrestrials because we don't know what languages they speak." Both of these are illogical claims because they depend upon what we don't know. Sometimes we must simply act on the basis of the knowledge we have, despite the gaps in it. In countering such claims, you can cite parallel cases and examples.

2. *Appeal to popular opinion (argumentum ad populum).* A frequent strategy is to **appeal to popular opinion** or to urge people to "jump on the bandwagon." This argument assumes that if everyone else is doing something, you should too—"But Christopher, everyone knows the world is flat!" or "But Dad, everyone else is going!" While these appeals may be useful in stating *valuative* claims, they're not the basis for *factual* claims. Even if most people believe or think something, it still may not be true. The world has witnessed hundreds of widely believed but false ideas, from the belief that night air causes tuberculosis to panic over an invasion by Martians.

3. *Sequential fallacy (post hoc, ergo propter hoc).* Literally translated from the Latin "after this, therefore because of this," the **sequential fallacy** is often present in arguments based on evidence from causal relations and it's often based on the assumption that if one event follows another, the first must be the cause. Thunder and lightning do not cause rain, although they often occur sequentially, and, even if you usually catch colds in the spring, the two are not causally related. That is, the season of the year does not cause your cold; a virus does.

4. *Begging the question (petitio principii).* **Begging the question** is rephrasing an idea and then offering it as its own reason. This kind of reasoning is a *tautology*, or circular thought. If someone asserts, "Abortion is murder because it is taking the life of the unborn," he or she has committed a fallacy by rephrasing the claim (it is murder) to form the reason (it is taking life). Sometimes questions can be fallacious, such as "Have you quit cheating on tests yet?" The claim, phrased as a question, assumes that you've cheated on tests in the past. Whatever your answer to the question, therefore, you're guilty. Claims of value are especially prone to *petitio principii.*

5. *Appeal to authority (ipse dixit).* *Ipse dixit* means "because he says it," and an **appeal to authority** occurs when someone who is popular but not an expert urges the acceptance of an idea or a product. Television advertisers frequently ask consumers to purchase products because movie stars or sports heroes endorse them. Celebrities promote everything from blue jeans to beer. The familiar figure provides name recognition, but not expertise. You can detect this fallacy by asking, "Is he or she an expert on this topic?"

Fallacies in Language

Finally, some fallacies creep into our arguments simply due to the ways in which we use words. Word meanings are flexible, so language can be used sloppily or manipulatively. Five **fallacies in language** are frequent in public debate.

1. *Ambiguity.* A word often has two or more meanings. Because of this **ambiguity,** some words can cause confusion and inaccurate claims. Suppose you hear, "Some dogs have fuzzy ears. My dog has fuzzy ears. My dog is *SOME* dog!" The problem here rests in the word *some.* In its first usage, it means *not all.* The word shifts meanings, however, so in the second usage it becomes *outstanding/exceptional.* Such shifts of meaning can result in flawed claims.

2. *Nonqualification.* It's all too easy through **nonqualification** to drop some important qualifications as an argument progresses. If such words as *maybe, might,* and *probably* fall by the wayside, the meaning of the argument can change. Advertisers often claim, "Our brand *may* result in fewer cavities *if* you follow a program of regular hygiene and professional dental care." When the qualifications are underplayed, the argument becomes verbally distorted.

3. *Is-Faults.* One of the trickiest verbs in English is *is.* "John is a man" and "John is a radical" are grammatically equivalent sentences; however, gender is a permanent characteristic of John, while his political leanings are not. We might expect political orientation to change, but not gender. Learn to recognize **is-faults,** distinguishing between the *is* of classification and the *is* of attribution.

4. *Persuasive definition.* In the heat of an argument, many advocates attempt to win by offering their own **persuasive definitions** of ideas or concepts. Value terms or abstract concepts are most open to special or skewed definitions. "Liberty means the right to own military weapons." "A good university education is one that leads to a good job." "Real men don't wear cologne." Each of these definitions sets up a particular point of view; each is capricious or arbitrary. If you accept the definition, the argument is over.[3] In order to challenge a fallacious argument, you can substitute a definition from a respected source.

5. *Name calling.* **Name calling** is the general label for attacks on people instead of on their arguments. *Argumentum ad hominem* is an attack on the special interests of a person: "Of course, you're defending her. You voted for her." *Argumentum ad personam* is an attack on a personal characteristic rather than on ideas: "You're just a dweeb" (or yuppie or chauvinist). Even dweebs, yuppies, and chauvinists sometimes offer solid claims. *Ideological appeals* link ideas or people with emotional labels: "Social security is really a Communist plot to overthrow America." This appeal links social security to something the listener considers sinister rather than examining social security on its own merits. Claims ought to be judged on their own features, not on the characteristics of the person who makes them.

These are some of the fallacies that creep into argumentation. A good basic logic book can point out additional fallacies.[4] Armed with knowledge of such fallacies, you should be able to construct sound arguments to protect yourself against unscrupulous demagogues, sales personnel, and advertisers.

TIPS FOR DEVELOPING ARGUMENTATIVE SPEECHES

As you get ready to pull all of your claims, kinds of evidence, and reasoning patterns together into coherent argumentative speeches, consider the following pieces of advice:

1. *Organize your arguments by putting the strongest first or last.* This strategy takes advantage of the *primacy-recency effects.* Arguments presented first set the agenda for what is to follow and a strong opening argument often impresses an audience with its power, thereby heightening the credibility of the arguer (the primacy effect). We also know that listeners tend to retain the most recently present idea (the recency effect), so you might put your strongest argument at the end of your speech so listeners remember your best shot.[5]

2. *Vary your evidence.* Different listeners are likely to prefer different kinds of evidence, and most listeners want supporting materials that are both logically relevant and psychologically motivating. For example, if you're arguing in favor of capital punishment, you can use statistical trends to signal the widespread problem of premeditated violence. To clinch this argument, though, more than sanitized facts are necessary. You'd be wise to provide descriptions of victims of premeditated crime to involve your audience in the human drama of the problem.

3. *Avoid personal attacks on opponents.* Maintain arguments on an appropriate intellectual level. This tactic enhances your credibility. If you can argue well without becoming vicious, you'll earn the respect—and perhaps the agreement—of your listeners; most know that the more someone screams, the weaker his or her arguments are. Work from strong, not loud, arguments.

4. *Know the potential arguments of your opponents.* The best advocates know their opponents' arguments better than their opponents do; they have thought about those arguments and ways of responding to them ahead of time. Having thought through opposing positions early on allows you to prepare a response and feel confident about your own position.

5. *Practice constructing logical arguments and detecting fallacious ones.* Ultimately, argument demands skill in operating the techniques of public reasoning. You need to practice routinely constructing arguments with solid relationships between and among claims, evidence, and reasoning patterns; and you need to practice regularly detecting the fallacies in other people's proposals. Critically examine product advertisements, political claims, and arguments that your neighbor makes in order to improve your communication skills—as both the sender and receiver of argumentative messages.

Sample Argumentative Speech

Policies are supported by particular factual assertions, as well as values. The advisability of a policy is based on the truth-value of the facts offered in its support, and on the audience's willingness to accept the value judgments being made. In many cases, it's necessary to attack conclusions drawn on the basis of factual data in order to argue for a reconsideration of a policy. Jenny Clanton of Southeastern Illinois College faced this problem in her analysis of NASA's continued willingness to use Plutonium 238 as its "fuel of choice" in launching space flights.

In developing her position that NASA's policy is flawed, Clanton used a combination of testimony from experts and argument from cause to demonstrate the level of risk that exists every time the shuttle is launched under current policy. Underlying her analysis is the value assumption that the level of risk is unacceptable. She began the speech with the startling observation that the *Challenger* disaster saved future lives. The next scheduled launch, in which the O-rings could have just as easily failed, could have produced a nuclear disaster.

In paragraphs 6–9, she demonstrated the risks attendant on the use of plutonium as a fuel. She concluded that continued use is "a crazy idea" unless all launches are perfectly safe. This led her to outline NASA's argument for safety in paragraph 10. In paragraphs 11–14, she offered a clear refutation of the presumed safety of plutonium. In the process, she highlighted the values underlying a policy that risks human life without due regard and found them inadequate as support. With the policy questioned through an analysis of factual claims about the potential hazards of plutonium use, she moved toward a resolution by posing questions about what Congress has been doing, what should be done, and what listeners can do. Her personal appeal was strengthened by a final rhetorical question that focused her listeners' attention on the risk involved.

THE CHALLENGER *DISASTER THAT DIDN'T HAPPEN*[6]
Jenny Clanton

Attention step
(Reference to subject)

On January 28, 1986, the American Space Program suffered the worst disaster in its more than 30 year history. The entire world was shocked when the space shuttle Challenger exploded seconds after lift-off, claiming the lives of seven brave astronauts and crippling our entire space agenda. I suppose the oldest cliché in our culture, spoken on battlegrounds and indeed virtually anywhere Americans die, is "We must press forward so we can say they did not die in vain." Rest assured. They didn't. The deaths of our seven

(Startling statement)

astronauts probably saved the lives of untold thousands of Americans. /1

(Explanation)

For, you see, if the O-rings had not failed on January 28, 1986, but rather on May 20, 1987, the next scheduled shuttle launch, in the words of Dr. John

(Testimony)

Gofman, Professor Emeritus at the University of California at Berkeley, you could have "kissed Florida good-bye." /2

(Specific instance)

Because the next shuttle, the one that was to have explored the atmosphere of Jupiter was to carry 47 lbs. of Plutonium 238, which is, again, according to Dr. Gofman, the most toxic substance on the face of the earth.

(Testimony)

Dr. Helen Caldicott corroborates Dr. Gofman's claim in her book, *Nuclear Madness,* when she cites studies estimating one ounce of widely dispersed Plutonium 238 particles as having the toxicity to induce lung cancer in every person on earth. /3

Today, when you leave this room, I want you to fully understand just what impact NASA's plans could have on this planet. I want you to become cynical. I want you to be a little scared. I want you to become angry. But most of all, I want you to begin to demand some answers. /4

(Forecasting)

To move you in this direction I would first like to explore with you just what plutonium is and what could happen if it were released in our atmosphere. Second, let's consider NASA's argument for the safety of the pluto-

(Statement of claim)

nium as used in the shuttle program. And finally, I want to convince you that NASA's conclusions are flawed. /5

Need step
(Significance of issue)
(Explanation)

So now, let's turn our attention to the nature of plutonium. Plutonium is a man-made radioactive element which is produced in large quantities in nuclear reactors from uranium. Plutonium is a chemically reactive metal, which, if exposed to air, ignites spontaneously and produces fine particles of plutonium dioxide. These particles, when dispersed by wind and inhaled by living organisms, lodge in the lungs. Lung cancer will follow—sooner or later. Once inside the human body, plutonium rests in bone tissue, causing

(Factual claim)

bone cancer. Plutonium 238 is so poisonous that less than one *millionth* of a gram is a carcinogenic dose. /6

(Qualifying expertise)

Last July, *Common Cause* magazine contacted Dr. Gofman at Berkeley and asked him to place Plutonium 238 in perspective. Before I share Dr. Gofman's assessment, please understand he's no poster-carrying "anti-nuke." Dr. Gofman was co-discoverer of Uranium 233, and he isolated the isotope

(Testimony)

first used in nuclear bombs. Dr. Gofman told Karl Grossman, author of the article "Redtape and Radio-activity" that Plutonium 238 is 300 times more radioactive than Plutonium 239, which is the isotope usd in atomic bombs. /7

(Testimony)

Dr. Richard Webb, a nuclear physicist and author of *The Accident Hazards of Nuclear Power Plants,* said in a similar interview that sending 46.7 lbs. of Plutonium 238 into space would be the equivalent of sending five nuclear reactors up—and then hoping they wouldn't crash or explode. /8

(Transition)

Dr. Gofman's final assessment? It's a crazy idea, unless shuttle launches are 100 percent perfect. Which is just about what NASA would have liked us to believe, and at first glance NASA's guarantees are pretty convincing. /9

(Opposing view)

NASA estimates the chance of releasing Plutonium into the environment, because of the possibility of a malfunction of the space shuttle, at .002 percent—that's not quite 100 percent perfect, but it's awfully close. NASA and the Department of Energy base their reliability figures on three factors:

(Specific instances)

1) the Titan 34D launch vehicle and its high success rate, 2) Energy Department officials in the March 10th *Aviation Week and Space Technology* magazine explain that the Plutonium would be safely contained in an unbreakable, quarter-inch thick iridium canister which would withstand pressures of over 2,000 pounds per square inch, and 3) in that same article, NASA explains there is "little public danger" because the Plutonium on board would be in the form of oxide pellets, each one inch in diameter. If you'll remember, the danger of Plutonium is in fine particles. /10

(Refutation of NASA position)
(Testimony/statistics)

Now, let's take a second glance. One month later, the April 28th issue of *Aviation Week and Space Technology* reported that two of the last nine Titans launched have blown up. Two failures in nine trips is great in baseball, but not when we're dealing with nuclear payloads. That same article estimates loss of orbiter and crew, not at .002 percent but at 1 in 25. /11

(Rhetorical questions)

With odds on the launch vehicle reduced to 1 in 25, the dual questions arise: just how breach-proof is that canister and, in a worst case scenario, what could happen if the pellets of 238 were released? For the answers to

(Qualifying expertise)

those questions we go to Dr. Gary Bennett, former Director of Safety and Nuclear Operations, who not only answers those questions, but also explains why NASA is so insistent on using plutonium. /12

(Testimony)

Last July, Dr. Bennett told *Common Cause* that there is concern within NASA and the Department of Energy that an explosion aboard the Galileo spacecraft, a Titan or other rocket, would, in turn, set off an explosion of the booster rockets. Bennett admitted that government tests in 1984 and 1985

(Causal argument)

determined that if the shuttle exploded, and then the booster rockets exploded, there would be a likelihood of breaching the iridium canister. The plutonium would then be vaporized and released into the environment; and there goes Florida. /13

(Satisfaction step)
(Rhetorical question)
(Explanation)
(Comparison/contrast)

But why would NASA take such a risk? It's really quite simple. On the one hand, Plutonium 238 is the one fuel that would enable space exploration beyond the limit of Mars. Without it, distant space exploration must wait for research to develop an equally effective, safe fuel. On the other hand, a worst case scenario would create the worst nuclear accident in history. In short, NASA weighed exploration now against the chances for disaster and opted to take the risk. The only problem is, I really don't like the idea of someone risking my life without consulting me—and I hope you don't either. By the way, there is evidence that NASA and the Department of Energy have projected some pretty horrible figures. Under the Freedom of Information Act rules, Karl Grossman was able to obtain agencies' estimates for the number of lives lost in a major accident. The only problem is that every reference to the number of people affected is blanketed out with liquid paper and the term Exempt #1 is written over the deletion. James Lombardo of the Energy Department explains the whiteouts were necessary for—you've got it—

(Qualifying expertise)

national security reasons. I would contend that national security would be threatened by mass anger over the callousness of the Energy Department, and justifiably so. Representative Edward Markey agrees, and when he was head of the House subcommittee on Energy, Conservation and Power, he uncovered most of the information I share with you today. /14

Visualization step
(Transition)
(Questions to struc-
ture following expla-
nation)

In a telephone interview last August, I asked Congressman Markey three questions. Why hasn't Congress done anything? What should be done? What can we do to help? /15

His answer to the first question was quite interesting. You may remember that shortly after the shuttle exploded and just when Congress was showing some interest in a thorough investigation of the space program, another larger, even more dramatic accident occurred—Chernobyl. The attention to Chernobyl as it related to our own power industry captured not only the attention of most Americans, but of Congress as well. Consequently, most of our nuclear experts are involved in working with Congress and the nuclear power industry. /16

And while Congress is focusing on one facet of the nuclear question, NASA and the Department of Energy are receiving much less attention. Which is why Congressman Markey helped found Space Watch. /17

Representative Markey is of the opinion that hysteria accomplishes nothing, but that all space flight should be halted until either Plutonium 238 can be made safe, which is highly unlikely, or until an alternative fuel can be found. The burden of proof should be on NASA to prove a safe fuel, and not on the public to prove it dangerous. /18

Action step
(Personal appeal)

This is where you and I come in. First, if by now you are sufficiently scared or angry, contact Space Watch through Representative Markey's office. Then, keep abreast of developments and exert pressure through your elected officials if Congress does nothing to interfere with NASA's plans. Send your objections not only to your own legislators, but to Representative Markey as well. Allow him to walk into the House with mailbag after mailbag of letters in opposition to NASA's unbridled desire to go to Jupiter. We have a friend in Congress who solicits help. The least we can do is give it to him. /19

(Pertinent quotation)
(Rhetorical question)

One last thought; as of November, Plutonium 238 is *still* NASA's and the Department of Energy's fuel of choice. Dr. Bennett's last words in that July interview were, "I think you should understand there's a degree of risk with any kind of launch vehicle." But isn't that the point? /20

CHAPTER SUMMARY

1. *Argumentation* is a process of advancing propositions or claims supported by good reasons and allowing others to examine those claims and reasons in order to test them or to offer counterarguments. Through *critical thinking*, a listener evaluates such claims and their support prior to accepting or rejecting them. Argumentation and critical thinking are both social processes, whereby people exchange views, and psychological processes, whereby individuals evaluate reasoning.

2. The process of arguing is governed by four major social conventions, or agreements: (a) *bilaterality*, (b) *self-risk*, (c) *reasonableness*, and (d) *rationality*.

3. Argumentation represents three levels of thought and action: (a) *the argumentative process*, during which proponents and opponents take turns addressing each other, offering constructive and refutative speeches; (b) *the argumentation speech* or the development of an introduction that sets out a position or claim, a body organized around a series of reasons that support the claim, and a conclusion that summarizes the positions; and (c) *the argumentative unit*, which consists of three building blocks—the claim, the evidence, and the reasoning pattern.

4. A unit of argumentation has three essential elements: (a) *the types of claims common to arguments—claims of fact, claims of value,* and *claims of policy;* (b) *the types of evidence or support that can be adduced*—rationally relevant evidence and motivationally relevant evidence; and (c) *the forms of reasoning that connect evidence and claims—reasoning from examples, reasoning from generalization or axiom, reasoning from sign, reasoning from parallel case,* and *reasoning from causal relation.*

5. Your primary job as a critical listener and arguer is to evaluate the claims, evidence, and reasoning of others. On one level, you're looking for ways in which the ideas and reasonings of others are important to your own thinking, and, on another level, you're examining the logical soundness of their thinking. A *fallacy* is a flaw in the rational properties of an argument or inference. Fallacies can be divided into three categories: (a) *fallacies in evidence*—including *hasty generalization, false division,* and *genetic fallacy;* (b) *fallacies in reasoning*—including *appeal to ignorance, appeal to popular opinion, sequential fallacy, begging the question,* and *appeal to authority;* and *fallacies in language*—including *ambiguity, nonqualification, is-faults, persuasive definition,* and *name calling.*

6. In developing argumentative speeches: (a) organize your arguments by putting the strongest first or last, (b) vary the evidence, (c) avoid personal attacks on opponents, (d) know the potential arguments of your opponents, and (e) practice constructing logical arguments and detecting fallacious ones.

KEY TERMS

ambiguity (p. 295)
appeal to authority (*ipse dixit*) (p. 294)
appeal to ignorance (*argumentum ad ignoratiami*) (p. 293)

appeal to popular opinion (*argumentum ad populum*) (p. 294)
argumentation (p. 278)

SKILLBUILDING ACTIVITIES

1. How influential are political debates in campaign years? In researching this question, consult Kathleen Hall Jamieson and David S. Birdsell, *Presidential Debates: The Challenge of Creating an Informed Electorate.* Present your critical summary in written form or as part of a class discussion on the role of argumentation in political decision making.

2. Prepare a ten-minute argumentative exchange on a topic involving you and another member of your class. Dividing the time equally, one of you will advocate a claim and the other will oppose it. Adopt any format you and your instructor choose. You might consider the following: (a) a Lincoln-Douglas format—the first person speaks for four minutes, the second speaks for five, and then the first person returns for a one-minute rejoinder; (b) an issue format—you both agree on a number of key issues, and then each of you speaks for two-and-a-half minutes on each issue; (c) a debate format—each speaker presents a constructive speech for three minutes, and then each speaker gives a two-minute rebuttal; (d) a heckling format—each speaker has five minutes to speak, but, during the middle of each speech, the audience or opponent may ask questions that the speaker must answer.

3. Turn the class into a deliberative assembly, decide on a motion or resolution to be argued, and then schedule a day or two for a full debate. Class members should assume argumentative roles: advocates, witnesses, direct examiners, cross-examiners, and summarizers. The deliberative assembly allows each speaker to be part of a team. Read about parliamentary procedure in Chapter 16. To read about the use of this format, see John D. Day, ed., *American Problems: What Should Be Done? Debates from "The Advocates"* (Palo Alto, Calif.: National Press Books, 1973).

REFERENCES

1. Harvey Siegel, *Educating Reason: Rationality, Critical Thinking, and Education* (New York: Routledge, 1988), 1–47. The importance of critical thinking has been

underscored in two recent national reports on higher education: The National Institute on Education, *Involvement in Learning: Realizing the Potential of American Higher Education,* 1984; and the American Association of Colleges, *Integrity in the College Curriculum: A Report to the Academic Community,* 1985. For a summary of research on critical thinking in the college setting, see James H. McMillan, "Enhancing College Students' Critical Thinking: A Review of Studies," *Research in Higher Education,* 26 (1987), 3–29.

2. A full discussion of the logical grounding of claims in evidence and reasoning is presented in the classic book on argumentation: Douglas Ehninger and Wayne Brockriede, *Decision by Debate,* 2nd ed. (New York: Harper & Row, 1978).

3. The original discussion of persuasive definition is found in Charles L. Stevenson, *Ethics and Language* (New Haven, Conn.: Yale University Press, 1944), chap. 9.

4. For an example, see Irving M. Copi, *Introduction to Logic,* 7th ed. (New York: Macmillan Publishing Co., 1986).

5. Most students of persuasion believe that the primacy and recency effects are equally potent; see Stephen W. Littlejohn and David M. Jabusch, *Persuasive Transactions* (Glenview, Ill.: ScottForesman, 1987), 235–236. Others, however, believe that because the primacy effect can color listeners' reactions to everything you say, your best argument should almost always come first; see Gary C. Woodward and Robert E. Denton, Jr., *Persuasion and Influence in American Life* (Prospect Heights, Ill.: Waveland Press, 1988), 299–300. More work that can explain why one position is more important than the other needs to be done.

6. Jenny Clanton, "The *Challenger* Disaster That Didn't Happen," *Winning Orations* (1988). Reprinted by permission of Larry Schnoor, Executive Secretary, Interstate Oratorical Association, Mankato State University, Mankato, Minn.

CHAPTER FIFTEEN

Speaking for Special Occasions

*R*andall Stevenson, the speech teacher, opened his class by asking each student the same question: "Who are you?" Everyone squirmed a little. The first student said, "I'm Caleb Portnoy," but Mr. Stevenson responded, "No, I mean who are you?" After getting the question a second time, students said, "I'm a college student," "I'm a New Yorker," "I'm one of the Jameson children from Fayetteville, Arkansas," "I'm an Italian Catholic," "I'm Jeremy Jackson's roommate," "I'm an American." Mr. Stevenson smiled, and said, "How interesting. Once we got past your name, your personal identification, each of you identified your base self in terms of social categories—geographical areas, social roles, parentage, religious orientation, and ethnic background. You didn't tell us anything unique about yourself except your name. Whenever any of us is pushed, we tend to rely on our groups for protection and identity."

As in Mr. Stevenson's speech class, groups and our consciousness of membership in them provide us with various aspects of our identity. They even have considerable authority over us. They can regulate our behavior because, after all, they often predate us; we are thrust into preexisting families, with their own rules or customs, and into social and political institutions that make claims upon our loyalty and actions from the day we are born. Social groups and institutions provide us with services, control our behaviors, and mark us for who we are. It's no wonder that Mr. Stevenson's students tended to identify themselves, when pushed, in terms of social categories.

In this chapter, we'll look at several kinds of speeches that you may give in the presence of, or as a representative of, some of those groups and institutions. Our focus will be on speeches that are given to or for *communities,* a word etymologically related to the idea of communication. First, we'll consider an individual's relationships to such communities and then we'll examine types of *speeches for special occasions*—speeches used to mark occasions that are particularly important to communities.

CEREMONY AND RITUAL IN THE COMMUNITY

The word *community* comes from the Latin *communis,* meaning *common,* or, more literally (with the *-ity* ending), *commonality.* A community is not simply the physical presence of people who live in the same town (their "local community") or who worship in the same place (although that place of worship is sometimes called a *religious community*). Physical presence is not the key to community membership, but psychological state is. A **community** is a group of people who think of themselves as bonded together, whether by blood, locale, nationality, race, occupation, gender, or other shared experience or attributes.

As we noted in Chapter 4, we all belong to a variety of demographic or social units—age stratum, social or work group, socioeconomic class, ethnic population, gender classification, place of worship, and so on. In a particular situation, one of those institutions may become important to us and

We tend to think of ourselves in terms of social groups and roles. How would you answer the question "Who am I?"

remind us that we belong to it. Thus, a middle-aged professor may dismiss an opinion you've expressed by retorting, "You won't be saying that when you're 45," reminding you that you belong to "the younger set." On Martin Luther King, Jr., Day, St. Patrick's Day, or Passover you may celebrate your ethnic heritage. In many late-evening dorm bull sessions, you may discuss your membership in a religious or ethnic group and you even may find that your membership is questioned. At such times, you'll be made conscious of community: your affinity with other, like-minded people.

Your relationships to groups are complex. Even though some groups come and go in your life—you're no longer a Cub Scout, Blue Bird, gang member, or high-school glee club singer—you always have some reference groups in your life. The key to their power is *salience*—the degree to which you perceive those groups and their standards as relevant to a particular situation. For example, you probably no longer see the Blue Birds as relevant to your life. That community has little salience for you; consequently, it rarely affects your decision making. Other reference groups do, however. You're currently being influenced by an educational institution. You're learning how to see things you had not seen before; to question some of your everyday assumptions about the world; and to reason your way to complex aesthetic, social, political, and evaluative judgments you've never made before. School is highly salient to your thinking. Furthermore, the things—and ways of thinking about them—you're now learning will become parts of your decision-making apparatus. Your educational institution will have less effect on you in later life, although you probably will find that, even when you're being influenced strongly by other groups, something out of your school experience will come to mind occasionally and affect a decision that you're making.

Reference groups make claims on individuals when they're seen as salient to a problem or event. Just as your group memberships change over time, so too does the power of a particular group to affect your life.[1]

So far, we've been talking in social-psychological terms—in terms of group-individual relationships understood psychologically. We now need to extend the discussion into the realm of speechmaking. That extension is easy: your sense of community is created in large part through public address. Social communities—family and friends—take shape through interpersonal, or one-on-one, talk, but most of your reference groups influence your life through public talk. You may have memorized and recited in a group the Boy Scout Law and oath, with each recitation reinforcing the Scouts' beliefs and values. Many religious groups have ceremonies involving group confession of sins and profession of faith, and most depend upon speechmaking—preaching—to instill and reinforce doctrine and morals.

Speeches for special occasions not only draw their themes and force from the beliefs, attitudes, and values of the group to whom they are addressed, but also are *ritualized,* structured in patterns standardized by that group. "Ritual action," to political scientist David Kertzer, "has a formal quality to it. It follows highly structured, standardized sequences and is often enacted at certain places and times that are themselves endowed with special symbolic meaning. . . . I have defined **ritual** as action wrapped in a

Waving the Bloody Shirt and the Burning Flag

The phrase "waving the bloody shirt" dates from the year 1868, when tax collector and school superintendent A. P. Huggins was roused from his bed, ordered to leave the state, and given 75 lashes by members of the Ku Klux Klan. Huggins reported the incident to the military authorities, and an officer took his bloodied shirt to Washington and gave it to Radical Republican Congressman Benjamin Butler of Massachusetts. Later, when giving a speech in support of a bill permitting the president to enforce Reconstruction laws with military force, Butler waved Huggins's shirt. From then on, Republican orators regularly "waved the bloody shirt," blaming the South for starting the Civil War and accusing it of disloyalty to the Union and to its flag.

Similarly, in the late 1980s and early 1990s people have burned the U.S. flag to protest nationalism and to call attention to threats to freedom of speech and the Bill of Rights. In reaction, many people have "waved the burning flag," denouncing flag burning as unpatriotic and as a symbol of anti-American sentiment. "Waving the bloody shirt" and "waving the burning flag" represent particular persuasive strategies in special occasion speaking. In special occasion speeches, you're likely to hear patriotic recitals of the lives of martyrs who died that we might enjoy freedom, of traditional values and their symbols, and of the United States as the democratic bulwark, impervious to the assaults of all other political systems around the world.

Buried in this kind of public speaking are difficult ethical moments. Certainly as Americans we should know our history and who our martyrs were; we should be able to openly discuss values and the topics of patriotism and allegiance; and the United States, for better or worse, is expected to play a significant role in the international scene.

1. But what if our definition of patriotism begins to preclude discussion of alternative viewpoints?
2. What if references to traditional American values halt the examination of values of other people's cultures?
3. When does the defense of democracy become cultural imperialism—an attack on all other cultures, economies, and political systems?

Special occasion speaking *is* a time for reflecting upon one's own culture and belief systems, but such situations can easily be used to batter someone else's culture and thoughts. What the Greeks called *epideictic* oratory, the oratory of praise and blame, is talk filled with ethical minefields. At what point does waving the bloody shirt or the burning flag stop, rather than encourage, dialogue?

web of symbolism."[2] If introductions of speakers often seem trite, it's because introducing someone into your community is a ritualized activity. If nomination speeches sound the same from campaign to campaign, it's because few of us want surprises in our campaign processes. Surprise can lead to change, and change, in turn, could upset our political system. In speeches for special occasions (except, as we shall see, speeches to entertain), the emphasis is upon ritualized tradition rather than revolutionary change.

Let's now look at three types of special-occasion talk: (a) speeches of introduction, (b) speeches of courtesy, and (c) speeches to entertain.

SPEECHES OF INTRODUCTION

Speeches of introduction are usually given by an individual who belongs to a community. They're designed to prepare the community (the audience) to accept the featured speaker and his or her message. A speech of introduction seems to ask permission for an outsider to speak; the decision to grant that permission, presumably, is based upon what the nonmember can contribute to the group: the group must *want* to hear the outsider before the featured speaker can be successful. Or, if the speaker is a member of the group, the introduction may serve as a reminder of his or her role and accomplishments within the community or organization.

Purpose

If you're invited to give a speech of introduction, remember that your main object is to create in your listeners a desire to hear the speaker you're introducing. Everything else should be subordinate to this aim. Don't bore your audience with a long recital of the speaker's biography or with a series of anecdotes about your acquaintance with him or her. Above all, don't air your own views on the subject of the speaker's message. You're only the speaker's advance agent; your job is to "sell" that person to the audience. Your goals should be to (a) arouse curiosity about the speaker and the subject in the minds of the listeners so that it will be easy to capture their attention and (b) motivate the audience to like and respect the speaker so they'll tend to respond favorably to the forthcoming information or proposal.

Formulating the Content

Usually, the better known or more respected a speaker is, the shorter your introduction needs to be; the less well known he or she is, the more you'll need to arouse interest in the speaker's subject and to build up his or her prestige. When presenting a speech of introduction, observe these principles:

1. *Be brief.* To say too much is often worse than to say nothing at all. For example, if you were to introduce the president, you might simply say, "Ladies and gentlemen, the President of the United States." The prestige of the person you introduce won't always be great enough for you to be so brief, but it's always better to say too little than to speak too long.

2. *Talk about the speaker.* Who is he? What's her position in business, education, sports, or government? What experiences has he had that qualify him to speak on the announced subject? Build up the speaker's identity, tell

what he knows or what she has done, but do not praise his or her ability as a speaker. Let speakers demonstrate their own skills.

3. *Emphasize the importance of the speaker's subject.* For example, in introducing a speaker who'll talk about the oil industry, you might say, "In one way or another, the oil industry is in the news every day—Middle East troubles, the ups and downs of the cost of heating oil, gasohol research, tanker spills, our energy needs for the twenty-first century. To help us make sense of the industry and the ways it impacts our daily lives, today's speaker. . . .'"

4. *Stress the appropriateness of the subject or the speaker.* If your town is considering a program to rebuild its main street area, a speech by a city planner is likely to be timely and appreciated. If an organization is marking an anniversary, a speech dealing with the group's progress and evolution through time is appropriate. References to relevant aspects of a speaker's background or the topic can tie speaker and speech to the audience's interests.

5. *Use humor if it suits the occasion.* Nothing puts an audience at ease better than laughter. Take care, however, that the humor is in good taste and does not negatively affect the speaker's credibility. The best stories are usually those shared by the introducer and speaker and told so as to illustrate a positive character trait of the speaker.

Sample Speech of Introduction

Under all circumstances, the four primary virtues of a speech of introduction are (a) tact, (b) brevity, (c) sincerity, and (d) enthusiasm. These virtues are illustrated in the following introduction.

INTRODUCING A CLASSMATE
Renata Ogilvie

A popular sport in the Student Union cafeteria is reading through lists of ingredients in prepared foods and candies, especially the chemical additives. One of the best players of this sport I've seen is our next speaker, Angela Vangelisti. Angela is amazing. Even with products like coffee whitener, which contain only one or two things I've even heard of, Angela can identify most of the emulsifiers, stabilizers, and flavor enhancers that comprise fake food. /1

While identifying chemical food additives passes the time in the cafeteria, there's also a serious side to the game. As Angela knows, there's a difference between blue dye numbers 1 and 2, and between good old yellow no. 5 and yellow no. 6; the cancer risk varies from one to the other. For example, the red dye no. 3 that you'll find in maraschino cherries is related to thyroid tumors. These are some of the reasons I was gratified to learn that Angela would share some of her technical knowledge as a nutrition major in a speech entitled "How to Read Labels and Live Longer." /2

SPEECHES OF COURTESY: WELCOMES, RESPONSES, ACCEPTANCES, AND TOASTS

Speeches of courtesy consist of explicit acknowledgement of the audience or of a member of the audience. When you extend a welcome to a political candidate who is visiting your class, or when you accept the Speaker of the Year award, for example, you are giving speeches of courtesy.

Typical Situations

Speeches of courtesy are given to fulfill one of four social obligations: (a) welcoming visitors, (b) responding to welcomes or greetings, (c) accepting awards from groups, and (d) toasting individuals with short speeches recognizing achievements.

Welcoming Visitors
When distinguished guests or visiting groups are present, someone extends a public greeting to them. For example, your basketball announcer might greet the opposing team and its supporters, or a fraternity chapter president might greet the representative from the national office who's visiting your campus. The speech of welcome is a way of introducing a stranger into a group or organization, giving them group approval, and making them feel more comfortable.

Responding to a Welcome or Greeting
Responses are ways for outsiders to recognize their status as visitors and to express their appreciation for admittance into the group or organization. Thus, the representative from the national office who's visiting a fraternity might respond to a greeting, in turn, by thanking the group for its warm welcome or recognizing its importance and accomplishments.

Accepting Awards
An individual who's presented an award usually must acknowledge the honor. Sometimes the award is made to an organization rather than to an individual in which case someone is selected to respond for the group. In all cases, however, the acceptance of awards via a speech is a way of thanking the group and acknowledging the importance of the activity being recognized; for example, people who receive Academy Awards (if they do more

Speeches of courtesy are given to welcome visitors, to respond to greetings, to accept awards, and to recognize an individual's achievements. In each case, the speaker acknowledges the group comprising the audience. What principles should guide a speaker on these occasions?

than blubber) thank the American Academy of Arts and Entertainment for the Oscar and often recognize the importance of making serious films on significant subjects.

Offering Toasts

While toasts offered to bridegrooms or others being "roasted" can become silly, the act of toasting is often an important ritual. Toasts are acts of tribute; through them, a group recognizes the achievements of an individual and expresses the hope that the person will continue to achieve distinction. After arduous negotiations, heads of state usually toast each other's positive personal qualities, accomplishments, and desire for future good relations. Ceremonially, toasts can unite separated peoples.

Purpose

The speech of courtesy has a double purpose. The speaker not only attempts to express a sentiment of gratitude or hospitality but also tries to create an aura of good feeling in the audience. Usually the success of such a speech depends on satisfying the listeners that the appropriate thing has been said.

Formulating the Content

The scope and content of a speech of courtesy should be guided by the following principles:

1. *Indicate for whom you are speaking.* When you act on behalf of a group, make clear that the greeting or acknowledgment comes from everyone and not from you alone.

2. *Present complimentary facts about the person or persons to whom you are extending the courtesy.* Review briefly the accomplishments or qualities of the person or group you are greeting or whose gift or welcome you are acknowledging.

3. *Illustrate; don't argue.* Present incidents and facts that make clear the importance of the occasion, but don't be contentious. Avoid areas of disagreement. Don't use a speech for courtesy as an opportunity to air your own views on controversial subjects or to advance your own policies. Express concretely and vividly the thoughts that are already in the minds of your listeners.

These virtues are illustrated in William Faulkner's "On Accepting the Nobel Prize for Literature," reprinted in Chapter 9, pages 185–186. Faulkner clearly indicates he's speaking *as* a writer *to* future writers. He honors those young writers in taking their compositional problems seriously; his own difficulties as a writer, which come out in the flood of metaphors and images that make up the bulk of his speech, stand not as arguments but as illustrations of the struggle he finds at the core of all good writing.

Speeches of courtesy are more than merely courteous talk. The courtesies expended in welcoming someone into your midst or in thanking someone for work done are really statements of your group's rules for living—its guiding principles. In extending courtesies to others, you're acknowledging the culture you share with them.

SPEECHES TO ENTERTAIN

Speeches to entertain present special challenges to speakers. As you may recall, we identified speeches of entertainment as an independent type of presentation in Chapter 3 because of the peculiar force of humor in speechmaking. Discounting slapstick of the slipping-on-a-banana-peel type, most humor depends primarily upon a listener's sensitivities to the routines and morals of one's society. This is obvious if you've ever listened to someone tell jokes from a foreign country. Often, humor cannot be translated, in part because of language differences (puns, for example, don't translate well) and in larger measure because of cultural differences.

Purpose

Like most humor in general, speeches to entertain usually work within the cultural frameworks of a particular group or society. Such speeches may be "merely funny," as in comic monologues, but most are serious in their force or demand on audiences. After-dinner speeches, for example, are usually more than dessert; their topics are normally relevant to the group at hand, and the anecdotes they contain usually are offered to make a point. That point may be as simple as deflecting an audience's antipathy toward the speaker or making the people in the audience feel more like a group, or it may be as serious as offering a critique of society.

Speakers seeking to deflect an audience's antipathy often use humor to ingratiate themselves. For example, Henry W. Grady, editor of the *Atlanta Constitution,* expected a good deal of distrust and hostility when, after the Civil War, he journeyed to New York City in 1886 to tell the New England Society about "The New South." He opened the speech not only by thanking the Society for the invitation, but also by telling stories about farmers, husbands and wives, and preachers. He praised Abraham Lincoln, a Northerner, as "the first typical American" of the new age; told another humorous story about shopkeepers and their advertising; poked fun at the great Union General Sherman—"who is considered an able man in our hearts, though some people think he is a kind of careless man about fire"; and assured his audience that a New South, one very much like the old North, was arising from the ashes.[3] Through the use of humor, Henry Grady had his audience cheering every point he made about the New South that evening.

Group cohesiveness can also be created through humor. (See Figure 15.1.) Politicians, especially when campaigning, spend much time telling humorous stories about their opponents, hitting them with stinging remarks. In part, of course, biting political humor degrades the opposition candidates and party; however, such humor also can make one's own party feel more cohesive. For example, Democrats collected Richard Nixon's 1972 bumper stickers which said, "Nixon Now," cut off the *w,* and put them on their own autos. Democrats did endless turns on the names Bush and Quayle in 1988. Similarly, Republicans poked fun at Michael Dukakis, laughing at a picture of him seated in a tank. Such zingers allow political party members to laugh at their opponents and to celebrate their membership in the "better" party.

Finally, speeches to entertain can be used not merely to poke fun at outsiders and to celebrate membership, but even to critique one's society. Humor can be used to urge general changes and reform of social practices.

Formulating the Content

When arranging materials for speeches to entertain, develop a series of illustrations, short quotations or quips, and stories, each following another in fairly rapid succession. Most important, make sure that each touches upon a central theme or point. An entertaining speech must be more than a comic monologue; it must be cohesive and pointed. The following sequence works well for speeches to entertain:

Figure 15.1. Checklist for Using Humor

These questions will help you determine the most effective way to use humor.

Purpose

_____ 1. Is my humor in good taste, or will it damage my credibility as a speaker?

_____ 2. Does my humorous story or anecdote have a point?

_____ 3. Does the point of my humor relate to the theme of my speech?

_____ 4. Has the story or anecdote been overused? Is it a cliché?

_____ 5. Am I choosing the humor simply for its own sake, or does it have a purpose within the speech?

_____ 6. Does the humor increase group cohesion?

_____ 7. Is my humor brief?

_____ 8. Where does the humor occur in the speech? Will it distract from the idea I want to clarify?

Delivery

_____ 1. Does the use of humor make me self-conscious, or it is natural?

_____ 2. Can I communicate the humorous story or anecdote spontaneously or does it sound artificial?

_____ 3. Is the punch line or point of the humor clear?

_____ 4. What will I do if my listeners don't respond appropriately to my humor?

_____ 5. Have I tested my stories or anecdotes on friends?

_____ 6. Do I risk reducing the impact of the humor by warning my listeners that they're about to be amused?

_____ 7. Will I copy another speaker's style of delivery, or will my delivery be my own?

1. Relate a story or anecdote, present an illustration, or quote an appropriate passage.
2. State the main idea or point of view implied by your opening.
3. Follow with a series of additional stories, anecdotes, quips, or illustrations that amplify or illuminate your central idea; arrange those supporting materials so they're thematically coherent.
4. Close with restatement of the central point you have developed; as in step 1, you can use a quotation or one final story that clinches and epitomizes your speech as a whole.

Sample Speech to Entertain

The following speech by cartoonist Garry Trudeau of *Doonesbury* fame illustrates the principles for arranging speeches to entertain and demonstrates pointedly that such speeches can have very serious purposes—in this case, a critique of American attitudes toward impertinence. Notice that Trudeau begins the speech with humorous observations, but then lets his point about impertinence emerge sharply with sarcasm through the latter portions of the speech. In all, this commencement speech delivered at Vassar College in 1986 suited his occupation, the times, and his audience.

THE VALUE OF IMPERTINENT QUESTIONS[4]
Garry Trudeau

Ladies and gentlemen of Vassar:

My wife, who works in television, told me recently that a typical interview on her show used to run 10 minutes. It now runs only five minutes, which is still triple the length of the average television news story. The average pop recording these days lasts around three minutes, or, about the time it takes to read a story in *People* magazine. The stories in *USA Today* take so little time to read that they're known in the business as "News McNuggets." /1

Now, the average comic strip only takes about 10 seconds to digest, but if you read every strip published in the *Washington Post,* as the President of the United States claims to, it takes roughly eight minutes a day, which means, a quick computation reveals, that the Leader of the Free World has spent a total of 11 days, 3 hours and 40 minutes of his presidency reading the comics. This fact, along with nuclear meltdown, are easily two of the most frightening thoughts of our times. /2

There's one exception to this relentless compression of time in modern life. That's right—the graduation speech. When it comes to graduation speeches, it is generally conceded that time—a generous dollop of time—is of the essence. This is because the chief function of the graduation speaker has always been to prevent graduating seniors from being released into the real world before they've been properly sedated. Like all anesthetics, graduation speeches take time to kick in, so I'm going to ask you to bear with me for about a quarter of an hour. It will go faster if you think of it as the equivalent of four videos. /3

I want to speak to you today about questions. About pertinent questions and impertinent questions. And where you might expect them to lead you. /4

I first learned about pertinent questions from my father, a retired physician who used to practice medicine in the Adirondacks. Like all parents racing against the clock to civilize their children, my father sought to instruct me in the ways of separating wheat from chaff, of asking sensible questions designed to yield useful answers. That is the way a diagnostician thinks. Fortunately for me, his own practical experience frequently contradicted his worthiest intentions. /5

Here's a case in point: A man turned up in my father's office complaining of an ulcer. My father asked the pertinent question. Was there some undue stress, he inquired, that might be causing the man to digest his stomach? The patient, who was married, thought about it for a moment and then allowed that he had a girlfriend in Syracuse, and that twice a week he'd been driving an old pick-up down to see her. Since the pick-up frequently broke down, he was often late in getting home, and he had to devise fabulous stories to tell his wife. My father, compassionately but sternly, told the man he had to make a hard decision about his personal priorities if he was ever to get well. /6

The patient nodded and went away, and six months later came back completely cured, a new man. My father congratulated him and then delicately inquired if he'd made some change in his life. /7

The man replied, "Yup. Got me a new pick-up." /8

So the pertinent question sometimes yields the impertinent answer. In spite of himself, my father ended up teaching me that an unexpected or inconvenient truth is often the price of honest inquiry. Of course, you presumably wouldn't be here if you didn't already know that. I'm confident that your education has been fairly studded with pertinent questions yielding impertinent answers. /9

But how many of you have learned to turn that around—to ask the impertinent question to get at that which is pertinent? /10

I first came across the impertinent question in the writings of that master inquisitor, Studs Terkel. He himself claims to have adopted it from the physicist Jacob Bronowski, who once told him, "Until you ask an impertinent question of nature, you do not get a pertinent answer. Great answers in nature are always hidden in the questions." When Einstein in 1905 questioned the assumption held for three hundred years that time is a given, he asked one of the great impertinent questions: "Why? How do I know that my time is the same as yours?" /11

The impertinent question is the glory and the engine of human inquiry. Copernicus asked it and shook the foundations of Renaissance Europe. Darwin asked it and is repudiated to this day. Thomas Jefferson asked it and was so invigorated by it that he declared it an inalienable right. /12

Daniel Defoe asked it and invented the novel. James Joyce asked it and reinvented the novel, which was promptly banned. /13

Nietzsche asked it and inspired Picasso, who restated it and inspired a revolution of aesthetics. /14

The Wright brothers asked it and their achievement was ignored for five years. Steven Jobs asked it and was ignored for five minutes, which was still long enough for him to make $200 million. /15

Whether revered or reviled in their lifetimes, history's movers framed their questions in ways that were entirely disrespectful of conventional wisdom. Civilization has always advanced in the shimmering wake of its discontents. As the writer Tristan Vox put it, "Doubt is precisely what makes a culture grow. How many of what we call our classics were conceived as the breaking of laws, exercises in subversion, as the expression of doubts about the self and society that could no longer be contained?" /16

The value of the impertinent question should be self-evident to Americans, for at no time in human history has it been asked more persistently and to greater effect than during the course of the American experiment. It is at the very core of our political and cultural character as a people, and we owe our vitality to its constant renewal. /17

Today, the need for that spirit of renewal has never seemed more pressing. There is a persistent feeling in this country that many of our institutions have not measured up, that with all our resources and technology and good intentions, we as a nation are still a long way from fulfilling our own expectations. The social programs that have failed to eliminate poverty, an educational system which has seen its effectiveness seriously eroded, the chemical breakthroughs that now threaten man's environment, the exploding booster rockets, malfunctioning nuclear power plants—these are but some of the images that have shaken our confidence. According to a recent poll, the only American institution that still enjoys the trust of a majority of college students today is medicine; only 44% of those polled trust educational institutions, 29% trust the White House, 23% trust the press and only 21% say they trust religion. /18

It's difficult to think of an institution in this country that has not had to reexamine its agenda, to ask impertinent questions about the purpose and the means of its mission. Society's leaders, whose number you join today, face a wall of public cynicism. As professionals, they have to speak more clearly about what they *can* do. As citizens, they have to speak clearly about what they *should* do. /19

Nowhere is the need for accountability more urgent than in what is shaping up to be the largest coordinated national undertaking of your generation—the Strategic Defense Initiative. It may well become the most fiercely contended issue of your times. Already 6,500 college scientists, including a majority of professors in 109 university physics and engineering departments, have declared their opposition to SDI and have signed a "pledge of non-participation" in a project they have called "ill-conceived and dangerous." The group, including 15 Nobel Prize winners, maintains that the weapons system is inherently destabilizing and that further pursuit of its development is likely to initiate a massive new arms competition. /20

The actions of these scientists constitute an extraordinary repudiation of the amorality of indiscriminate weapons research. Science, since it leads to knowledge, has all too frequently led its practitioners to believe that it is inherently self-justifying, that there is nothing dangerous about splitting atoms in a moral vacuum. These attitudes are held in abundance by some of the brightest people of your generation, who are already hard at work on what nearly *all* of them concede is a dangerous fantasy. /21

Listen to these comments from the young Star Warriors still in their 20s working on particle beams and brain bombs at Lawrence Livermore National Laboratory: /22

This from the inventor of the atomic powered x-ray laser, "Until 1980 or so, I didn't want to have anything to do with nuclear anything. Back in those days I thought there was something fundamentally evil about weapons. Now I see it as an interesting physics problem." /23

His co-worker, another brilliant young physicist, says he has doubts about the wisdom of SDI but concurs that "the science is *very* interesting." /24

A third member of the team had this to say: "I think that the great majority of the lab's technical people view the President's (Star Wars) speech as somewhat off the wall and the programs being proposed as being, in the end, intrinsically rather foolish. But obviously, the lab is benefiting right now and will continue to benefit, and everybody's happy with the marvelous new work." /25

Marvelous new work, indeed. As a TRW recruiting brochure put it recently, "We're standing on the first rung of a defense development that will dominate the industry for the next 20 years." Why? Because weapons manufacturers think Star Wars will work? On the contrary, at a recent trade show, McDonnell Douglas boasted on one wall its Star Wars hardware while on a facing wall, it displayed proposed Star Wars countermeasures, including a "maneuvering re-entry vehicle" and a "defense suppression vehicle." GA Technologies is already marketing the latest in "survivable materials" to protect American missiles from a *Soviet* defensive system. /26

No one in the defense industry seriously believes in a "peace shield"; in fact they're betting against it. If an American SDI is big business, then the hardware needed to overcome the anticipated Soviet response is even bigger business. The industry is further encouraged by the mindless momentum of the program, as evidenced by the recent admission of Reagan's undersecretary of defense that he pulled the $26 billion price tag out of the air. /27

Said the official, "I tried to figure out what the hell we're talking about. [Congress] wanted a number and kept on insisting on having a number. OK. First year was $2.4 billion, and I figure, OK, best we could handle is maybe a 20%–25% growth." /28

Little wonder that during the program's first year, the money could not be spent fast enough to use up the yearly appropriation. Undeterred, the following year the administration asked for $2.5 billion, greater than its request for all the basic research financed by the National Science Foundation and Department of Energy combined. /29

It should not surprise us that so many in the scientific establishment find this obscene. Said computer scientist David Parnas, who recently quit an SDI advisory panel, "Most of the money spent will be wasted; we wouldn't trust the system even if we did build it. It is our duty . . . to reply that we have no technological magic (that will make nuclear weapons obsolete). The President and the public should know that." /30

To question the rationale of the SDI enterprise should be, as Mr. Parnas suggests, a question of simple duty. It shouldn't have to be an impertinent question, but that's exactly what it's becoming. The Star Wars juggernaut may already be unstoppable. $69 billion dollars will be spent by 1994. A representative of Hughes Aircraft recently predicted, "By 1988, it may be institutionalized." Lobbies are already being mobilized, interests are becoming entrenched, foreign governments are already being involved, on the sound theory that Star Wars will be harder to stop if it becomes part of Allied diplomacy. And all around the country, some of the most talented men and women of your generation are being recruited to solve "an interesting physics problem." /31

The impertinent question. We need it now more than ever. /32

And yet, sadly, healthy skepticism is at odds with the prevailing sentiment of our times. As Tristan Vox sees it, "arguments abound to the effect that a nation does not grow great by doubting itself, indeed that self-criticism was the trap that American democracy had laid for American greatness." /33

We've been here before. It was called the '50s. This supposedly conservative doctrine holds that the very qualities from which this country has traditionally drawn its strength—idealism, openness, freedom of expression—are naive and dangerous in a cold war struggle. It maintains that America's raucous squabbles, our noisy dissent—in short, its very heritage—have weakened us as a nation and caused it to lose its unchallenged supremacy. /34

As the *New Republic's* Mike Kinsley put it, "Talk about blaming America first." /35

In such an atmosphere, the impertinent question comes with risks. Ask the two engineers at Morton Thiokol who protested the launch of the doomed Challenger space shuttle. Ask any Pentagon procurement whistleblower. Ask David Stockman. The mere fact of this president's widespread popularity casts suspicions on the motives of even the loyalest of oppositions. There is, of course, no question that this president seems to have fulfilled a deep yearning in many Americans to feel positively about their country. And yet, the Reagan presidency often reminds me of a remark made by a woman to sportscaster Heywood Broun following the victories of the great racehorse Secretariat in the Triple Crown. After the trauma of Vietnam and Watergate, she told Broun, Secretariat had "restored her faith in mankind." /36

I would submit to you that Ronald Reagan is the Secretariat of the '80s. He has restored our faith in ourselves, and for that, we are all in his debt. It does not, however, exempt his administration from criticism from concerned citizens who love their nation as much as he does. One of the things that has always distinguished this country from most others is that we've always challenged ourselves to do better. As a satirist, I can't foresee any administration, Republican or Democratic, under which the basic message wouldn't be the same—that it's possible to do better. /37

This is the true glory of America. This hope is what stirs me as a patriot—not a winning medal count at the Olympics, not the ability to drop 9,000 servicemen on a Caribbean golf course, not jingoistic commercials that tell me that the pride is back, America, when for many of us the pride never left, and certainly not by the fantasy of 1,000 laser rays criss-crossing the heavens in software-orchestrated precision, obliterating a swarm of supersonic projectiles. /38

Skeptical? You bet. You're looking at a man who has attended 16 graduations, at four of which, including one technical college, the microphone failed. /39

The impertinent question. The means by which we reaffirm our noblest impulses as a people. But what about the impertinent question as it pertains to us as individuals? Bronowski had an addendum to his comments on the subject. "Ask the same kind of question," he charged Studs Terkel, "not about the outside, but the inside world; not about facts but about the self." /40

This is impertinence of the gravest sort. The inner life finds very little currency in this, the age of hustle. David Stockman has written of a leadership circle which is intellectually inert, obsessed by television, bored by introspection and ideas of substance. Meanwhile, all across town, the sad stories of sleaze abound, 110 to date, all pointing [to] the new prevailing ethic of corner-cutting and self-advancement, whose only caveat is the admonition not to get caught. /41

It can seem a pretty grim picture. Indeed, as you look around you, you see very little to distract you from this narrow path. And yet that is exactly what your liberal education—with its emphasis on ideas, on inquiry, on humanist values—sought to do. As the president of my alma mater once observed, "The whole point of your education has been to urge you to see and feel about the connectedness among things and how that connectedness must be fostered so that civilization is sustained." /42

Our understanding of the interdependencies of the human experience is the only force which keeps a society from fragmenting. The extent to which you seek that understanding is the extent to which you will be strong enough to repudiate the callousness you see around you. /43

This won't please you, but let me share a little of what one of the more astute voices of your generation, 24-year-old David Leavitt, has written about his peers: "Mine is a generation perfectly willing to admit its contemptible qualities. But our contempt is self-congratulatory. The buzz in the background, every minute of our lives, is that detached ironic voice telling us: At least you're not faking it, as they did, at least you're not pretending as they did. It's okay to be selfish as long as you're up-front about it." /44

This is a pretty bleak portrait of the values of a generation, and my guess is I'm staring at hundreds of exceptions. My further guess is that the yearning for moral commitment is as intense as it always was, but that the generation with no rules, the generation that grew up in the rubble of smashed idealism, fallen heroes and broken marriages is deeply suspicious. /45

Columnist Ellen Goodman has speculated that this is why apartheid and the soup kitchen have emerged as the causes of choice; they offer that stark unambiguous clarity that World War II offered their grandparents, that sense that there is no good news about the other side of the argument. But Goodman, being incorrigibly of her era, also believes that micro evolves into macro; that to be involved inevitably leads to decisions between imperfect options; that many of you will take risks, make mistakes, and become citizens in spite of yourselves. /46

I'm afraid there's simply no other way. If ours becomes a society intolerant of failure and uncompassionate in the face of suffering, then surely we are lost. With the uncertainties of the future hedging in on you, you need to assess your commonalities. You need to say how you would treat other people, and how you would have them treat you back. /47

The best your college education can do for you now is to remind you that it's one thing to be self-absorbed and quite another to be self-aware. It comes down to a matter of being open, of seeing. It comes down to a matter of remaining intrigued enough by life to welcome its constant renewal. In short, it comes down to the impertinent question. /48

From those of us floundering out here in the real world, to those of you preparing to enter it, may I just say, welcome. We need you. /49

Thank you and good luck. /50

CHAPTER SUMMARY

1. Speeches on special occasions are usually grounded in ceremonies or *rituals* for defining and reinforcing a community's fundamental beliefs and values. We define ourselves by and live up to standards of behavior established by groups and institutions; thus, special-occasion speeches define and reinforce a *community* in important ways.

2. Typical speeches on special occasions include (a) *speeches of introduction*, (b) *speeches of courtesy* (welcomes, responses, acceptances, and toasts), and (c) *speeches to entertain.*

3. In speeches of introduction and courtesy, we see efforts to recognize and work within a group's standards for conduct.

4. In speeches to entertain, we see attempts to deflect a group's reservations, to create group cohesiveness, and even to critique and reform a group's practices.

KEY TERMS

community (p. 305)
ritual (p. 306)
speeches of courtesy (p. 310)

speeches of introduction (p. 308)
speeches to entertain (p. 312)

SKILLBUILDING ACTIVITIES

1. Your instructor will give you a list of special-occasion, impromptu speech topics, such as:
   a. Student X is a visitor from a neighboring school; introduce him or her to the class.

b. You are Student X; respond to this introduction.

c. Present your speech-critique forms to the state historical records office.

d. You have just been named Outstanding Classroom Speaker for this term; accept the award.

e. You are a representative of a Speechwriters-for-Hire firm; sell your services to other members of the class.

You will have between five and ten minutes in which to prepare and then present a speech on the topic assigned or drawn from the list. Be ready to discuss the techniques you used in putting the speech together.

2. Using the four-step procedure outlined on page 314, prepare and present to your classroom audience a simple speech to entertain based on one of the following topics or a similar one:

   a. You can't take it with you
   b. The portion of campus I would not show a visitor
   c. What this country really needs is _____
   d. My most idiosyncratic professor
   e. The role of television in my life

3. During the next round of classroom speeches, you'll be asked to introduce one of your classmates. Follow the suggestions in this chapter, and, after learning the speaker's topic, plan an introduction that emphasizes its importance.

REFERENCES

1. For a discussion of the kinds of group activity that reinforce the power of groups over your life, see James E. Combs, "The Functions of Ritual," *Dimensions of Political Drama* (Santa Monica, Calif.: Goodyear Pub. Co., 1980), 20–22; see also Philip G. Zimbardo, *Psychology and Life*, 12th ed. (Glenview, Ill.: ScottForesman, 1985), 631.

2. David I. Kertzer, *Ritual, Politics, and Power* (New Haven, Conn.: Yale University Press, 1988), 9.

3. Henry W. Grady, "The New South," *American Public Addresses: 1740–1952*, A. Craig Baird, ed. (New York: McGraw-Hill Book Co., 1956), 181–185.

4. Garry Trudeau, "The Value of Impertinent Questions," *Representative American Speeches 1986–1987*, Owen Peterson, ed. (New York: H. W. Wilson Co., 1987), 132–142.

CHAPTER SIXTEEN

Public Group
Communication

*W*hen Carrie's public speaking instructor emphasized how much time people
normally spend working in groups, Carrie was skeptical. Then, Carrie's
instructor asked everyone to reflect on what they'd done during the previous
week. Carrie's week began with her comparative religions study group and a
choir meeting. On Monday, her biology class broke down into lab groups and
then she met with several of her sorority sisters after class to discuss plans for
homecoming. During the rest of the week, Carrie participated in a chapter of the
Sierra Club, delivered a group report on an advertising campaign in her marketing class, worked as a volunteer leader with her troop of Girl Scouts, and
gathered with some friends to study for a French examination. As she thought
about it, Carrie began to realize how often she worked with groups of people.

Throughout this book, we've discussed public speaking with a particular
vision in mind—that of a single speaker addressing an audience. However,
as Carrie discovered, there are public speaking arrangements in which
you'll be participating in a different role—as part of a group.

An essential characteristic of the public speaking roles we'll examine in
this chapter is your relationship to others—as part of a group seeking
knowledge or making decisions; as a member of a group or team making a
collective presentation to an audience; or as a representative of a group
making announcements and answering questions. Your role may be to participate in the discussion of an idea or problem; to function as part of a

323

panel or symposium; or to address the public as a group representative or spokesperson.

We call this chapter *Public Group Communication* because, in each case we examine, your messages are presented to a public—the rest of your group or society at large—and because your messages are generated within a group.

GROUP DISCUSSIONS

Businesses and other professional organizations depend heavily on oral communication for their success. Businesspeople and professionals rely on committees, task forces, and more informal groups to formulate ideas, evaluate courses of action, and put proposals into effect. These exchanges are generally termed **group discussions.** A group discussion is a shared, purposive communication transaction in which a small group of people exchanges and evaluates ideas and information in order to understand a subject or to solve a problem.

There are two major types of discussions: (a) *learning discussions* and (b) *decision-making discussions.* Participants in **learning discussions** seek to educate each other and to come to a fuller understanding of a subject or problem. Amateurs interested in art, literature, or coin collecting, for example, may gather to share thoughts and information. Book clubs, genealogical societies, and religious instruction classes are also learning groups. Businesses use learning or study groups to educate new employees and to explore problems creatively.

In **decision-making discussions**, participants seek agreement on what the group should believe or do. These groups may also discuss ways of implementing their decisions. In discussions of this kind, participants examine conflicting facts and values, evaluate differences of opinion, and explore proposed courses of action for their practicality. The goal is to arrive at a consensus. A neighborhood homeowners' association may gather periodically to decide on projects to undertake. A city council might plan for meeting federal housing standards. A subcommittee of an insurance association might search for ways to expand markets. Once their decisions are made, these groups may discuss ways to implement their plans.

Responsibilities of Participants

When you participate in group communication, the most important requirement is that you *have a knowledge of the subject* at hand. If you know what you're talking about, you're better prepared to contribute to the group process.

It's equally important for you to *pay attention to the discussion* as it progresses. Unless you listen to what's going on, you'll forget what's already been said or lose track of the direction in which the group is moving. As a result, you may make redundant or irrelevant comments, require the

You will probably be involved in many group discussions during your lifetime. What are the various kinds of group discussions?

restatement of points already settled, or misunderstand the positions taken by other participants. In any case, you won't be adding to the progress of the discussion.

You also should *be aware of the dynamics of the group and its members.* To the extent that you can acquaint yourself with group members' values and interests, you'll be able to judge more accurately the importance of their remarks. You'll also be able to determine the role you must play in order to make the group process profitable.

Responsibilities of Leaders

Effective group leadership requires many talents. The leader of the group must be alert, quick-witted, and clear-thinking—able to perceive basic issues, to recognize significant ideas, to sense the direction of an interchange, to note common elements in diverse points of view, and to strip controversial matters of unnecessary complexity. Most importantly, a good discussion leader must periodically summarize the results of the discussion or highlight essential points.

A discussion leader must also be *impartial.* The leader needs to ensure that unpopular viewpoints are allowed expression. The leader must make sure that participants phrase questions and comments in neutral terms. Through the example of the leader, a spirit of cooperation and conciliation will be promoted among participants who may disagree.

To ensure that all participants are involved in a democratic, representative way—especially if the discussion is formal or involves many people— the leader should have a working knowledge of parliamentary procedure and the commonly used motions. For a brief discussion of parliamentary procedure and a table of such motions, see pages 330–333.

Finally, a discussion leader should *encourage active participation*. There are times, such as at the beginning of a discussion, when individuals may be hesitant to state their opinions. Provocative questions may stimulate them to participate. A leader whose manner conveys confidence in them may encourage group members who have ideas to contribute.

DEVELOPING A DISCUSSION PLAN

In group discussions, individuals may lose much time by needlessly repeating points already made or by aimlessly wandering from point to point. A carefully developed discussion plan will guard against these dangers.

Ideally, the entire group will cooperate in framing the discussion plan, but sometimes a leader must take the responsibility for formulating it. There are separate plans for learning discussions and decision-making discussions. Although these plans can be used in most situations, they may occasionally have to be modified.

A Plan for Learning Discussions

Learning discussions characteristically seek answers to questions of fact or value. Sometimes a learning discussion is based on a book, a study outline, or a syllabus. In these cases, the discussion should follow the organizational pattern used in the book, outline, or syllabus. The organization of the discussion should be modified to accommodate the experiences of the group members and should emphasize the most important facts and principles being studied. If the group finds that prepared materials are outdated or incomplete, it should add the missing information or points of view.

When learning discussions are not based on prepared materials, the group must *phrase the subject for discussion as a question*. Sometimes the question is framed before the actual discussion begins. If not, the members of the group must work it out together. Ordinarily, the subject is phrased as a claim of fact or of value. (See pages 283–284.) Questions of fact seek an addition to or a clarification of knowledge, such as "What is this community doing to increase the number of small businesses in town?" or "What range of courses and internship experiences are important to a public relations or advertising major?" Questions of value seek judgments, appraisals, or preferences, such as "Is the United States' Middle Eastern policy effective?" or "Are there viable alternatives to this school's traditional academic grading system?"

The following steps should help you to develop a satisfactory discussion plan for questions of fact or value.

Step 1: The Introduction
The introduction is a statement of the discussion question by the leader. One or two examples may be provided to show the question's significance.

Occasionally, it's necessary to add a brief history of the problem that has led to the discussion of the question.

Step 2: The Analysis

The analysis is the group's exploration of the nature and meaning of the question and the narrowing of the scope of the discussion to its most important topics. The following considerations are pertinent here:

1. Into what major topical divisions may this question conveniently be divided (see pages 124–128 for some suggestions)?
2. To which of these topics should the discussion be confined?
   a. Which topics are of most interest and importance to the group?
   b. On which topics are the members of the group already so well informed that detailed discussion would be pointless?

At this point, the leader should summarize the discussion by listing in a logical sequence the particular topics that have been chosen for discussion.

Step 3: The Investigation

In the investigative phase of the discussion, the members focus on the topics they have chosen in the preceding step. Under each topic, they may consider the following questions:

1. What terms need definition? How should these terms be defined (see Chapter 8 for types of definitions)?
2. What factual material needs to be introduced as background for the discussion (historical, social, geographic, and so on)?
3. What personal experiences of group members might illuminate the discussion?
4. What basic principles or causal relationships can be inferred from this information and these experiences?
5. On which facts or principles is there general agreement? On which points is information still lacking or conflicting?

Step 4: The Final Summary

At the close of the discussion, the leader briefly restates (a) the reasons given for considering the topics chosen and (b) the essential points brought out under each of the main topics. A summary need not be exhaustive. Its purpose is to review the more important points and make clear their relationship to each other and to the general subject.

A Plan for Decision-Making Discussions

Decision-making discussions characteristically raise claims of policy. (See page 284.) "What can be done to give students a more effective voice in the affairs of our college?" "How can our company meet competition from foreign imports?"[1] Answering questions of policy requires answering secondary questions of fact and value.

The five steps in the following plan for decision-making discussions are adapted from John Dewey's analysis of how we think when we are confronted with a problem.[2] This plan is one of several possible ways of deciding on a course of action and is intended to be suggestive rather than prescriptive. Any plan that's developed, however, should probably follow a problem-solution order. Steps in this plan should always be stated as a series of questions.

Step 1: Defining the Problem

After the leader makes introductory remarks stating the general purpose of the discussion and its importance, the group should consider the following questions:

1. How can the problem for discussion be phrased as a question (note: usually the question has been phrased before the discussion begins; if not, it should be phrased at this time)?
2. What terms need defining?
   a. What do the terms in the question mean?
   b. What other terms or concepts should be defined?

Step 2: Analyzing the Problem

This step involves evaluating the problem's scope and importance, discovering its causes, singling out the specific conditions that need correction, and setting up the basic requirements of an effective solution. The following sequence of questions is suggested for this step:

1. What evidence is there that an unsatisfactory situation exists?
   a. In what ways have members of the group been aware of the problem, how have they been affected by it, or how are they likely to be affected?
   b. What other people or groups does the situation affect, and in what ways are they affected?
   c. Is the situation likely to improve itself, or will it become worse if nothing is done about it?
   d. Is the problem sufficiently serious to warrant discussion and action at this time (if not, further discussion is pointless)?
2. What are the causes of this unsatisfactory situation?
   a. Are they primarily financial, political, social, or what?
   b. To what extent is the situation the result of misunderstandings or emotional conflicts between individuals or groups?
   c. Why hasn't anything been done?
3. What specific aspects of the present situation must be corrected?; what demands must be met and what desires satisfied?
   a. What evils does everyone in the group wish corrected?
   b. What additional evils does a majority in the group wish corrected?
   c. What desirable elements in the present situation must be retained?

4. In light of the answers to Questions 1, 2, and 3 above, by what criteria should any proposed plan or remedy be judged?
   a. What must the plan do?
   b. What must the plan avoid?
   c. What restrictions of time, money, and so on must be considered?
5. In addition to the above criteria, what supplementary qualities of a plan are desirable, although not essential?

At this stage the leader summarizes the points the group has agreed on thus far. A clear statement of the agreements reached on questions 4 and 5 is particularly important since these set forth the criteria for judging proposed remedies. Agreement on the criteria tends to make further discussion more objective and to minimize disagreements based on personal prejudices.

Step 3: Suggesting Solutions

In Step 3, a wide range of possible solutions are presented. The group asks the following questions:

> What are the various ways in which the difficulty could be solved (if the group is meeting to discuss the merits of a previously proposed plan, it asks what alternatives to the proposed plan exist)?
> a. What is the exact nature of each proposed solution? What cost, actions, or changes does it entail or imply?
> b. How may the various solutions best be grouped for initial consideration? It is helpful to list all solutions, preferably on a chalkboard.

Step 4: Evaluating the Proposed Solutions

After the group members have suggested solutions, they examine and compare these solutions and try to agree on a mutually satisfactory plan. The group may consider the following questions:

1. What elements are common to all the proposed solutions and are therefore probably desirable?
2. How do the solutions differ?
3. How do the various solutions meet the criteria set up in Questions 4 and 5 of the analysis step (this question may be answered either by considering each plan or type of plan separately in the light of the criteria agreed on, or by considering each criterion separately to determine which solution best satisfies it)?
4. Which solutions should be eliminated and which ones retained for further consideration?
5. Which solution or combination of solutions should finally be approved?
   a. Which objectionable features of the approved solution or solutions should be eliminated or modified?

b. If a number of solutions are approved, how may the best features of all the approved solutions be combined in a single superior plan?

As soon as agreement is reached on these matters, the leader sums up the principal features of the accepted plan. In groups that have no authority to act, this statement normally concludes the discussion.

Step 5: Deciding How to Put the Approved Solution into Operation

When a group has the power to put its solution into operation, the following additional questions are pertinent:

1. What persons or committees should be responsible for taking action?
2. When and where should the solution go into effect?
3. What official action, what appropriation of money, and so on is necessary (note: if divergent solutions are suggested, the group may need to evaluate each briefly to decide on the most satisfactory one)?

When these matters have been decided, the leader briefly restates the action agreed on to ensure that it's clear and acceptable to the group.

Discussions Governed by Parliamentary Procedure

Sometimes, especially when groups are large or formal, your discussions are governed by parliamentary procedure. **Parliamentary procedure** is a set of technical rules that prescribes what may be said by whom, when, and to whom; these rules are designed to keep groups from being disorganized or dominated by a few overly powerful people. Among the most common of these technical rules are those recorded in *Robert's Rules of Order.* (See Table 16.1 on pages 332–333.) Because these technical rules are important and because you will probably encounter them, we'll discuss them briefly.

As noted, parliamentary procedure limits *what* you can say (some motions are "out of order"), *whether* you can say it (you may not discuss an idea if your motion is not seconded), and even *when* you can say it (everything you say must be germane to the motion under consideration). The essential details of parliamentary procedure for handling motions are shown in the chart on pages 332–333.

If you're taking part in a meeting that is governed by parliamentary rules, there are several things you can do to increase your effectiveness:

1. *Know the appropriate rules yourself.* Don't depend on a good chairperson to keep you informed about the process. The more knowledgeable you are, the less confused you'll become as the parliamentary process unfolds. Also, you'll be able to counteract efforts to use the rules to create an unfair advantage for one or more persons.

2. *Listen carefully.* Be aware of what's going on. If the chair does not keep the group on track by constantly reminding members of what's pending, you may need to take that responsibility. A conscientious leader should keep you and others informed regarding what's on the floor.

3. *Ask questions.* If you aren't sure about the procedures or become lost in the parliamentary thicket, don't hesitate to raise a question of personal privilege. Be specific in asking the chair or the parliamentarian (if one has been appointed) what's on the floor or what motions are appropriate under the circumstances.

4. *Speak to the motion.* Limit your remarks to the specific motion on the floor. Don't discuss the entire main motion if an amendment is pending; instead, comment directly on the merits of the amendment.

5. *Avoid unnecessary parliamentary gymnastics.* If the members of a group yield to the temptation to play with the rules, parliamentary procedure becomes counterproductive. The rational process of decision making is undermined by such game playing. Refrain from piling one motion on top of another, cluttering the floor (and the minds of members) with amendments to amendments. Also guard against raising petty points of order. Parliamentary procedure is intended to ensure equal, fair, controlled participation by all members. It provides a systematic way to introduce and dispose of complex ideas. Unnecessary "gymnastics" will impede rather than foster group decision making.

One final point must be made: the key to successful group communication experiences is interdependency. Even though discussions are sometimes competitive or hostile, they are ultimately a cooperative activity. You share with others; they share with you. Your ideas are deflected, reshaped, or accepted by others. In the end, they belong to everybody in the group. All group members leave parts of themselves in the final outcome. You are changed, even if just a little, by having worked as part of a mini-society or team. And, of course, you leave a group more experienced at cooperative and competitive communication behavior. When group members promote a sense of interdependency, the result is positive and productive.

PRESENTATIONS IN TEAMS: PANELS AND SYMPOSIA

When a group is too large for effective roundtable discussion or when its members are not well informed on the topic, a **panel** of individuals may be selected to discuss the topic for the benefit of others, who then become an audience. Members of a panel may be particularly well informed on the subject or may represent divergent views.

Table 16.1 Parliamentary Procedure for Handling Motions
Speakers should be familiar with parliamentary procedure.

Classification of motions	Types of motions and their purposes	Order of handling	Must be seconded	Can be discussed	Can be amended	Vote required [1]	Can be reconsidered
Main motion	To present a proposal to the assembly	Cannot be made while any other motion is pending	Yes	Yes	Yes	Majority	Yes
Subsidiary motions [2]	To postpone indefinitely, to kill a motion	Has precedence over above motion	Yes	Yes	No	Majority	Affirmative vote only
	To amend a motion	Has precedence over above motions	Yes	When motion is debatable	Yes	Majority	Yes
	To refer a motion to committee	Has precedence over above motions	Yes	Yes	Yes	Majority	Until committee takes up subject
	To postpone discussion of a motion to a certain time	Has precedence over above motions	Yes	Yes	Yes	Majority	Yes
	To limit discussion of a motion	Has precedence over above motions	Yes	No	Yes	Two-thirds	Yes
	Previous question (to take a vote on the pending motion)	Has precedence over above motions	Yes	No	No	Two-thirds	No
	To table (to lay a motion aside until later)	Has precedence over above motions	Yes	No	No	Majority	No
Incidental motions [3]	To suspend the rules (to change the order of business temporarily)	Has precedence over a pending motion when its purpose relates to the motion	Yes	No	No	Two-thirds	No
	To close nominations [4]	[4]	Yes	No	Yes	Two-thirds	No
	To request leave to withdraw or modify a motion [5]	Has precedence over motion to which it pertains and other motions applied to it	No	No	No	Majority [5]	Negative vote only
	To rise to a point of order (to enforce the rules) [6]	Has precedence over pending motion out of which it arises	No	No	No	Chair decides [7]	No
	To appeal from the decision of the chair (to reverse chair's ruling) [6]	Is in order only when made immediately after chair announces ruling	Yes	When ruling was on debatable motion	No	Majority [1]	Yes
	To divide the question (to consider a motion by parts)	Has precedence over motion to which it pertains and motion to postpone indefinitely	[8]	No	Yes	Majority [8]	No
	To object to consideration of a question	In order only when a main motion is first introduced	No	No	No	Two-thirds	Negative vote only
	To divide the assembly (to take a standing vote)	Has precedence after question has been put	No	No	No	Chair decides	No

Privileged motions						
To call for the orders of the day (to keep meeting to order of business) [6, 9]	Has precedence over above motions	No	No	No	No vote required	No
To raise a question of privilege (to point out noise, etc.) [6]	Has precedence over above motions	No	No	No	Chair decides [7]	No
To recess [10]	Has precedence over above motions	Yes	No [10]	Yes	Majority	No
To adjourn [11]	Has precedence over above motions	Yes	No [11]	No [11]	Majority	No
To fix the time to which to adjourn (to set next meeting time) [12]	Has precedence over above motions	Yes	No [12]	Yes	Majority	Yes
Unclassified motions						
To take from the table (to bring up tabled motion for consideration)	Cannot be made while another motion is pending	Yes	No	No	Majority	No
To reconsider (to reverse vote on previously decided motion) [13]	Can be made while another motion is pending [13]	Yes	When motion to be reconsidered is debatable	No	Majority	No
To rescind (to repeal decision on a motion) [14]	Cannot be made while another motion is pending	Yes	Yes	Yes	Majority or two-thirds [14]	Negative vote only

1. A tied vote is always lost except on an appeal from the decision of the chair. The vote is taken on the ruling, not the appeal, and a tie sustains the ruling.

2. Subsidiary motions are applied to a motion before the assembly for the purpose of disposing of it properly.

3. Incidental motions are incidental to the conduct of business. Most of them arise out of a pending motion and must be decided before the pending motion is decided.

4. The chair opens nominations with "Nominations are now in order." A member may move to close nominations, or the chair may declare nominations closed if there is no response to his or her inquiry "Are there any further nominations?"

5. When the motion is before the assembly, the mover requests permission to withdraw or modify it, and if there is no objection from anyone, the chair announces that the motion is withdrawn or modified. If anyone objects, the chair puts the request to a vote.

6. A member may interrupt a speaker to rise to a point of order or of appeal, to call for orders of the day, or to raise a question of privilege.

7. Chair's ruling stands unless appealed and reversed.

8. If propositions or resolutions relate to independent subjects, they must be divided on the request of a single member. The request to divide the question may be made when another member has the floor. If they relate to the same subject but each part can stand alone, they may be divided only on a regular motion and vote.

9. The regular order of business may be changed by a motion to suspend the rules.

10. The motion to recess is not privileged if made at a time when no other motion is pending. When not privileged, it can be discussed. When privileged, it cannot be discussed, but can be amended as to length of recess.

11. The motion to adjourn is not privileged if qualified or if adoption would dissolve the assembly. When not privileged, it can be discussed and amended.

12. The motion to fix the time to which to adjourn is not privileged if no other motion is pending or if the assembly has scheduled another meeting on the same or following day. When not privileged, it can be discussed.

13. A motion to reconsider may be made only by one who voted on the prevailing side. It must be made during the meeting at which the vote to be reconsidered was taken, or on the succeeding day of the same session. If reconsideration is moved while another motion is pending, discussion on it is delayed until discussion is completed on the pending motion; then it has precedence over all new motions of equal rank.

14. It is impossible to rescind any action that has been taken as a result of a motion, but the unexecuted part may be rescinded. Adoption of the motion to rescind requires only a majority vote when notice is given at a previous meeting; it requires a two-thirds vote when no notice is given and the motion to rescind is voted on immediately.

Another type of audience-oriented discussion is the **symposium.** In a symposium format, usually three to five speakers present short speeches on different facets of a subject or offer different solutions to a problem. This format is especially valuable when recognized experts are the speakers. The symposium is commonly used at large-scale conferences and conventions.

Various modifications of the panel and symposium are possible. Sometimes the two formats may be successfully combined. Frequently, the speeches of the symposium are followed by an informal exchange among the speakers. Then the meeting might be opened up for audience questions, comments, and reactions. The essential characteristic of both the panel and symposium is that a few people discuss a subject or problem for the benefit of a large audience.

When you're asked to participate in a panel or symposium, remember that the techniques you use don't vary substantially from those you use in other speeches. Keep in mind, however, that you're participating as a member of a group that's focusing on a specific topic or problem. Therefore, you have an obligation to function as part of a team. With this important caution in mind, we can discuss techniques useful in preparing for and participating in panels and symposia.

Preparing for Panels and Symposia

As part of a panel or symposium team, it's important that you take others into account as you plan your remarks. The team approach involves several constraints that you don't face in other speaking situations. First, you have to *fit your comments into a general theme.* Suppose the theme of your panel is "The Role of the University in the Economic Development of the State." This topic places certain substantial and stylistic limits on you. You'll be expected to mention university programs and the needs of the state. You'll also be expected to talk about programs that aid in the creation of jobs, the attraction of new capital, and the growth of tax revenues.

Second, remember that *you may be responsible for covering only a portion of a topic or theme.* In most panels and symposia, speakers divide the topic into parts to avoid duplication. This also provides your audience with a variety of viewpoints. You might divide the responsibilities of a five-member panel as follows:

The Role of the University in the Economic Development of the State

Speaker 1: Constitutional requirements for university service to the state
Speaker 2: Potential university contributions to the growth of hi-tech and bio-tech business expansion
Speaker 3: Potential university contributions to an increase in foreign trade
Speaker 4: Potential university contributions to plans for attracting new manufacturers to the state
Speaker 5: The dangers of focusing too many university resources on economic growth

Third, *the more you know about the subject under discussion, the better.* You should be ready to discuss many facets of the topic in addition to the part of the discussion for which you are responsible. For each aspect of the subject or implication of the problem you think may be discussed, make the following analysis:

1. *Review the facts you already know.* Go over the information you've acquired through previous reading or personal experience and organize it in you mind. Prepare as if you were going to present a speech on every phase of the topic. You'll then be better qualified to discuss any part of it.

2. *Bring your knowledge up to date.* Find out if recent changes have affected the situation. Fit the newly-acquired information into what you already know.

3. *Determine a tentative point of view on each of the important issues.* Decide what your attitude will be. Should the university retain patent rights on any inventions or advances made by university personnel? Is the university in danger of being run by the state? Will the university be enslaved to an economic model if too many resources are tied to economic growth? Should the state remain separate from the ivory tower? Stake out a tentative position on each issue that is likely to come before the group. Have the facts and reasons that support your view clearly in mind. Be ready to state and substantiate your opinion whenever it's most appropriate, but also be willing to change your mind if information or points of view provided by other participants are convincing.

Fourth, *anticipate the effect of your ideas or proposals on the other members of the group or the organization.* Will your proposal make someone lose money or force someone to retract an agreement? Will it put certain groups at a disadvantage? Some forethought may enable you to adjust to possible opposition. The more thoroughly you relate your facts to the subject and listeners, the more effective your contributions to the discussion will be.

Participating in Panels and Symposia

Your delivery will, of course, vary with the nature and purpose of the discussion and the degree of formality that is being observed. In general, however, *speak in a direct, friendly, conversational style.* As the discussion proceeds, differences of opinion may arise, tensions may increase, and some conflict may surface. You should be sensitive to the evolution of the discussion and make adjustments in the way you voice your ideas and reactions.

Present your point of view clearly and succinctly. Participation in a panel or symposium should always be guided by one underlying aim: to help the group think objectively and creatively so that it can analyze the subject or solve the problem at hand. To this end, you should organize your contributions in a way that will best stimulate people to think for themselves.

Inquiry order or elimination order work well. Begin by stating the nature of the problem as you see it; next, outline the various hypotheses or solutions that occurred to you; then, tell why you rejected certain solutions; and state your own opinion and explain the reasons for it. In this way, you give other group members a chance to examine your thinking and to add other ideas. At the same time, you'll be making your contribution in the most objective and rational manner possible.

Remain sincere, open-minded, and objective. Above all, remember that a serious discussion is not a stage for prima donnas or an arena for settling personal problems. When you have something to say, say it modestly and sincerely. Always maintain an open, objective attitude. Accept criticism with dignity and treat disagreement with an open mind. Your primary purpose is not to get your own view accepted, but to work out the best group decision. The best result is a team effort.

RESPONDING TO QUESTIONS AND OBJECTIONS

Direct feedback from listeners is often a part of public group communication. In meetings, listeners are usually given a chance to ask questions. Panelists frequently direct questions to each other; professors ask students to clarify points made in classroom reports; club treasurers are often asked to justify particular expenditures; and spokespersons usually field questions about statements they've made.

Sometimes, questions require only a short response—a bit of factual material, a *yes* or *no,* or a reference to an authoritative source. But at other times, questions from listeners require more fully developed responses. For example, some questions call for *elaboration* and *explanation.* After an oral report, you might be asked to elaborate on some statistical information you've presented. Other questions call for *justification* and *defense.* Politicians must often defend positions they've taken. In open hearings, school boards seeking to cut expenditures justify their selection of school buildings to be closed. At city council meetings, the city manager might be asked to defend specific decisions. In these special situations, a brief speech is called for in response to questions and objections.

Techniques for Responding to Questions

Responses to questions that call for elaboration and explanation are, in many ways, equivalent to informative speeches. Think about your responses as short informative speeches in which you offer listeners ideas and information in response to their needs and interests. Consider the following points on how to turn your responses into effective informative speeches:

1. *Give a whole speech.* Your responses should include an introduction, a body, and a conclusion. Even though a response is an impromptu speech,

Some audience members may ask for elaboration or explanation. What are the best ways to respond?

you're still expected to structure ideas and to present information clearly. An elaborated remark might take the following form:

a. *Introduction:* a rephrasing of the question to clarify it for the other audience members; an indication of why the question is a good one; a forecast of the steps you will take in answering it.

b. *Body:* first point—often a brief historical review; second point—the information or explanation requested.

c. *Conclusion:* a very brief summary (unless the answer was extraordinarily long); a direct reference to the questioner to see if further elaboration or explanation is required.

2. *Directly address the question as it has been asked.* Nothing is more frustrating to a questioner than an answer that misses the point or drifts from the query. Suppose that, after you have advocated a "pass-fail" grading system for all colleges, you are asked how graduate schools can evaluate potential candidates for advanced degrees. The questioner is calling for information and an explanation. If your response is a tirade against the inequities of letter grades or the cowardice of professors who refuse to give failing grades, you'll probably not satisfy the questioner. A better response would include all of the factors—letters of recommendation, standardized tests, number of advanced courses taken, and so on—that graduate schools can use to evaluate candidates. If you're unsure what the point of the question is, ask before you attempt an answer.

3. *Be succinct.* While you certainly don't want to give a terse "yes" or "no" in response to a question calling for detail, neither should you talk for eight

minutes when two minutes will suffice. If you really think a long, complex answer is needed, you can say, "To understand why we should institute a summer orientation program at this school, you should know more about recruitment, student fears, problems with placement testing, and so on. I can go into these topics if you'd like, but for now, in response to the particular question I was asked, I'd say that. . . ." In this way, you're able to offer a short answer, yet leave an opportunity for additional questions from other listeners.

4. *Be courteous.* During question periods, you may be amazed to hear a person ask a question that you answered during your talk. Or another person may ask for information so basic that you realize your whole presentation was probably too complex. In these situations, it's easy to become flippant or overly patronizing. Avoid those temptations. Don't embarrass a questioner by pointing out that you've already answered the question. Don't insult your listeners. If you really think it would be a waste of the audience's time for you to review fundamental details, simply say that you're willing to talk with those individuals after the meeting.

Techniques for Responding to Objections

A full response to an objection has two parts: (a) it answers the objection (**rebuttal**) and (b) it rebuilds the original ideas (**re-establishment**). Suppose that at an office meeting you propose that your division institute a "management-by-objectives" system of employee evaluation. With this approach, the supervisor and employee together plan goals for a specified period of time. You contend that the approach tends to increase productivity, make employees feel they are taking part in determining their own futures, and make company expectations more concrete. During a question period, someone objects, saying that the approach means more busywork, that supervisors aren't really interested in involving employees in work decisions, and that job frustration rather than job satisfaction is the more likely result.

Your rebuttal rests on the results of studies at other companies similar to your own (*reasoning from parallel case*). You say that those studies conclude that paperwork doesn't increase, that supervisors like having concrete commitments on paper from employees, and that employee satisfaction probably increases because job turnover rates usually go down (*reasoning from sign*). Following your rebuttal, you reestablish your original arguments by reporting on the results of interviews with selected employees in your own company. They think the system would be a good one. Successful respondents tend to adhere to the following communicative techniques:

1. *Be constructive as well as destructive when responding to objections.* Don't simply tear down the other person's counterarguments. Constructively bolster your original statements as well. Reestablishment rationally shores up your position and, consequently, increases your credibility.

2. *Answer objections in an orderly fashion.* If several objections are raised by a single questioner, answer them one at a time. This approach lets you respond to each objection and helps listeners sort out the issues raised.

3. *Attack each objection in a systematic fashion.* Refutation usually proceeds in a series of four steps:

a. *State the claim that you seek to rebut:* "Joe has said that a management-by-objectives system won't work because supervisors don't want input from their underlings."

b. *State your objection to it:* "I'm not sure what evidence Joe has for that statement, but I do know of three studies done at businesses much like ours, and these studies support my position."

c. *Offer evidence for your objection:* "The first study that reinforces my point was done at the XYZ Insurance Company in 1987. This study was duplicated by subsequent studies at several other companies in 1989 and 1990."

d. *Indicate the significance of your rebuttal:* "If our company is similar to the three I've mentioned—and I think it is—then I believe our supervisors will likewise appreciate specific commitments from their subordinates, quarter by quarter. Until Joe can provide us with more support for his objection, I think we will have to agree that my position is most feasible."

4. *Keep the exchange on an impersonal (intellectual) level.* Counterarguments and rebuttals can degenerate into name-calling exchanges. Little is settled in verbal battles. Effective decision making is more likely to occur when the calm voice of reason dominates than when group members squabble.

Answering questions and responding to objections is a vital part of the group communication process because it allows us to interact directly with others. We are made accountable for what we say by questioners and counterarguers. Through verbal exchanges we can begin to weed out flaws in logic, insufficient evidence, prejudices, and unfeasible plans of action. By testing our ideas in the give-and-take of the public forum, we ultimately contribute to the group process.

We've now come full circle. We've reviewed the forms of everyday public oral communication in this textbook. We've concentrated on the steps for constructing and delivering informative, persuasive, and specialized speeches. And, we've examined samples of the public discourses that comprise our world of work and social interaction.

While you can't learn everything there is to know about public oral communication in a single course or in one brief book, you're now prepared to take up the challenges of public oral expression. As you think through the rhetorical decisions that you make each time you rise to speak, we hope you'll find a wealth of personal fulfillment and public service. You'll then be putting the principles of speech communication to work in your life. If you do, we'll have accomplished our purposes.

CHAPTER SUMMARY

1. A *group discussion* is a shared, purposive communication transaction in which people exchange and evaluate ideas and information in order to understand a subject (study or learning discussion) or to solve a problem (action or decision-making discussion).

2. To be a successful participant in a discussion, you must know the subject, pay close attention to the progress of the discussion, and acquaint yourself with the other participants.

3. To be a successful discussion leader, you need effective expression, impartiality, and an encouraging or permissive attitude toward others. You may also be responsible for developing a discussion plan.

4. A plan for learning discussions requires four steps: (a) an *introduction,* (b) an *analysis,* (c) an *investigation,* and (d) a *summary.*

5. A plan for a decision-making discussion require five steps: (a) *defining the problem,* (b) *analyzing the problem,* (c) *suggesting solutions,* (d) *evaluating the proposed solutions,* and (e) *deciding how to put the approved solution into operation.*

6. Discussions following parliamentary procedure are governed by the technical rules recorded in *Robert's Rules of Order.*

7. When speaking as part of a panel or symposium, fit your comments to the general theme, cover your portion of the theme, and develop a broad base of knowledge so that you can work well within the group.

8. When speaking on a panel or at a symposium, present your viewpoint clearly, succinctly, and fairly; and maintain an attitude of sincerity, open-mindedness, and objectivity.

9. When responding to questions, give a brief but complete speech and answer the questions as they are asked.

10. When responding to objections, be both constructive and destructive, answer them in an orderly manner, attack each objection in a systematic fashion, and keep the exchange on an impersonal level.

KEY TERMS

decision-making discussions (p. 324)
group discussions (p. 324)
learning discussions (p. 324)
panel (p. 331)

parliamentary procedure (p. 330)
rebuttal (p. 338)
re-establishment (p. 338)
symposium (p. 334)

SKILLBUILDING ACTIVITIES

1. Join four or five of your classmates and select a topic for a learning or decision-making discussion. Prepare a panel forum to present to your class. Decide on the degree of audience involvement you will allow, the kind of interaction

among panelists you will encourage, and the desirability of having audience members critique you after the discussion. The following are possible topics:

    a. How effective is our freshman orientation program?

    b. How are American cities solving their traffic problems?

    c. What features make a novel/play/film/speech great?

    d. What are the social and ethical implications of organ transplant surgery?

    e. How can we reconcile the demand of both the ecological and energy crises in this country?

    f. What can be done about America's child abuse problems?

    g. How can the basic public speaking course be improved?

    h. What reasonable legal controls should be placed over pornography?

    i. What has the United Nations accomplished?

2. Conduct press conferences. Speakers will select or be given a description of a particular press conference situation. They will prepare an opening statement, and the rest of the class will serve as members of the press, asking clarifying or probing questions. You could, for example, pretend to be the president, disagreeing with legislation Congress has passed or a board chair indicating that your company has signed a trade agreement with China.

3. As a class, pick a controversial topic. Then divide the class into groups pro and con. Begin with a spokesperson from one group who will give an impromptu argument on the topic. Alternate to a spokesperson from the other side who will refute the argument and offer another. Continue alternating from one group to the other until everyone has had a chance to practice rebuttal and reestablishment of arguments.

REFERENCES

1. Not all discussions of this kind deal with problems or policies over which the group has immediate control. For example, a decision-making group may ask, "Should we de-emphasize intercollegiate athletics?" or "What can the government do to ensure a stable food supply at reasonable prices?" The systematic investigation of these subjects, however, requires the same steps as would the exploration of matters over which the group does have control. The only difference is that, instead of asking, "What shall *we* do?" the group, in effect, asks, "What shall we *recommend* to those in authority?" or "What *would* we do if we were in positions of authority?"

2. See John Dewey, "Analysis of Reflective Thinking," *How We Think* (Boston: D.C. Heath, 1933), chap. 7. See also pages 263–270 of this textbook, where these steps are discussed in connection with the motivated sequence.

APPENDIX

Sample Speech Materials

A Speech to Inform

Some speeches to inform give listeners detailed information, instructions, and background data. Other speeches to inform, however, try to *orient* audiences. Rather than concentrate on detail, these particular informative speeches offer ways of thinking about and looking at an idea, event, or object.

Architect Myron Goldsmith's speech, *We Shape Our Buildings, and Thereafter They Shape Us,* is an example of an informative speech whose purpose is to orient. Goldsmith's speech opened a symposium on the revised architectural master plan for the city of Columbus, Indiana. His informative speech was designed to orient the audience to the value of the dual architectural concerns for utility and aesthetic appeal. Notice that Mr. Goldsmith (a) uses his introduction to stress the importance of his subject and to forecast the development of his speech; (b) carefully divides the body of his talk into "utilitarian" and "aesthetic" considerations; and (c) presents a short conclusion (because the other presenters at the symposium presumably will develop more particular conclusions). The resulting speech is short, clear, and effective.

WE SHAPE OUR BUILDINGS, AND THEREAFTER THEY SHAPE US
Myron Goldsmith

The theme of our symposium is "We Shape Our Buildings, and Thereafter They Shape Us." I would like to explore the truth of that statement in terms of architectural merit and the architecture of your community. /1

Scholars all over the world study the impact of environment on human behavior. It is a new and burgeoning field of research activity for anthropologists, sociologists, psychologists, and communication specialists. For these scholars, it is a fresh area of inquiry that is enjoying a surge of attention and scrutiny. It is widely covered and discussed in journal literature, in publications, and in symposiums such as the one we enjoy today. /2

But the impact of environment on human behavior is *not* a new idea to architects: It's something we've known for hundreds of years. I will address its significance in reference to the two broad aspects or dimensions of architecture—the utilitarian and the aesthetic—and I will explain why I think great architecture combines both of these. /3

First, the utilitarian. In the field of domestic architecture, we know that some houses are easier and more pleasant to live in than others and promote positive interaction among family members. The large kitchen of our past and its legacy in the post-World-War II family room encourage family interaction. On the other hand, a too-formal and forbidding room can discourage use. A similar effect occurs in a neighborhood. Arrangement of houses in a common cul-de-sac promotes interaction among families and children in the cul-de-sac. Or, dwellings can be set back—behind fences, through gates. Such devices provide greater privacy and security; they convey messages that say: Stay Out. /4

In places of work, we know that a pleasant, well-organized factory or office fosters better efficiency, happier employees, and less absenteeism. The layout of a building can promote or restrict accessibility to people. In some banks, for example, the president is in the open, accessible to any person who wants to discuss something. The opposite can also be true, where top executives are on the upper floor of a building, reached only through a battery of receptionists and secretaries, or even in a separate building with separate dining and parking facilities. This too affects interaction, the style of management, and the priorities of the corporation. /5

I know of a conglomerate that was nearly ruined because all the top managers of the constituent companies were moved to a single, isolated building on the theory that the interaction of the top management was the most important priority. For them, horizontal communication at the upper echelons was more important than vertical communication. And meanwhile, no one was minding the company store. /6

In other words, we have learned and are learning by trial and error about architectural spaces—public and private, accessible and formal. We understand more about what makes a building function well and efficiently. /7

What about the aesthetic? In the best architecture, the utilitarian is combined with the aesthetic. And when that occurs, architecture represents more than the sum of its parts. While it is easy to define and evaluate the functional aspect, it is much more difficult to define and evaluate the aesthetic aspect. To do this, we must be able to recognize and make informed judgments about aesthetics and decide how much we are willing to invest in it.

The return may be many times the investment in the improved quality of life. /8

How does the aesthetic aspect serve us and our community? Does it only give people pleasure? Or does it meet other basic human needs as well? The most dramatic example of this concept is the church or cathedral. How can one explain Chartres Cathedral, built 700 years ago in a town the size of Columbus, Indiana? What prompted the prodigious effort in engineering and craftsmanship, in art and architecture? What made those people build a nave over 120 feet high, the height of a 12-story building, and towers almost 300 feet high? If the utilitarian dimension was the sole criterion, they could have built a nave 15 to 20 feet high. But there were other things at stake in the 13th century—the glory of God and civic pride, to name but two. The worship of God was heightened and exalted by the beauty of man's unparalleled artistic achievement. And the pride of the community was enhanced by the size, the proportions, and the majesty of the cathedral—bigger and more beautiful than its counterpart in Paris, only 40 miles away. /9

But we need not go to thirteenth century France to see a proper example of the combination of the utilitarian and the aesthetic in historic architecture. Your own county courthouse, built in 1874, is a good example. Not to put it in the same class as Chartres, but it is a fine building. It provides centralized, efficient working space for the county functions, but it also aesthetically represents a good example of late nineteenth century civic architecture. Buildings constitute a large part of the tangible reality we experience. Size and scale are not necessarily the measure of their significance. /10

Your own town is a notable example of the impact of a distinguished architectural environment on the quality of community life: where informed clients and distinguished architects have confronted with honesty and solved with integrity the problems of space and use, where the functional and aesthetic aspects of architecture have forged a standard of excellence that any community in the world might envy. Through a combination of clear vision, good fortune, and unusual circumstances, you have provided for your citizens the finest our profession has to offer in churches, schools, and buildings—public, commercial, and industrial. You have given your young people something beautiful to grow up with, and you have given your own population something beautiful to live with. /11

So, then, what value do we place on the environment where we live and work and learn? How important is it that the community as well as the leadership—clients, architects, teachers, and business people—are knowledgeable about architecture and have some aesthetic judgments? It is of immense value and in Columbus you are better informed about architecture than any city I know of. Columbus is the proper training ground for the architects and clients of the future. You shape your buildings, and thereafter they shape you. /12

Many students are tempted to devote all of their speeches to the "big" topics—death, pestilence, and destruction. Some of the most interesting speeches, however, come out of our own backgrounds. Maria Battista of Clarion University in Pennsylvania concentrated on the "small" topics of life as she prepared a persuasive speech for the 1989 Interstate Oratorical Association contest. Her speech featured the neighborhood bully. The topic was a good one because student audiences are young enough to remember bullies and yet old enough to know that we ought to be able to handle the problem.

Paragraphs 1–2 of Battista's speech refresh our memories of childhood bullies, and the third paragraph assures us that bullies still exist today. Battista then uses a quotation to verbalize the claim of her speech. Paragraph 4 forecasts the speech, and paragraphs 5–15 develop the need step. Paragraph 16 offers a transition to the satisfaction step. Then Battista presents plans for action in three phases: paragraphs 17–20 examine solutions to the bully problem, paragraph 21 reviews sources of information about the problem, and paragraphs 22–26 outline solutions that communities generally can pursue. Paragraph 27 serves as the visualization step, considering the bully examples in a then-current film, *Lord of the Flies.* Finally, because this is a persuasive rather than an actuative speech, the action step in paragraph 28 is limited to a general plea for audience concern.

THE SCHOOLYARD BULLY
Maria Battista

Who can forget them? They were usually the biggest kids in the group, intimidating everyone around them. The smiles on their faces were not friendly ones, but were used to express the pleasure they received as a result of their tyrannical personalities. You've all seen them and may even have been one of their victims. What I'm describing is the schoolyard bully. /1

Unfortunately, the type of child you may remember as being labeled a troublemaker in school is still around today. Not only do they still exist as children, but they may also be adults who are raising a bully of their own. /2

In *People's Weekly,* April 13, 1987, the findings of a 22-year-old study conducted by psychologists Rowell Huesmann and Leonard Eron revealed that of the 294 30-year-olds involved in this study, "Children who were identified as troublemakers at age 8 were more likely at age 30 to batter spouses, commit crimes and be unemployed." The bottom line these researchers noted in *USA Today,* February 23, 1987, was "don't assume a 'bully' stage will pass, leaving no long-term adult effects. 'Parents should try to change this behavior, getting outside help if necessary.' " /3

To fully understand the complexity of the schoolyard bully problem and the possible ways to approach it, it is important first, to realize the seriousness of this situation; second, to see what characteristics are common to bullies and what causes them to be this way; and finally, to stop running away from the problem and suggest some possible approaches to help alleviate the aggression displayed by bullies. /4

In the *San Francisco Chronicle,* November 25, 1987, Ronald D. Stephen, Executive Director of the National School Safety Center, cited a Scandinavian study which said "one in seven students is either a bully or the victim of a bully." /5

Dr. Dan Olweus, Head of Personality Psychology at the University of Bergen in Norway, wrote in the NSSC's fall journal of 1987 that approximately 4.8 million American schoolchildren are affected—2.7 million as victims and 2.1 million as bullies. /6

Because of the alarming number of children involved in bully-victim problems it is necessary to see what type of child constitutes being labeled a bully, and what factors are distinctly pervasive and inherent to a child developing this undesirable behavior. /7

Both girls and boys can be bullies, but abuse is most frequently committed by the latter. While girls practice social bullying, boys, on the other hand, often express their aggression in physical confrontations or verbal abuse. The effects of bullying can range from trivial to tragic. /8

Of all the research done on bullies, they are generally bigger, stronger and older than their victims. They are also of average intelligence, but display below average school performance. Other factors that may further brand a child as a bully are quickness to anger, the use of force or the desire to dominate others as was noted in *Parents Magazine,* April, 1988. The American Psychiatric Association's official diagnostic manual categorized a bully's aggressive behavior as a "conduct disorder," which includes a variety of behaviors ranging from defiance of rules to fighting, stealing, lying and other antisocial acts. /9

Psychologist Kenneth Dodge of Vanderbilt in *The New York Times,* April 7, 1987, noted that "Bullies view the world with a paranoid's eye. They feel justified in retaliating for what are actually imaginary harms." Dr. Lochman, Psychologist, at Duke University, (*NYT,* previously cited) has stated that "Bullies do not seem to realize how aggressive they are." These two perceptual distortions, first, seeing a threat everywhere and, second, seeing themselves as noncombative, are key links to the belligerance of bullies which sets them apart from their classmates. /10

Indeed, these children are different from others, but the problem stems more from the home environment than from school. Dr. Albert Bandura, in his book *Aggression: A Social Learning Analysis,* has found that aggression is a learned response. Therefore, children who are exposed to an aggressive model will most likely acquire the same behavior. /11

Furthermore, according to the *Chicago Tribune*, June 20, 1986, "often bullies have been abused, or have witnessed the parent beat up his spouse or other children in the home." Also, in *Psychology Today*, February, 1988, mothers who had the characteristics of a bully as a child, manifest their aggression by punishing their children harshly. This type of behavior displayed by parents inadvertently teaches youngsters that aggression and violence are an effective means to reach a goal. /12

The process of victimization carried out by bullies as a result of their aggressive behavior may range on a continuum from teasing to the death of the victim. The bully starts out teasing his victim with playful joking and pranks. In the second phase, the bully blames and criticizes the victim. Ridicule, namecalling and sarcasm are a few of the behaviors displayed by bullies in the third phase. This usually results in the fourth phase where the victim feels humiliation and embarrassment, especially among fellow classmates. Schoolyard bullying usually ends in the fifth phase which includes physical abuse, beating and hazing. However, in some instances, victimization by the bully may lead to scapegoating and witchhunts, or even sacrifice which includes ritual death, murder and execution. /13

Now that we have an insight into how many children are affected, the characteristics of bullies, and what causes them to be this way, let us now look at some possible solutions to this serious problem. /14

Dr. Nathaniel Floyd, a psychologist for the Board of Cooperative Educational Services (BOCES) of Southern Westchester, New York, has done extensive research on why bullies act the way they do. After several phone conversations and correspondence with Dr. Floyd, I was enlightened with ways to help bullies and their victims. /15

In one of the articles Dr. Floyd wrote, which appeared in *The Pointer*, Winter 1985, he offered many incentive programs to help both the bully and victim. Three of the most significant incentive programs include the following: /16

1. *The Winning Ticket*, which in essence is a simple incentive system designed to help students learn how to control undesirable behavior. /17

2. A *Ten Dollar Token*, which is a more complex system designed to modify behavior by having students, for example, trade in a "Ten Dollar" token for free time, or even a free lunch. /18

3. *Behavioral Contracts*, which basically are signed agreements reached through informal negotiations between students and other parties, such as parents, teachers, or school personnel. This provides everyone involved with a sense that they have some control over what is agreed to. /19

Furthermore, Dr. Floyd has also made available diagnostic checklists to help teachers identify potential bullies and victims. /20

I have copies available of these diagnostic checklists and incentive programs for any of you who would be interested in promoting such ideas in your own community and school districts. Also, I have included an address of the Agency for Instructional Television which provides a 15-minute color film on bullies that may be used within the classroom for instructional purposes. /21

However, you may still be asking yourself the question, "What can the general public do to control aggressive youth?" When I asked Dr. Floyd this very question, he gave me the following advice: /22

1. Educators need to have news articles, press releases, television discussions, seminars and conferences in order to increase public awareness of the problem and its causes. /23

2. Parents need to be trained how to raise children relative to discipline, nutrition and caring. /24

3. Students need to be involved in peer leadership programs. These can include internships that require tolerance for others, caring for the sick, and, in general, being involved in community functions. /25

4. School/Community partnerships need to be developed and maintained. For example, athletes could be recruited to speak in schools on non-violent ways to solve problems. /26

If such actions are not taken to alleviate the pervasiveness of the problem with schoolyard bullies, we may not only recognize the reality that schoolyard bullies and their victims exist, but perhaps one day the fiction novel, *Lord of the Flies,* written by William Golding, will become the new future. In this book, we see that children unsupervised by adults will obtain leadership and power by threatening and killing the weaker children. The lesson learned in this novel is enough to warrant that aggression in children is not something to ignore and label as "kids just being kids." /27

The objective of all civilized societies is to help children realize their potential in an environment that is secure and free of all unnecessary violence. /28

A Speech to Actuate

Snitching is something we've all had ambiguous feelings about since we were children. The ambiguity of our feelings stems from societal pressures both to conform and to stand out. A thoughtful speaker can help guide listeners through ethical dilemmas regarding "whistleblowing" that they will face throughout their lives.

Shannon Dyer of Missouri's Southwest Baptist University tackled the topic of whistleblowing in the 1989 Interstate Oratorical Association contest. Dyer began his speech with references to the Challenger disaster and the Bhopal accident, both of which could have been prevented by whistleblowers. Dyer focused on whistleblowing in paragraph 3 and stated his claim in paragraph 4. In paragraph 5 he forecast the "who/what/how" structure for his speech, and in paragraphs 6–9 he developed the need for action. Paragraph 10 summarizes the general dimensions of the problem and serves as a transition into the satisfaction step. Paragraphs 11, 12, and 13 explore a three-part plan. In the visualization step, Dyer presents the example of Roger Roijoly, a senior engineer on the Challenger project, who must wrestle interminably with his conscience since he did not blow the whistle (negative visualization). In paragraph 15 Dyer appeals directly to fear as visualization blends into the call for action.

THE DILEMMA OF WHISTLEBLOWERS
Shannon Dyer

Millions of Americans, including most of us in this room, watched with anticipation the 1986 historic flight of the space shuttle, Challenger. Suddenly, a ball of smoke and flames filled the screen. Dazed, we began to realize that seven people had died as we watched. /1

In Bhopal, India, a toxic gas leak was discovered at the Union Carbide plant, but not before it left a grotesque and prolific path of destruction of over 2,000 dead. /2;

Facing two of the greatest tragedies of our time, we are amazed to find that these failures were not due to technology or safety. In fact, safety engineers had fully warned company officials, yet, in neither case was any attempt made to correct the problem. Instead the engineers were labeled troublemakers. /3

Today, there are countless numbers of these time-bomb tragedies waiting to ignite. It is only the conscience of ethical workers that can defuse the bomb or blow the whistle on these potential disasters. Unfortunately, most employees who do try to warn us never survive the traumatic experience. /4

Thus, let's examine the dilemma of the whistleblowers. First, who are whistleblowers? Then, what is the high personal price of their warnings? And finally, how can we protect these citizens—the watchdogs of our nation's safety? /5

Who are they? Whistleblowers are simply employees who object in a situation they feel is dangerous or illegal. They are social workers such as Irvin Levin of the Brooklyn Office of Special Services for Children who reported that serious cases of child abuse and even death were not being properly investigated. They are medical personnel, such as Dr. Grace Pierce of a New Jersey pharmaceutical company who protested the production of a new drug for infants which she believed would have dangerous—even fatal—side effects. They are security officers such as John Berter of the Veterans Administration Hospital in Cincinnati who following his conscience exposed two of his superiors for repeatedly beating patients. But whistleblowers are also you and I when we see something illegal or dangerous going on in our professions and we just can't look the other way. /6

Inevitably, these reports aren't always welcome to employers, thus, whistleblowers become "troublemakers" and "traitors." *Psychology Today* in August of 1986, tells us that objectors are driven by feelings of professional ethics, religious values or allegiance to the community. In fact, *Nation's Business* explains that we often become whistleblowers out of a concern for our company. Understanding who whistleblowers are allows us to expose the heart of the problem—the high personal cost to the employee. /7

Judith Penley paid the price of a clean conscience with her life. Immediately after taking part in an outside investigation of her employer, the Watts Bar Nuclear Power Plant, several attempts were made on her life. Scared and confused, Judith told investigators she knew of no one who would even want to hurt her. The next day, Judith was brutally gunned down as she waited for a friend. "With echoes of Karen Silkwood," *Newsweek* reports that investigators drew an obvious connection. /8

Not all whistleblowers pay such a high price. Most just lose their jobs, some lose vacation time and yet others are demoted to menial or demeaning tasks. No matter what form it takes, "nearly all whistleblowers can count on some form of retaliation." David Ewing, author of *Do It My Way Or You're Fired!,* estimates that at least 500,000 employees are fired unfairly each year. "Since the burden of proof usually falls on the whistleblower, legal bills may mount rapidly. [T]hey may be heavily in debt and face the loss of home, spouse, children (and) friends." /9

In spite of documented injustice, it has only been in the last two years that Congress has even considered legislation to help reinstate and give redress to these victims. But these efforts have been the equivalent to applying a band-aid where a tourniquet is needed. Of the two government agencies designed to protect these citizens, the *Economist* reports only 1% of the cases filed "make it through the Office of Special Council's fine sieve," and GAP, the Government Accountability Project, can only "handle 100 cases a year," turning down 95% of its requests. So how can we protect these citizens who are only trying to protect us? For our final question, there is a three-fold answer. First, stop the retaliation; second, those vital warnings must be heard; and finally, as potential objectors, we must be prepared. /10

To stop the retaliation Russell Mokhiber of the Center for the Study of Responsive Law explains that the problem is legal deterrence. Corporations have adopted limited liability, thus, no single individual in management can be held accountable for destroying the employee's life. "(But) if you personalize the crime," he explains, "people will start holding management to the kind of moral standards the larger society has." Therefore, we must call for stiff prosecution of individuals responsible for the retaliation. /11

Second, these vital warnings must be heard and separated from everyday complaints. Corporations such as IBM and AT&T have found that the most effective early warning system is a formal "ombudsman" system. A senior executive operates outside the normal chain of command. He is permanently available at the end of a hot line to deal with employee grievances and alarms on a confidential basis. /12

And finally—and perhaps most important—we should be prepared. We must realize that objecting to our employers will bring retaliation. Is the situation serious enough—dangerous or illegal? Does it warrant the risk? If so, we seek the advice of several veteran whistleblowers. In a recent interview in *Technology Review:* seek immediate legal council, and if possible, find an anonymous route to make your warnings heard. /13

Realizing what it means to become a whistleblower and the high personal price it exacts, we should demand protection for these workers who literally hold the safety of our nation in their hands. Unfortunately, it's too late for the 2,000 people in Bhopal, and for the crew of the Challenger, but not for Roger Roijoly. Roger was Senior Engineer of the shuttle who desperately tried to warn his superiors to postpone that fatal flight. As you and I sat bewildered at the explosion, Roger went to his office and wept—he knew exactly what had happened. Amid sleepless nights, Roger testified before the Presidential Commission investigating the disaster. And yes, he was fired. But now Roger takes his warning on ethical decision making to the college lecture circuit, for the ethical training of engineers. "From where I sit," he states, "the agency is following the same principles that got it into trouble on the shuttle. When I see someone approaching the edge of a cliff, should I whisper—or should I scream?" /14

How many lives will it take for us to learn this lesson? Two thousand more like Bhopal? Or just yours in a needless auto accident? Or mine in an airplane that was improperly tested? Or someone we love who was given a "lifesaving" drug that kills due to medical negligence in testing? If we do not attempt to protect our objectors now, then our endangered species of whistleblowers will become extinct as will the conscience and safety of our nation. /15

An Argumentative Speech (Claim of Policy)

In a technology-intensive society, especially one caught up in innovation, it is difficult to stop a stampede toward new labor-saving devices and money-saving processes. That stampede was what Samantha Hubbard of Anchorage Community College faced when she fought the Food and Drug Administration's recent approval of food irradiation as a preservation process.

Notice how she set up her argumentative speech: paragraphs 1–3 provide basic orientation to the problem area; paragraphs 4–5 offer her claim and forecast; and paragraphs 6–7 offer historical background on present policy. Hubbard is now ready for the argumentative core of the speech: paragraph 8 outlines the affirmative case for irradiation while paragraphs 9–11 bolster the negative case in support of her claims. Paragraph 12 then adds some additional support, and her concluding paragraph requests that her position be recognized by Congress.

IRRADIATION OF FOOD
Samantha L. Hubbard

On December 12, 1985, the United States Food and Drug Administration approved the irradiation of food—a method of preservation so controversial it has been debated for thirty years. /1

Irradiation is a process by which the food is taken to a nuclear plant and bombarded with gamma rays or machine generated electrons. This activates the electrons within the food—which begin moving around, thereby changing the chemical makeup of the food itself. The Food and Drug Administration, the FDA, is now allowing the food industry to irradiate fruits and vegetables. Margaret Heckler, former Secretary of the U.S. Department of Health and Human Services, is one of the strong proponents, calling the use of irradiation a promising new technique. /2

However, the opponents argue that the FDA has failed to prove this technique to be safe for the consumer. The Health Research Group for the Public Citizen contends that the FDA loses whatever scientific credibility it may have by declaring irradiation to be safe. In response, Sanford Miller, Director of the FDA's Center for Food Safety and Applied Nutrition, claims that people might be less worried if they knew that irradiation has been used for years to sterilize hospital equipment. Of course, we don't *eat* hospital equipment. /3

Today I would like to urge you to recognize the startling lack of safety of this proposal and to help you see how unnecessary the "Federal Food Irradiation Development and Control Act of 1985" is. /4

I will focus on the following areas: The history of its use, the pros and cons of this technique, and the importance of this issue to each and every one of us. /5

The idea of using irradiation as a preservation technique was conceived more than thirty years ago. In 1953, during the Eisenhower Administration, the FDA okayed the U.S. Army to test the feasibility of irradiation as a means to prevent food spoilage. The Army spent 51 million dollars on testing between 1953 and 1978. It is estimated that 80 million dollars has now been spent by the U.S. Government on irradiation research. In 1958, the FDA classified irradiation as a food additive, thereby requiring users to test its safety as they would have to for any chemical additive. Then, in 1960, it was approved for use to disinfest wheat and limit sprouting potatoes; and then approved for use on bacon on the basis of U.S. Army test results in 1963. But this approval was reversed in 1968 when it was discovered that the test used in collecting the data had not been carried out scientifically, and in some cases was blatantly fraudulent. The further implication of this discovery is that it puts all the test data collected by the Army between 1953 to 1963 in question. In 1971, when the Army was ready to abandon the project, Congress unexpectedly granted a contract for long term animal feeding studies to be carried out by Industrial Biotest Laboratories, I.B.T., who had—by the way—conducted several of the Army studies. Tests were carried out by I.B.T. until 1977, and in 1983 three of their top executives were convicted of falsifying data. /6

Irradiation has now been approved for use on fruits and vegetables . . . but in the near future possibly grains, meat, fish, and poultry. Included in these proposals are plans to reclassify irradiation so that it will no longer be considered a food additive. This means that irradiated foods may not have to [be] labeled. /7

Let us look at the affirmative argument for the use of irradiation. When food is irradiated, the movement of the electrons damages the DNA, which is why radiation is so harmful to humans. This retards cell division, slows ripening, allows fruits and vegetables to be shipped farther, and allows longer shelf lives. The irradiation process also kills any insects which may have infected crops. In fact, the recent outlawing of ethyline dibromide as a pesticide , because of its carcinogenic properties, has made irradiation seem to look more attractive at this time. /8

But the argument against this technique is much stronger. First, not enough is known about the chemical changes that take place within the food when it is exposed to radiation. The movement of the electrons breaks chemical bonds—new chemical substances are created called radiolytic products; some of these are entirely unique to the food and there is no test data available at this time to show the implications of such new chemical creations. *Science Digest* of October, 1984, reported that the irradiation process may kill insects but promotes the growth of mold which produces aflatoxins . . . Aflatoxins are currently considered by the Environmental Protection Agency as being 1,000 times more carcinogenic than EDB. Furthermore, there are no guarantees that these crops will not become reinfested. Also, the irradiation process may kill organisms which cause smell and other signs of spoilage without killing the harmful organism itself. This means that irradiated food might look and smell perfectly fine, but may be rotten. In addition, animal feeding studies showed severe kidney disease, cancerous body lesions, chronic reproductive problems, and mutagenic assault. In fact, as of August, 1985, the FDA itself had to stop animal feeding studies because the laboratory animals were either dying or becoming violently ill after ingesting irradiated food. The United Nations Committee on Food Irradiation admits the possibility of these effects in humans, which might be latent and not become evident for 20, 30, or even 40 years. At present, tests involving food irradiation and humans have not been sufficiently long term. /9

Environmental factors also must be considered. First, food has to be irradiated in nuclear plants, governed by the Nuclear Regulatory Commission whose record is poor insofar as protecting the workers is concerned. Also,

Cobalt 60, a highly radioactive substance, has to be transported to and from these plants, presumably by the nation's highways. And there is no technique available at this time to deal with the waste generated. This is no *small* problem. One irradiation plant has the potential to generate as much radioactive waste as all government and commercial nuclear facilities in 1981. /10

This issue effects [sic] us all. We are already receiving foods treated by all the known methods of preservation. For example, fruits and vegetables that are picked while still green, and bananas that are gassed to make them yellow before they are ripe. Irradiated foods are now going to be put on our shelves . . . food that has been changed enough to inhibit nutritive value. This means that we could conceivably eat a diet of what we think is only fresh fruit, vegetables and grains and still suffer the consequences of a poor diet. /11

After reviewing both sides of this issue, I am outraged at the prospect of irradiated foods. While the food will not be radioactive, it will not be what it appears to be. The fact that the FDA is willing to allow this process despite the fact that 80 million dollars of research has not provided any proof that this technique is safe or necessary seem[s] to me to be in complete disregard of its role as a protective agency. What of the laboratory animals that died during testing and the mortality rate of their offspring? If the FDA will not protect us, we must protect ourselves. Oppose the "Federal Food Irradiation Development and Control Act of 1985." Ban the sale of irradiated food and the construction of irradiation facilities. /12

It should now be apparent to all that, even though this bill has just been passed in the U.S. Senate, we must seek to repeal it. The FDA has not proven this technique to be safe or necessary. Without an outcry from the public, irradiated foods are going to be imposed on us . . . and if not banned now, we will have to suffer the consequences in the next generation. /13

An Acceptance Speech

"Brutus is an honourable man"—Mark Antony used that phrase four times in his speech at the reading of Caesar's will in Shakespeare's play *Julius Caesar* (*III.ii*). The more he used it, the more ironic became the assertion and the more the crowd called for revenge. In 1964, too, after a heart-rending film tribute to John F. Kennedy was shown to the Democratic National Convention, then-vice-presidential nominee Hubert H. Humphrey presented a rousing speech to bring the delegates back to practical politics. He used a refrain—"But not Mr. Goldwater!"—to attack the GOP candidate, and, within five minutes, the auditorium was rocking to that refrain. In the speech that follows, songwriter Marilyn Bergman uses a refrain—"Interesting things, words"—with humor and irony when talking to an audience of women in film. The refrain involves the audience with her thoughts, it shows off her own verbal skills, and it provides a structure for a speech that, because of its short length, would have been difficult to structure otherwise.

INTERESTING THINGS, WORDS
Marilyn Bergman

Thank you. This award is particularly meaningful to me as it comes from women in film—both very important in my life—women and film. Not *girls* in film. Not *ladies* in film. But *women* in film. /1

Interesting things, words. /2

Girl: non-threatening, unimpowered, non-authoritative. According to Webster: "A female servant." /3

Lady: identifying class or social position. Not free—belonging to, a mistress of a lord. Webster again: "well-bred, of refined and gentle manner." /4

Woman: clearly and cleanly identifying gender. Independent, responsible, empowered. According to Webster: "an adult female person." /5

Interesting things, words. /6

I've had a love affair with them for as long as I can remember. As a writer, I spend my days in pursuit of the right word. Words can be used to express or repress, to release or restrain, to enlighten or obscure. Through words we can adore each other and abhor each other. Nations can offend or befriend one another. Words can enslave and keep people in their place. They're easy prey for those who would tamper with the integrity of their meaning. Like those who use the words "peacekeeper" for an instrument of death and destruction—who refer to the contras of Nicaragua as "freedom fighters." And "moral majority." To my mind, neither moral nor the majority. Or those who call themselves "pro-life," a word which makes it appear that those who oppose them are anti-life. /7

Interesting things, words. /8

How stealthily they can enter the vocabulary and lose their real identity in the crowd. "Fall-out" for example: a word that was born with the bomb. Meaning radioactive particles in the atmosphere as a result of nuclear explosion. How benign the word has become through usage. We use it now to mean, "the result of something"—a meeting, a conversation—with no positive or negative implication, and certainly no danger. "Melt-down"—I dare say before too long it will wend its way into the vernacular, stripped of its malignant meaning. /9

Are we not creating a language with which to describe the indescribable? To make thinkable the unthinkable. And the sinister innocent, so that people are not outraged. So that these horrors are taken as a part of life, a fact of life. When in reality they are the facts of death and we should not accept them. /10

Interesting things, words. /11

Message movies: That invariably means that a movie is not commercial and is left of center. And yet, aren't "Rambo" and "Cobra" perfect message movies? Their message is loud and clear: "Violent solutions are the only solutions." According to the *New York Times* review of "Cobra," its message is: "the good guys can't win if they have to play by the rules." In this case, the rules are the Constitution of the United States, the courts, and the laws of due process. All drowned in blood—in orgies of murder and weapon worship, and all for the almighty buck. Aren't we selling our souls? /12

I remember the "Grapes of Wrath," about the hungry and homeless in America in the 1930s. "To Kill a Mockingbird," about racism. "Doctor Strangelove," which addressed the insanity of war, and "Tootsie," perhaps one of the most insightful movies about sexism ever made. Highly successful, all of them. /13

Sure we want to entertain and be entertained, and made to forget the fear, the violence, the wars, slums, the greed. The sounds of people devouring each other and the earth. But don't we have to make sure that there's always a place for films that reaffirm the best in us? That elevate, that illuminate. That call upon us to hold out a vision of ourselves in relationship to others—to *all* others. To not deny the problems of our times, but to raise questions in our work and perhaps even help find some answers. /14

We are the communicators. We deal with words and images. We must remember that words need the resonance of ideas—of thought. Otherwise they wear out—become deprived of their levels, their richness. We live in an atmosphere of slogans—where content is not questioned, and unless something can be reduced to a bumper sticker or a ten second news bite it is discarded. /15

We help provide the mirror into which America—if not the world—looks to see itself. That's power—and with it comes responsibility. /16

I remember when I first read Rachel Carson's *The Silent Spring* in which she warned us of the consequences of destroying the balance of nature. I remember thinking: "but *they* won't allow that to happen. *They* know better. *They* won't allow the seas to die, the air to become polluted. *They* won't allow the food chain to become poisoned." I was wrong. Not only has all that happened, but who are "*they*?" /17

I've come to think that there is no "they." Trusting that there is, is a way of abdicating responsibility, of copping out, of leaving it to others. But we mustn't. For it's becoming more and more clear, that "we" are "they." /18

Thank you again for this wonderful award and for letting me get all these words off my chest. /19

After-dinner speeches usually are one of two kinds: Some speakers try for humor organized loosely around a theme; others go for an inspirational theme appropriate to the audience being addressed. Richard L. Weaver II, Professor of Interpersonal and Public Communication at Bowling Green State University, used that second tactic when talking to the school's Golden Key National Honors Society. He talked about creativity to creative people—a topic designed to please the audience. He organized the speech around two foci—the characteristics of creative people and the means that a person can use to achieve his or her full potential. The characteristics and means were easy to understand, well illustrated, and organized so they could be remembered. The result is a pleasant, satisfying, and even elevating speech; it is light enough to follow dinner, yet strong enough to interest a bright audience.

SECOND WIND: CAPITALIZING ON YOUR FULL CREATIVE POTENTIAL

Richard L. Weaver II

First, I want to thank all of those people who were involved in the decision to have me come and speak. I want to thank you because this opportunity gives me a chance to say something important to people who should *really* care. I like talking to the crème de la crème of our students. Congratulations to all of you. /1

Let me begin with a story: "A Zen master invited one of his students over to his house for afternoon tea. They talked for a while, and then the time came for tea. The teacher poured the tea into the student's cup. Even after the cup was full, he continued to pour. The cup overflowed and tea spilled out onto the floor. /2

"Finally, the student said, 'Master you must stop pouring; the tea is overflowing—it's not going into the cup.' " /3

"The teacher replied, 'That's very observant of you. And the same is true with you. If you are to receive any of my teachings, you must first empty out what you have in your mental cup.' " /4

The moral to this story is that we need the ability to unlearn what we know—*and* the important ability to go well beyond (flow over) what we already know. We need second wind. /5

Our minds are cluttered with ready-made answers; we do not have the freedom to strike off the beaten path in new directions. Our attitudes, approaches, and responses have created mental locks. We need to be able to unlearn some of what we know, and we need to learn to go well beyond (flow over) what we already know. This flowing-over process will help us unlearn and learn again. We need second wind. /6

"Creativity," by definition, means artistic or intellectual inventiveness. Inventiveness . . . bringing things together in new ways, for example. We need to find ways to stimulate insight. Insight is the wisdom of the soul. And insight comes to the *prepared* mind. See, that's why I enjoy talking to you—people with prepared minds. You have laid the foundation—at least some of the essential footings—for developing creativity—or, for capitalizing on your full creative potential. Who better than *you,* as a prospect for creative endeavor? Who better than you to capitalize on second wind? /7

All right, let me give you a little quiz. When was the last time you came up with a creative idea? This morning? Yesterday? Last week? Last month? Last year? What was it? What is it that motivates you to be creative? /8

Some of the answers might be: "I found a new way to debug a computer program." "I decorated my room with a new poster." "I got a unique idea for a paper I had to write, or a speech that I had to give." "I found a new way to make lasagna taste even better." "I found a quicker way to get from my dorm room to McDonald's or Wendy's." Being creative is fun, and being creative results in change. /9

Do you know what a "creative self" looks like? There are four character-istics. Ask yourself if any of these (or all of these!) fit you: (1) Creative people are *more adventurous*. They dare and are willing to fail. They are more experimental; they're curious to see what happens. Sometimes they're even considered to be rebellious. Let me share with you a great quotation about failing. This is one you can hang onto and state, forthrightly, to your parents as you traverse the creative path: "If you're not failing occasionally, then you're not reaching out as far as you can." /10

In addition to being adventurous, (2) creative people are also *more spon-taneous*. They don't fear expressing their thoughts and feelings. That's how we generate reactions and discussions. Most people stop and ask, "How good is this thought?" Or "How will it make me look?"—then they suppress the thought. You need to take to heart the folk wisdom of Will Rogers, who said, "Everybody is ignorant, only on different subjects." Most people will be open and receptive to your ideas if you will just share them. Spontaneous people are people who stick their neck out; if they never stick their neck out, they'll never get their head above the crowd. James B. Conant, a famous educator and former president of Harvard University, had a poster on his office wall of a turtle. It read, "Behold the turtle, he makes progress only when he sticks his neck out." /11

In addition to being adventurous and spontaneous, (3) creative people have *more of a sense of humor*. Humorous situations often result from see-ing the old in a new way. I think we take life too seriously. When our primary goal is to get good grades, our vision is blurred and our goal blocks out the beauty, variety, and richness of our lives. One of the best things people can have up their sleeves is a funny bone. One thing I've noticed is that people are about as happy as they make up their minds to be. If you change your self and the way you come at the world, your work will seem different. /12

In addition to being adventurous, spontaneous, and having a sense of humor, (4) creative people *have and use intuition,* and have the courage to express it. Intuition equals instantaneous apprehension. Intuition comes from experience. The broader the experience, the more the materials we have to draw upon. Experience provides the materials of creativity. And the courage and confidence to express our ideas comes, too, from knowing more. Listen to this advice of an anonymous sage:

> You can't control the length of your life—but you can control its width and depth. You can't control the contour of your face—but you can control its expression. You can't control the weather—but you can control the atmosphere of your mind. Why worry about things you can't control when you can keep yourself busy controlling the things that depend on *you.* /13

Adventurous . . . spontaneous . . . having a sense of humor . . . and having and using intuition . . . how many of you see yourselves as having at least three out of the four characteristics of the creative person? [Ask for a show of hands.] I thought so; perfect candidates for second wind. /14

We know what creativity means, and we know what the creative self looks like. Now, how can you capitalize on your full creative potential? There are numerous suggestions and many possibilities; let me share just three that, if followed, will change you from a caterpillar into a butterfly: the launching pad to freedom of flight. /15

To begin with, we need *courage.* Creative people are *not* necessarily talented people. Talent suggests that you have an area in which you are accomplished—like music, writing, athletics, art, etc. A talented person can write prose, for example, that is fine, clear, and proper—but creative people can make it soar! It's more a matter of degree. /16

Courage means willingness to frolick in new territory. Opening your mind to the unaccustomed. Trying things you've never tried before. Courage means taking risks. Courage means feeling something strongly enough and having the courage to try it. Putting yourself on the line. Passionate involvement. Living life with both arms—not with one attached to something secure *before* reaching out with the other. Let me share a personal story. Since ninth grade I had wanted to go into medicine—from the time we had to write our career projects in ninth-grade social studies. It was both a personal *and* a public commitment for me. In my sophomore year of college, I had to take a required speech course as part of my pre-medical program at the University of Michigan. It was *courage,* as I look back on it now, that caused me to break a six-year commitment to medicine and to become a speech major. It was a break that, once made, became a passionate commitment. /17

I ask you, how do *you* know what you'd really like until you've experienced more, seen more, done more, tried more? I am a teacher of speech not a doctor of medicine because I had the courage to open myself to a new possibility. It is the courage of second wind. /18

Are you in a rut? Someone described a rut as a grave with both ends pushed out. Want to try something new? Did you know that there are more than 130 student organizations on this campus? How many have you tried? Explore more; be active. Read more, travel more, make more friends, do more things because the more you experience the more you will have to bring to each new encounter. /19

In addition to courage, we need *curiosity*. Curiosity is a state of mind. Curiosity will stimulate your imagination. We need new visions—new ways of looking at things. Acts of creation are often unstructured and loose. And we've been taught to be so organized, routinized, formal—follow the rules. Let me read you what one frustrated 16-year old boy wrote:

> He always wanted to explain things
> But no one cared.
> The teacher came and spoke to him.
> She told him to wear a tie like all the other boys.
> He said it didn't matter.
> After that they drew.
> And he drew all yellow and it was the way he felt about the morning
> And it was beautiful.
> The teacher came and smiled at him.
> "What's this?" she said. "Why don't you draw something like Ken's drawing
> Isn't that beautiful?"
> After that his mother bought him a tie.
> And he always drew airplanes and rocketships like everyone else.
> And he threw the old picture away.
> And when he lay out alone looking at the sky
> It was big and blue and all of everything.
> But he wasn't anymore.
> He was square inside and brown
> And his hands were still
> And he was like everyone else.
> And the things inside that needed saying didn't need it anymore.
> It had stopped pushing.
> It was crushed.
> Stiff
> Like everything else.

Just after writing this, this 16-year-old boy committed suicide. Curiosity stifled. No chance for second wind. /20

What makes creativity difficult is fear. Fear of retribution; fear of authority; fear of breaking the rules; fear of failure. We need to allow our minds to wander into fantasy, daydreams, and reverie—fanciful imagination. We need to let our minds roam. A preoccupation with grades keeps us safe and secure—structured and rigid. We're doing what society expects; what our parents want; what our teachers think is right. But do you know what? We can have it both ways! Listen to your inner voices. *We* are our own biggest hurdle, our biggest handicap, our biggest restriction, our biggest burden. We need to loosen the bridle that society has placed on us, and we need to remove the chains that shackle us. We need the freedom to experience second wind. /21

We need courage; we need curiosity; and, third, we need to *think beyond*—to flow over. So often, insights have occurred because we have been willing to ask, "What else?" We are restricted in our creativity by people who say, "It can't be done," "That's absolutely impossible," "It goes against the facts," or "This is the only way to do it." Most new ideas *are* at variance with what is known as the "facts." The airplane is, perhaps, the best example. "If God had intended that man should fly," they said, "He would have given him wings." The development of the rifle was another; bows and arrows were thought to be far superior when the rifle was first introduced. But the more experiences we have, the more our ideas can flow over. Just look sometime at the resources that creative people depend upon—they are pulling ideas from everywhere. They depend upon *all* their resources and they are limited only by the extent of their ability to imagine. What is it that is stopping us? Fear that we may be wrong? The person who is never wrong is one who never does anything—wrong *or* right! Enthusiasm is the lubricant that oils the machinery of action. Ask the questions "What if?" and "What about?" but don't stop there. Ask, "But what else?" and then keep on asking, "But what else?" /22

The reason I jumped at the opportunity to talk with you is because you are students who have already established a base of operations. Everybody in this room knows what you can do with your first breath—your first wind. That's why you're here! Let me end with a brief story: "A certain youth was fond of swimming but he had never swum farther than one-half mile in his life. One day he was challenged to attempt a five-mile swim. When he passed the first half-mile, he naturally began to lose his wind. Very soon his heart began to pound, he gasped for breath, and his face assumed an agonized look. Just as he was about to give up, he suddenly drew a deep breath, then another and another, and his troubles were gone. Since he had never before experienced "second wind," it seemed a miracle to him. His new-found strength propelled him on and on and he finished the five miles tired of muscle, but breathing easily and confidently. /23

"To him this was a new discovery, for he had never known that power was within him. It's true that every distance runner knows the power of second wind. In every long race the runners are tempted to give up, just before second wind comes. Always they go through the breathless stage, and always follows the miracle to carry them onward. Yes, here is a power, unknown to many, that can take men *ten times as far* as most people can go. /24

"In every man not only is there a vast lung power in reserve, but there is also an amazing reserve supply of mind power and general physical power." /25

Ahhhh, yes, we all know what you can do with first wind. Your presence here is evidence of that. To capitalize on *your* full creative potential . . . to put yourself together in a new way—inventiveness—you need to discover second wind. It's that amazing reserve supply of power—creative power—at *your* command. Just remember, it's what you can do with second wind that counts! /26

CREDITS

Literary Credits: 59–61—"Looking Out for Number Two" by Diane M. Schleppi. Reprinted from *Winning Orations* by special arrangement with the Interstate Oratorical Association, Larry Schnoor, Executive Secretary, Mankato State College, Mankato, Minnesota; 91–92—From "Dirty Business: Money Laundering and the War on Drugs" by Helen K. Sinclair in *Vital Speeches of the Day,* April 15, 1990. Reprinted by permission of the author; 93–94, 98—From "U.S. Perspectives on the Pacific Rim: Compete and Learn" by John F. Copper in *Vital Speeches of the Day,* June 1, 1990. Reprinted by permission of the author; 94—From "Adolescents: Their Needs and Problems" by Joseph A. Califano, Jr., from *Vital Speeches of the Day,* vol. XLIV, August 15, 1978. Reprinted by permission of *Vital Speeches of the Day;* 97—"Where Were You 12 Years Ago?" by Joseph N. Hankin in *Vital Speeches of the Day,* March 1, 1988; 98—"A Crossroads in U.S. Trade Policy" by Ronald K. Shelp in *Vital Speeches of the Day,* August 1, 1987; 149—From "America, the Arts and the Future" by Arthur M. Schlesinger, Jr., *Representative American Speeches, 1987–88,* edited by Owen Peterson, 60:127. Reprinted by permission of Arthur M. Schlesinger, Jr.; 149—From "The Barriers Come Tumbling Down" by Russell J. Love. Given at the Harris-Hillman School Commencement, Nashville, Tennessee, May 21, 1981. Reprinted by permission; 150—From "The Free Burn Fallacy" by Nicholas Flynn. Reprinted from *Winning Orations* by special arrangement with the Interstate Oratorical Association, Larry Schnoor, Executive Secretary, Mankato State College, Mankato, Minnesota; 150—From "Reflections from the Grassroots" by Liz Carpenter, as it appeared in *Representative American Speeches, 1987–88,* edited by Owen Peterson, 60:181–182. Reprinted by permission of the author; 150—From a speech presented to the Christian Life Commission of the Southern Baptist Convention by Anson Mount. Reprinted by permission of the Christian Life Commission; 151—From "Health Care for a Caring America: We Must Develop a Better System" by Horace B. Deets in *Vital Speeches of the Day,* August 1, 1989. Reprinted by permission of the author; 151, 349–51—"The Dilemma of Whistleblowers" by Shannon Dyer. Reprinted from *Winning Orations* by special arrangement with the Interstate Oratorical Association, Larry Schnoor, Executive Secretary, Mankato State College, Mankato, Minnesota; 152—From "Integrity: An Event Whose Time Has Come" by Ronald W. Roskens in *Vital Speeches of the Day,* June 1, 1989. Reprinted by permission of the author; 152–53—From "Global Marketing" by George V. Grune in *Vital Speeches of the Day,* July 15, 1989. Reprinted by permission; 154—From "Have You Checked Lately?" by Deanna Sellnow. Reprinted from *Winning Orations* by special arrangement with the Interstate Oratorical Association, Larry Schnoor, Executive Secretary, Mankato State College, Mankato, Minnesota; 156—From "Employee Involvement" by Allen A. Schumer in *Vital Speeches of the Day,* July 1, 1988. Reprinted by permission of the author; 157—From "The Hidden Legacy of the Arms Race" by Tim Dolin. Reprinted from *Winning Orations* by special arrangement with the Interstate Oratorical Association, Larry Schnoor, Executive Secretary, Mankato State College, Mankato, Minnesota; 157—From "Memo to the Press" by Everette E. Dennis in *Vital Speeches of the Day,* June 1, 1988. Reprinted by permission of the author; 158—From "The Flood Gates of the Mind" by Michael A. Twitchell. Reprinted from *Winning Orations, 1983,* by special arrangement with the Interstate Oratorical Association, Larry Schnoor, Executive Secretary, Mankato State College, Mankato, Minnesota; 181–82—From "Duty, Honor and Country" by General Douglas MacArthur. Delivered at the United States Military Academy, West Point, N. Y., on May 12, 1962; 182—*The Kandy-Kolored Tangerine-Flake Streamline Baby* by Tom Wolfe. New York: Farrar, Straus and Giroux, Inc., 1965; 183–84—From "The Strangler" by Charles Schaillol. Reprinted from *Winning Orations* by special arrangement with the Interstate Oratorical Association, Larry Schnoor, Executive Secretary, Mankato State College, Mankato, Minnesota; 185—"Love, Law and Civil Disobedience" by Martin Luther King, Jr., 1961; 186—From *Essays and Public Letters by William Faulkner* by William Faulkner, edited by J. Meriwether. Copyright © 1965 by Random House, Inc. Reprinted by permission of Random House, Inc.; 247–50—Speech by Barbara Seidl in *1988 Championship Debates and Speeches,* edited by John K. Boaz and James R. Brey. Copyright © 1988 by the American Forensic Association. Reprinted by permission; 298–300—"The *Challenger* Disaster That Didn't Happen" by Jenny Clanton. Reprinted from *Winning Orations* by special arrangement with the Interstate Oratorical Association, Larry Schnoor, Executive Secretary, Mankato State College, Mankato, Minnesota; 315–21—Speech "The Value of Impertinent Questions" by Garry B. Trudeau. Reprinted with permission of Garry B. Trudeau and Universal Press Syndicate; 342–44—"We Shape Our Buildings and Thereafter They Shape Us" by Myron Goldsmith. Reprinted by permission of Myron Goldsmith; 352–54—"Irradiation of Food" by Samantha L. Hubbard, *Winning Orations 1987.* Reprinted by permission of Larry Schnoor, Executive Secretary, Interstate Oratorical Association, Mankato State University, Mankato, Minn.; 345–48—"The Schoolyard Bully" by Maria Battista. Reprinted by permission of Larry Schnoor, Executive Secretary, Interstate Oratorical Association, Mankato State University, Mankato, Minnesota; 355–56—"Interesting Things, Words" by Marilyn Bergman. Delivered to Women in Film, Los Angeles, California, May 30, 1986. Reprinted by permission of Freedom, Kinzelberg & Broder; 357–62—"Second Wind: Capitalizing on Your Full Creative Potential" by Richard L. Weaver II.

Photo Credits: *Photographs not credited are the property of ScottForesman (T—top and B—bottom);* 9—Brownie Harris/The Stock Market; 17—G. Rancinan/Sygma; 24T—Paul Conklin/Uniphoto; 24B—Bob Daemmrich/Uniphoto; 29—Alan Oddie/Photo Edit; 55—Bob Daemmrich/Uniphoto; 73—David Wells/The Image Works; 80—Bob Daemmrich/Stock Boston; 82—Kirk Schlea/Berg & Associates; 113—Elizabeth Crews/Stock Boston; 115—Tony Freeman/Photo Edit; 126—Gabe Palmer/The Stock Market; 142—Margaret C. Berg/Berg & Associates; 153—Bob Daemmrich/Tony Stone Worldwide; 159—Arnie Sachs/Sygma; 173—Loren Santow/Tony Stone Worldwide; 177—Ken Ballard/Tony Stone Worldwide; 184—Frank Siteman/Uniphoto; 194—Courtesy of Pearson Yachts, Portsmouth, R.I.; 203—John Maher/The Stock Market; 208—Jon Feingersh/Uniphoto; 209—Novosti/Sygma; 217—Bak/Shooting Star; 230—Sepp Seitz/Woodfin Camp & Associates; 239—Charles Gupton/The Stock Market; 253—Andrew Holbrooke/Black Star; 262—Courtesy of Foote, Cone & Belding; 280—Bob Daemmrich/Uniphoto; 286—Dallas & John Heaton/Uniphoto; 305—Dilip Mehta/Contact Press Images/Woodfin Camp & Associates; 311—Margaret C. Berg/Berg & Associates; 325—Robert Frerck/Tony Stone Worldwide; 337—Don & Pat Valenti/Tony Stone Worldwide.

Index